The Government of Time

Historical Materialism Book Series

The Historical Materialism Book Series is a major publishing initiative of the radical left. The capitalist crisis of the twenty-first century has been met by a resurgence of interest in critical Marxist theory. At the same time, the publishing institutions committed to Marxism have contracted markedly since the high point of the 1970s. The Historical Materialism Book Series is dedicated to addressing this situation by making available important works of Marxist theory. The aim of the series is to publish important theoretical contributions as the basis for vigorous intellectual debate and exchange on the left.

The peer-reviewed series publishes original monographs, translated texts, and reprints of classics across the bounds of academic disciplinary agendas and across the divisions of the left. The series is particularly concerned to encourage the internationalization of Marxist debate and aims to translate significant studies from beyond the English-speaking world.

For a full list of titles in the Historical Materialism Book Series
available in paperback from Haymarket Books, visit:
https://www.haymarketbooks.org/series_collections/1-historical-materialism

The Government of Time

*Theories of Plural Temporality
in the Marxist Tradition*

Edited by
Vittorio Morfino
Peter D. Thomas

Haymarket Books
Chicago, IL

First published in 2017 by Brill Academic Publishers, The Netherlands
© 2017 Koninklijke Brill NV, Leiden, The Netherlands

Published in paperback in 2018 by
Haymarket Books
P.O. Box 180165
Chicago, IL 60618
773-583-7884
www.haymarketbooks.org

ISBN: 978-1-60846-017-5

Trade distribution:
In the US, Consortium Book Sales, www.cbsd.com
In Canada, Publishers Group Canada, www.pgcbooks.ca
In the UK, Turnaround Publisher Services, www.turnaround-uk.com
All other countries, Ingram Publisher Services International, ips_intlsales@
ingramcontent.com

Cover design by Jamie Kerry and Ragina Johnson.

This book was published with the generous support of Lannan Foundation
and the Wallace Action Fund.

Printed in the United States.

10 9 8 7 6 5 4 3 2 1

Library of Congress Cataloging-in-Publication data is available.

Contents

Tempora multa

Vittorio Morfino and Peter D. Thomas

Beyond the Circle and the Line

It has become customary to counterpose Greek and Christian conceptions of time by means of the metaphors of the circle and the line: while the Greek world was supposedly dominated by a circular conception of both natural and historical time, Christian time had an origin (in the birth of Christ) and an orientation. In the case of the Greeks, while the situation was undoubtedly more complex, it is nevertheless difficult to deny that the circle seems to have been the dominant metaphor for conceiving of time's progress.[1] The 'likely story' of Plato's *Timaeus*, for instance, affirms the primacy of time over movement, to the extent that the demiurge 'first' generates 'time [as] the mobile image of eternity', and 'second' the circular movement of the stars and planets, as signs of its flow, as the unit of measure of the different parts of time.[2] In Aristotle's conception, on the other hand, there is a primacy of movement over time, in terms of 'number of movement in respect of the before and after'.[3] Nevertheless, in both cases the sphere is the geometric figure that dominates the cosmology and the circle is the figure that traces the flow of time. Eternal repetition of the identical, mimesis of a perfection that Plato situates beyond the sensible, and which Aristotle locates in the celestial world. The circle was dominant as a paradigm not only of cosmological time, but also of historical time: it is enough to think of, on the one hand, the Stoic conception of cosmic cycles according to which every historical event is repeated in an identical way an infinite number of times, and, on the other, the Polybian theory of anacyclosis which, following Platonic and Aristotelian models, thinks the forms of government in a sequence that revolves around itself.

Christianity breaks with a circular conception of time. The figure of Christ constitutes a watershed, between a before and an after, between prehistory and history, a point of no return. The advent of Christ announces the coming future

---

1   See, for example, Momigliano 1966 and Vegetti 2000.

2   Plat. Tim. 37d–38c.

3   Aristot. Phys. 220a25–26.

of his reign and 'opens' the time of history that leads to it. Examined closely, things are extremely complex also in this case, but perhaps two fundamental paradigms can be individuated: that exemplified by the sequence of kingdoms of Joachim of Fiore (whose third kingdom makes Augustine's *civitas dei* immanent to history) and that of the sudden eruption, of the 'God who comes like a thief in the night', of Paul of Tarsus. Modernity will witness precisely a secularisation of these two models of temporality: on the one hand, the philosophies of the history of humanity in which linear time is oriented towards a telos, and, on the other hand, the so-called discontinous philosophies, in which an homogenous and empty time is interrupted by the eruption of an eschaton. The one and the other are nevertheless founded on a common presupposition: the divine creation that institutes the temporal line, even if in order to excede it or interrupt it.

Whether thought under the Greek form of the circle or the Christian form of the line oriented towards the future (presented as either telos or as eschaton), time is a single time that finds its metaphysical foundation in the Platonic idea of eternity, in the Aristotelian movement of the sphere or in the continuous creation of the Christian God. The plurality of times, that is, is traced back to the unity of a foundation, whether cosmological, metaphysical or theological. What would happen if this foundation were undermined? This is the famous question that Augustine poses in order to oppose the reduction of time to motion:

> I once heard a learned man say that time is simply the movement of the sun and moon and stars. I did not agree. For why should not time rather be the movement of all bodies? Supposing the light of heaven were to cease, and a potter's wheel still turn round: would there be no time by which we might measure those rotations and say either that it turned at equal intervals, or, if it moved now more slowly and now more quickly, that some rotations were longer and others shorter?[4]

Is it possible to delineate a materialist tradition that could respond positively to Augustine's question, that is, with the answer that time cannot be thought without motion and that every motion has its specific temporality? In what ways could such a materialist tradition of plural temporalities help to transform our understanding of the Marxist tradition's capacity to think the specificity of historical time? And what metaphors could these traditions provide that might help us to move beyond the circle and the line as dominant temporal figures?

---

4 Augustine 1993, p. 225 (*Confess.* XI, 23) (translation modified).

There were some of the questions that motivated a permanent seminar held at the University of Milan Bicocca between 2009 and 2011, dedicated to the topic of the plural temporalities of and within the Marxist tradition. Despite recurrent claims of Marxism's inherent teleology, naïve historicism, and linear progressivism, we were convinced that the Marxist tradition – both its 'heterodox' currents as well as its supposedly orthodox and canonical formulations – offers other resources for theorising a plurality of historical times. This was not a question of asserting 'Marxism' conceived as a closed system already containing within itself a fully elaborated theory of plural temporalities, or of denying those real tendencies towards temporal linearity and unity that have marked its historical existence. Rather, we aimed to investigate how the Marxist tradition itself could be transformed and renewed by reconnecting with the 'subterranean currents' of plural temporalities that have traversed it throughout its development, seeking both to valorise neglected resources from this contradictory history and also to read against the grain some of its dominant modalities. Reconnecting with – or rather, constructing – an equally subterranean materialist tradition of reflections on the plurality of time within which our discussions could be oriented therefore seemed to constitute a necessary point of departure – and perhaps, in the alternative metaphors, figures and concepts that it provided, simultaneously also a terrain of refoundation.

'The Only Materialist Tradition'

In atomistic philosophy and in Epicurus the infinity of worlds does not allow the *reductio ad unum* of times. The Aristotelian number of movement according to a before and after doesn't find in Epicurus either a metaphysical anchorage in substance, or a cosmological anchorage in the movement of the sphere of a finite universe. In atomism every sustance is a temporary aggregation and every sphere is situated in an infinite universe without either outside or beyond. Time is the 'accident of accidents'. As Lucretius writes:

> Therefore besides void and bodies no third nature
> can be left self-existing in the sum of things
> [...]
> Time also exists not of itself, but only from the things
> is derived the sense of what has been done in the past,
> then what thing is present with us, further what is to follow after.
> Nor may we admit that anyone has a sense of time by itself
> separated from the movement of things and quiet calm.

> [...]
> [...] You may perceive that things done [*res gestae*]
> do never at all consist or exist in themselves as body does,
> nor are said to exist in the same way as void;
> but rather that you may properly call them
> accidents [*eventa*] of body, and of the place in which the things are
>   severally done.[5]

The complex texture of things, the *textura rerum*, cannot be reduced to a single time. Every conjugation of atoms has its own rhythm, but simultaneously does not exist in isolation, being always intertwined with innumerable others. Time is nothing but the symptom of this plurality of rhythms, the infinite intertwining of which does not permit an absolute foundation. As Lucretius writes again:

> For whatever has happened may be called an accident [*eventum*],
> be it of a land or be it of the people itself [*aliud terris, aliud regionibus ipsis*].[6]

What Epicurus and Lucretius propose at a cosmological level, the deconstruction of the hypostasis of a single time, is pursued by Machiavelli on the terrain of politics and history. In *The Discourses* he not only deconstructs both the Polybian theory of anacyclosis as well as the temporal line of biblical narration, but also pushes the definition of the object of his research much further. Rome is not thought of as the 'mixed form' able to subtract itself from the cycle, or as a humanistic ideal, or even as the simple origin of a philosophy of history. Its grandiose history is analysed by beginning from the primacy of the material over form, by the primacy of the case and of conflict over the mixed form to which it gives rise, beginning from the plurality of forces that underlie unity. In *The Prince*, then, politics is thought as an historical horizon that appears precisely as a 'variation of times', as *fortuna*, and in which occasion offers itself to virtue (itself plural, encounter of the fox, man and the lion) not in the form of a kairos, in which a destiny is revealed, but in the material form of the intertwining of a plurality of rhythms.[7]

---

5   Lucretius 1924 (*De rer. Nat.*, I, vv. 445–82).

6   Lucretius 1924 (*De rer. Nat.*, I, vv. 469–70; translation modified).

7   On this dimension of Machiavelli's thought, see Del Lucchese 2004 and Morfino 2005 and 2012a.

In Spinoza this discourse is projected from an historico-political to an onto-logical level, from biblical criticism, in which the imaginary statute of the temporal line of the narration of the book is demonstrated, to the deconstruction of theology and of the metaphysics of the tradition implicated in a theory of substance whose immanence to the modes makes unthinkable any form of anchoring in an absolute that can found the claim of a single time. Spinoza's substance is not presence, it is not the Newtonian time that guarantees the absoluteness of space and time. Rather, it is the *ordo* of the *connexiones* of durations, an intertwining of rhythms with respect to which time, conceived as the Aristotelian order according to a before and after, is nothing but the imaginary absolutisation of one rhythm, taken as a measure of the others, and for which eternity does not constitute a panoramic point of view, an absolute anchoring, but the precise deconstruction of the possibility of such a perspective. In this sense, knowledge *sub specie aeternitatis* is precisely a knowledge that relativises, to the extent to which it exhibits the relational texture of any singular thing, its being a rhythm among rhythms, composed of rhythms, traversed by rhythms, not one that absolutises like a Medusa's glance that petrifies the modes in an abyssal *nunc stans*. To know *sub specie aeternitatis* the history of the Hebrew people means precisely to refuse the imaginary identification of the time of narration of the Book and the time of the world, to know the material texture, the political and economic organisation, the ideological apparatuses (and rituals) and the conflicts that traverse it and within which narration itself acquires its conjunctural meaning.[8]

Finally, in Darwin, on the level of the history of life, we witness the rejection of the idea of a single time as a law of the evolution of species. Darwin's theory makes unthinkable not only the circular time of the reproduction of living forms, which mimic in the sublunar world the movement of the heavenly world (what will later, after Darwin's rupture, be defined as fixism), but also a time-line on which their teleologically oriented evolution unfolds (an element misunderstood in the readings of Darwin in the late nineteenth century). Darwinian time is plural because it corresponds to the multiplicity of forces that confront each other in the struggle for existence, which nevertheless must be understood in a metaphorical way, as a complex network of relations that gives rise to the continuity or discontinuity of natural history:

[...] in the long-run the forces are so nicely balanced, that the face of nature remains for long periods of time uniform, though assuredly the merest trifle would give the victory to one organic being over another.

8   See Morfino 2009.

Nevertheless, so profound is our ignorance, and so high our presumption, that we marvel when we hear of the extinction of an organic being; and as we do not see the cause, we invoke cataclysm to desolate the world, or invent laws on the duration of the forms of life![9]

In other words, for Darwin in the beginning was complexity, the plurality of forces that interact through a web of complex relations, even when nature appears to be unvaried for long periods: simplicity, that is, is one of the possible effects of complexity, never the rule, never the law of order.

Lucretius, Machivelli, Spinoza, Darwin. A very heterogenous tradition: a Latin Poet, a Florentine Secretary, a Dutch Jewish Philosopher and an English Naturalist. In reality, it constitutes a 'selective tradition' only retrospectively, that is, only to the extent to which it offers a toolbox of instruments to use, on an ontological, physical, biological, historical or political level, in order to think the question of plural temporality within the Marxist tradition. In the process, the internal relations of force of both the materialist and Marxist traditions are transformed. It is thus a virtuous circle: because if it is true that it is the questions posed by Marxism that constitute this tradition *après coup*, it is also true that the answers thus solicited retroact on the Marxist tradition itself, making visible what was previously invisible or visible only in a partial and confused way.

The Marxist Tradition

The question of plural temporality was certainly a marginal question in the Marxist tradition, largely dominated by a philosophy of universal history and by the hegemony of a single time: the Hegelian synthesis of the becoming subject of substance by means of the concept transforming itself into time guides the historical progress of humanity until the transparency of communism, a secularisation of the messiah. It is in this sense that the transition from the realm of necessity to the realm of freedom, from pre-history to history, as Marx writes in the celebrated 'Preface' of 1859, has often been understood.

Humanity thus inevitably sets itself only such tasks as it is able to solve, since closer examination will always show that the problem itself arises only when the material conditions for its solution are already present or at least in the course of formation. In broad outline, the Asiatic, ancient,

---

9 Darwin 1988, p. 59. For a reading of Darwin's 'philosophy', see Morfino 2007.

feudal and modern bourgeois modes of production may be designated as epochs marking progress in the economic development of society. The bourgeois mode of production is the last antagonistic form of the social process of production – antagonistic not in the sense of individual antagonism but of an antagonism that emanates from the individuals' social conditions of existence – but the productive forces developing within bourgeois society create also the material conditions for a solution of this antagonism. The prehistory [*Vorgeschichte*] of human society accordingly closes with this social formation.[10]

A single time, the temporal line of universal hisory, on which the various epochs are successively arranged. From the great fresco of the *Manifesto of the Communist Party* to the pages of the 'Preface' of 1859, to *Anti-Dühring* and the determinism of the Second International and the imposition of the Bolshevik model in the Third International and, *dulcis in fundo*, in Stalinist Histo-Mat; but also in so-called 'Western Marxism', from *History and Class Consciousness* to *Dialectic of Enlightenment*, to *Eros and Civilization* and the Italian workerism of the 1960s and 1970s, to Negri's *Insurgencies*, history is thought in terms of a single and directed temporal line. Nevertheless, within this tradition it is possible to find traces of a different attempt, often in the form of a symptom of the insufficiency of the paradigm of single time, of the philosophy of history.

In the young Marx's 'Contribution to the Critique of Hegel's Philosophy of Right. Introduction', plural temporality appears in order to explain the different historical developments of France, Germany and England in terms of anticipations and delays, making Germany a crucible of many times. Germany is contemporary with the past of other European peoples on the social level, contemporary with their present in terms of the theory of the state, and contemporary with their future in criticism, in philosophy.[11] The theme returns in the final pages of the 'Introduction' of 1857 in the attempt to problematise the question of the relations between structure and superstructure in the form of a series of points to be developed:

> The uneven development of material production relative to e.g. artistic development. In general, the concept of progress [is] not to be conceived in the usual abstractness [*gewöhnlichen Abstraktion*]. In modern art etc. this dis-

---

10   *MEW* 13, p. 9.

11   See Frosini 2009, pp. 47–62.

proportion [is] not as important or so difficult to grasp as within practical-social relations themselves. E.g. the relation of education. Relation of the *United States* to Europe. But the really difficult point to discuss here is how relations of production develop unevenly as legal relations. Thus e.g. the relation of Roman private law (this less the case with criminal and public law) to modern production.[12]

Plural temporality finally reappears in some of the pages of the 'mature' Marx. The chapter on primitive accumulation, for instance, far from being a dialectic of violence condensed in the conclusion of the chapter by the formula of the expropriation of the expropriators (the negation of the negation), is in reality a genuine archaeology of this dialectic. The term 'violence' is the summary and generic form of a plurality of real processes that range from conquest to subjugation, from assasination to theft. It is not a univocal directional indicator of a process of transition from one society to another occuring simultaneously everywhere. It dissolves some forms of existence of feudal society, liberating elements that come together in giving rise to capitalist society, but never by means of a model of simple and transitive causality.

The English proletariat (and the localisation of the process is already a methodological caution against totalised philosophies of violence) is the effect of a plurality of causes that was not immanent to those causes in advance (the dissolution of feudal orders, the enclosure of the common lands for the feeding of sheep, the theft of ecclesiastical property in the Reformation, the clearing of estates, that is, the expulsion of tenant farmers by landlords). Each of these processes should be analysed in its specific temporality. For instance, there is a difference between the relative simultaneity of the theft of ecclesiastical property and the clearing of the estates in the Scottish Highlands and in Ireland, and the drawn out process of the expropriation of the common lands from the fifteenth century to the eighteenth century, even though it changed from 'violent individual action' to the use of the 'law [as a] vehicle of theft'. Violence thus acquires meaning only in a history written in the *futur anterior*, *ex post*, in which the fluctuation that preceded the conjugation is imprisoned in a linear and teleological time.[13]

Plural temporality once again appears in Marx's so-called 'Ethnological Notebooks', the theoretical core of which has been described as a 'multilinear

---

12   *MEW* 42, p. 43.
13   See Morfino 2004–5.

model of historical development',[14] and in a famous letter to Vera Zasulič in which Marx questions the thinkability of the Russian rural commune [*obščina*] within the theoretical frame of stagist development. In particular, in the first draft of the letter to Zasulič we find an important reflection on primitive communities.

> The history of the decline of primitive communities (it would be a mistake to place them all on the same level; as in geological formations, these historical forms contain a whole series of primary, secondary, tertiary types, etc.) has still to be written. [...] But in any event the research has advanced far enough to establish that: (1) the vitality of primitive communities was incomparably greater than that of Semitic, Greek, Roman, etc. societies, and, *a fortiori*, that of modern capitalist societies; (2) the causes of their decline stem from economic facts which prevented them from passing a certain stage of development, from historical surroundings not at all analogous with the historical surroundings of the Russian commune of today.[15]

Marx's desire to avoid a rigidly stadial conception of history is evident in this attempt to think time by means of the metaphor of geological strata. History is certainly a succession, but also a stratification of times, and in this sense the *obščina* does not represent simply the archaic – a residue of the past condemned to die – but a temporal stratum that is present and active, and in this sense thus also the real possibility of an alternative to Western capitalist modernisation.[16]

But it is perhaps in the analysis of temporality in *Capital* that we find Marx's most systematic attempt to liberate himself from a single and linear concept of time. Althusser strongly emphasised this aspect: in *Capital*, Marx shows how the time of economic production cannot be read in terms of the continuity of the time of life or of the clock. It is a case instead of a complex and non-linear time, a time of times that has to be constructed beginning from the actual structures of production, from the diverse rhythms that mark production, distribution and circulation.

Tombazos has studied this question in depth in the different volumes of *Capital*.[17] Bracaletti's chapter in this book also focuses on the different tem-

---

14   Anderson 2002, p. 90.

15   *MEW* 19, p. 386.

16   On this theme, see Tomba 2011.

17   Tombazos 1994.

poralities presented in the three volumes. In the first volume we encounter a time in which every capital is juxtaposed to the others and is isolated in the 'abstract synchronicity of a spatialised time in which only production exists'.[18] In the second volume, we instead find a cyclical temporality in which the 'concept of the turnover of capital' is central, which includes the intertwining, without pre-established harmony, of the cycles of money capital, of commodity capital and productive capital, but also the different temporal modalities with which fixed capital and circulating capital enter into the productive cycle: 'with this cyclical temporality there are intertwined [...] forms of simultaneity and non-simultaneity'.[19] Finally, in the third volume we find a temporality that Tombazos defines as 'organic' and that Bracaletti proposes (arguably more precisely) to define as 'mixed', in the sense that we here find the contradictory co-presence of previously discrete temporalities. In this sense, 'in the complex overlaying of simultaneity and non-simultaneity, of linearity and cyclicality [...], the time of capital turns out to be a time of disequilibrium'.[20]

A critique of a classical theory of singular time can be found in all the philosophical production of Ernst Bloch, from the *Spirit of Utopia* to *Experimentum mundi*. However, it is in *Heritage of Our Times* that this moves into the foregound, in response to the difficulty of explaining the rise of an historical phenomenon like Nazism by means of a Marxist model of the contradiction between the productive forces and relations of production. After all, what 'type' of developmental stage could Nazism represent in the logic of a linear time teleologically oriented towards communism? In the central essay of this collection, 'Non-contemporaneity and Obligation to its Dialectic', Bloch proposes precisely a multispatial and multitemporal dialectic able to account for the objective and subjective non-contemporaneities co-present in German society, of times that 'get in the way', so to speak, of the principal contradiction of capital/labour. Bloch returns to these themes a few years later in the context of the German Democratic Republic of the postwar period in 'Differentiations in the Concept of Progress', in order to elaborate a critique of the Eurocentric model of the philosophy of history. At the same time, he aims to put into crisis the dominant Soviet ideology of stages of development by means of a model of multilinear progress, a carriage led by many horses, a multiversum that refuses both the temporal sequence of stages of societal development, ordered accord-

---

18   Bracaletti in this volume.
19   Ibid.
20   Ibid.

ing to a historical-geographical hierarchy, as well as the contemporaneity of the different elements that constitute any society, and also finally the couplet of nature-history, which makes the former the simple non-temporal environment of the latter.

Around the same time that Bloch wrote the articles that compose *Heritage of Our Times*, Gramsci wrote in a fascist prison the notes that would later be collected in his *Prison Notebooks*. Beyond the historicist interpretation that was given to them by Togliatti in the postwar period, there can be found in Gramsci's work important elements for thinking the structural non-contemporaneity of the present and the 'fractured' nature of historical time. For instance, the Gramscian theory of the individual (the *persona*) posits it as a 'living archaeological site' in which the historical process 'has left an infinity of traces', depositing layers of sedimentation. Similar themes can be found in Gramsci's reflections on language, which he thinks not as a static and homogenous reality, but rather, as a stratified social production, heterogenous, transformed in different ways and with diverse rhythms (a distinction beween 'molecular' and 'mass' effects) by the different languages spoken by various classes and strata of the population. This innovation, this continuous acquisition of terms of new metaphorical meanings that differ from the original ones, means that language is at the same time a living reality and a museum of fossils of previous life and civilisations. Further traces of these themes can be found in Gramsci's reflections on the interplay between national languages and dialects, marked by different temporalities that are linked in the last instance to the relation of subaltern and hegemonic forces, though without thinking dialects as residual and separated from the national language. If, on the one hand, Gramsci attributes to dialects the characteristic of being the vehicle of fossilised and anarachonistic conceptions of the world, he also maintains that dialects exercise a strong influence on the national language and can also constitute a possible incubator for linguistic innovations. Finally, plural temporalities are apparent in Gramsci's considerations on the present of nation states, fractured from within by urban centres and rural peripheries and from without by non-contemporaneity on an international level, precisely because hegemonic relations relegate some social formations to function as the 'past' of others. Here, Gramsci's privileged example is the difference between East and West, founded not on the basis of a progressive linear time in which the West would be 'advanced' and the East 'underdeveloped', nor on the notion of an ideal-typical model of the state, present in the West and absent in the East. Rather, Gramsci sees these temporal distinctions as the result of imperialist expansion that imposes an essential unity of the disparity of historical national experiences. According to Gramsci, this non-contemporaneity of the present, this temporal stratification, this plurality of times, is the symptom par excellence of the class struggle.[21]

Pasolini also refers to a non-contemporaneity of the present in *Gramsci's Ashes* [*Ceneri di Gramsci*], in which he counterposes the bourgeois form of life, which posseses history (the most exalted of bourgeois possessions), and the life of the popular neighbourhoods.

> corporeal, collective presence;
> not living, but surviving
> – perhaps more joyous than living – like
> a nation of animals, within its mysterious
> orgasm there would be no other longing
> than that for daily action,[22]

Pasolini opposes the two forms of life as spirit opposed to nature, in a sort of inverted Hegelianism in which true life is not that of history, of spirit, but the popular life, of the popular neighbourhoods, immersed in the intemporality of nature:

> How much more empty
> – in this void of history, in this
> humming pause in which existence holds its tongue –
> is each ideal, clearly better is
> the immense, bronzed voluptuousness,
> almost Alexandrian, which illuminates
> and impurely ignites all [...],[23]

This is the suspension of history that Pasolini first portrayed in *Racconti e cronache romane*, in *Accattone* and in *Mamma Roma*, before revisiting it in other moments, with *Medea*, *The Thousand and One Nights*, and the *Gospel According to Matthew*. Nevertheless, Pinzolo, beginning from an analysis of the scholarship on the linguistics and semiology of Pasolini's cinema, invites us not to read this opposition in a naïve way, as the opposition of the modern and the primitive, the natural. Instead, it is modernity itself that constitutes the primitive, as a residue, a survival or leftover, a multiplicity of strata of surpassed civilisation. Pasolini proposes a hermeneutics of this modernity:

---

21   For a reading of Gramsci that goes in this direction, see Thomas 2009, p. 285.
22   Pasolini 1957, pp. 72–3; cf. Pasolini 2005b.
23   Pasolini 1957, p. 73; cf. Pasolini 2005b.

The problem for Pasolini was to consider the insertion of the heterogeneous into the homogeneous, starting from class struggles understood as the continuous displacing and bifurcating of temporalities, subjects and places. The development of capitalism, with the ensuing need for enlarging the army of the labour force and of consumers, led to the urbanisation of rural populations and to the creation of a sub-proletariat. The occupation of spaces brings about a plurality of tempos and leads to a paradoxical phenomenology of class struggle, which finds itself confronted by an absolute conflict where no recognition between the conflicting parties is possible and where there is no common stake. It is the conflict between those who fight and those who are always already excluded from the fight, on the margins of it. What is a fight between those who live in a temporality oriented towards the goal of progress and development, and consequently look and fight for *something*, and those who do not fight because they live in a temporality from which the idea of becoming is absent? In fact, it can only be a frozen conflict where the fighting attitude of one part meets only the preliminary surrender of the other.[24]

To a certain extent, this reading of Pasolini is similar to the reading that Althusser proposes of Strehler's staging of *Nost Milan* by Bertolazzi. Althusser sees represented two forms of temporality that alternate on the stage without any apparent causal nexus: the empty time of the misery of Milanese popular life and the full, instantaneous, dramatic time of the development of a story, a dialectical time in which a telos guides the contradictions that traverse it. According to Althusser, it is precisely the absence of relations that constitutes the true relation. The originality of Strehler's production consists, that is, precisely in representing and making live this absence of relations, demonstrating that the drama is not at the centre, but at the margins:

> The paradox of *El Nost Milan* is that the dialectic in it is acted marginally, so to speak, in the wings, [*latéralement, à la cantonade*], somewhere in one corner of the stage and at the ends of the acts: this dialectic (although it does seem to be indispensable to any theatrical work) is a long time coming: the characters could not care less about it. It takes its time, and never arrives until the end ...[25]

---

24 See Pinzolo's chapter in this volume.

25 Althusser 1996, p. 138; Althusser 1969, p. 138.

This critique of dialectical temporality, here only sketched out, is taken up again in other essays in *For Marx* and in 'The Object of Capital' within a project of a general rethinking of Marxism in an anti-Hegelian sense (but perhaps it would be more exact to say 'non-Hegelian', as Frosini has suggested),[26] which clearly had the goal of attacking both Soviet Marxist ideology as well as so-called Western Marxism (historical materialism as a theory of stages, on the one hand, and the humanist tale of the journey of humanity from alienation to transparency, on the other). In 'The Object of Capital', Althusser proposed to think – or rather, to constitute – the specific concept of Marxist historical time in its difference from Hegelian time founded on contemporaneity and succession. To think society as a structured complex whole means to think its temporality not in the form of an essential contemporaneity, of which every element is an expression, but rather in terms of a structural non-contemporaneity; structure here is understood as the rejection of a fundamental time in relation to which other times would be anticipations or delays, and points instead towards a precise articulation of times in a given social formation (that is, the autonomy of levels is relative, but not absolute). To think politics and philosophy according to the model of 'relative autonomy' within the French Communist Party in the 1960s meant, on the one hand, to liberate politics from the flux of the historical current and, on the other, to liberate philosophy, theory, from the immediate link with politics: that is, it meant, on the one hand, to deny politics the legitimation of historical destiny, and, on the other, to think philosophy not in terms of the legitimation of a given political line, but as a critical force.

Finally, more recently, a number of scholars from a variety of intellectual and geographical backgrounds, grouped together in the generic category of postcolonial studies, have proposed a critique of singular time and of universal history as ideology of colonialism and imperialism.[27] Edward Said's *Orientalism* criticised the classic division of the Orient and the Occident, a division constructed from the point of view of the West and which inclues an implicit hierarchy that makes the Orient the prehistory of the West. Ranajit Guha, founder of *Subaltern Studies*, showed how Hegelian *Weltgeschichte* constitutes an absolute limit both in spatial and temporal terms between the space of civilisation, Europe, and the space of barbarism, the colonised continents. Chakrabarty and Chaterjee provide a critique of the temporality of modernity founded on the repression, in the service first of colonialism and then of nationalism, of all these heterogenous temporalities. In *Provincializing Europe*, Chakrabarty pro-

---

26   Frosini, *per litteras.*

27   For a critical reconstruction of this current of thought, see Mezzadra 2008.

poses a critique of historicism as an ideology of progress centred on the idea of a capitalism and of a modernity that would constitute the telos towards which non-European temporalities would tend. They are therefore thought in the form of a 'not yet', that is, always as a 'figure of lack', of a still incomplete transition to modernity.

Developing a distinction of Marx, Chakrabarty proposes to call 'History 1' the homogenous and empty time posited by capital, the time of abstract labour, and 'History 2' the plural heterogenous temporalities that pre-exist capital. He proposes not to think History 2 as the other of History 1, but rather, to think them together, destroying the topological distinction between an 'inside' and an 'outside' of capitalism and making any model of capitalism a provisional compromise between History 1 and History 2 (that is, there is no universal model of capitalism – such as Weber's protestant ethic – that could posit itself as a telos of the others). History 2 has precisely the function of constantly interrupting the totalisation of History 1, revealing the fractured and plural nature of the present: subaltern histories, in other words, are inscribed within the history of capital and nevertheless do not have to be thought by means of the model of transition, but rather, of translation, in a way that makes it possible to comprehend their specificity.

Echoing the reading of *Hamlet* proposed by Derrida in *Specters of Marx*, Chakrabarty affirms that time is in itself 'out of joint', that within the moment, in the present, there inheres necessarily a plurality, an absence of closure, a constant fragmentation that cannot be comprehended by means of the model of anachronism, that is, by assuming that residues of the past are contemporaries of the present. We must think instead the moment, the present, as structurally non-one, that is, without the promises that a principle can one day close up this heterogeneity and incompletion into a totality: History 2 fractures the homogenous and empty time of History 1 by means of a future that is already present within it, and that nevertheless is structurally plural, that is, it does not carry within it any closure of the totality and instead is precisely what makes this impossible.

The plural futures of History 2 make the moment perpetually fragmented, without it being possible for one fragment to be added to another in order to prefigure a totality. According to Chakrabarty, the archaic enters modernity not as a 'remnant' of another time, but as constitutive of the present. Chatterjee, in *The Politics of the Governed*, has emphasised how the empty and homogenous time of capital, of modernity, transforms any other time that opposes it into a premodern resistance, into a residue, an archaism, giving rise to the repression of the heterogenous time of real space, characterised by different densities, a genuine plurality of times that are not the relic of a premodern past, but are co-present and therefore constitute some of the possible vectors of conflictuality. It is in order to think this co-presence in Indian society that, both following and modifying Guha's pioneering work as well as appropriating some of Gramsci's terminology, Chatterjee introduces his own distinctive concept of 'political society', in order to provide an account of the politics of the governed in the Indian postcolonial reality (and in what he characterises as 'most of the world'). The homogeneity of the nation and the citizenship that finds its foundation in individualistic civil society, the field of action of the politics of the elite, is set against the social heterogeneity of the population in which Chatterjee claims governmentality (understood in a broadly Foucauldian sense) is operative. Political society then constitutes, according to Chatterjee, an environment of negotiation and contestation of heterogeneous groups of the population whose paralegal action does not constitute the pathological aspect of a backward modernity, but rather, an element of the historical constitution of modernity.

Premodern Time, Postmodern Time and Lived Time

It should thus be clear from this survey the particular way in which the texts collected in this volume confront the question of plural temporalities. In different ways, the various chapters attempt to read the Marxist tradition through the materialist tradition, trying to propose some responses to the question of plural temporality. Naturally, the answers given are not univocal. Nevertheless, our seminar discussions led us to delimit a problematic, to trace some lines of demarcation in relation to other plural conceptions of time.

First, it was noted that no return to a premodern conception of time is possible, or, in the terms of Koselleck's *Begriffsgeschichte*, no return to the *Historiae* that preceded the formation of the collective singular of *Geschichte* is possible; or, in Marxist terms, no return to a moment 'before' the formation of the global market. A theory of plural temporalities today constitutes a point of departure for the future of Marxist theory rather than a summation of its past; only by confronting and thinking through coherently the implications of this theory for a materialist conception of history can a properly Marxist concept of historical time be developed.

Second, we were concerned to trace out with precision the distance of our attempt from tendencies that also seem to posit a multiplicity of times and narrations, but which ultimately conceive such multiplicity as composed of unrelated and indifferent elements. In this context, some of Derrida's observations in an interview from the early 1970s about Althusser's thought are extremely interesting.

Althusser's entire, and necessary, critique of the 'Hegelian' concept of history and of the notion of an expressive totality, etc., aims at showing that there is not one single history, a general history, but rather *histories* different in their type, rhythm, mode of inscription – intervallic, differentiated histories [*il n'y a pas une seule histoire, une histoire générale mais des histoire différentes dans leur type, leur rythme, leur mode d'inscription, histoires décalées, différenciées, etc.*].[28]

And Derrida adds: 'I have always subscribed to this'. Derrida found in Althusser his own refutation of a linear scheme of the development of presence expressed in *On Grammatology*. Not a history, therefore, but numerous histories, as Derrida summarises and agrees. But in the subsequent passage he also indicates a distance:

To ask another kind of question: on the basis of what minimal semantic kernel will these heterogeneous, irreducible histories still be named 'histories'? How can the minimum that they must have in common be determined if the common noun history is to be conferred in a way that is not purely conventional or purely confused? [...] As soon as the question of the historicity of history is asked – and how can it be avoided if one is manipulating a plural or heterogenous concept of history? – one is impelled to respond with a definition of essence, of quiddity, to reconstitute a system of essential predicates, and one is also led to refurbish the semantic grounds of the philosophical tradition. A philosophical tradition that always, finally, amounts to an inclusion of historicity on an ontological ground, precisely. Henceforth, we must not only ask what is the 'essence' of history, the historicity of history, but what is the 'history' of 'essence' in general? And if one wishes to mark a break between some 'new concept of history' and the question of the essence of history (as with the concept that the essence regulates), the question of the history of essence and the history of the concept, finally the history of the meaning of Being, you have a measure of the work which remains to be done.[29]

The risk, according to Derrida, is the metaphysical re-appropriation of the concept of History. For Derrida, this character is linked not only to linearity, but 'to an entire *system* of implications (theology, eschatology, elevating and inter-

---

28   Derrida 2002, p. 50 (1972, p. 79).
29   Derrida 2002, p. 51 (1972, pp. 80–1).

iorizing accumulation of meaning, a certain type of traditionality, a certain concept of continuity)'.[30] For the concept of history, as for any other concept, Derrida adds, 'cannot be subject to a simple and instantaneous mutation': 'we must elaborate a strategy of the textual work which at every instant borrows an old word from philosophy in order immediately to demarcate it'.[31]

Derrida's acute reflections mark the beginning of many discourses that would later become associated with the postmodern, even as they take a clear distance from their periodising implications. Nevertheless, these reflections are arguably founded on the repression of a fundamental aspect of Althusser's discourse. The question is not simply the plurality of times, the plurality of rhythms, the plurality of histories, but the articulation of this plurality. Above all, it is not a question of narration, but of the material structures of different levels (material in the sense in which the different practices and their incorporation of power relations are material). Just as Bloch refused a theory of cycles of culture that have an isolated development à la Spengler, so Althusser refused to think the temporality of different social levels as unrelated. If there is never intra-expressivity between levels, there is neverthelesss always articulation, although given in the problematical form of a determination of a last instance 'whose lonely hour never comes'.

Third, a final line of demarcation should be noted with respect to philosophies of experience or philosophies of lived experiences. The multiversum, the plurality of temporalities, the different rhythms, the intertwinings, the ruptures and the discontinuities are not to be thought in subjective terms, or within a stream of consciousness in which there would be many times present. The problematic of plural temporality explored in this volume should in this sense not be confused with themes elaborated by, for example, James, Bergson, Dilthey or Husserl. In other words, we are not dealing here with the multiple temporalities of subjective consciousness, but with the materiality of the different levels of the social structure. Subjective consciousness, like any form of narrativity, is an effect of this materiality of the social structure, a material effect of dispositifs and apparatuses that model the social imaginary by means of which subjects 'live' their own world. If the subject is given as a multiversum, it has to be thought always as a result and not as originary. The stratification of the temporalities of the subject is neither the ultimate foundation nor the mirror of a given social totality, but the effect of its being constituted and traversed by social relations always in a given position, that is, of its being always already

---

30   Derrida 2002, p. 50 (1972, p. 77).

31   Derrida 2002, p. 51 (1972, p. 80).

positioned within determinate relations of forces and caught up in determinate narrations that are unfolded on many temporal levels. As Althusser sometimes remarked, *on nait toujours quelque part* ...[32] We are made of time, of strata of time, of intertwinings of time. And it is within these intertwinings that political action becomes possible.

---

32   Althusser 1969, p. 74.

CHAPTER 1

The Temporality of the General Will

Augusto Illuminati

Rousseau makes a clear distinction between the time of individual will (and of the totality of wills pursuing private interests, *la volonté de tous*) and the time of the *volonté générale*, which expresses itself in public deliberation. The former is inconstant and floating; the latter is as constant and uniform as divine eternity, similar to the feeling of ecstatic suspension of time achieved by Jean-Jacques in contact with nature. 'In our most intense enjoyments, there is hardly an instant when the heart can genuinely say to us: *I would like this instant to last forever!*'.[1] In the *nunc stans* of time the representation becomes self-referential identity.

I intend here to measure the differential in temporality between the two contrasting versions of the collective *volonté* that are evoked simultaneously: the *volonté générale* and the *volonté de tous*. The plural nature of the collective allows us to represent the synchronisation of time, or its absence: do things fall together, is it an intuition, an expression, or rather a reflection, or mediation? Retroactively, we will see that individual will is also divided by a temporal split, and that the people, in at least one of the two definitions given, behaves like an individual, relinquishing the caution they should have learned from Spinoza: the multitude, *quae una veluti mente ducitur* ... The fact is that there we had *multitudo*, here we have a *peuple*. Subjugated by itself, but subjugated nonetheless.

I shall start with the passage in the *Social Contract* where a strange discussion interrupts the communitarian compactness, supposedly created by the *nouvelle association*, already mentioned at the end of the second *Discourse*. The distinction is antinomical and paradoxical. The core of the argument is to be found in Book II, chapter 3, and is anticipated, with many significant details, in the first version known as the *Geneva Manuscript*, Book I, chapters 2 and 4, which are, respectively, on and against the *General Society of the Human Race* and on the definition of the inalienable nature of sovereignty. 'In fact, each individual, as a man, may have a particular will contrary or dissimilar to the general will which he has as a citizen',[2] where wickedness is this opposi-

---

1 Rousseau 2000, p. 46 (*Fifth Walk*).
2 Rousseau, 2003, p. 7.

tion of a particular will to the public will, as is clearly stated in the *Political Fragment* III, 7.[3] 'It follows from what has gone before that the general will is always right and tends to the public advantage; but it does not follow that the deliberations of the people are always equally correct',[4] because an individual always aims at his or her own good but is not always capable of seeing it, and the people, the sum of single individuals, can be deceived. We are talking of a people that is already 'constituted' and that therefore must not be deceived. However, the *constitution* of a people, in the rare cases where the social contract is possible and can be established, consists in both building and manipulation, in that the Legislator does not act with violent means (counter-productive) nor does he use rational means (inapplicable), but acts with a careful, almost Machiavellian, mix of benevolence and seduction. Deception is unavoidable in the constituent phase, but is deplorable in the constituted people. A messy situation, a stain that remains in the artificial eternity of the general will correctly formed.

Consequently, the general will is stuck in the *always*, while the particular will fluctuates in time. The incoherent assembling of the particular wills (which lacks that constancy provided by the *always*) produces, against the general will, the will of all.

> There is often a great deal of difference between the will of all and the general will; the latter considers only the common interest, while the former takes private interest into account, and is no more than a sum of particular wills: but take away from these same wills the pluses and minuses that cancel one another, and the general will remains as the sum of the differences.[5]

Here Rousseau clarifies (see the author's note) that the balance between differences, without which there would be no common, is not a statistical-liberalist kind of balance, but the result of an *art politique*, as is the case with artificial bodies. How can the balance between the pluses and minuses, between the many *petites différences*, result in the stable middle-way of the collective will? For the deliberation to be a good one, in its impartial immediacy, it is necessary that when the people hold their deliberations, 'being furnished with adequate information' (by whom?), the citizens 'have no communica-

---

3 Rousseau 1964, vol. III, p. 483.
4 Rousseau 2003, p. 3.
5 Rousseau 2003, p. 17.

tion one with another'. In particular, it is necessary to prevent the forming of factions, permanent lobbies ('partial associations formed at the expense of the great association'), the 'sects' deplored by Machiavelli, ruled by centralism which binds its members and is against loyalty to the State, with the result that legislative voting is determined by very few actors in accord with their areas of interest. This means no political parties: every citizen must vote, being informed (how?) but also ignoring the opinion of other people: 'that each citizen should think only his own thoughts'. How does one 'think'? Perhaps making sure that all other citizens' thoughts suffer no interference, watching them closely, and being at the same time watched, something envisaged by the immense auto-Panopticon stadium designed by the Jacobin visionary architect Boullée and intended for popular deliberations. A sinister fantasy, which anticipates the way similar constructions were recently used for containing the dangerous masses.

Apart from the operative evidence of the conclusion – which the *fin de siècle* Rousseauian French revolutionaries applied in their own way, allowing their own clubs to flourish while condemning other factions, in particular preventing workers' trade-union organisations – the text of the *Social Contract* is quite enigmatic if it is not integrated with other assumptions made elsewhere by the author, either earlier or later, beginning with the first draft of the *Social Contract*. Let us then turn to the *Geneva Manuscript*, which very clearly illustrates the nature of that *always [toujours]* that characterises the general will in the *Social Contract*, Book II, chapter 3. It must be pointed out that there is no general society of the human race,[6] that is, a compact social body; rather, there is a swarm, a fluctuating and unstable group made up of thousands of reciprocal relations. In a state of nature, an individual is never the same in two different moments of her or his life, and this leads to the misery and weakness of the multitude, unable to achieve the common good, and calls for an *artificial* reorganisation in line with a political project that introduces morality and rationality. The common strength of the state, founded in such a way, is directed by the general will and is called sovereignty.[7] We must therefore expect to run into the same aporias and contradictions that characterise the *dispositif* of sovereignty.

However, now comes the interesting part. Not only does private interest always tend towards preference and the public will towards equality, reproducing on a collective scale the tormented opposition between legitimate

---

6   Rousseau 1964, *Geneva Manuscript*, I, p. 2.

7   Rousseau 1964, *Geneva Manuscript*, I, p. 4.

amour de soi-même (instinct of self-preservation, Spinoza's *conatus*) and harmful *amour propre* (spirit of emulation, Hobbes's *vain-glory*), but an additional temporal gap appears.

Even if it were possible to reach an agreement between the two types of will, how would it be possible for such an agreement to last? What would stop these two kinds of will from separating after one moment, from going back to the state of nature, to the fluctuating identity of the individual in a multitude? Human order is subject to numerous transformations: ways of thinking and of doing change so easily it would be risky to say that tomorrow we will want the same thing we want today. It is true that the collective will is less subject to this kind of inconsistency, but nothing can guarantee the sameness of the particular will. Even if the social body (artificial) could say it now wants the same thing a single man wants, it could not say the same for the future. The general will that directs the state is not the will of the past but of the present, and the true nature of sovereignty is a permanent agreement in time and space, its effects being always the same, with no interference by singular changes: public acts continue to be valid because of tacit consensus until they are revoked or modified by other acts of the same nature. The play between wanting and not wanting is arrested, is in a state of arrest, in the punctual event of the *volonté générale*, an impersonal *katechon* which restrains the dissolution of society, in the same way that Kant's categorical imperative restrains inclinations.

In other words: law, the expression of the general will removed from the changeable fluidity and from the schemes of the *volonté de tous*, has the quality of the divine eternity-instant, the *nunc stans*. Authenticity is the object of ecstasy. This is supported by Rousseau's private experience, and even autobiographical writings, which are characterised by the psychotic structure of primitive temporality, the opposite of social temporality. My thesis is that the schizoid implications highlight the historical and theoretical contradiction that Rousseau brilliantly identifies when writing the catechism of democratic sovereignty, of post-absolutist obedience, which follows the neutralisation of conflict.

In order to illustrate this psychotic deviation, it will be enough to read the episode described in the first *Promenade* [Walk], which sets the key for all the *Rêveries du promeneur solitaire*, the terminal outcome of the Rousseauian production in every sense:

> I am now alone on earth, no longer having any brother, neighbour, friend, or society other than myself. The most sociable and the most loving of humans has been proscribed from society by a unanimous agreement. [...] Everything is finished for me on earth. People can no longer do good

or evil to me here. I have nothing more to hope for or to fear in this world; and here I am, tranquil at the bottom of the abyss, a poor unfortunate mortal, but unperturbed, like God Himself. Everything external is henceforth foreign to me. [...] I am on earth as though on a foreign planet onto which I have fallen from the one I inhabited.[8]

The flagellation goes on, an even more introverted replica of the *Confessions*, where he declares that he is 'nothing among men', has no relations or interaction with them, and that 'to abstain has become my sole duty and I fulfil it as much as it is in me to do so'.

Inaction first suspends time, the corporeality which supports the perception of duration is dissolved in a vortex of resentment and monumental innocence. The Platonic and gnostic *allógenos* has definitely installed itself in the Parisian desert of modernity and evasions are positioned at the geographical margins.

The first ecstatic experience appears on the stage during the second *Promenade*. On 24 October 1776, Rousseau leaves the house in the afternoon (in rue Plâtrière, today named after him, near the Temple), walks through the Marais very slowly, then takes rue du Chemin-Vert and starts climbing up Ménilmontant. Fields and vineyards, as the name of the street indicates, a classic excursion in the areas today overwritten by the urban development that changed Paris in the nineteenth century (XI and XX *arrondissements*), the neighbourhoods of the extreme barricades of the Paris Commune, celebrated by *Temps des cérises*, now home to the *bobos*. He heads towards Charonne, passing through a landscape which announced the arrival of winter at the end of the grape harvest, a sweet and sad metaphor of age and of the destiny of a self-pitying wanderer:

> I saw myself at the decline of an innocent and unfortunate life, my soul still full of vivacious feelings and my mind still bedecked with a few flowers – but flowers already wilted by sadness and dried up by worries.[9]

On his way back he walks along Haute-Borne, the present-day rue Oberkampf, where in front of the Galant Jardinier a great Danish dog leaps up at him, causing him to faint and fall hurt to the ground. He is assisted and taken home. This is what he says about the experience of waking up after the incident:

---

8   Rousseau 2000, pp. 1–90.

9   Rousseau 2000, p. 10.

Night was coming on. I perceived the sky, some stars, and a little greenery. This first sensation was a delicious moment. I still had no feeling of myself except as being 'over there'. I was born into life at this instant, and it seemed to me that I filled all the objects I perceived with my frail existence. Entirely absorbed in the present moment. I remembered nothing; I had no distinct notion of my person nor the least idea of what had just happened to me; I knew neither who I was nor where I was; I felt neither injury, fear, nor worry. I watched my blood flow as I would have watched a brook flow, without even suspecting that this blood belonged to me in any way. I felt a rapturous calm in my whole being; and each time I remember it, I find nothing comparable to it in all the activity of known pleasures.[10]

The translucent innocence of inaction is caught in a sense of guilt which permeates the opacity of any practice.

In 1749, while walking through the Bois de Vincennes on a sweltering afternoon, slightly to the south of the route just described, on his way to see his friend Diderot who was confined in the Vincennes prison, he read the advertisement published by the Academy of Dijon and immediately grasped the ideas which were to develop into the first *Discourse*. Illumination of Vincennes: social injustice revealed, but also a fall into writing and fame, the loss of innocence. All subsequent disgraces originated here. We are at the end of a cycle, dereliction and adherence to vegetative life, though always in the form of an involuntary contraction of time.

And finally the fifth *Promenade*, which is rather an insular description, revolving around the Isle de Saint-Pierre (or Île de La Motte) at the centre of the lake Bienne. The shores of the lake are romantic and wild, pristine and uncontaminated, not touched by human cultivation or by travellers. The two small islands are even more solitary, although they are farmed and occasionally inhabited, sometimes the destination for day trips and local festivals. The environment is similar to the artificially natural surroundings depicted in *New Heloise*. Here Rousseau experiences the most tranquil happiness:

Now what is this happiness and in what did its enjoyment consist? From the description of the life I led there, I will let all the men of this century guess at it. The precious *far niente* was the first principal enjoyment I wanted to savor in all its sweetness, and all I did during my sojourn was in

---

10   Rousseau 2000, p. 11.

effect only the delightful and necessary pursuit of a man who has devoted himself to idleness.[11]

Botanising, family life with Thérèse, gardening, personal consumption and solitary boat trips when the water is calm:

> and there, stretching myself out full-length in the boat, my eyes turned to heaven, I let myself slowly drift back and forth with the water, sometimes for several hours, plunged in a thousand confused, but delightful, reveries, which, even without having any well-determined or constant object, were in my opinion a hundred times preferable to the sweetest things I had found in what are called the pleasures of life. Often, warned by the setting of the sun that it was the hour of retreat, I would find myself so far from the Island that I was forced to work with all my might to get back before the nightfall.[12]

When the water is agitated he lies down on the banks and drifts into oblivion until nightfall.

> There, the noise of the waves and the tossing of the water, captivating my senses and chasing all other disturbance from my soul, plunged it into a delightful reverie in which night would often surprise me without my having noticed it. The ebb and flow of this water and its noise, continual but magnified at intervals, striking my ears and eyes without respite, took the place of the internal movements which reverie extinguished within me and was enough to make me feel my existence with pleasure and without taking the trouble to think. From time to time some weak and short reflection about the instability of things in this world arose, an image brought on by surface of the water. But soon these weak impressions were erased by the uniformity of the continual movement which lulled me and which, without any active assistance from my soul, held me so fast that, called by the hour and agreed-upon signal, I could not tear myself without effort.[13]

The creases of time and the reflections induced are muffled by the same rhythm. So intense is the desire to replicate the experience that one surrenders

---

11   Rousseau 2000, p. 42.
12   Rousseau 2000, p. 44.
13   Rousseau 2000, p. 45.

to the repetition compulsion: going to bed and wishing for the next day to be exactly the same. Instead of the flow of fugitive instants we have a simple and permanent state, similar to death, though of ecstatic happiness. A muffled apology of Thanatos, a return to inertia from the mundane flow. The present lasts always, without marking its duration and leaving no trace of sequence, ataraxic and self-fulfilled. Anticipating Faust, Jean-Jacques Rousseau declares: 'As for happiness which lasts, I doubt that it is known here. In our most intense enjoyments, there is hardly an instant when the heart can genuinely say to us: *I would like this instant to last forever!*'.[14]

That fixed moment, however, has no life of its own, being similar to death, an allegorical projection of the most stationary sovereignty. Goethe borrows from the *Promenade* in his *Faust*, Part II, Act V. The protagonist, now 100 years old, has become a businessman and is managing a large plot of reclaimed land, in the style of an enclosure, having transformed a stretch of sea into arable soil. It is a celebration of the industrial revolution which does not, however, forget to mention the price paid. The good old Baucis and Philemon, whose small cottage is right in the middle of the estate, on an elevated spot from where it is possible to survey the dried-out land as if in a panopticon, are easily dispossessed: they are burned alive. Faust is taken by remorse, and, now blind, mistakes the noise of the undertakers digging his grave for that of workmen intent on digging a gully; he then implores time to stop, leading Mephistopheles to believe he is now in his power. The arrest of the present is no longer ecstatic, it is complex and contradictory (in 1831 Goethe had read Hegel's *Phenomenology* and the passage on the 'here and now'). Modernisation, which in Rousseau was presented as the antinomic couple of transparency-opacity, is now an unresolved element even from a socialist-utopian point of view, a Saint-Simonian one, a view shared by the old Poet. The 'Act' that characterised the beginning (*im Anfang war die Tat ...*) now displays all its aporiai. Faust is saved by the intervention of the Eternal Feminine, of the victim Gretchen, who recapitulates the victim Julie. It is an exaggerated denouement.

Let us go back to the lacustrine ecstasy. The next passage is revealing: 'What do we enjoy in such a situation? Nothing external to ourselves, nothing if not ourselves and our own existence. As long as this state lasts, we are sufficient unto ourselves, like God'.[15] Instant happiness is transparency with no reflection, divine acquiescence, party-like euphoria, self-representation where precisely

---

14   Rousseau 2000, p. 46.
15   Rousseau 2000, p. 46.

nothing is represented because all is translucent, the people see themselves in the immediacy, not in an estranged and alienating spectacle.[16] Ordinary temporality is opacity, *funeste hasard* of the development of humanity which progresses in stages, sequence of the passions and interests which fragment the *volonté générale* and break it up into *volonté de tous*, the sum of affects driven by *amour propre*. The legislator, he who must establish the right contract with his charismatic constituent power and then disappear, is almost a divine being, nearly invisible, appearing now in the indifferent Wolmar in the *New Heloise*, an elusive and ataraxic spectator, *oeil vivant*, in Jean-Jacques as legislator or organiser of village surprise parties, or exiled in the uniform and lulling rhythm of nature ... More examples of the theological drift can be inferred from the rationalism *sui generis* which characterises the *Profession de foi* of the Savoyard Vicar, *exemplar divinae vitae* within that *exemplar humanae vitae* represented by *Émile*, the equivalent of the diffidence towards parties and political representation in the *Social Contract*, or in the article 'Économie politique' in the *Encyclopédie*, where it is said that the most general will is always the most just also, and the voice of the people is in fact the voice of God.[17] The *délibération publique* must never deviate from the *volonté générale*, because the people are seduced by particular interests and the social body or *moi commun* is dismembered into tacit or legal sections.

Two observations enable us to offer a provisional conclusion:

First, Rousseau constructs an ideology and sumptuous rhetoric of the *nunc stans* on the basis of a conception of human development which progresses through casual leaps, where it is evident that he is borrowing from Diderot – and this means a shift from agnosticism to Platonic deism. Rousseau was fascinated by Diderot's idea that the universe could well be the result of a long series of throws of dice.[18] The second *Discourse* and *On the Origins of Language*

---

16   See Rousseau's *Letter to M. D'Alembert on the Theatre.*

17   Rousseau 1964, Vol. III, p. 246.

18   See Diderot 1916, *Thought 21* pp. 38–40: 'I open the pages of a celebrated professor and I read: "Atheists, I concede to you that movement is essential to matter; what conclusion do you draw from that? That the world is the result of a fortuitous concourse of atoms? You might as well tell me that Homer's Iliad or Voltaire's Henriade is the result of a fortuitous concourse of written characters." I should be very sorry to use that argument to an atheist; he would make quick work of the comparison. According to laws of the analysis of chances (he would say) I ought not to be surprised that a thing happens, when it is possible and the difficulty of the result is compensated by the number of throws. There is a certain number of throws in which I would back myself to bring 100,000 sixes at once with 100,000 dice. Whatever the definite number of letters with which I am invited fortuitously to create

are governed by the arbitrary – Althusser insisted on this point, identifying the underground current of aleatory materialism in these writings – and a certain autobiographical element can be found in the passage from the 1748 project for the literary journal *Le Persifleur* where Rousseau-Diderot claims that 'nothing is less like me than myself; that is why it would be useless to attempt to define my character by anything other than variety ... In a word, a Protean, a chameleon and a woman are all of them creatures less changeable than I'.[19] (Diderot uses the same formula for Rameau's nephew!). Furthermore, in the never composed *La morale sensitive ou le matérialisme du sage*, of which Book 9 of the *Confessions* gives us a draft, he claims: 'It has been remarked that most men are in the course of their lives frequently unlike themselves, and seem to be transformed into others very different from what they were'. The identification of his happy self in the panic flow of things is a later and alternative outcome. Here we are dealing with a discontinuous temporality which still recurs in the characters of *New Heloise*.

Second, what kind of political representation is involved here? On the one hand, the rejection of plural temporality (*volonté de tous*) reinforces the criticism of liberal representation, inhibiting even that limited pluralism required by the political and economic market of modernity; on the other hand, the illumination of the *nunc stans* exalts the perfect and self-referential representation of the contract. 'I can see no viable middle path between the rawest democracy and the most complete Hobbesian system', Rousseau wrote to Mirabeau on 26 July 1767. It is a retrospective reference that accounts for both the con-

---

the Iliad, there is a certain definite number of throws which would make the venture advantageous to me; indeed, my advantage would be infinite if the number of throws permitted me were infinite. You grant me that matter exists from all eternity and that movement is essential to it. In return for this concession, I will suppose, as you do, that the world has no limits, that the multitude of atoms is infinite, and that this order which causes you astonishment nowhere contradicts itself. Well, from these mutual admissions there follows nothing else unless it be that the possibility of fortuitously creating the universe is very small but that the quantity of throws is infinite; that is to say, that the difficulty of the result is more than sufficiently compensated by the multitude of throws. Therefore, if anything ought to be repugnant to reason, it is the supposition that matter being in motion from all eternity, and there being perhaps in the infinite number of possible combinations an infinite number of admirable arrangements, none of these admirable arrangements would have ensued, out of the infinite multitude of those which matter took on successively. Therefore, the mind ought to be more astonished at the hypothetical duration of chaos than at the actual birth of the universe'. On this protean phase in Rousseau's work, see Starobinski 1971 and 1988.

19   Rousseau 1964, vol. I, p. 1108.

tinuity and the contradictory nature of sovereignty. In this sense, D.F. Wallace is right when in the delirious monologue at the beginning of *Infinite Jest* he says: 'I believe Hobbes is just Rousseau in a dark mirror'.[20]

The act which unites the *pactum unionis* and the *pactum subjectionis* without delegating to a third party, the act by which a subject renounces his person and goods to regain them from the community, can be likened to the way Julie leaves her past behind her and is reborn in the matrimonial pact, founded on loyalty to order and on the exercise of a constant will [*volonté constant*].[21] The whole scene, which opens with the solemn *incipit* describing the emotion experienced for the first time on her arrival at the church, evokes the *Être Eternel* which is not only the God of philosophers but also the God in the Bible. The fragmentary, heterogenous and passionate past of Julie will, however, resurface and cause the failure of the union and the ruin of the protagonists' lives.

The couple Émile-Sophie also breaks up at the end of the pedagogical novel. Despite its solemn prefiguration, the social contract would not know a better fate. Rousseau – not by chance but because of fate – will be able to experience the *nunc stans* only on the fluctuating waves of the lake, where we have eternity exposing the death drive, not death opening up into eternity.

---

20   Wallace 1996.
21   Rousseau 1997, letter XVIII.

CHAPTER 2

The French Revolution and the Temporality of the Collective Subject between Sieyès and Marx

Luca Basso

The Problem of the French Revolution

While the French Revolution needs to be interpreted historically – it was an event concluded in itself – it also triggered a number of aspects that reach beyond a specific period, fixed in time. We are faced with a veritable 'battle field' of historical and political analysis: positioning ourselves in relation to this event is also crucial with a view to understanding the present situation. Moreover, from a strictly historical perspective, it is important to remember that the French Revolution was a complex event, containing a number of interrelated revolutions within itself: the revolution of the Third Estate, that of the *sans-culottes* in the city and that of the peasants in the countryside. The old Marxist interpretation of the French Revolution as a bourgeois revolution undoubtedly pinpoints one aspect of the problem, but arguably fails to highlight its distinctive characteristics.[1] Moreover, various scholars have noted that, strictly speaking, the Revolution was sparked off by the *officiers*, and hence by bourgeois intellectuals and professionals, rather than by the 'capitalist' bourgeoisie.[2] So the relationship between the French Revolution and capitalist development should be problematised; the theory according to which the French Revolution led to the realisation of the interests of the bourgeoisie thus no longer appears so clear-cut and indisputable. With regard to studies of the Revolution, alongside a number of important nineteenth-century texts (such as Thiers, Michelet, Tocqueville), we must not forget Jaurès's *Histoire socialiste de la Révolution française*, which appeared for the first time between 1901 and 1904, and which was extremely influential, particularly in the French context.[3] Notwithstanding its limitations, the time-honoured work of Georges Lefebvre is still unsurpassed. This author perceived the French Revolution as a bourgeois revolution,

---

1   See Soboul 1975.
2   For example, Cobban 1964.
3   See Jaurès 2015.

but avoided schematisms and inflexibility, instead providing a complex, multi-causal interpretation: for Lefebvre, the bourgeois nature of the Revolution did not exclude antagonism and compromises between the various components.[4] Lefebvre's analysis is also interesting for interweaving the conflicts in the countryside and in the city: the former, in many cases, were distinguished not only by an anti-feudal character, but also by an anti-capitalist one.[5]

At this stage, I shall examine the 'stakes' of the French Revolution from two perspectives: that of Sieyès and that of Marx. The former, Sieyès, an influential theoretician of the Revolution, 'ideologist' of the Third Estate, played a crucial role in the initial years of the Revolution; the latter, in many ways, adopted the French Revolution – the Revolution *par excellence*, the mother of all revolutions – as a model for the communist revolution. But the comparison between the two thinkers focuses on the question of political temporality. This comparison aims to underline the clear difference, from a temporal perspective, between the collective subject of Sieyès and that of Marx, using the common reference to the French Revolution as a starting point.

Sieyès and the French Revolution

We shall start with a reference to the pamphlet of the Abbé Joseph-Emmanuel Sieyès, *Qu'est-ce que le Tiers-Etat?* [*What is the Third Estate?*], a work published in January 1789 and which played a decisive role in the French Revolution.[6] Born into a bourgeois family, Sieyès played a fundamental role in transforming the Estates-General into a National Assembly and, together with Mirabeau, opposed the King's order to dissolve the assembly on 23 June 1789. He then left the Jacobin Club to join the 'Society of 1789', founded in 1790 by Condorcet, Lafayette and Mirabeau with his inspiration. On 17 June 1790, Sieyès was applauded by the Parisian crowd that had assembled at the *Palais Royal* to celebrate the first anniversary of the National Assembly. The celebration had been organised by the 'Society of 1789'. The first interesting aspect to underline is that the pamphlet in question, which has been interpreted as a manifesto of the Revolution, is presented by the author as a work of constitutional-political science, in which a decisive role is attributed to the problems related to the limitation of legislative power. In actual fact, Sieyès could not be appreciated

---

4   See Lefebvre 1962.
5   See also Richet-Furet 1970 and Vovelle 1984.
6   Sieyès 1970.

THE TEMPORALITY OF THE COLLECTIVE SUBJECT

either by those who longed for the return of the *ancien régime* or by advocates of the Terror. The work on which this article is based, *What is the Third Estate?*, is preceded by two other significant texts, *Views of the Executive Means* and *Essay on Privileges*: the latter is based on the refusal of the idea that privilege entitles its holder to a position of pre-eminence within a nation. The distinctive characteristic of privilege is that of being outside of the common laws.[7]

The world-famous opening words of *What is the Third Estate?* are as follows: 'What is the Third Estate? – Everything. What has the Third Estate been until now? – Nothing. What does it want to be? – Something'.[8] Here the author underlines the need for political recognition of the Third Estate, which is indeed considered as being 'Everything'.[9] In this sense, the link between the Third Estate and the nation is close. But 'what is a nation? A body of associates, living under a common law [*loi commune*] and represented by the same legislature'.[10] The constitutive reference to the common law, and thus to the element of the nation, implies, for Sieyès, a radical criticism of the logic of privileges.[11] With regard to the Third Estate, he makes three requests. First, that the representatives of the Third Estate be chosen from among the citizens that belong to the Third Estate itself.[12] Second, that the representatives of the Third Estate be equal in number to the sum of the other two orders.[13] And finally, the Third Estate demands that 'the Estates-General vote by heads and not by Orders'.[14] Returning to the first request, it is important to note that Sieyès explains that, in order to belong to the Third Estate, a person must demonstrate that they do not enjoy any privileges, or, if they are holders of privileges, they must be prepared to give them up.[15] He returns again to the idea of the absolute contraposition between the medieval logic of privileges and the logic of the nation: 'Above all, beware, I beg you, of the multifarious agents of feudalism. It is to

---

7   On Sieyès, see particularly Bastid 1970, the comprehensive work of Bredin 1988, Pasquino 1998, and Scuccimarra 2002, which focuses, however, on a phase of Sieyès's reflections subsequent to that dealt with in this investigation.

8   Sieyès 1970, p. 119. Further on, Sieyès states that 'the Third Estate embraces [...] all that which belongs to the Nation' (Sieyès 1970, p. 126).

9   Sieyès 1970, p. 126.

10   Ibid.

11   See Sieyès 1970, pp. 130–1: 'Any privilege [...] runs contrary to common laws [*droit commun*]; hence all those who enjoy privileges, without exception, constitute a separate class opposed to the Third Estate'.

12   Sieyès 1970, p. 137.

13   Sieyès 1970, p. 144.

14   Sieyès 1970, p. 151.

15   Sieyès 1970, p. 137.

the odious remnants of this barbaric system that we still owe the division of France, to her misfortune, into three mutually hostile orders'.[16] In this context, worship of the state means the full political recognition of the people and the radical criticism of any privileges:

> We can be free only with the People and by the People [...] Day by day, the influence of reason [*empire de la raison*] spreads further, increasingly necessitating the restitution of the rights that have been usurped. Sooner or later, every class will have to withdraw inside the boundaries of the social contract [*contrat social*], the contract which concerns everyone, and binds all the associates one to the other [...].[17]

The passage quoted contains two particularly important terms: *empire de la raison* and *contrat social*.[18] With regard to the latter, it is significant to note, among other things, the recurring references to the element of the social contract in the writings of this period and in the debates of the National Assembly, from the reference to Rousseau but also the experience of the American Revolution. In this sense, we see a total refusal of the Medieval, of the 'shadows', of obscurity; the 'Enlightenment' of modernity means, on the other hand, the affirmation of the people, an unacceptable element for the ruling classes:

> We expect you to submit to the common laws, not to offer a token of insulting pity for an Order which you have treated mercilessly for so long. But it is for the Estates-General to discuss this matter; today's question is how to constitute it properly. If the Third Estate is not represented in the Estates-General, the voice of the nation will be mute in that Assembly. And none of its acts will be valid.[19]

Thus the Third Estate-nation, and the radical contraposition of this element to the privilege system, comes to signify the negation of the feudal structure. Moreover, this is one of the aspects that also exists in Marx, particularly in his early writings, in which he highlights the overthrow of feudalism by the French Revolution: from this perspective, the event in question would appear to carry to extremes the process already started by absolutism, and to be aimed at the

---

16   Sieyès 1970, pp. 140–1.
17   Sieyès 1970, p. 157.
18   See Baczko 1997.
19   Sieyès 1970, p. 160.

construction of the state-form, 'one step ahead' compared to Medieval times. According to more traditional, 'orthodox' Marxism, the French Revolution was interpreted purely and simply as a bourgeois revolution, with the power to clear the final obstacles hampering the full realisation of political modernity. This element also provided a point of contact between the various interweaving French Revolutions in the city and the country. But, as became evident later, this way of approaching the problem overlooks a series of important elements.

However, to return to Sieyès, it is essential to point out that the Third Estate is not simply a part of but corresponds to the nation; therefore, the good of the Third Estate becomes *salus publica*:

> The public health demands that the common interest of society be kept pure and uncontaminated. And on the basis of this point of view – the only good, truly national point of view – the Third Estate will never lend its authority to admitting several different orders into a so-called House of Commons, because the very idea of a House of Commons made up of different Orders is a monstrosity.[20]

From this perspective, there is an authentic identification of the Third Estate with the nation, so that the will of the Third Estate constitutes the will of the nation as a whole, and not just the will of a specific part. But 'what is the will of a Nation? It is the result of individual wills, just as the Nation is the aggregate of the individuals who compose it'.[21] The will of the nation, the common will, which presents as its purpose the public good, is identified with the sum of individual wills. In this sense, there is no contraposition between the individual dimension and the common dimension.

---

20   Sieyès 1970, p. 168. See also Sieyès 1970, p. 197: 'Mark the enormous discrepancy between the assembly of the Third Estate and those of the other two Orders [...] The former represents twenty-five million people and deliberates over the interests of the Nation'.

21   Sieyès 1970, pp. 204–5. See also Sieyès 1970, pp. 207–8: 'In a National Assembly, particular interests are bound to remain isolated, and the will of the majority must always be in accordance with the general good [...] We know what the true dream of a National Assembly is: not to pursue the private interests of citizens, but to consider them in their entirety in terms of the common interest'; Sieyès 1970, p. 210: 'It is certain therefore that only the non-privileged members of society are entitled to be electors and deputies [...] All privileges then are, in the very nature of things, unjust, odious and opposed to the great end of all political society. A privileged class is to the Nation what individual advantages are to the citizen. Like them, it is something that cannot be represented'.

However, the individual will is exactly that of a subject who is free and equal to others, and so the will of the nation as the sum of the individual wills clashes radically with the privilege system, as clearly emerges from the conclusion of the work:

> Do not ask what is the appropriate place for a privileged class in the social order. It is like deciding on the appropriate place in the body of a sick man for a malignant humour that torments him. It must be neutralised. The health and the order of the organs must be restored, so as to prevent the formation of noxious combinations that vitiate the essential principles of life itself. But the word has gone round: you are not fit enough to be healthy! And to this aphorism of aristocratic wisdom, you give credence like a pack of Orientals consoling themselves with fatalism. Sick as you are then, so remain![22]

It is important to stress the relevance of this criticism of privilege: the affirmation of national sovereign power, of the general will, can only take place through the exclusion from the field of politics of all those considered as enemies of the nation. On the other hand, the Third Estate possesses in itself all that is necessary for the formation of a 'complete nation': so what is not a nation must therefore be excluded. The figure of Rousseau's legislator is disregarded here: the Third Estate, for the reasons described, claims for its representatives the full exercise of constituent power. The figure of the legislator is archaic, outdated by the existence of a representative Assembly, which combines all the functions in itself and thus exercises constituent power.

But the question investigated opens up a theme of fundamental interest for Sieyès, namely, that of representation:

> Like civil rights, political rights derive from a person's capacity as a citizen. These legal rights are identical for every person, whether his property happens to be great or small. Any citizen who satisfies all the formal requirements for an elector has the right to be represented [...] The right to be represented is single and indivisible. All citizens enjoy it equally.[23]

Representation is founded on equality, which is based on the negation of privilege: 'The privileged classes are to the great body of citizens what exceptions

---

22   Sieyès 1970, p. 218.
23   Sieyès 1970, p. 145.

are to the law. Any society must be governed by common laws and submitted to a common order'.[24] This latter statement represents a negation of the privilege system, with its particularistic character of the elimination of any communality. However, the question is certainly not based on an idea of absolute freedom.[25] From this perspective, the discussion of freedom is a discussion on the limitations posed to freedom itself. But a new and extremely important aspect is introduced by Sieyès: the relationship between the question of representation and the dimension of work. In fact, the theme of the representation of the Third Estate is connected with a social and economic element:

> Some people have supposed that they reinforce the difficulty of which we have just disposed by submitting that the Third Estate does not contain enough intelligent [*éclairés*] or courageous members and so forth competent to represent it, and that it has no option but to call on the leading figures [*lumières*] of the aristocracy [...] So ridiculous a statement deserves no answer. Look at the available classes [*classes disponibles*] in the Third Estate; and like everyone else I call 'available' those classes where some sort of affluence enables men to receive a liberal education, to train their minds [*raison*] and to take an interest in public affairs [*affaires publiques*]. Such classes have no interest other than that of the rest of the people [*people*].[26]

Here, with respect to the representatives, Sieyès refers to the 'available classes', and therefore to bourgeois exponents with 'a liberal education'. This line of reasoning implies the existence of major economic changes and hence the division of labour: 'Towns have increased in number and size. Commerce and arts have, as it were, created new classes thronging with prosperous families of educated and civic-minded citizens'.[27] Sieyès refers to the most dynamic, the most hard-working classes, and therefore the Third Estate: 'The Third Estate, which had been reduced to nothing, has reacquired by its industry something of what had been seized from it by the offence of those in power'.[28] Faced with this state

---

24 Sieyès 1970, pp. 148–9.
25 See Sieyès 1970, p. 139: 'In no circumstances can any freedom or right be unlimited. In all countries, the law prescribes certain qualifications without which one can be neither an elector nor eligible for election [...] Political liberty, therefore, has its limits, just as civil liberty has'.
26 Sieyès 1970, pp. 143–4.
27 Sieyès 1970, p. 149.
28 Sieyès 1970, p. 150.

of affairs, it is no longer possible to be intimidated by the nobility, which is only a shadow of its former self. Sieyès states that the Third Estate is not asking to participate, but to have its identity acknowledged: it constitutes a nation, which is entitled to the initiative of the Constitution. This assumption is based on a purely economic argument, inspired by physiocrats, but especially by Smith and Locke. In particular, Sieyès read Smith in depth; references to political economy, modern science *par excellence*, echo throughout his writings. So he considers the representative system as a special case of the rational division of labour that constitutes the fundamental principle of social life. Indeed, Sieyès conceives of the division of labour as a special application of representation. Since economic progress is founded on an ever more rational division of labour, which gives greater individual freedom to everyone, the political system can only progress by means of a generalisation of the representative system. Politics constitutes a specialised activity, suitable for the division of labour, the representative system implements all that befits 'modern nations'. The Third Estate is distinguished by its social utility, bearing the weight of the labours through which man exercises his freedom. So this justifies its request to have representatives in the Estates in a number equal to the sum of those of the Nobility and the Clergy. The Third Estate constitutes a complete nation, inasmuch as it organises all the social labour, within the complex structure of its various functions.[29]

In order to understand this structural link between representation and the division of labour, it is not sufficient to draw on the English model, and hence on the English constitution, conceived as a paradigm.

> I am very much afraid that this much-vaunted masterpiece cannot withstand an impartial examination based on the principles of a genuine political order [...] Consider the system of national representation and how bad all its elements are, as the English themselves admit! [...] I do not deny that the English Constitution was an astonishing piece of work at the time [...] I would still dare to submit that instead of displaying all the simplicity of good order, it rather reveals a scaffolding of precautions against disorder.[30]

---

29   See Negri 1999.

30   Sieyès 1970, p. 172. See also Sieyès 1970, p. 174: 'But it is surely a mistake to attribute everything good about England to the sole power of the Constitution [...] It is not difficult to see that the English Nation is [...] the only nation that is able to be free without having a good Constitution'.

From this perspective, it is not a question of copying the English system but of aspiring to create new models.

> No people, it is said, have done better than the English. But even if this is true, does it mean that at the end of the eighteenth century the products of the political art should be what they were at the end of the seventeenth century? Just as the English did not fall below the level of Enlightenment [*lumières*] of their age, so we should not fall below the level of our own. Above all, we should not be discouraged by finding nothing in history that seems to fit our own position. The true science of the state of society [*science de l'etat de société*] is not at all that old.[31]

In this sense, we are concerned with a new situation, consequent to the founding and development of the 'true science of the state of society'. Sieyès's argument is not, therefore, directed towards a re-proposal of the English constitutional structure,[32] but rather towards creating something radically new and absolutely unprecedented in history.

If the argument's starting point is the novelty of the 'science of the state of society', an element that did not exist in the seventeenth century, it is important to investigate what society actually is, by 'examining the various parts one by one, and then joining them mentally together, one after another'.[33] Three phases are, nonetheless, discernible in the formation of political society: the first is distinguished by the 'interplay of the individual wills', the second by the 'action of common will [*volonté commune*],' and the third by the 'representative common will [*volonté commune representative*]'.

> The associates want to give consistency to their union; they want to fulfil its aim [...] We see that power, then, belongs to the community, them. The community needs a common will; without singleness of will it could not succeed in being a willing and acting body. It is certain, also, that this body has no rights other than such as derive from the common will.[34]

At any event, the common will is considered as the sum of the individual wills, identifying itself with the majority of the individual wills: 'If for the slightest

31 Sieyès 1970, p. 175.
32 See Pasquino 1998, which underlines the substantial compliance of Sieyès's argument with the English constitutional model. See also Bastid 1970.
33 Sieyès 1970, p. 178.
34 Ibid.

moment one loses sight of this self-evident principle that the common will is the opinion of the majority and not of the minority, there is no point in carrying on the discussion'.[35] Here he seems to rediscover elements of his own in Rousseau's reflections regarding the relationship between particular – or individual – will, and general – or common – will. If we examine the question more closely, in actual fact we realise that common will, rather than corresponding to the 'general will', actually corresponds to Rousseau's 'will of all', that is, the will of the majority of individual wills. But Sieyès, in defining the third epoch, takes another step that distances him further from Rousseau: 'The associates are too numerous and occupy too large an area to exercise their common will easily by themselves'.[36] Hence emerges the concept of representative common will.[37] Also from this perspective the distance from Rousseau is apparent, the aforementioned having flatly denied the possibility of a representative general will, given the fact that the general will, being always in operation, cannot be other than what it is, and hence cannot be represented: representing it would mean alienating it. Sieyès uses the concept of representative general will against the Republican party, recalling in some ways Montesquieu's distinction between 'despotism' and 'legitimate government'.[38] It is perhaps no coincidence that authors with liberal sympathies such as Constant appreciated various aspects of Sieyès's arguments. In this way, Sieyès links the inalienable sovereignty of the general will with the idea of the exercising of this will by the representatives of the nation.

Posing the question of the representative general will means posing the question of the constitution:

> It is impossible to create a body [*corps*] for any purpose without giving it the organisation [*organisation*], procedures and laws appropriate for it to fulfil its intended functions. This is called the constitution [*constitution*] of this body [...] So each representative government must have its constitution [...] Thus the assembly of representatives which is entrusted with

---

35   Sieyès 1970, p. 189.

36   Sieyès 1970, p. 178.

37   See Sieyès 1970, p. 179: '1. The will is not full and unlimited in the body of representatives, is nothing but a large portion of the common national will. 2. Delegates do not exercise as their right but it is the rights of an other. The common will is there in committee [*en commission*]'.

38   See Pasquino 1998. It is, however, important to point out that Pasquino underlines the fact that Sieyès defines the question of the separation of powers in different terms from that of Montesquieu and from that of Madison.

the legislative power, i.e. the exercise of the common will, exists only in the form which the Nation has chosen to give it. It is nothing without its constitutive forms; it acts, proceeds, or commands only by way of those forms.[39]

According to Sieyès, the legislative activity should be entrusted to elected representatives. The electoral principle assumes the function which Hobbes attributed to the principle of authorisation, justifying at the same time the heteronomy of the law, which is the will of representatives provided with a free mandate, and the identity between the will of the legislator and the common will. As clearly emerges, Sieyès's argument moves on a constitutional level. The Third Estate is, so to speak, 'constitutionalised'. As pointed out by a number of interpreters, Sieyès is the politician who most strongly perceived the artistic nature of social creation,[40] and of the State-form, and he is indeed the inventor of modern public law.[41]

If we move from natural law to positive law,[42] the theme of the constitution becomes central. 'Neither aspect of the Constitution is the creation [*ouvrage*] of the constituted power [*pouvoir constitué*], but of the constituent power [*pouvoir constituent*]. No type of delegated power can in any way alter the conditions of its delegation'.[43] Within this scenario,

> a nation can only be constituted in virtue of natural law [*droit naturel*]. A government [*gouvernement*], on the other hand, is only fruit of positive law [*droit positif*]. The nation is all that it can be, by the very fact that it exists [...] Not only is the Nation not subject to a constitution, but it cannot be and it must not be.[44]

Even if the Nation forms the basis of the argument developed, the relevance attributed by Sieyès to the constitutional moment is crucial: the Third Estate is 'constitutionalised', and therefore, in a certain sense, 'blocked' in substantial fixity. Although the description of society is complex, dynamic and well-

---

39 Sieyès 1970, pp. 179–80.
40 See Groethuysen 1956.
41 See Bredin 1988.
42 Sieyès 1970, p. 180: 'The Nation is prior to everything. It is the source of everything. Its will is always legal; indeed it is the law itself. Prior to and above the nation, there is only *natural law [droit naturel]*'.
43 Sieyès 1970, pp. 180–1.
44 Sieyès 1970, pp. 181–3.

structured, the overall representation of the Third Estate is not. Underlying the argument is a conception of property as an element that cannot be touched by revolutionary power. The labour element is not connected, in Sieyès, with class dynamics. If, up to that moment, the Estates-General presented an unfair criterion for representation, it is necessary, on the contrary, to give sufficient power to those performing a critical social function. At any event, to create the order in question, it is not so much a case of taking the English constitution, fruit of the seventeenth century, as a model, but rather of applying science: the latter produces the dissolution of the imperative mandate, and the development of representation, which implies the separation of the representative from the represented.[45] Starting from this definition of representation, Sieyès comes to the key concept of constituent power, which should structure society politically, placing it in an appropriate relationship with the nation itself.[46] This is at the origin of the fundamental laws that innervate the constitutional bodies. This constituent power is only valid if it is representative power, within which the electoral body becomes a corporation of owners. This marks the transition from Rousseau's position to that of Montesquieu. The subsequent evolution of Sieyès's thought focuses on establishing further limitations to constituent power. There is no irremediable fracture between Sieyès's early writings and his later ones.[47] At this stage it is, however, important to avoid a misinterpretation: the interest for the constitution is outlined by Sieyès in different terms compared to Montesquieu, since the constitutional reference to tradition is rejected, in favour of the construction of something radically new. The aim is to create a social space; underlying the argument there is a constitutional imagination.

Returning to the central theme of this chapter, namely the relationship between the collective subject and temporality, it is important to observe that in Sieyès the position of Rousseau is only apparently resumed: in actual fact, however, the concept of representative general will distances him from Rousseau, bringing him closer to Montesquieu. But the fundamental novelty of Sieyès is that he has placed himself on the level of the division of labour, and hence in search of a political form appropriate to the division of labour. With

---

45   On the centrality of the question of representation, see Bredin 1988, p. 541: 'Representation will be the foundation of social organisation, it will lead to the business of government, perhaps even to the formation of what will be termed a "political class". Such is the modernity, and the insight, of Sieyès'.

46   See Negri 1999. On the concept of constituent power, see, among others, Zweig 1909; Steiner 1966; Häberle 1987.

47   See Scuccimarra 2002.

regard to the latter, however, no form of radical criticism exists. On the contrary, as pointed out earlier, the collective subject, embodied by the Third Estate, presents an expansive character with regard to the old privilege system, but not with regard to the order founded on the division of labour. There is a strong 'constitutionalisation' of the argument, blocking any expansive temporality, that calls into question the division of labour. The collective subject, the Third Estate, is rendered adequate to the dynamics of labour, to the requirements of the most productive classes, once the most reactionary part, full of privileges, namely the *Ancien régime*, has been purged. However, the continuation of Sieyès's thought should not be viewed as a negation of the previous phases. As time passes, Sieyès becomes obsessed with the problem of 'concluding' the Revolution. His aim becomes that of drawing up a constitution which, using the representative system, is able to block, or 'seal', the political system. In this area, as we shall see, the distance from the Marxian solution is considerable.

Marx and the French Revolution

If Sieyès was the real theoretician of the initial phase of the French Revolution, for Marx the interpretation of the French Revolution was a thought that tormented him throughout his life, a veritable obsession. Marx never ceased to brood upon the French Revolution, even though he never dealt with the question in an extensive, systematic manner.[48] My intention here, however, is not to make a 'textual' comparison between the two thinkers, also because Marx rarely refers to Sieyès. Notwithstanding this, however, a very important 'stake' emerges between Sieyès and Marx, in relation to the French Revolution, and to the question of the collective subject raised by it. One of the few passages in which Marx refers to Sieyès is found in a section of *The German Ideology*, dedicated to the criticism of the representatives of 'real' socialism: 'Cabet greatly embarrasses his bourgeois opponent by numbering Sieyès among the forerunners of communism, by reason of the fact that he recognised equality of rights, and considered that only the state sanctions property [...]'.[49]

---

48   Two texts entirely dedicated to the relationship between Marx and the French Revolution are Bongiovanni 1989, and Furet 1986. The following studies are also very important, for different reasons: Balibar 1992, which dwells on the Marxist analysis of the *Declaration*, and Hobsbawm 1990, which focuses attention on interpretations of the French Revolution, considered as the mother of all revolutions.

49   Marx and Engels 1975b, p. 526.

Marx is not only ironic towards Sieyès, however; he also praises him for having understood 'modern politics': 'Proudhon's treatise *Qu'est-ce que la propriété?* is as important for modern political economy as Sieyès' work *Qu'est-ce que le tiers état?* for modern politics'.[50] The relevant point here is not so much the specific evaluation that Marx gives of Sieyès, but rather the acceptance of the novelty introduced by the element of the Third Estate, with its disruptive consequences. The crux of the matter resides in the attempt to discern some distinctive characteristics of the Marxian position, without however giving a totally organic and 'systematic' interpretation of the question given the fact that, notwithstanding the elements of continuity in his analysis, there are nonetheless various aspects of discontinuity. But there is another reason why it is necessary to avoid an excessively 'theoretistic' approach to the problem. Marx's interpretation of the French Revolution cannot be reduced to a historical judgement in the strict sense of the term, nor does it appear as the fruit of a complex philosophical expression; rather it emerges as a way of taking a position, on each occasion, within a given situation. It is a question of 'thinking in the conjuncture', starting from the 'actual truth of the matter', to quote Machiavelli's famous words.[51] But what profoundly distances Marx from Sieyès is the question of the expansive temporality of the collective subject of the French Revolution, a temporality which is excluded and 'blocked' by Sieyès in a constitutional apparatus, which opens the revolution but then closes it immediately, attempting to curb its most 'subversive' aspects and rendering it functional to the division of labour. For Sieyès, the revolution must end; for Marx, on the other hand, it must expand and develop.

Marx never dedicates a specific essay to the French Revolution and to Jacobinism: despite this, he never stops inquiring into its meaning. It is interesting to observe that the studies on the French Revolution carried out by historians who were certainly not progressive thinkers, such as Guizot, Mignet and Thiers, played an important role in Marx's formation. Our analysis can begin with his early writings, and in particular *On the Jewish Question* [*Zur Judenfrage*, 1844], which deals with the issue of the individual separation of *citoyen* and *bourgeois*, deriving from the 'mundane scission [*die weltliche Spaltung*] between political state and civil society'.[52] For the man of civil society, the *bourgeois*, 'the life in the state is nothing more than an appearance [*Schein*] or a momentary exception to the essential nature of things and to the rule'.[53] In comparison with the

---

50   Marx and Engels 1975a, p. 31.

51   See Basso 2012.

52   Marx 1975b, p. 137.

53   Marx 1975b, p. 220.

real value of civil society, the State appears as a *Schein*, appearance, or, at any event, in a transitory exception. Within this scenario, the *bourgeois* and *citoyen* come to represent the actual man and the true man:

> Man [...], is taken to be the real man, man as distinct from the citizen, since he is man in his sensuous, individual and immediate existence, whereas political man is simply abstract, artificial man, man as an allegorical, moral person. Actual man [*der wirkliche Mensch*] is acknowledged only in the form of egoistic individual and true man [*der wahre Mensch*] only in the form of the abstract citizen.[54]

If the individual separation between *bourgeois* and *citoyen* is a distinctive feature of modernity, the Marx of *On the Jewish Question* is interested in understanding when this *Trennung* [separation] has reached its peak: the event of the French Revolution was a turning-point in this process. In the *Kritik* Marx had already asserted that the French Revolution 'was the process completed in which the estates were transformed into social classes, i.e. the class distinctions in civil society became merely social differences in private life, of no significance in political life. This accomplished the separation [*die Trennung*] of political life and civil society'.[55] In *On the Jewish Question* Marx deepens his analysis of the French Revolution, and examines some of the fundamental principles of the *Declaration of the Rights of Man and Citizen* [*Déclaration des droits de l'homme et du citoyen*] of 1789 and 1791, which will later become articles of the Constitutions of 1791 and 1793, as well as American constitutional texts. In a 'guided' reading of the *Déclaration*, Marx sharply differentiates between the rights of man and the rights of the citizen. The rights of the man concern the bourgeois, that is, man as member of civil society, the egoistic man who is 'separated from other men and from the community [*vom Menschen und vom Gemeinwesen getrennten*]'.[56] These rights do no more than note and confirm the existing *Trennung* of bourgeois civil society, where each man is separated from the other and it is impossible to give life to a *Gemeinwesen* [community]. The freedom of *bürgerliche Gesellschaft* is indifferent to the needs of the 'common being'; on the contrary, it hinges on the pursuit of self-interest, the real

---

54   Marx 1975b, p. 234. See Gilbert 1981, p. 33, which notes the 'gap' produced by the French
      Revolution between man as an individual member of civil society and man as a modern
      citizen.

55   Marx 1975a, p. 146.

56   Marx 1975b, p. 230.

goal of the bourgeois. In the *Déclaration*, only one limit is imposed on bourgeois freedom: the respect of every other bourgeois's freedom. This conception of freedom reflects an atomistic view of civil society: 'The liberty we are dealing with is that of man as an isolated monad who is withdrawn into himself. [...] But the right of man to freedom is not based on the association of man with man, but rather on the separation [*Absonderung*] of man from man. It is the right of this separation, the right of the restricted individual, restricted to himself'.[57] The individual of civil society, an atom unconnected to other atoms, is at the centre of this argument. The rights of man, an outcome of revolutionary events, according to Marx, totally endorse this state of affairs. But Marx's separation between man and citizen proves to be rather problematic. In actual fact, these two elements continuously recall one another. A closer examination of the articles of the *Déclaration* reveals that the two terms are interpreted as one, as a sort of hendiadys: the 'and' interposed between 'rights of man' and 'rights of the citizen' seems to point to an identification of the terms, rather than their separation.[58] This makes it difficult to interpret the *citoyen* as an individual who belongs to a realm of mere illusion.

According to Marx, the French Revolution leads the process of destruction of feudal society, which had begun with Absolutism, to its extreme consequence:

> Political emancipation is at the same time the dissolution of the old society on which there rested the power of the sovereign, the political system as estranged from the people [*das dem Volk entfremdete Staatswesen*]. The political revolution is the revolution of civil society. What was the character of the old society? It can be characterised in one word: feudalism. The old civil society had a directly political character.[59]

The events after 1789 significantly shook up the *status quo*, raising the affairs of the state to the level of those of the people and eliminating all intermediate organisms. Thus, the premises of Absolutism were fulfilled: for this interpret-

---

57   Marx 1975b, p. 232. See McLellan 1970; Maihofer 1992, p. 94.

58   Reference is made to Balibar 1992, who believes the foundation of the French Revolution to be the *citoyen* rather than the *bourgeois*, the private individual, bearer of interests that are outside of sociality; the revolutionary solution consisted in identifying these two concepts. The *Declaration* is based on the reclaiming of the universal right to politics. Miaille 2001 problematises the notion of a clear separation between the elements in question. See Hincker 1990; Hunt 1975, p. 73; Feher 1990. For an analysis of the *Declaration*, see also Gauchet 1989, in particular pp. 73–4; Picavet 1996, pp. 249–71.

59   Marx 1975b, p. 232.

ation, the French Revolution is the revolution of the 'political' that becomes autonomous from civil society. Earlier on, Tocqueville had maintained that the revolution constituted the continuation of the work initiated by the monarchy.[60] Many years later, in *The Civil War in France* (1871), Marx states that 'the gigantic broom of the French Revolution of the 18th century swept away all these relics of bygone times, thus clearing simultaneously the social soil of its last hindrances to the superstructure of the modern state edifice [...]'.[61] This process led to the primacy of private individuals in civil society, and, released from the latter, the political realm 'found refuge' in the sphere of the state. During the French Revolution two dynamics simultaneously unfold: on the one hand, civil society is divided up into independent individuals, bearers of particular interests; on the other hand, the political sphere becomes autonomous from civil society. So the ambivalence of the French Revolution has to be acknowledged: while its character is expansive and propulsive, it simultaneously sanctions a substantial dependence of the *citoyen, qua* member of the State, on the *homme, qua* egoistic member of the *bürgerliche Gesellschaft*.

> The political revolution dissolves civil life into its component parts without revolutionising the parts and subjecting them to criticism. It regards civil society, the world of needs, of labour, of private interests and of civil law, as the foundation of its existence [...].[62]

The *Déclaration* is an extremely important document, because it fully reflects the emergence and heightening of both a separation in the individual due to the events of the French Revolution, and above all the crucial role of the sphere of civil society, where freedom is merely a function that enables the coexistence of different unhindered whims. But the very arbitrariness in itself is not questioned. The protection of private property is the necessary consequence of the notion of *Freiheit* outlined earlier.[63] Freedom finds its natural outlet in the institution of private property, which represents 'the right to enjoy and dispose of one's resources at will [*à son gré*], without regard for other men and independently of society: the right of self-interest'.[64] Marx aims to remove the 'veils' that mystify the picture of the present in the *bürgerliche Gesellschaft*,

---

60   On Tocqueville, also in relation to his analysis of the French Revolution, see Chignola 2004.

61   Marx 1986, p. 328.

62   Marx 1975b, p. 234.

63   See Basso 2008/2009, in particular pp. 69–73.

64   Marx 1975b, p. 229. See also Michel 1983, p. 42; Arnold 1990, p. 56.

presented as the guarantor of universal rights whilst being, in fact, the protector of particular interests.[65] The affirmation of the 'illusory' character of the rights of man and, in particular, the right to freedom, does not prevent Marx from recognising their crucial function in the abolition of feudal privileges. Marx's critique of modern *bürgerliche Gesellschaft* is not nostalgia for previous social formations. This constitutes the greatest point of contact with the analysis conducted by Sieyès: the French Revolution emerges as a negation of the privilege system. From this standpoint, *liberté, égalité, fraternité*, the 'motifs' of the French Revolution, cannot be seen as merely unreal, even though in earlier writings Marx often denounced their illusory character *sic et simpliciter*. In actual fact, the circumstances were the fruit of a practice of emancipation from a series of ties and ecclesiastic and aristocratic-hierarchical structures. At the same time, however, it was far from neutral. It was thus necessary to demystify their universality, and understand it as a function of the interests of the *bourgeois*, rather than simplistically as a non-existence. Marx's attitude towards the French Revolution is thus structurally two-fold: on the one hand, he recognises its propulsive role, the overcoming of mediaeval privileges and the creation of a juridical establishment founded on freedom, equality, property and security; on the other hand, he criticises its 'bourgeois' character, its connection, however dissimulated and hidden, to the interests of the *bourgeois*, the interests of man as a member of *bürgerliche Gesellschaft*, in relation to whom the *citoyen* only occupies a secondary and derivative role. While for Sieyès it was necessary fully to maintain freedom, equality and property, in contrast with the medieval privilege system, Marx, on the other hand, develops an immanent critique of those elements. In fact, in Marx's opinion, the revolution may be considered as 'progress' [*Fortschritt*] provided that this term is not interpreted according to a totally linear understanding or an abstract set of principles, but rather by recognising the duplicity and, therefore, the incipient contradictions as they arose particularly strongly during the Reign of Terror, when its exponents invested in the impossible task of subjecting the *bourgeois* to the *citoyen*.

At this stage, the way in which Marx defines the Reign of Terror, and his relationship with the earlier phases of the French Revolution, require deeper examination. Of significance is the fact that, in his early writings, Marx regards the French Revolution and Terror as examples of 'political understanding', often returning to Hegel's thoughts on this issue. In the *Phenomenology of Spirit* in particular, Hegel refers to absolute freedom, and to what prevents internal

---

65   See Balibar 1993.

difference, thus resulting in total unmediated negation. It is in this sense, in the *King of Prussia and Social Reform*, that Marx debates with the exponents of the Terror:

> The classical period of political understanding is the French Revolution. Far from identifying the principle of the State as the source of social ills, the heroes of the French Revolution held social life to be the source of political problems [...] Thus Robespierre regarded great wealth and great poverty as an obstacle to pure democracy. He therefore wished to establish a universal system of Spartan frugality. The principle of politics is the will. The more one-sided, i.e. the more perfect, political understanding is, the more completely it puts its faith in the omnipotence of the will. The blinder it is towards the natural and spiritual limitations of the will, the more incapable it becomes of discovering the real source of the evils of society.[66]

In *The Holy Family* the Jacobins are accused of a lack of rigorous social and historical analysis, of a purely subjectivist and voluntarist approach.[67] Traditional 'orthodox' Marxism followed this approach, emphasising the fact that Robespierre longed for a society based on a free association of producers, not a proletarian state.

This issue cannot be approached from a 'theoretistic' standpoint; it must be played out in practice. If we agree to approach the question in this way, it becomes necessary to investigate the development of the 'revolutionary practices' into the Reign of Terror. Already in *The Holy Family*, confirming the fact that contrasting tensions co-exist in the same text, Marx points out that

> the right to freedom ceases to be a right as soon as it enters into conflict with political life, whereas in theory political life is simply the guarantee of the rights of man, the rights of individual man, and should be abandoned as soon as it contradicts its goal, these rights of man [...] Even if we were to assume that the relationship is properly expressed in revolutionary practice, the problem still remains to be solved as to why the relationship is set upon its head in the minds of the political emancipators so that the end appears as the means and the means as the end.[68]

---

66   Marx 1975d, p. 413.
67   Marx and Engels 1975a, p. 95. On this subject, see Negri 1999.
68   Marx and Engels 1975a, p. 231.

The development of 'revolutionary practice' into the Reign of Terror seems to question the idea of the domination of the *bourgeois* over the *citoyen* held in 'theory'.[69] Thus the dynamics of the French Revolution, in its 'practice' rather than the abstract principles of the *Déclaration*, led to the emergence of a truly despotic domination of the 'heavens' of politics, the realm of the state, over the 'earth' of civil society, the social sphere. In this regard, the *Holy Family* (1845), in contrast with previous writings, contains an important theoretical development. In his argument against the idealistic representation of Bauer, a powerful acknowledgement of the French Revolution emerges.

> The revolutionary movement which began in 1789 in the *Cercle Social*, which in the middle of its course had as its chief representatives Leclerc and Roux, and which finally with Babeuf's conspiracy was temporarily defeated, gave rise to the communist idea which Babeuf's friend Buonarroti re-introduced in France after the Revolution of 1830.[70]

In recognising the event in question, Marx does not limit himself to a general statement on the necessity of the historical process, on the basis of concepts of the philosophy of history, but goes further, considering the French Revolution as a model, a reference point, however abstract, for the 'communist idea'. In their discussion on Jacobinism in the section of *The German Ideology* on Stirner, Marx and Engels describe Robespierre and Saint-Just as the real representatives of revolutionary power, 'i.e. of the only truly revolutionary class, the innumerable masses'.[71] Marx reproaches Stirner for having said nothing about 'the actual empirical grounds for the cutting off of heads – grounds which were based on extremely worldly interests – though not, of course, of the stockjobbers, but of the innumerable masses'.[72] In *The King of Prussia and Social Reform*

---

69   See Maguire 1978, pp. 9–11; Löwy 1989, in particular pp. 115–16, which attributes the apparent contradiction between 'theory' and 'revolutionary practice' to an obvious difficulty – experienced by Marx – of interpretation of the Terror: 'If Marx's analysis of the bourgeois character of the revolution is extraordinarily clear and consistent, the same cannot be said of his attempts to interpret Jacobinism and the Terror of 1793. Confronted with the mystery of Jacobinism, Marx hesitates [...] The Terror is a moment when the political becomes autonomous and comes into direct conflict with bourgeois society'. Löwy hits the nail on the head when he highlights the hesitant and uncertain attitude of Marx in interpreting the Terror.

70   Marx and Engels 1975a, p. 230.

71   Marx and Engels 1975b, p. 297.

72   Ibid.

he refers to the decisive outbreak of the Silesian revolt, through which the 'disastrous isolation' of men from the community emerged. While discussing this event, he refers to the French Revolution:

> We have shown that in the Silesian uprising, there was no separation of thoughts from social principles. That leaves the 'disastrous isolation of men from the community'. By community is meant here the political community, the State [...] But do not all rebellions without exception have their roots in the disastrous isolation of man from the community? Does not every rebellion necessarily presuppose isolation? Would the revolution of 1789 have taken place if French citizens had not felt disastrously isolated from the community? The abolition of this isolation was its very purpose.[73]

The crux of the matter under question is the subjective realm, in a practice directed at abolishing 'the present state of things',[74] to quote the famous words of *The German Ideology*. The upsurge of the notion of the proletariat in the *Contribution to the Critique of Hegel's Philosophy of Law, Introduction* (1844), with its partisan universality, can be interpreted as a radicalisation of the question of the collective subject in the French Revolution, with its unstoppable temporality. In the conclusion of the text, a direct reference is made to the French Revolution as a paradigm for the German revolution. 'When all the inner conditions are met, the day of the German resurrection will be heralded by the cock of Gaul'.[75] In texts written before or contemporaneously with these, Engels interprets the French Revolution as the origin of European democracy, with its ambivalent character: on the one hand, it has an expansive role and opens up scenarios that had been unthinkable until then; on the other hand, it becomes its own opposite when it turns into a dictatorship. Babeuf and Napoleon represent the two opposite 'poles' of this debate. Be that as it may, for Engels, 'the French Revolution was a social movement [*eine soziale Bewegung*] from beginning to end, and after it a purely political democracy became a complete absurdity'.[76] So, in Engels, the French Revolution emerges as a fluid, dynamic process that sanctioned the shift from *politische* to *soziale Demokratie*. Thus, also in Engels's analysis, the French Revolution cannot be reduced to a merely

---

73 Marx 1975d, p. 295.
74 Marx and Engels 1975b, p. 49.
75 Marx 1975c, p. 187.
76 Engels 1975, p. 5.

'political' revolution.[77] The French Revolution is investigated in terms of its expansive temporality, which affects the social relations: unlike in Sieyès, it is the subjective component, with its permanent mobilisation, that punctuates the argument, not its constitutional 'closure'.

This 'thinking in practice' cannot but find further reinforcement in the decisive conjuncture of 1848. In *Moralising Criticism and Critical Morality*, which he wrote just before 1848, Marx forcefully underlines the fact that 'the first manifestation of a truly active communist party is contained in the French Revolution, at the moment when the constitutional monarchy was abolished'.[78] Within the French context, Babeuf and Buonarroti had radically insisted on these social questions, and on the need to question property relations.[79] So the idea developed with ever increasing conviction that the Terror was a turning-point, from the political standpoint, for the organisation of the proletariat into a party. In 1848 Marx points out that 'the Jacobin of 1793 has become the Communist of the present day'.[80] Thus the interpretation of the Terror as a form of domination of 'political understanding' is clearly put behind: in the historical and political texts in particular, the radicalism of the Terror is pregnant with consequences for the working class movement. In various Marxian texts, the 1848 revolution is interpreted as a repetitive pattern of the revolution *par excellence*, the 1789 revolution, but in the form of a caricature, a parody.[81] This, however, does not mean interpreting the French Revolution as a proletarian, anti-bourgeois revolution (this would be devoid of sense); an excerpt from *The Bourgeoisie and the Counter-Revolution* (December 1848) is eloquent on this subject: in 1789 '[...] the bourgeoisie was the class that *really* headed the movement [...] *All French terrorism* was nothing but a *plebeian way* of dealing with the *enemies of the bourgeoisie*, absolutism, feudalism and philistinism'.[82] Furthermore, in *The Bill Proposing the Abolition of Feudal Obligations*, issued in July 1848, Marx comments that

> [...] the German revolution of 1848 is merely a *parody of the French revolution of 1789*. On August 4, 1789, three weeks after the storming of the Bastille, the French people, in a single day, got the better of the feudal

77   It is also for this reason that my argument is totally incompatible with the interpretation of Furet 1986.

78   Marx 1976, p. 312.

79   Ibid.

80   Marx and Engels 1976, p. 545.

81   On the question of repetition, see Assoun 1978.

82   Marx 1977b, p. 161.

obligations. On July 11, 1848, four months after the March barricades, the feudal obligations got the better of the German people [...] The French bourgeoisie of 1789 never left its allies, the peasants, in the lurch [...] The German bourgeoisie of 1848 unhesitatingly betrays the peasants [...].[83]

On the other hand, Marx subsequently points out, in *The Eighteenth Brumaire of Louis Napoleon* (1852), that

Hegel remarks [...] that all facts and personages of great importance in world history occur, as it were, twice. He forgot to add: the first time as tragedy, the second as farce. Caussidière for Danton, Louis Blanc for Robespierre, the Montagne of 1848 to 1851 for the Montagne of 1793 to 1795, the Nephew for the Uncle.[84]

Be that as it may, as Marx later remarks, the exponents of Terror, whilst evoking the *polis* and *res publica* in their speeches, had no intention of rebuilding them. Their real aim was to build a bourgeois society.

Camille Desmoulins, Danton, Robespierre, St. Just, Napoleon, the heroes as well as the parties and the masses of the old French Revolution, performed the task of their time – that of unchaining and establishing modern bourgeois society – in Roman costumes with Roman phrases.[85]

In its 'highest phase',[86] 'political enlightenment' protected the rights to private property and therefore the interests of the *bourgeois* from whom it had declared its independence, finding its 'profane' realisation in the government of the Directorate, in which 'civil society [*die bürgerliche Gesellschaft*] – the revolution had freed it from feudal bonds and had recognised it officially, although the Terror had sought to sacrifice it to an ancient political regime – explodes in powerful vital currents'.[87] From this standpoint, the Directorate represents the inevitable outcome of the one-sidedness of the Jacobin Terror, with its negation of the realm of the particular. If the French Revolution had led to extreme consequences, the process of separation in the individual, and the subordination of his political to his civil, bourgeois, side, the Reign of Terror attempted to invert

---

83   Marx 1977a, pp. 294–5.
84   Marx 1979, p. 103.
85   Marx 1979, p. 104.
86   Marx and Engels 1975a, p. 126.
87   Marx and Engels 1975a, p. 126.

this process, to the advantage of an all-powerful, totalising political realm. Despite the intentions of its exponents, it constituted, to use an expression from *The German Ideology*, an 'energetic bourgeois liberalism [*Bourgeoisliberalismus*]'.[88] The fact that, over the course of time, Marx tended to increasingly apply the notion of 'thinking in practice' to the question of the French Revolution does not mean that he abandoned the idea of the French Revolution as a bourgeois revolution that swept away the last surviving remnants of the feudal system.

So it is not a question of attempting to bend the Marxian vision towards an idea of the French Revolution as a bourgeois revolution,[89] nor of turning Marx into an apologist of the Terror, as though there were a kind of full theoretical identification between Jacobinism and communism. In the first volume of *Capital* Marx states this clearly:

> During the very first storms of the revolution, the French bourgeoisie dared to take away from the workers the right of association but just acquired. By a decree of June 14, 1791, they declared all coalition of the workers as 'an attempt against liberty' [...].[90]

In any event, the relationship between Marx and the Terror is extremely complex: in many ways, Jacobinism is an 'unthought' of Marx's theory. In Marx's interpretation of the Terror, there are two conflicting elements: the first concerns its (presumed or real) anti-proletarian nature (suffice it to mention the *maximum* wage issue), while the second concerns the impetus given to the mobilisation of the masses, particularly at a 'plebeian' level, decisive for the constitution of a communist party. From the standpoint of an overall historical schema, both approaches can remain open. But a change of tactics is required in the investigation, with a 'thinking in practice' approach to the question of the French Revolution, on the basis of coordinates that are never wholly predictable.

---

88   Marx and Engels 1975b, p. 99.
89   From this perspective, the interpretation of Soboul 1975, while highlighting a fundamental
      aspect of the Revolution, is, however, rather restrictive, inasmuch as it does not grasp the
      extreme internal complexity of the subjective emergences present in it.
90   Marx 1996, p. 730.

Tempora Multa?

From the analysis conducted, the problem of the relationship between temporality and subjectivity emerges. To this effect, the experience of the French Revolution is of crucial importance, with its unstoppable temporality, with its impetuous acceleration, with its striving towards the future. Here, the distance between Marx and Sieyès appears evident: the latter does not fully appreciate the expansive temporality of the revolution as a permanent, inexhaustible movement. Moreover, this element is rooted in the 'social', and finds its field of application in the 'social'. Here there is, at one and the same time, a point of contact but also of distance between the two thinkers. The point of contact consists of the reference to the division of labour, and hence of the relationship between the French Revolution and the division of labour. The distance resides in the fact that Sieyès does not criticise the power relationships within society, and even wishes to draw up a constitution that would facilitate the development of private property. Marx, on the other hand, deconstructs these elements.

In this analysis, modern temporality is considered an inevitable acquisition, but at the same time an ambivalent and problematic element, and not as a state of affairs to be accepted without criticism. Within the perspective outlined, there are two polemical targets of my argument. The first is provided by some eighteenth- and nineteenth-century currents of thought – supported by the idea of a totally linear and cumulative temporality – characterised by the idea of the unstoppable progress of humankind. However, in Marx there are various ambiguities in this regard. The second polemical target is provided by Messianic approaches: here, there is a dimension, albeit paradoxical, albeit non-orthodox, of transcendence. But the structured argument turns out to be totally immanent, and therefore denies any reference to a Messiah. So it is not a question of juxtaposing to linear temporality an element of absolute – and hence transcendent – alterity with respect to it, on the basis of a Messianic 'flash'.

In conclusion, whether this expansive temporality, entirely immanent, possesses a character of plurality or otherwise, needs to be investigated. Meanwhile, it is important to remember, as a crucial reference, although not without internal difficulties, the shift in modern times from the plurality of *Historiae* – typical of the pre-modern vision – to *Geschichte* as 'collective singular', with the accelerated tempo that it exerts over the course of events.[91] If we thus refuse

---

91   See Koselleck 2004.

the 'backward-looking' imagination, it becomes senseless to consider returning
to the pre-modern plurality of the *historiae*. Rather, the element of plurality, if
employed, must be interpreted on the basis of the new coordinates. To this end,
two observations arise. In the first place, the Marxist variation of the temporality of the collective subject is connected with a specific logic of determination,
of the 'actual truth of the matter', of the singularity of the issue.[92] In this sense,
there is a 'situated' temporality that cannot be transformed into a general law.
In the second case, on examining the singular event of the French Revolution,
with its devastating character, it is clear to see that it has a complex internal
structure. In a certain sense, it could even be said that there were 'several'
French Revolutions: the revolution of the Third Estate, the *bourgeois* revolution
(well illustrated in Sieyès's analysis), the revolution of the *sans-culottes*, and the
revolution of the peasants. The revolutions in question have certain aspects in
common (e.g. the anti-feudal question), but also important divergences (e.g.
the Third Estate was, on the whole, favourable to capitalistic modernisation,
whereas the peasants were critical of this approach). The Marxian approach,
also in relation to the French Revolution, aims to reject both a sort of *reductio
ad unum* of the temporal dimensions, and a definition based on a plurality of
times, which would, in any case, presuppose the existence of a unique time that
would act as a paradigm. Sometimes these elements meet or clash, sometimes
they do not, but it is impossible to define the matter once and for all in a clear
sense.

The reference to the French Revolution interests Marx not so much for the
purpose of reconstructing the crucial importance and complexity of that historical period, but more for the purpose of making the emergence of subjectivity contained in it 'explode', by 'replaying it' in relation to the Silesian revolt and
to 1848 revolution. For Marx, the French Revolution was a contemporary event,
or rather it was situated in a much more 'expansive' perspective compared to
that typical of the German situation contemporary to him. Thus the theme of
temporality is not examined in an abstract fashion, in a theoretistic way, but
applied to practice, so that it is brought into play in a given situation. The problem in question consists of politically defining the action of the working class,
rejecting any kind of 'oligarchic' option, and creating a movement charged with
'subversive' temporality with the power to destroy the *status quo*.[93] This '*prise de
parole*',[94] on the one hand, continues along the lines of the French Revolution,

92   See Althusser 1999.

93   See Marx and Engels 1989, p. 517: 'The emancipation [*Befreiung*] of the working class must
      be the act [*Werk*] of the workers themselves'. See Basso 2015, in particular pp. 146–201.

94   See de Certeau 1994.

the 'mother' of all revolutions, in its capacity to deploy all categories of politics; but, on the other hand, tends to go beyond its constitutive limits, disrupting the bourgeois distinction between the 'social' and the 'political', with new, unprecedented coordinates, that can never be fully predicted and the path of which is always open to review:

> The social revolution of the nineteenth century cannot take its poetry from the past but only from the future [...] The former revolutions required recollections of past world history in order to smother their own content. The revolution of the nineteenth century must let the dead bury their dead in order to arrive at its own content.[95]

---

95   Marx 1979, p. 106.

CHAPTER 3

Layers of Time in Marx: From the *Grundrisse* to *Capital* to the Russian Commune

Massimiliano Tomba

It would be easy to find in Marx many passages that assume a deliberate philosophy of history [*Geschichtsphilosophie*].[1] What is more difficult, though necessary, is to understand why the late Marx was able to free himself from a progressivist philosophy of history. If Marx was eventually able to expunge a philosophy of history from his reflections, this is not because he reconsidered the philosophical presuppositions of his idea of history, but rather because the unilinear conception of historical development became incompatible with his own theoretical and political perspective.

The *Grundrisse* (1857–8) might be considered a 'research laboratory' in which Marx brilliantly analysed both the anthropological transformation and the development of the modes of production from the perspective of the supersession of capitalism. His perspective, however, is still characterised by a philosophy of history that allowed him, on the one hand, to prefigure, problematically, the collapse of the capitalist mode of production within the development of capitalism itself, and, on the other hand, and even more problematically, to stress the emancipatory and civilising force of capital in relation to an ambiguous view on colonialism. For instance, he 'emphasised the "revolutionary" role of British free trade, basing himself upon a general expectation that it would destroy the framework of the old society which was an obstacle to the growth of productive forces, and would generate in its place the kind of development that would lay the basis for a new society'.[2]

When, in the 1860s, Marx rethinks the notion of socially necessary labour in relation to value, the more evidently *geschichtsphilosophische* perspective of the *Grundrisse* becomes impracticable. The impact of the economic crisis at the end of the 1850s and the failure of the hoped-for revolution in Europe oblige Marx to rethink the entire categorical framework of his own analysis. In *Capital*, the Promethean emphasis on technological development based on the

---

1   This chapter draws freely on Tomba 2013a.

2   Mohri 1979, p. 35; see also Anderson 2010.

productive force of innovation and machinery, still evident in the *Grundrisse*, no longer has as its outcome the immediate transition to communism. Already in 1858, retackling the same problem, Marx interprets *crisis* no longer as the engine of the revolutionary process, but as an element with the power to bring about capitalist accumulation and development. In his late works Marx began to pay attention to how different forms of production synchronically interact with each other and, finally, he abandoned the scheme of unilinear development based on the unfolding of predetermined historical stages. Historical phenomena, Marx wrote in a letter of 1877, cannot be understood with 'the *passe-partout* of an historical-philosophical theory whose great virtue is to stand above history'.[3]

In this chapter I analyse Marx's reflections on the categories of the capitalist mode of production and his views on history as two interrelated sides of his intellectual and political development. Marx's theory is strictly intertwined with his philosophy of history and, therefore, it is not possible to consider one without the other. I argue that Marx's oeuvre contains layers of time: not only is Marx's intellectual development composed of different temporal and theoretical layers, but his conception of history is also layered with different and, at times, fundamentally incompatible approaches to history.

Into Marx's Laboratory

Science, both in its description in *Capital* and in the *Grundrisse*, works as a productive force objectified in fixed capital. What changes between the two descriptions, between those of 1857–8 and that of 1867, is the categorical context.[4] Considering an increase in the productive force, Marx encounters a number of difficulties, which comes from the consideration of exchange value as labour time effectively objectified in a product, and *not* as socially necessary working time. In the *Grundrisse* Marx often confuses the rate of surplus value with the rate of profit and does not distinguish between value and exchange value. These problems, together with some brilliant intuitions, converge in the so-called *Fragment on Machines*,[5] in which some read-

---

3 Marx 1989, p. 201.

4 Heinrich 2009.

5 The origin of the so-called 'Fragment of Machines' goes back to Renato Solmi's translation in the fourth issue of the Italian journal *Quaderni Rossi*, published with this title in 1964. It corresponds to the Notebooks VI: 43–44 and VII: 1–3 of the manuscript of the *Grundrisse*. See Wright 2002.

ers have noticed an extraordinary theoretical anticipation of late capitalist society.[6]

In those pages of the *Grundrisse*, Marx outlines capitalist development as a process that involves the accumulation of knowledge in the social brain, so that at a certain stage of development it is neither the direct human labour that the worker performs, nor the time during which he works, but rather the appropriation of his own general productive power, his understanding of nature and his mastery over it by virtue of his presence as a social body.[7] This also applies to the development of the *social individual* as counterbalanced by individuality limited by nature.[8] These forms, which are believed to constitute the real wealth of the individual, can only be deployed after destroying that which produces them and, at the same time, limits them: capital. This contradiction is traced back by Marx to an *immanent contradiction* in the capitalist mode of production, in contrast to the real wealth manifested in the disproportion between the labour time applied and the power of the production process. Modern industry, increasing productivity through the use of machinery, has reduced labour time to a minimum. These two poles constitute the dialectic that Marx shapes into a philosophy of history: 'As soon as labor in the direct form has ceased to be the great well-spring of wealth, labor time ceases and must cease to be its measure, and hence exchange value must cease to be the measure of use value'.[9] Having identified the way in which 'capital thus works to dissolve itself',[10] eroding the law according to which labour is the measure of value, Marx must conclude that 'with that, production based on exchange value breaks down'.[11] The *Grundrisse* outline a theory of the crisis that is closely linked to that of the collapse of capitalism. The *image* of the collapse, that is, the collapse as an image, is the focus of Marx's analysis. It is the point at which the various lines of Marx's crisis analysis converge, as in a lens in which theoretical analysis merges with practice in the act of suspending itself.

During the 1860s Marx reconsidered his previous perspective on value and the problem posed in the *Grundrisse* regarding the collapse of the law of value became senseless: not only do 'machines create no new value',[12] but their

---

6   On the *Fragment* and the history of its interpretations, see Bellofiore and Tomba 2013a; Heinrich 2013.

7   Marx 1987, p. 91; *MEW* 42, p. 601.

8   Marx 1987, p. 92 and p. 133; *MEW* 42, p. 601 and p. 641.

9   Marx 1987, p. 91; *MEW* 42, p. 601.

10   Marx 1987, p. 86; *MEW* 42, p. 596.

11   Marx 1987, p. 91; *MEW* 42, p. 601.

12   Marx 1996, p. 390; *MEW* 23, p. 408.

diffusion in a given branch of production also eliminates the possibility of obtaining the extra surplus value that their sporadic introduction permitted:

> As the use of machinery becomes *more general* [*Verallgemeinerung*] in a particular industry, the social value of the product sinks down to its individual value, and the law that *surplus value does not arise from the labour-power that has been replaced by the machinery, but from the labour-power actually employed in working with the machinery, asserts itself.*[13]

When a technological innovation has been diffused, the growth of the productive powers of labour obtained through its use becomes socially dominant and the possibility of gaining higher quantities of social surplus-value by means of the production of relative surplus-value is reduced. Machines, therefore, Marx argued during the 1860s, do not create value; they transfer their own value to the product. These artificial forces are, however, able to extend the working day beyond all natural limits: not only until the workers are physically and mentally worn out, turning day and night into a continuum, but also, through increased productive force, until 30-hour days have been obtained within the natural limits of 24 hours. Newton's absolute time ceases to be the 'natural measure'. It is replaced by socially necessary labour-time, the universal measure of human labour subsumed in capital.

In the *Grundrisse*, Marx seeks to view the relationship between the new forms of production triggered by the dominion of capital and the transformation of human nature *into a new subject* dialectically, in which increased leisure time is, on the one hand, an expression of the technological innovation of production and, on the other, an engine for the ever increasing automation of production. Prometheanism trusts in the tendency of capital, insofar as it constitutes a permanent revolution: all that is needed is to pinpoint this tendency, intensify it, and then deliver the final blow. Development, tendency, crisis, communism: these are the coordinates that emerge from the *Grundrisse* holding together the Notebooks IV on the pre-capitalist modes of production and the final pages of *The Fragment on Machines* in the Notebook VII. The pre-capitalist economic forms, in which individuals are prisoners of existing relationships, have their *natural* limit, and cannot produce the 'free and full development' of the individual and of society.[14] For Marx, only the capitalist mode of production creates the basis for the *social individual*: an individual who has severed

---

13   Marx 1996, pp. 409–10; *MEW* 23, p. 429.
14   Marx 1987, pp. 410–11; *MEW* 42, p. 395. See Wainwright 2008; Mohri 1970.

the umbilical cord that bound him to nature and makes society his own nature. The Marxian concept of the *social individual* evokes a sort of zenith of capitalist development, the point at which the development of the productive forces even transforms human nature. This issue is taken up again in *The Fragment on Machines*. Here, individual development is interpreted in relation to the development of machine-related production in an ever increasing *geschichtsphilosophische* tension and finally directed towards the breakdown of production based on the exchange value.[15] Again in Notebook VII, Marx seeks to create a dialectical polarity between the 'rich development of the social individual' and the development of the productive forces. The tension produced is directed towards the suppression of the 'self-valorization of capital' and finally towards the 'violent overthrow of capital' itself.[16] The historical sketch of pre-capitalist forms is used in a projective manner:

> These indications, together with the correct grasp of the present [*richtige Fassung des Gegenwärtigen*], then also offer the key to the understanding of the past [*Verständnis der Vergangenheit*] – a work in its own right, which we hope to be able to undertake as well. This correct approach, moreover, leads to points which indicate the transcendence of the present form of production relations, the movement coming into being, thus foreshadowing the future [*foreshadowing der Zukunft*].[17]

Verständnis der Vergangenheit combined with a *richtige Fassung des Gegenwärtigen* should shed light on the future – *foreshadowing der Zukunft*. Reading the *Grundrisse*, it is important to pay attention to certain sintagmas, to their collocation in contexts of sense. We cannot bypass those pages as we might in a self-service restaurant. We cannot choose a dish and leave the vegetables. We are served the whole menu. The philosophy of history affects the entire framework of the *Grundrisse*. It should be read with the benefit of hindsight.

Marx's emphasis on the 'overthrow' manifests his political intention to force his analysis in order to intervene and open up revolutionary possibilities in the middle of the crisis; but it also bears the signs of categorical opacity on points which are absolutely fundamental to an understanding of the relationship between absolute and relative surplus-value.[18] Indeed, during the 1850s, Marx had not yet defined the notion of value. The opening of the *Grundrisse* –

---

15   Marx 1987, p. 91; *MEW* 42, p. 601.
16   Marx 1987, pp. 133–4; *MEW* 42, pp. 641–3.
17   Marx 1987, p. 389; *MEW* 42, p. 373.
18   See Tomba 2013b, pp. 139–50.

'11. Money' – refers to the first chapter, *not yet written*, on value. This theoretical work is brought to completion during the 1860s. In the first edition of *Capital* (1867) there are still theoretical problems that are partially revised in the appendix written at the suggestion of Engels and partially further developed in the second edition (1873).[19] But for the purpose of the question posed in the *Fragment*, it is significant that here Marx had still not defined his own idea of *socially necessary labour* as labour which, in a given quantity, is objectified in exchange value.

The Forms of Exploitation within the World Market

In a letter of 8 October 1858, after having written about a hundred pages of the *Grundrisse* and after having seen the crisis dissolve without any kind of overthrow of the capitalist mode of production, Marx drafts for Engels an initial statement on the reorganisation of capital after the crisis:

> There is no denying that bourgeois society has for the second time experienced its 16th century, a 16th century which, I hope, will sound its death knell just as the first ushered it into the world. The proper task of bourgeois society is the creation of the world market [*Weltmarkt*], at least in outline, and of the production based on that market. Since the world is round, the colonisation of California and Australia and the opening up of China and Japan would seem to have completed this process. For us, the difficult question is this: on the Continent revolution is imminent and will, moreover, instantly assume a socialist character. Will it not necessarily be crushed [*gecrusht*] in this little corner of the earth, since the *movement* of bourgeois society is still in the *ascendant* over a far greater area?[20]

This letter set the course for Marx's theoretical and political work throughout the 1860s. Marx raised at least three crucial issues. The 'second sixteenth century' of capitalism forces us to think of accumulation as a long-term process. Capitalist accumulation cannot, therefore, be limited to the protohistory of the capitalist mode of production. Second, not only theoretical analysis, but also political analysis, has to be thought in terms of the world market. The

---

19   Hecker 1987, pp. 166–8.
20   Marx and Engels 1983, pp. 347–8.

world is round, and the world-market creates connections between different geographic areas and different forms of exploitation. Capitalism cannot be analysed simply by looking at the nations where it is most highly developed. Neither should we imagine that these nations are the locomotive that tows the other cars of the train. Finally, and, indeed, as a result of these reflections, Marx asked himself, as well as his friend Engels, what possibilities of success a revolution might have – and *not* only in one single country but *even* a European revolution – in the face of the globalisation of the market. Without an international perspective, the revolution would necessarily be crushed. These three points, which made up Marx's frame for his work over the following years, were to be ignored in much of twentieth-century Marxism – with serious consequences. Whereas after the crisis at the end of the 1850s, while investigating the relationships between the various forms of exploitation, Marx sought a categorical and political repositioning in terms of the world market, much of Marxism opted for the *complementary* roads to socialism, either in one country alone, or to communism at the high points of capitalist development.

With these problems to consider, Marx began to rethink the entire categorial framework of his own analysis. These analyses, and the comparison of different forms of production and different forms of uprising, are what opened new perspectives for Marx, even if he did not always explore all of them fully. It became possible for him to imagine the capitalist mode of production not according to a pattern defined by *origin, development* and *crisis,* but rather as a constantly concurrent combination of those three moments and of their temporalities. *Original* accumulation [*ursprüngliche Akkumulation*] was to be conceived *not* as an initial form, but rather as an always-present method of the extortion of surplus-labour.[21] Some Marxian reflections that measure up to the standard of *Capital* develop in this direction. However, Marx did not always develop them to their fullest extent. Herein lay the possibility of a non-historicist interpretation of the different modes of production.[22]

When, in *Capital,* Marx analyses *ursprüngliche Akkumulation,* he has a different objective from that which characterised the analysis of pre-capitalist production forms in the *Grundrisse.* There Marx was seeking a theory for the breakdown of a form of production and the transition to a superior form. In

---

21   See Dussel and Yanez 1990; Marini 1991; Bagu 1949.

22   These themes have been taken up again today in the context of postcolonial studies. According to Chakrabarty, to speak of a residue means to think in historicist terms. Challenging the theories of *uneven development,* he holds that it is historicist to consider the distinction between formal and real subsumption of labour 'as a question of historical transition' (Chakrabarty 2000, pp. 49–50).

Capital, his attention is focused elsewhere. So much so that, compared to the first edition, in the second edition of the first volume he tones down some statements on the history of capitalist development [*Entwicklungsgeschichte*]: the 'succession of historical processes' [*Reihe historischer Prozesse*] cedes its place to an analysis of the English case,[23] where the transition to the capitalist mode of production is investigated, concentrating on the 'violent levers' [*gewaltsame Hebeln*] that made it possible. Indeed, the violence of the state [*Staatsgewalt*] takes powerful action in order to demolish the feudal system and to discipline the new 'formally free' labourer. The historical subdivisions expounded by Marx correspond with the chronicles of this event:

- the 'dissolution of the feudal bands of retainers' of the fifteenth and sixteenth centuries had hurled great masses of men as free and 'unattached' proletarians [*vogelfreie Proletarier*] on the labour market;[24]
- 'The process of forcible expropriation of the people received ... a new and frightful impulse from the Reformation, and from the consequent colossal spoliation of the church property. ... The suppression of the monasteries, &c., hurled their inmates into the proletariat';[25]
- after the restoration of the *Stuarts*, the landed proprietors abolished the feudal tenure of land.[26] If a mass of proletarians had been generated through the dissolution of the feudal system, it now had to be disciplined, made to move, not at the pace of the Church, but at the chronometrical pace of the market;
- at the end of the fifteenth century, a '*bloody legislation* against vagabondage' takes hold throughout Europe;[27]
- in *1530* Henry VIII ordains whipping and imprisonment 'for sturdy vagabonds'. 'They are to be tied to the cart-tail and whipped until the blood streams from their bodies, then to swear an oath to go back to their birthplace or to where they have lived the last three years and to "put themselves to labor." ... For the second arrest for vagabondage the whipping is to be repeated and half the ear sliced off; but for the third relapse the offender is to be executed as a hardened criminal and enemy of the common weal';[28]

---

23 Compare the first edition of *Capital* (1867), in MEGA² II/5, 581, with the text of the fourth edition (1890) in MEW 23, p. 751. See Regina 2009.

24 Marx 1996, pp. 708–9; MEW 23, p. 746.

25 Marx 1996, p. 711; MEW 23, pp. 748–9.

26 Marx 1996, p. 713; MEW 23, p. 751.

27 Marx 1996, p. 723; MEW 23, p. 762.

28 Marx 1996, pp. 762–3; MEW 23, pp. 762–3.

- in *1547* Edward VI 'ordains that if anyone refuses to work, he shall be condemned as a slave to the person who has denounced him as an idler';[29]
- in *1572* Elizabeth ordains that 'beggars above 14 years of age are to be severely
  flogged and branded on the left ear *unless someone will take them into service
  for two years* ... but for the third offence they are to be executed without
  mercy as felons';[30]
- James I (1603–25) ordains that 'incorrigible and dangerous rogues are to be
  branded with an R on the left shoulder and set to hard labor'.[31]

As the case of the American colonies shows, the flight of workers was the fundamental problem of the accumulation of capital from 1500 to 1800.[32] The
purpose of English legislation in the sixteenth and seventeenth centuries is
the immobilisation and disciplining of labour power, even through slavery
which, 'far from representing an abnormal excrescence in the colonies ... constitutes an authoritarian, homogenous response of control of the mobility on
the European and North-American labor-market, of which indenture is a particular declination'.[33] Capitalist slavery does not concern men who are not free;
it arises, rather, from the control of free wage labour. It is a disciplined vari-
ant. It is not the slave trade that produces the slave, but bonded wage labour
that produces the modern forms of slavery.[34] Accumulation is not confinable
to a historical moment located at the dawning of the capitalist mode of production,[35] but is constantly reproduced by the capitalist mode of production
itself. The problem that Marx manages to pose at the end of the 1860s, in
contrast with what he wrote in the section of the *Grundrisse* entitled 'Forms
Preceding Capitalist Production', regards the co-existence of various forms of
exploitation, their interweaving as regards the relationship between absolute
surplus-value and relative surplus-value, on the basis of the capitalist need to
obtain ever increasing quantities of absolute surplus-value able to support the
labour intensified through technological innovations. Hence, the importance
of extra-economic means in order to manage to squeeze as much surplus-value
as possible out of the great mass of workers: the disciplinary power of the state

---

29   Marx 1996, p. 724; *MEW* 23, p. 763.
30   Marx 1996, p. 725; *MEW* 23, p. 764.
31   Marx 1996, pp. 725–6; *MEW* 23, p. 764.
32   Boutang 1998, p. 25.
33   Boutang 1998, p. 175.
34   Boutang 1998, p. 244.
35   The analyses of de Angelis also move in this direction: see De Angelis 2001. See also
      Glasmann 2006; Hall 2012; Bonefeld 2014, pp. 79–100.

on Chinese workers;[36] new forms of forced labour around the world; racism and the generation of insecurity in migrant workers in the Western metropolises.[37] The process of accumulation is characterised, as Rosa Luxemburg realised in 1913, by the intervention of extra-economic elements. An important difference from Luxemburg's argument is that accumulation does not necessary require non-capitalist areas. Accumulation's processes also take advantage of the differences between wages, intensity and productivity of labour-forces. These differences are also created by extra-economic factors, such as the imposition of new ethnic divisions of labour or the total blackmailing of migrant workers who are without residence permits. Thus, alongside the terrorism of separation of the workers from the means of production, there is also the continual recourse to violent extra-economic means to increase the absolute exploitation of the workforce both in terms of intensity and hours worked. The globe was the theatre for the genesis of the capitalist mode of production, founded on extermination, enslavement and the 'hunting of black-skins'.

> The discovery of gold and silver in America, the extirpation, enslavement and entombment in mines of the indigenous population, the beginning of the conquest and looting of the East Indies, the turning of Africa into a warren for the commercial hunting of black-skins, signalised the rosy dawn of the era of capitalist production. These idyllic proceedings are the *chief moments of primitive accumulation*. On their heels treads the *commercial war* of the European nations, with the globe for a theatre.[38]

According to Marx, the different moments of original accumulation distribute themselves now more or less in geographical and 'chronological order' [*zeitliche Reihenfolge*], from Spanish colonialism to the European trade wars; they arrive at a 'systematical combination' in England, 'embracing the colonies, the national debt, the modern mode of taxation, and the protectionist system'.[39] All these systems used state force. Hence, Marx's attention is drawn to the 'violent levers' of the state.

---

36   Ngai 2005.
37   Gambino and Sacchetto 2013.
38   Marx 1996, p. 739; *MEW* 23, p. 779.
39   Marx 1996, p. 739; *MEW* 23, p. 779.

Violence and History

Capital is written in strata that are in tension with each other. Its chapters should not be read in the order of progression because some of the later chapters act as detonators for the earlier ones. One of the fuses is located in the chapter on accumulation. It is necessary to pull apart the chapter on factory legislation and put these pages next to those concerning so-called primitive accumulation. We could then note the attention that Marx pays to state interventions in relation to class struggle and the dissolution of the pre-existing social forms.

> If the general extension of factory legislation to all trades for the purpose of protecting the working-class both in mind and body has become inevitable, on the other hand, as we have already pointed out, that extension hastens on the general conversion of numerous isolated small industries into a few combined industries carried on upon a large scale; it therefore accelerates the concentration of capital and the exclusive predominance of the factory system. It destroys both the ancient and the transitional forms, behind which the dominion of capital is still in part concealed, and replaces them by the direct and open sway of capital. But thereby it also generalizes the direct opposition to this sway.[40]

If the state violence interventions from the sixteenth century onwards had favoured the formation of an army of salaried workers and contributed to the destruction of class power, Marx seeks to understand the ambivalence of the state's interventions on the subject of factory legislation. These interventions requested by the workers to improve their labour conditions also produced a concentration of capital. During this process economic and authoritative social forms are dissolved, so that class antagonism assumes a form that is more openly capitalist. These are tendencies that contradict each other inasmuch as they originate from the clash with the counter-tendencies of the class struggle. The materialist historiographer demonstrates the possibility of a new social formation within the revolutionising elements of the old society.[41] State force is considered to be a moment of ambivalence: although it destroys forms, it also opens new possibilities for those who manage to understand how that state action is the relatively autonomous product of the struggle against the class

---

40   Marx 1996, p. 504; *MEW* 23, pp. 525–6.
41   Marx 1996, p. 504; *MEW* 23, pp. 525–6.

struggle. It is in this sense that Marx defines force [*Gewalt*] as 'the midwife of every old society pregnant with a new one'.[42] This statement of Marx, that is considered to be so scandalous that it has been stigmatised as a violent philosophy of history or as an apology for violence *tout court*, refers precisely to the power of the state. This concentrated, organised force acted as an 'economic power' [*ökonomische Potenz*] where it contributed to the process of transformation of the feudal mode of production into the capitalist mode. This concerns colonial violence, the treatment of the populations of the colonies by Christian Europe, the colonial administration of Holland, the stealing of men in Celebes to procure slaves for Java.[43] The colonial system promoted the development of the industrialist capitalist system, but this was hardly progressive history.[44] The historical material assembled by Marx in these pages is used to tell the counter-history of a development that was possible through the 'great slaughter of the innocents'.[45] Capital comes into the world dripping with blood, displaying its deadly side right from the start: 'Wherever they (the Dutch) set foot, devastation and depopulation followed'.[46] This extreme violence occurs 'in plantation-colonies destined for export trade only, such as the West Indies, and in rich and well-populated countries, such as Mexico and India, that were given over to plunder'.[47] The tones on the civilising nature of British colonialism of the 1850s are long gone. Marx instead now wants to understand the entanglement of different forms of production like slavery and the capitalist mode of production. Indeed, slavery, subsumed in the capitalist mode of production inasmuch as it becomes labour destined for world commerce, takes on a new form in which the *rhythm* and *intensity* of labour are regulated by the clocks of the world stock markets. Thus, the development of the 'international character of the capitalistic regime', leads to the 'entanglement of all peoples in the net of the world market'.[48] Insofar as forms of slave labour enter the world market, they can no longer be considered as having been left over from former times.[49] The network of the world market not only supports various forms of exploitation by simultaneously combining them, but it also puts different working populations in contact with one another.

---

42   Marx 1996, p. 739; *MEW* 23, p. 779.

43   Here Marx also quotes historical documents such as Howitt 1838 and Stamford Raffles 1817.

44   See Anderson 2010.

45   Marx 1996, p. 745; *MEW* 23, p. 785.

46   Marx 1996, p. 740; *MEW* 23, p. 780.

47   Marx 1996, p. 741; *MEW* 23, p. 781.

48   Marx 1996, p. 750; *MEW* 23, p. 790.

49   On the 'plurality of temporal strata' of slavery, see Tomich 2003.

Here Marx indicates not only a scheme of historical analysis in terms of the present, i.e. the combination of the forms of exploitation in the world market, but he also indicates the level that the organisation of labour must assume. At the same time, demonstrating how state violence worked as an *economic power*, he also demonstrates the possible counter-use to which the workers have put the state. Maintaining the tension between the chapter on so-called originary accumulation and that on modern industry, it is possible to analyse the history of the role of state *Gewalt* within the social and political forms. The pages on factory legislation and on the obligation to attend school can be reinterpreted as initiatives aiming at changing social relationships, as episodes in the class struggle in which the working class succeeds in forcing the state over to its own side.

In the conflicting dynamics that led to factory legislation, the state appears to possess relative autonomy. The state is at the service of the ruling class, which is implicated in the class struggle, since its function is to neutralise the conflict, but in the performance of its function it has a relatively autonomous role. The dynamics of the conflict and the forces at play can push the state to issue legislation that limits the autocracy of capital in the factory and its destructive nature inside and outside the factory.

State intervention, which is not neutral, must be seen as part of the class struggle. It is not always reducible to the interests of the ruling class. It should be understood in the ambivalence of its own relative autonomy. Marx was interested in its use by workers, for instance, in securing legislation on the working day or on the family. In fact, through a universal law on the working day, a victory of the working class in a sector of production or in a series of battles applied to the entire working class. They therefore become political victories of the working class. An entire paragraph of the fourth section of *Capital* is dedicated to the *factory laws*. Marx shows how the dynamic of this legislation was forced on capital against its wishes. Indeed, because of its relative autonomy, the state does not directly coincide with the interests of the capitalist class. It can also enter into conflict with capital. As a direct consequence of the Factory Act of 1864 which, with the authority of the state, imposed health and hygiene measures for workplaces, the small workshops were converted into factories.[50]

Analysing the originary accumulation of capital, Marx shows the 'series of forcible methods' that punctuate history. The chapter on the accumulation of capital is not at the beginning, but at the end of the first book of *Capital*. In

---

50   Marx 1996, p. 485; *MEW* 23, p. 506.

the final pages Marx outlines the historical tendency of capitalist accumulation. For Marx the tendencies only have substance when in tension and in counter-position with the counter-tendencies. So if there is a tendency towards the centralisation of capital and the increase in exploitation, there is also an increase in the 'rebellion of the working class',[51] in the sense that the capitalist tendency is not a straight line, but a line dotted with the syncopated temporality of the working class struggle.

Marx's historiography is political and has to be fixed in an image with the power to evoke and take upon itself the old and new working class uprisings. The history of the capitalist mode of production can only be written through those images. The capitalist form is the way we see it today not because it has followed the immanent development of the concept of value, but because it was brought by the proletarian uprisings into an antagonistic relationship with the process of valorisation. It is the counter-histories that make history and the counter-tendencies that create the tendency.[52]

When Marx writes that 'capitalist production begets, with the inexorability of a law of nature [*Notwendigkeit eines Naturprozesses*], its own negation', these words should be taken seriously. Marx is not naturalising a historical fatality. In the context of chapter 24, he is reasoning on the historical tendencies of the capitalist mode of production and hence, on its counter-tendencies. He puts it in Hegelian terms. The *Naturprozess* is the production of the identical and the non-identical. *Value* is like the *telos* of the valorisation process, and *living labour* is like the life-blood vampirised by capital, on the one hand, and resistance to exploitation, on the other.[53] The vampire lives off the blood of mortals, but as soon as they can, they plant a wooden stake in his heart. *Capital* recounts this historical *multiversum*. Living labour is the condition of the possibility of capital, but it is also its negation. The 'negation of the negation' to which Marx refers is not, as orthodox Marxists and their liberal critics maintain, a dialectical law applied to history. On the contrary, it expresses the possibility of an asymmetrical uprising. Capital cannot exist without living labour, while living labour can exist and even realise itself without capital. In this tension, the possibility of the *novum* arises. The *Negation der Negation* is therefore the instant of a struggle, the action of the counter-tendencies on the tendency, the suspension of the law of value.

---

51   Marx 1996, p. 750; *MEW* 23, p. 790.
52   On this subject, see Bensaïd 1995a and Bensaïd 1995b.
53   Among the few, particularly in Italy, to take the Marxian metaphors concerning the critique of political economy seriously is Bellofiore 2009.

In the final pages of section IV dedicated to machines and modern industry, after having illustrated the prison regime of modern industry, Marx paints another picture of the consequences of the new industrial regime on the lives of the workers:

> But if modern industry, by its very nature, therefore necessitates *variation of labour*, fluency of function, universal mobility of the labourer, on the other hand, in its *capitalistic form*, it reproduces the old division of labour with its ossified particularisations. We have seen how this *absolute contradiction* ... dispels all fixity and security in the situation of the labourer; how it constantly threatens, by taking away the instruments of labour, to snatch from his hands his means of subsistence, and, by suppressing his detail-function, to make him superfluous. We have seen, too, how this antagonism vents its rage ... in the incessant human sacrifices from among the working-class, in the most reckless squandering of labour-power and in the devastation caused by a social anarchy. This is the negative side. But if [*Wenn aber*] ...⁵⁴

If all the above is the negative side, this '*aber*' heralds something positive. It is not a dialectical reversal. On the contrary, it represents the co-existence of antithetical forces within the real situation. Since the form of the capitalist mode of production is characterised by an antagonistic relationship with the working class, the traces of this antagonism must be evident also in the institutional forms. That 'but' does not indicate the point of reversal, but the opening words of the second item of the series.

> But if, on the one hand, variation of work at present imposes itself after the manner of an overpowering natural law, and with the blindly destructive action of a law of nature [*blind zerstörenden Wirkung eines Naturgesetzes*] that meets with resistance at all points [*überall auf Hindernisse stößt*], modern industry, on the other hand, through its catastrophes imposes the necessity of recognising, as a fundamental law of production, variation of work, consequently fitness of the labourer for varied work, consequently the greatest possible development of his varied aptitudes. It becomes a question of life and death for society to adapt the mode of production to the normal functioning of this law. It becomes a question of life and death ... to replace the detail-worker [*Teilindividuum*], grappled by life-

---

54   Marx 1996, pp. 489–90; *MEW* 23, p. 511.

long repetition of one and the same trivial operation, and thus reduced to the mere fragment of a man by the fully developed individual [*das total entwickelte Individuum*], fit for a variety of labours, ready to face any change of production. One step already spontaneously taken towards effecting this revolution [*Umwälzungsprozess*] ... is the establishment of technical and agricultural schools, and of *écoles d'enseignement professionnel* in which the children of the working-men receive some little instruction in technology and in the practical handling of the various implements of labour. Though the Factory Act [*Fabrikgesetzgebung*], that first and meagre concession wrung from capital, is limited to combining elementary education with work in the factory, there can be no doubt that when the working-class comes into power, as inevitably it must, technical instruction, both theoretical and practical, will take its proper place in the working-class schools.[55]

The Factory Act does not fall from the sky, it is not the concession of a paternalistic state, but one of the victories of the working class on the solid terrain of the class struggle. This is the reason for the final crescendo of Marx's pages on the conquest of power by the working class and education, both theoretical and practical, for the workers. Education is a victory. In the same way, the detail-worker [*Teilindividuum*] cedes his place to the fully developed individual [*das total entwickelte Individuum*] not within a linear process of capitalist development, but as part of a dynamic interwoven with the countermelody of the working class and what it manages to gain in the struggle from capital. However, left free to proceed according to its nature, capital mortifies the working class and brings it to physical and spiritual exhaustion. But the blindly destructive action [*blind zerstörenden Wirkung*] of its law meets with resistance at all points [*überall auf Hindernisse stößt*], which reorient and divert it, forcing it to come to a compromise. Here there emerges Marx's argument for compulsory education, which seeks to save the children from the mental stupor and the physical catastrophe of factory labour occupying the entire day. Using those incomplete documents which are the factory inspectors' *Reports*, Marx describes the young substitutes of the labour power in the London printing works as 'utter savages and very extraordinary creatures', who as soon as they get too old for such work, 'become recruits of crime' and 'attempts to procure them employment elsewhere, were rendered of no avail by their ignorance and brutality, and by their

55   Marx 1996, p. 490; *MEW* 23, pp. 511–12.

mental and bodily degradation'.[56] Marx's purpose in using the *Reports* was not to raise a moral scandal. These work conditions were recorded by the factory inspectors and Marx's additions to them were negligible. What Marx did do was to edit and assemble this material so that it became an integral part of critical theory. Marx's editing technique still needs to be studied. The pages in which Marx recopies the factory inspector reports should be read and understood in the context of his categorical account. If this is omitted, the specific objective of *Capital* cannot be fully grasped. It is transformed into a work of political economy, and not the *critique of political economy* that it actually is. Marx does not describe capital and the capitalist relationships with the composure of an entomologist investigating the object of his research; he assumes the viewpoint of the object, or rather, the subjective side of the object.

Taking apart and reassembling those *Reports* until he has transformed them into theoretical material, Marx develops an idea of critique that is not indignation in the face of degradation, but a historiographical strategy, on the one hand, geared to demonstrating what in reality acts as a possibility,[57] and, on the other, ready to trigger off the explosive charge of the past in the present. Marx shows the *basso continuo* of *extra-economic violence* without which the capitalist mode of production would not manage to sustain itself and would never have succeeded in getting off the ground. But in this appalling story of violence, Marx also demonstrates how the working class was not a mass of inert victims. On the contrary, it interacted with the state force, exerting its own force. The force exerted by the working class plotted the vectors of the counter-tendency: the *contretemps* of capitalist development. And if there is still a world today, we owe it to the force of these counter-tendencies. Marx works constantly to construct an electrical arc between the force exerted in the *past* by the working class and the struggles of the *present*. The spark can only ignite within this tradition, taking sides with the counter-history of the struggles of the working class movement. The historiography inaugurated by Marx had already grasped the extent to which a historiography of the victims would have been inauspicious.

Inasmuch as it is characterised by the valorisation of its own end, the capitalist mode of production can undoubtedly be described in terms of tendency, but this on its own is as abstract as the dominion of value. A tendency as such of the capitalist mode of production is never given. The tendency must

---

56   Marx 1996, pp. 487–8; *MEW* 23, p. 509.

57   'Factory labour may be as pure and as excellent as domestic labour, and perhaps more so (*Reports of Ins of Fact. 31st Oct. 1865*, 129)' (Marx 1996, p. 493); *MEW* 23, p. 514.

always be formulated within the contingency, in the sum total of the tendencies and counter-tendencies. The history of capital is always subjected to the discontinuous times of relations of exchange, of exploitation and domination, showing a process of rhythmical determination constantly inverting new harmonies and disharmonies.[58] The capitalist mode of production, left free to develop itself, to realise its own tendency, would present itself as an immense process of destruction that would not only lower wages to the absolute minimum necessary for workers' survival, but would also turn the entire planet into a desert. There are, however, counter-tendencies that continually reorient this tendency. When Marx speaks of *tendency*, therefore, he does so in the same way that a painter begins to paint the background before painting the subjects of the picture. The counter-tendencies are, in reality, the only elements that really define the tendency.

Conclusion: Towards a Historiography of the Layers of Time

In his mature writings, Marx becomes particularly attentive to the possibilities of a political combination of historical layers. Ever since Marx's reply to the editor of *Otecestvennye Zapiski*, his problem consists in identifying an alternative route from that of the capitalist civilisation embraced by Western Europe. This is the question that prompts Marx to read and annotate *Ancient Society* (1877) by L.H. Morgan. In his annotations, Marx refers constantly to the Slavs in relation to the communist organisation of the primal families.[59] And in the first draft of his letter to V. Zasulič (1881), he wrote: 'history of the decline of primitive communities (it would be a mistake to place them all on the same level [*sur la même ligne*]; as in geological formations [*formations géologiques*], these historical forms contain a whole series of primary, secondary, tertiary types, etc.) has still to be written'.[60] Investigating the origin of the German 'agricultural commune' as the 'the most recent type of the archaic form of societies [*formation archaïque des sociétés*]',[61] Marx reinterprets the historical develop-

---

58   Bensaïd 1995a.

59   Between 1880 and 1881 Marx reads and annotates *Ancient Society* by Lewis Morgan. The notes are published in Marx 1972. An edition of all the historical and anthropological notes of this period is expected with the publication of volume IV/27 of *MEGA*. On Marx's interpretation of Morgan, see Shaw 1984.

60   See Marx to V. Zasulič, First draft, in Marx 1989a, p. 358; *MEW* 19, p. 386. See Wada 1983.

61   Marx 1989a, p. 352; *MEW* 19, p. 388.

ment of Western Europe as a period of transition from communal property to private property, as a period of transition from the *primary* to the *secondary* formation, depending on the geological metaphor employed.[62] In the historiographical draft of Marx, there are two acquisitions that should not be missed: on the one hand, this passage, limited to the history of Western Europe, does not determine in any way whatsoever a historical law on the dissolution of communal property;[63] on the other hand, the geological metaphor expresses an overlapping of layers, not a succession of strata. The *secondary* layer is superimposed on the *primary* layer without cancelling it out. The materialist historian, treating historical periods like geological eras, can render the various strata visible at one and the same time. The historical forms, arranging themselves not according to the linearity of the past and present but as 'geological formations' in which the *then-and-there* co-exists alongside the *here-and-now*, makes it possible to think in terms of the simultaneous presence of temporalities on a plane and not according to the image of a linear vector. The encounter between different historical temporalities can ignite new possibilities of liberation, in which the Russian commune can represent a form of non-capitalist economy. Moreover, quoting Morgan, Marx wrote that modern societies tend towards 'a revival in a superior form of an archaic social type'. He then notes that 'we must not let ourselves to be alarmed at the word "archaic"'.[64] Indeed, the elimination of capitalist production can be understood as 'the return of modern societies to an "archaic [*archaïque*]" type of communal property'.[65] Marx's perspective is not romantic. The archaic, being contemporary, is not condemned to die, but can be combined with the temporality of the working class struggles, thus giving rise to a new social formation that is alternative to the capitalist modernity.

---

62   On the spatial connotation of history, Koselleck observes that the spatialisation metaphor, which makes it possible to pluralise the concept of time, has an advantage. The concept of 'temporal strata [*Zeitschichten*] gestures, like its geological model, towards several levels of time [*Zeitebenen*] of different duration and differentiable origin, which are nonetheless present and effectual at the same time' (Koselleck 2000, p. 9). Anderson writes that the theoretical kernel of Marx's *Ethnological Notebooks* consists in the 'multilinear model of historical development' as opposed to a unilinear model: Anderson 2002, p. 90. See also L. Krader, *Introduction*, in Marx 1972, pp. 1–85.

63   'But does this mean that in all circumstances [and in all historical contexts] the development of the "agricultural commune" must follow this path? Not at all' (Marx 1989a, p. 352; *MEW* 19, p. 388).

64   Marx 1989a, p. 350; *MEW* 19, p. 387.

65   Marx 1989a, p. 350; *MEW* 19, p. 387.

Marx's 'geological' vision, in layers, of historical periods does not derive from a reflection on the philosophy of history. Rather, it arises, on the one hand, from the need to construct a historiographic paradigm appropriate to the competition between capitals and the combination of different forms of exploitation,[66] and, on the other, from the need to consider the entire globe: the European corner of the world together with the three-quarters of the planet, where the former's wealth is a product of its plunder of the latter.

---

66   Fineschi 2009.

CHAPTER 4

Temporality in *Capital*

Stefano Bracaletti

Diachronic and Synchronic Processes, Mixed Temporalities

As a work of economic theory, *Capital* exhibits many references to temporal processes and more generally to dynamics in which time has an essential role. However, unlike the different approaches characteristic of neoclassical thought which thematise 'time' as an object of economic inquiry in itself, in *Capital* these processes and dynamics remain 'hidden', so to speak, within the folds of the analysis of the production and circulation processes and their intertwining. Starting from some intuitions of Stavros Tombazos,[1] in this chapter I seek to spell out these temporal processes and present them within a comprehensive framework.

The time of capital is a macroeconomic time wherein individual choices of consumption and investment are always connected to macro-processes linked to the intertwining of production time and circulation time, to their phases, and above all – in the mechanisms of the reproduction of the economic system – to the intertwining dynamics of use value and exchange value and to the substantial role of money in economic reproduction. In the complex overlapping of simultaneity and non-simultaneity, and the resulting linearity and cyclicality, the time of capital turns out to be a time of disequilibrium, as emerges clearly from the analysis of monetary phenomena that mediate the reconstitution of aggregate social capital.

Starting from these general lines, we can attempt to define different types of temporality in *Capital*. First, we have the linear and abstract temporality of the process of immediate production, the object of analysis in Volume 1. This process begins at point t with the acquisition of labour power and means of production, and finishes at point $t + 1$ with the sale of a commodity, after which the process begins anew, as if it were a segment within many perfectly similar segments arranged one after another. The problems of realisation and the relationship with other capitals are not posed. It is taken for granted that every single capital finds what it needs on the market in the phase of pur-

---

1 Tombazos 1994.

chase – labour power and means of production – and that it actually finds a buyer in the phase of selling. Every single capital co-exists alongside the others and is 'isolated' from them in the abstract synchronicity of a spatialised time in which only production exists. The categories of this abstract and linear temporality are those we know well from Volume 1: value, surplus value, rate of surplus value, constant and variable capital. They capture the way value is transferred to the product (as we know, constant capital transfers all of its value to the product, while variable capital adds value depending on the labour time expended beyond necessary labour time) as well as the capacity of capital's valorisation, but exactly as specified above – in an abstract way, without posing the problem of how or over what actual time this value can be realised.

This does not preclude various analytic developments of fundamental importance such as those concerning the working day and the various combinations between its prolongation or reduction in relation to the increase and reduction in the intensity of labour, whose factors influence the rate and quantity of surplus value. Even accumulation, in Volume I, is considered as a linear process based on the inexorable increase in the organic composition of capital, that is, the substitution of variable capital by fixed capital.

After the linear and synchronic temporality of Volume 1, we encounter the cyclical temporality of Volume 2, where the concept of the turnover of capital, which shows the dynamic of valorisation in its concreteness, is central. As we will see, inside of this temporality, forms of simultaneity and non-simultaneity are interwoven. In Volume 2 there is also what seems to be a linear process of accumulation, but it is instead integrated by the cyclical processes of the reconstitution of various parts of the social product both from the point of value and use value. These cyclical processes define other determinations of the process of capitalist production.

Finally, in Volume 3 there are economic categories as they appear to the agents of production – price of production and cost, profit, rate of profit, ground rent – and a set of forms capital assumes in the process of circulation such as commercial capital and credit capital. At this level of analysis, the attention focuses on a set of misleading phenomena that derive from the intertwining of production and circulation. These phenomena give the false idea that surplus value also comes from circulation, or in any case not entirely from the use of labour power inside the productive process beyond necessary labour time: 1) the subdivision of profit into interest and entrepreneurial gain and the fact that the latter pays exactly a quota to the money capitalist, making it appear as if what remains is his reward for his contribution to the productive process; 2) wages, according to Marx, enter into the cost of production as something given a priori, defined in the contract before the goods that contain the equivalent of corresponding value are produced. In the same way, the capitalist finds in front of him, as a given of the economic system, an average rate of profit that pre-exists the particular process of production that he will implement. In order to determine what the price will be on a competitive market, he must add the rate of profit and the cost of production. For this reason, these quantities will appear to him not as the result of a division of the value of goods but as 'factors' that determine value itself; 3) in capitals that differ only by the time of circulation, a longer time of circulation is the basis for higher prices. This happens because a longer time of circulation means that the agents of circulation must be paid more and therefore the prices imposed on the products are higher.

Tombazos defines the temporality in Volume 3 as 'organic'. In my view, it is perhaps more of a contradictory co-presence of the different temporalities defined earlier. In other words, the temporality in Volume 3 is a mixed temporality. What actually prevail are simultaneous processes and the contradictory overlapping of tendencies linked to different temporalities.

For example, commercial capital reduces the selling time and therefore the turnover time. However, in doing so it attempts to reinsert a linear temporality (reproducing the money form so as to begin a new productive process) into a form of cyclical temporality, breaking the latter or creating the illusion that it is accomplished (industrial capital selling commodities to the wholesaler has completed the cycle M-M' and can therefore recommence producing new commodities independently of the sale of the first amount, with the risk, after a certain period, of accumulating unsold commodities).

Credit capital has its origin in the necessity to accumulate money not for speculative purposes but as an integral part of the unfolding of the different phases in the productive cycle itself. Credit capital also imposes a linear temporality (indirectly using money unutilised by a certain capital for other productive processes, producing more, and more quickly, when the market is favourable or when unexpected opportunities suddenly open in new or hitherto stagnant sectors) on a cyclical mechanism, avoiding the hoarding of unproductive money and shortening the time in which the various anticipations that mediate the exchange between Departments 1 and 2 (means of production and consumption) flow back. Credit capital also imposes a linear temporality on the reconstitution of fixed capital, through various financial instruments. With the elimination of the necessity of real money, however, the cycle is rendered more vulnerable at various points. This is particularly the case when credit is not recuperated, or if there are external events that interrupt the normal course of the cycle.

Other examples of contradictory temporality, which are, however, only linked to the mechanisms of circulation in an indirect manner, are the processes that lead to the fall of the rate of profit and the equalisation of the rates of profit. Regarding the first problem, abstractly, the deep structure of capitalist accumulation involves the increase of fixed capital, which, in a linear and abstract dynamic, would lead to the fall of the rate of profit. The antagonistic tendencies and those that Marx defines as 'the intrinsic contradictions of the law (the law of the tendency of the rate of profit to fall)' lead instead, substantially, to a theory of the cycle. In this case a partially cyclical temporality is imposed onto a linear temporality. The deep linear dynamic otherwise makes its effects felt because the inherent contradictions in it can manifest themselves on a wider scale. Regarding the second problem, the mechanisms of credit (that is, mechanisms linked to circulation) favour the mobility of capitals and the equalisation of the rates of profit and therefore the formation of the prices of production. It is a process that cannot be defined as either cyclical or linear. If the neoclassical convergence towards equilibrium is rejected, we can say that the process takes place through disequilibria and continuous disproportions.

Dimensions of Cyclical Temporality: Simultaneity and Non-Simultaneity in the Turnover of Single Capital

If we focus now on the cyclical temporality that characterises Volume 2, we see that it gives rise to a set of fundamental problems for understanding both the analysis of Volume 3 and more generally several dynamics of a developed capitalist economy. Starting from the money form with which labour power and means of production are purchased, capital goes through different phases, some specific to production and others to circulation, in order then to return to the money form. The fulfilment of these phases constitutes a turnover. Actually, as we have observed (and it is a point that should constantly remembered), capital as value-in-process is always contemporaneously in each of the different phases. It should also be noted that, in the analysis of the process of circulation, various references to the productive process enter exclusively as categories of circulation/turnover. As Tombazos notes, the circulation of value involves a series of categories which regard the production process as one moment in the temporality of circulation.[2] Thus, while variable and constant capital are categories of production and its linear temporality, fixed and circulating capital

---

2 Tombazos 1994, p. 147.

are categories that define a cyclical temporality in which circulation is added to production.[3] 'These two categories exclusively belong to the sphere of the production of capital – for only productive capital can be fixed or circulating – but they are categories of productive capital insofar as productive capital is a moment of the total circulation of capital or its turnover'.[4]

The categories of fixed and circulating capital that concern the way in which the means of production, or more precisely their value, accomplish a turnover, constitute the analytic basis for specifying the concept of turnover time (in more detail, the average turnover time), and permit the concretisation and rendering operative of the concept of the rate of valorisation (rate of profit) – or rather the passage from a synchronic level in which the rate of valorisation is calculated in any instant of time, to a diachronic level that takes into account the turnover, or in fact different turnovers, of the different component parts of capital.[5] In practice, turnover time is a given magnitude: the shorter the time of circulation, the longer the time of production.

Marx distinguishes first of all between *permanence in the sphere of production* and *actual production*.[6] Capital has a tendency to render the process of production as continuous as possible for the purposes of valorisation, but this absolute continuity represents only an ideal limit. Leaving aside the rhythms and natural pauses, in fact, unforeseen interruptions and pauses can occur in which the means of production remain inactive while remaining in the sphere of production. A fundamental aspect of this distinction is represented by inventories and the way they are managed (ensuring a vast amount in the place of production in order to address unforeseen situations, as in the Fordist system, or instead reducing them to the minimum, integrating producers and suppliers in a different way, as in lean production).

---

3 The distinction between fixed and circulating capital defines the different type of turnover of the various constitutive parts of productive capital. Fixed capital (in general, plants and machinery) remains 'fixed' in its form through different periods of production and gives value to the product little by little. Conversely, the circulating part (raw and auxiliary materials, such as electricity) is completely consumed in every cycle, thereby losing its original form. In the same time during which fixed capital accomplishes a turnover (five years, for example), circulating capital accomplishes several turnovers.

4 Tombazos 1994, p. 160.

5 The more technical problematics of turnover, which we will not focus on here, are treated by Marx in the following chapters: 7, 'The Turnover Time and the Number of Turnovers'; 9, 'The Aggregate Turnover of the Capital Advanced. Cycles of Turnover'; 15, 'Effect of Turnover Time on Magnitude of Advanced Capital'; and 16, 'The Turnover of Variable Capital'.

6 Marx 1981a, p. 202.

The turnover of the process of production (that is, production time) is divided into *the working period* and *the production period*.[7] The first is the labour period in which the material is effectively subjected to the action of human labour. This phase is usually longer in industries that require a high monetary disbursement for fixed capital, such as railroads. The second refers to those productive branches in which, beyond human labour, the action of natural processes that do not require human labour is fundamental. Examples of these branches are the production of wine, leather tanning, forestry, and various types of animal raising. In these cases the commodity, before being ready to be sold, must remain in the sphere of production for a certain time. The period of production can therefore be longer than the working period.

As regards turnover in the process of circulation (that is, the time of circulation),[8] the distinction is between the *selling time* and the *buying time*. With respect to the selling time, an objective aspect is represented by the costs of conservation,[9] and the costs of transportation,[10] of the commodity from the place where it is produced to the places where it can actually be sold. It is unnecessary to specify that the interest of every capitalist is to reduce both the time and costs associated with these phases. Other costs of circulation are those linked to bookkeeping and to the means of circulation (that is, money). The latter represents a cost that must be reduced through its substitution by electronic means. The most difficult moment, of course, is the actual sale itself. As to this aspect there is therefore a correlated series of strategies for intervening on the most problematic link in turnover time, the consumer. As we will see, these strategies also aim at 'integrating' the consumer into the productive process as much as possible. Another fundamental aspect of the reduction of the selling time is the use of credit. The buying time (understood as the time required to buy – that is, have available – the components necessary to launch a productive process) is naturally less problematic. Even here, however, hiccups can arise that prolong the turnover time, such as when a company does not recuperate its credits. As we will see, in order at least partially to resolve problems of this type, schemes such as factoring were devised.

Here is a schema of the movements of capital in its turnover:

---

7   Marx 1981a, pp. 200–1, and more specifically with regard to the labour period, pp. 306–15; and with regard to the time of production, pp. 316–25.

8   Marx 1981a, pp. 202–4 and more specifically, pp. 326–33.

9   Marx 1981a, pp. 214–25.

10   Marx 1981a, pp. 225–36.

Turnover time = (A) production time + (B) circulation time
If the turnover time is a given magnitude, as B decreases A increases
Premise: distinction between permanence in the production sphere and actual production

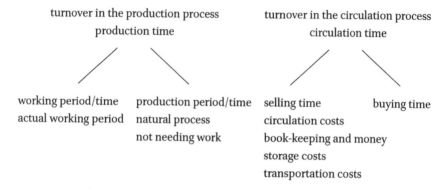

| turnover in the production process | turnover in the circulation process |
| production time | circulation time |

working period/time   production period/time   selling time   buying time
actual working period   natural process   circulation costs
                         not needing work   book-keeping and money
                                         storage costs
                                         transportation costs

In fact, it should not be forgotten that the cyclical temporality we are examining contains a form of essential simultaneity that is fundamental in order to understand the concept of value-in-process expressed in the analysis of the three cycles in the first section of Volume 2,[11] the cycle of money capital, of productive capital, and of commodity capital. The set of these cycles is the actual cycle of industrial capital.[12]

Cycle of money capital
M–C (means of production + labour power)...P...C′–M′

Cycle of productive capital
P...C–M–C...P

Cycle of commodity capital
C′–M′–C...P...C′

---

11   Marx 1981a, pp. 167–79.

12   M is a certain quantity of money. M′ is the increased quantity at the end of the cycle. P stands for the process of production and C is a certain quantity of commodities. Without focusing on this aspect here, we can recall that the cycle of commodity capital already begins with C′, value increased with surplus value; the cycle of capital therefore also includes the circulation of surplus value, destined to be both consumed by individual capitalists and reinvested. Precisely because it enables us to grasp the intertwining of these different circuits, the cycle of commodity capital is the form at the basis of the analysis of the reproduction of aggregate social capital.

From a certain point of view, the subtitle 'process of circulation' is therefore misleading, because what is analysed is the movement of capital as a 'thing in process', that is, the unity of the process of production and circulation. The first part on the three cycles seeks to fix and develop precisely this point, although at a high level of abstraction (which at times renders it difficult to follow the many distinctions developed by Marx). Every capital finds itself contemporaneously in each cycle and must fulfil all three of them. In other words, every capital fulfils all three of the cycles, not one after another, but rather contemporaneously to one another.[13]

This dynamic can be expressed in an appropriate manner through the concept of 'supervenience'.[14] The specific property of capital to be a thing in process, a value that is valorised, cannot be fully manifested in any of the cycles considered in isolation, but is an emergent property/function on the basis of the necessary presence of a fraction of capital in all three of the cycles according to the modalities just explained (sequentiality and contemporaneity). The emergent function is represented by the valorisation that cannot be related to any of the three forms considered in isolation, but is manifest in the fact of assuming them and leaving them behind one after the other and contemporaneously. Any analysis that isolates and absolutises one of the three cycles (treating capital as a sum of money, or else as the means of production together with labour power) lapses into a reductionism and a partial vision of economic reality.[15]

---

13   Marx 1981a, pp. 180–2.

14   Arthur 1997.

15   However, if they are not abstractly absolutised, the fact of choosing one of the three cycles rather than the others is useful for different purposes of analysis. Thus, the cycle of money capital is fundamental for understanding all of the mechanisms linked to turnover, because only through M-M′ can it be quantitatively and tangibly grasped that the initial monetary value has been reconstituted, as well as the time it took to do it. The money form is also necessary (abstractly, in its currency form) in order to constitute, in a definite and predictable time, the fund for the reconstitution of fixed capital, thus allowing it to accomplish its turnover. The cycle of commodity capital, which already begins as C′ (that is, as valorised capital), helps to understand the movement of aggregate social capital. In this movement, the circulation of surplus value is also included, and therefore the cycle of commodity capital grasps the intertwining of various capitals. Each one of the three cycles, finally, covers the various more concrete determinations of the cyclical temporality mentioned earlier. Even if each cycle contains the others and therefore comprehends all of the concrete determinations, the buying and selling time is embraced in a more specific

In this way, the mercantilist conception absolutises the circuit of money capital, trivially observing how 'money gives birth to money' without grasping its illusory aspects when the circuit is considered separately from the other two circuits. Mercantilism therefore sees the accumulation of money in the material sense as the most secure and tangible form of wealth that any nation must have as its aim, abstaining as much as possible from consumption.[16]

Classical economics instead absolutises the cycle P...P. It sees the money form as an inessential intermediate passage of productive activity, and focuses exclusively on the continuity of production: the objective is to produce the greatest quantity of possible use values at the lowest price. In this way it confuses the process of valorisation with a natural-material process of growth and does not grasp its specific social form.[17] Most recently, a modern example of reductionism which absolutises the circuit of commodity capital is Piero Sraffa's approach in his famous *Production of Commodities by Means of Commodities*. Sraffa completely neglects the determinations of value, and therefore the social relations of production. The entire cycle of capital is then reduced to the movement of a set of commodities between a point of departure and a point of arrival. Prices are understood as simply co-efficients of the equilibrium that permits the reproduction of the economic system in strictly physical terms. Class relations vanish from the productive process understood as a simple function of production, and only reappear in distribution. There are thereby no difficulties linked to valorisation, and the transition from c' to c' in commodity capital is simply linked to technical co-efficient determinations and as such is not problematic at all. One merit of Sraffa's model, however, rests in the fact that since it is based on the circuit of commodity capital, it grasps the intersections between various Departments of production at the basis of the analysis of aggregate capital (as was recalled above), that is, the fact that an input must have necessarily been the output of some other circuit of capital.[18]

The analysis of the three cycles according to the characteristics we have seen therefore have, among other things, precisely the objective of eliminating the ideological vision of the process of capitalist production that appears in the

---

manner in c-c'; in p-p the production period and the working period; in m-m' the whole turnover cycle in terms of a company's accounting procedures (in particular the fund of accumulated fixed capital).

16   Marx 1981a, pp. 138–9.
17   Marx 1981a, pp. 172–3.
18   Arthur 1997, pp. 108–9.

abstractions we have considered. According to Patrick Murray, these abstractions carry a false vision of the process of capitalist production as if it were constituted by two separate spheres: on one side, simply circulation, a simple commodity exchange mediated by money aimed at satisfying needs; and on the other, production of wealth, of use values, in the greatest possible quantity at the lowest possible price. Together, the analysis of Volume 2 therefore aims to show that: 1) all commercial transactions are 'mixed up' in the circuits of capital and its valorisation; and 2) a developed, commercial economy is necessarily a capitalist economy. No generalised circulation of commodities exists that is not a circulation of capital, that is, that does not have the mechanisms of the valorisation of capital at its base.[19] The three circuits are therefore not simple contemporaneous movements/flows, but precisely impose a cyclical time in which a comparison must be made between the preceding and the present moment before their repetition.[20]

To conclude our analysis with a paradox, we can observe that in an ideal economy without time and competition, every capitalist would completely carry through the time of production of his productive process and, even if particularly rigid natural obligations were present in such processes, would begin the time of circulation and would wait until, when it is over, the advanced money flows back, in order to evaluate whether to begin a new process, and, if so, on what scale. In fact, as we know, production time and circulation time are intertwined. Capital – or more precisely, a fraction of capital – therefore contemporaneously assumes the form of money capital, commodity capital, and productive capital, and this imposes quantitative equilibriums among the

---

19   Murray 1997, pp. 33–4.

20   However, Murray specifies that this type of representation cannot be considered a sheer and misleading appearance. Capitalist circulation, in fact, with its determinations, encompasses within itself simple circulation and its definite figures/forms: commodities, money, buyers, sellers, and the exchange of commodities mediated by money for the satisfaction of needs. Among other things, capital, before subverting the mode of production, works in its original form of industrial capital and finance capital according to the laws of simple circulation. In addition, different functions which are necessary for the reproduction of capital are still governed by the laws of simple circulation: the money spent in an unproductive way by the consumer (both the capitalist and the salaried worker) simply represents money, not money capital. The labour power sold on the market represents for its owner simply a commodity, not a commodity-capital. These forms, and the representation of the economy to which they give rise, are therefore not an evanescent appearance but represent a partial aspect of the overall reality of the capitalist economy. As such, if absolutised, they hinder a correct understanding of it in its essential determinations. See Murray 1997, p. 35.

different parts that can easily be neglected. Each of the three cycles moves in relative autonomy, confronting its own problematics, even though each one is still conditioned by the others, and the conclusion of each one entails a comparison between an initial and final moment. Only this comparison, which happens in the form of a comparison of money quantities but inevitably makes reference to quantities of final commodities and productive input for bookkeeping purposes, can render valorisation tangible. This intertwinement of different temporalities – simultaneity and consequentiality – effectively grasps the real movement and shows how Marx detaches himself from the analysis of equilibrium in neoclassical terms.

As observed earlier, the temporality of Volume 1 is intentionally a linear temporality, abstracted from a production that is detached from the problematics of the actual sale of the products and the requirements of the productive process at the global level. In this framework, use value enters in a very poor and general way: a commodity must simply have a determinate utility for someone.

The categories of circulation and the cyclical temporality they define (not simply identical repetition but comparison between different periods in order to bring the quantitative difference before the repetition itself to light) shows, instead, among other things, the importance of use value in economic analysis as a category that is indissolubly linked to value. Regarding such use value, an aspect often forgotten, but obviously fundamental for defining the process of capitalist production, is the intrinsic characteristic of labour power, namely, the fact it presents itself on the market as such, separately from the means of production. In this way, labour power cannot directly produce use value for its own personal consumption or for sale. Starting from here, it is easier to define the fundamental aspect that identifies the relation between non-possessors and possessors of labour power, expressed on a global level by a division into the two Departments of the means of production and means of consumption. This aspect consists in the fact that workers are separated from the means of production while capitalists possess them. In this sense, then, the exchanges that take place between the two Departments are defined by this class relation and at the same create and re-create it, for the means of production always remain in the hands of the capitalists, guaranteeing the key condition of capitalist production: namely, that the workers continue to be able to do nothing other than sell their labour power.

Another aspect, widely noted and studied, and in which the importance of use value is reaffirmed, is the analysis of the costs of circulation and their division into productive (inasmuch as value is added to the product) and unproductive expenditures. Transportation costs are productive because only through transport can commodities get to the place where their use value can be realised, that is, where they are actually consumed. Even the costs of conservation, inside a certain limit (the average selling time in normal conditions), are productive because they keep the product unspoiled and therefore sellable and consumable.

Another point in which the aspect of use value enters in a substantial way is the distinction between fixed and circulating capital, even if this is for different reasons, in the sense that the difference between the first and the second is based on the way in which the value of a certain material entity present in the productive process circulates (and not on its own material properties and functions). Indeed, as noted, for ideological reasons classical political economy does not distinguish and correctly define the categories of circulating and fixed capital. The fact that, from the point of view of turnover, labour power is circulating capital – or more exactly the similarity of the forms that variable and circulating capital present from the point of view of the turnover of capital – conceals their differences from the point of view of valorisation.

However, on the margins of the various traditional aspects just mentioned, it can be affirmed that *time* itself, within the cyclical mechanisms inherent to the turnover of capital, is actually the use value of primary importance. This aspect is defined, beyond the distinction between fixed capital and circulating capital (categories relevant, as noted, to the way in which the means of production turnover), also in the distinction between the various phases of the process of circulation previously examined.[21]

Regarding the categories of fixed and circulating capital, the durations of the different components in turnover have a profound effect on the rate of surplus value and its realisation, distribution, and accumulation. Essentially, the more these durations are reduced, the more the possibility of capitalist valorisation improves. These durations depend on a set of factors that include: the availability of labour power and materials, the capacity of combining them in a profitable way, the way in which scientific and technological development influence production time, the speed of communication, and transportation, and finally the efficacy of marketing strategies (selling time) and financial instruments, both to avoid leaving fractions of capital inactive in the money form and to favour consumption (buying and selling time). In relation to the dynamics of cyclical temporality inherent to the turnover of capital, there is therefore the incentive and even the necessity for capital to: 1) reduce the time of turnover; 2) reduce the expenses associated with storage within the process of production as well as within circulation itself; and 3) reduce the costs linked

---

21   Murray 1997, pp. 47–50.

to money and bookkeeping. Furthermore, it is important to highlight other ways of materially intervening in the time of circulation in order to reduce it. Examples include the strategy of management to secure the right combination of means of production and labour power, as well as to split the processes of production into different sections, so that their expansion can happen through small increments. This avoids having to find or have available considerable sums of money, and the problems associated with credit that follow from this need. Today, these tendencies are gathered together under the concept of lean production, which we will examine in more detail later.[22]

Concluding the analysis of this section, we can observe that, beyond the strictly productive-financial-managerial level, there is also a juridical level on which instruments for accelerating turnover time are realised. In particular, an instrument such as factoring helps to speed up buying time by ensuring that a company recuperates advanced capital more quickly. Factoring is an instrument of outsourcing the management of loans. Through factoring, which falls under the category of atypical contracts, a company transfers the credit to a third component (the factor), paying a commission and obtaining the nominal value immediately or at a deadline. The third component assumes the responsibility for bookkeeping and for obtaining payments as well as for the risk of non-fulfilment. In this way, the company that stipulates the factoring contract takes on a debt towards the factor but has the financial resources at its disposal for other investments, paying dividends, or adjusting the balance sheet, and therefore another turnover can begin.[23]

Dimensions of Cyclical Temporality: Simultaneity and Non-Simultaneity in the Turnover of Aggregate Social Capital

After the turnover of single capital, Marx analyses the turnover of aggregate social capital in the third section of Volume 2. Here the problems and implications stressed at the level of single capital remain valid, and new determinations are posed. In this case, too, we are dealing with a cyclical temporality concerning how, in production, over a given period of time such as one year, the quantities in terms of value and necessary material elements reappear in order to begin a new cycle and a new turnover. Here it is important to under-

---

22   Murray 1997, p. 54.

23   There is also a more limited form of factoring in which it is not the credit that is transferred to the factor, but just the possibility of autonomously managing it.

stand how value is actually replaced, that is, how the value of various parts of the social product return to money form. In single capital and its turnover, the form of use in which it exists can be casual (except for the earlier distinctions, where use value has, as pointed out, a very important function, but from a general point of view, that is, concerning how the different typologies of means of production and products influence their turnover).

On the contrary, in the turnover of aggregate capital, the aspect of use value is substantial because social capital must be divided into two very general but specific categories of use, not by virtue of the different typologies of turnover but due to the needs connected to the subsistence of society as a whole. Such categories of use are, of course, means of production and means of consumption.

Marx poses the problem in the following terms: 'How is the capital consumed in production replaced in its value out of the annual product, and how is the movement of this replacement intertwined with the consumption of surplus value by the capitalists and of wages by the workers?'[24]

We have just affirmed that, even in the analysis of aggregate social capital, a cyclical temporality emerges that regards the mechanisms through which in production, over a long period of time such as one year, the quantities in terms of value and necessary material elements reappear in order to begin a new cycle and a new turnover. As recalled in the preceding analysis, at the level of single capital, the simultaneity wherein each capital finds itself in the three cycles imposes quantitative balances among the various fractions that can be easily neglected. In the case of the reproduction of social capital, the focal point actually becomes the *non-simultaneity* inside of the cyclical process of reproduction, linked to the way money mediates a series of key passages in the turnover of aggregate capital. In my view, rather than the alleged analysis of equilibrium in the exchange between two sections and models of balanced development in enlarged reproduction – on which many interpretations have focused – the fulcrum of Marx's analysis of the reproduction of aggregate capital is precisely the analysis of the function of money as an essential factor of mediation (and therefore the intimate money-character of the capitalist economy), and at the same time, inescapably, of the disequilibrium that affects even the simple and normal flowing of the process.[25] In order to understand this function, in Volume 2 Marx abstracts from the phenomena of credit (even

---

24   Marx 1981a, p. 469.
25   This is roughly the position of Fred Moseley (1997). I had outlined some aspects of this
       interpretation, analysing in detail what Moseley calls, here and in other texts, Smith's
       dogma, in Bracaletti 1990.

if he considered it necessary in a developed capitalist economy) and departs ideally from the circulation of actual money (even if it is not necessarily currency) in order to show how money is absolutely essential to the functioning of the capitalist economy to mediate a set of phenomena in the production process. Marx therefore proposes an endogenous theory of money. Money arises from the very form of the capitalist economy, which is necessarily a monetary economy. Money is therefore not a veil which conceals the real phenomena, as in the neoclassical view. Conceiving of it in this way means not grasping the essential aspect of the capitalist economy and reducing it to an economy based on the simple exchange of goods, an exchange that money would only render more fluid without fulfilling an essential role. The process of circulation can instead suffer breakdowns, interruptions, and crises for reasons intrinsic to its endogenous mechanisms and not for reasons inherent to the system of credit. Or, looking at things from another point of view, the system of credit does no more than accentuate the intrinsic disequilibrium in these mechanisms but has in them its origin and its structural base, first of all in order to employ in a productive way the money accumulated at various parts of the productive process so that it is not left inactive. This accumulation assumes various forms.[26] It can occur, above all, for the needs of circulation (the unforeseen necessity of money in front of sudden contraction, in the phase of selling in particular; or sudden changes of the prices of various types of materials used; or, finally the necessity of money for unforeseen expansions of production when facing an unexpected increase in demand, or for work that requires an early, large disbursement).

An additional necessity of accumulation is linked to the fact that only beyond a certain quantity can money function as capital. Until this quantity is reached, it must be subtracted from circulation. In this way, the fund comes to be constituted on the side of the money used for the functioning of the normal productive process, and it is necessary because the continuing expansion of production, and therefore new projects of investment, is an essential characteristic of capitalist production.

In discussing the three cycles of capital, I have emphasised the fact that there is constantly an element of capital present in each of them: commodity capital, productive capital, and monetary capital. Because the money form, even if it is necessary, represents a 'suspension' of the production and circulation of commodities, the ideal situation would be for capital to assume it as seldomly as possible. However, this is able to happen only if (as in the schemas and previ-

---

26   Campbell 1997, pp. 138–41.

ous considerations) production and circulation time are perfectly harmonised, that is, if one begins exactly when the other ends. This does not happen for a variety of reasons, in particular the possibility of hiccups in various phases. The presence of money in liquid form is therefore always necessary in order to guarantee continuity, so that, for example, a process of production can recommence when a process of circulation is completed. According to Marx, this fraction of capital is fundamental, but it was neglected by the classical economists.

A final necessity of money accumulation, probably the most important and with more consequences on the structural level, concerns the reproduction of fixed capital. This process requires the constitution of a monetary fund for a variable number of years, sometimes very high. This involves unilateral sales in various sectors which must be counterbalanced by unilateral purchases in other sectors. This temporal lag is at the origin of deep phenomena of disequilibrium and clearly shows that the reproduction of the economic system cannot be conceived as a simple exchange of the parts of annual product with respect to which money only has an inessential role of convenience. In a capitalist economy, money is instead materially necessary in order to 'recompose' this lag.

In general, to repeat once again, the key point for understanding this set of processes is the fact that the accumulation of money never simultaneously occurs at all points of the system. Precisely this fact is the presupposition of possible equilibrium. This equilibrium is placed at an ideal point of an aleatory whole between an absolute non-simultaneity and an absolute simultaneity that would render the reproduction process possible. The necessity of money accumulation does not lapse with the credit system. Rather, it assumes the form of the application of various types of financial instruments that mediate this dialectic of simultaneity and non-simultaneity. If, for several political reasons, the monetary access to these instruments became problematic, capitalists would return to money accumulation for the necessity of production and circulation.[27]

The point of departure of Marx's analysis, aiming to understand as a fundamental point the global movement of money, is the subdivision of production into two Departments: 'production of the means of production' and 'production of the means of consumption'. The central problem is precisely that of defining the exchange between these sections on the global level.

Simple reproduction is an abstract hypothesis at the basis of capitalism, because one part of surplus value must always be employed to increase pro-

---

27   Campbell 1997, p. 137.

duction. However, Marx takes it into consideration because it enables him to highlight the conditions of the form of every reproduction. Even in the case of accumulation, it represents a 'real factor', that is, the necessary presupposition for securing at least the continuation of the process on its given basis.

Behind the various passages that Marx highlights, what must be taken into account is the fundamental problematic that characterises the analysis of aggregate social capital, that is, the intertwining of the dynamics of value and use value, two aspects which are constantly in conflict in capitalist production. However, this intertwining, as has been observed many times, is not relevant for the analysis of individual capital. In social capital, on the contrary, the macroeconomic relations between quantities of value are necessarily intertwined with quantities of use value. At the global level, one part of social labour must be dedicated to the means of consumption, and one part to the means of production. Although the ultimate goal is the valorisation of capital, it finds a generalised constraint in this subdivision.

As Geert Reuten observes, this conflict between these two aspects – the reproduction of use value necessary for the material survival of society and the dynamics of value and its increase, necessary for the survival of the capitalist form of production (or more banally, capitalism itself) – shows no traces in orthodox post-Keynesian economics. The latter deals with this problem by splitting it into two completely separate aspects or reducing it to only one of them, either monetary or physical (in the second case, the two aspects are rendered homogenous through index numbers).[28]

Let us now consider the following table.[29]

c = constant capital
v = variable capital
sv = surplus value

Department I. Production of means of production:[30]

capital: 4000 (c) + 1000 (v) = 5000
commodity product: 4000 (c)
+ 1000 (v) + 1000 (sv) = 6000
existing in means of production

---

28   Reuten 1997, p. 192.
29   Marx 1981a, p. 473. The organic composition of capital is 4/1 and the rate of surplus value
      is 100%. In conformity with his framework, Marx reasons here in terms of value.
30   It should be noted that the money (in the form of gold) necessary for the realisation of the

Department II. Production of means of consumption:

> capital: 2000 (C) + 500 (V) = 2500
> commodity product: 2000 (C)
> + 500 (V) + 500 (SV) = 3000
> existing in means of consumption

To recap, the annual aggregate commodity-production is:

> I 4000 (C) + 1000 (V) + 1000 (SV) = 6000
> means of production

> II 2000 (C) + 500 (V) + 500 (SV) = 3000
> means of consumption

We can now see how the exchange between the two Departments occurs, for now limited to commodity-flows.[31]

500 (V) and 500 (SV), which represent the part of the product that corresponds to the workers' salaries and capitalists' profits, remain inside of Department II. Taking into account monetary mediation, we can say that 500 (V), the workers' wage, and 500 (SV), the capitalists' of Department II's income, are spent in the means of consumption inside Department II, through thousands of reciprocal transactions. 4000 (C) in Department I represents the constant capital that must reconstitute what was consumed during the process of production. As for the 500 (V) and 500 (SV) of Department II, it also represents both supply and demand, and as such remains inside of Department I, fulfilling its function through the thousands of trades by capitalists in Department I.

Therefore, there remains in Department I 1000 (V) + 1000 (SV) and in Department II 2000 (C). 1000 (V) + 1000 (SV) represent respectively the wages of the workers and the income of the capitalists in Department I and must be real-

---

process belongs to the means of production and is directly introduced by the capitalist class as a result of the production of a specific branch. This quantity also includes the money for the circulation of surplus value. The question of several economists (which Marx takes as an object of critique) regarding the quantity of money necessary for the monetisation of surplus value – how is it possible that the capitalists extract more money from the sphere of circulation than they put in? – is badly posed and conceals the substantial misunderstanding of this point.

31   Marx 1981a, p. 474.

ised in the means of subsistence. Since 1000 (v) + 1000 (sv) exist, however, in the form of means of production, they must necessarily be exchanged with the products of Department II: they represent therefore only demand. 2000 (c) in Department II represents the value of constant capital (here we consider it composed exclusively of circulating capital and exclude for the moment the replacement of fixed capital) to be replaced. Through various considerations, Marx arrives at the conclusion that 'I (v + sv) can be realised only in II c, just as II c can be realised only in its function as a component part of the productive capital by way of this realisation'.[32] I (v + sv) must therefore be equal to II c and this is the fundamental presupposition of simple reproduction.

Relying on the formulation of Paul Sweezy, the series of relations between the Department of the means of production and the Department of the means of consumption presented by Marx can be schematised as follows:

c = constant capital
v = variable capital
s = surplus value

Value-product of Department I = $c_1 + v_1 + s_1$
Value-product of Department II = $c_2 + v_2 + s_2$

The conditions for simple reproduction:
The aggregate constant capital must be equal to the product of Department I.
The aggregate social need of means of consumption must be equal to the product of Department II.

$$c_1 + c_2 = c_1 + v_1 + s_1$$
$$v_1 + s_1 + v_1 + s_2 = c_2 + v_2 + s_2$$

After eliminating the members that appear on both sides in the two equations (which represent both the supply and demand inside of one Department), we obtain the equation $c_2 = v_1 + s_1$ (in Marx's terminology, II c = I [v + sv]).[33]

Before touching on some aspects of the monetary dynamics, let us examine the equation $c_2 = v_1 + s_1$. This equation is often construed by various interpreters as a condition of equilibrium. In my view, however, this is not its most significant aspect (and as a condition of equilibrium, it is rather poor). Rather,

32   Marx 1981a, p. 484.
33   Sweezy 1942, pp. 76–7.

through this equivalence Marx manages to highlight a key point that had not been understood by previous economists: the *double temporal level* which must be taken into account if one wants to identify the more general condition, purely at an accounting level, that allows the economic system to go through the same phases, that is, the exchange of one part of the past working day with one part of the present working day. Understanding these aspects requires the passage from a microeconomic to a macroeconomic perspective. In other words, based on the correct formulation of the relationship between use value and exchange value, understanding these aspects in relation to aggregated social capital requires the transition to a mode of analysis different from that employed for individual capital. Behind the different impasses in which the analysis of classical economics gets stuck, we actually find the missing elaboration of this transition.

In this way, Adam Smith transfers to the aggregate social capital determinations that are valid only for individual capital. Only the latter, as stated above, can be considered in the abstract simultaneity of a linear temporality. Smith correctly resolves the single product into its constituent parts – C + V + SV – without forgetting, beyond the value added by new labor, the constant part which represents the value of the means of production consumed. However, he affirms that the constant part (C) can also be resolved in labour, that is, in V + SV, thereby laying the foundations for an infinite regress that, while posing no problems in the *abstract simultaneity* of the analysis of individual capitals, makes the constant part disappear in the analysis of aggregate social capital. It is as though aggregate social capital were resolved in V + SV and therefore, paradoxically, as if the entire annual labour (V + SV precisely) produced exclusively means of consumption (the products that can enter the income of capitalists and workers), while constant capital (the raw material and machinery used) were reconstituted on its own at the beginning of every productive cycle, without a quota of annual labour being dedicated to it. The key point for overcoming this impasse is precisely the different type of formulation necessary in order to analyse the process of the reproduction of aggregate social capital.[34]

---

34 'A correct point in all this is that in the movement of the social capital – i.e. of the totality of individual capitals – things look different from the way they do when each individual capital is taken separately, i.e. from the standpoint of each individual capitalist. For the latter, commodity value can be resolved into (1) a constant element (a fourth element, as Smith says) and (2) the sum of wages and surplus value, i.e. profit and rent' (Marx 1981a, pp. 460–1). This misunderstanding of the nexus of social capital 'overlaps', so to speak, with the misconception regarding the subdivision of value, expressed in the famous 'trinity

Let us now consider any capital that is given in any use value. On the one hand, this capital finds the elements necessary for reproduction on the market: the machines, raw material, and means of consumption for workers and capitalists. On the other hand, aggregate capital, as a totality – the sum of all the single capitals producing different use values – of course, cannot be exchanged against another capital. Therefore, while in the case of a single capital its different parts exist in an indifferent use value, reappearing after the sale of this use value, in the case of aggregate capital, precisely because no exchange can be presupposed, the constant part and the variable part must be represented immediately in their material form, without the mediation of any sale. Marx specifies that this is one of the difficulties confronted in the analysis of aggregate capital: the constant part of value manifests itself in a different use value (means of production) than the use value of the variable part (means of consumption).[35]

In order to resolve this problem it is therefore necessary, precisely, to pose it from a different point of view than that of single capital, understanding how in the process of the reproduction of complex capital

> the product in which wages and surplus value are realised, i.e. all value newly added in the course of the year, can replace its constant value portion and still be reducible to a value defined simply by revenues; how, moreover, the constant capital consumed in production can be replaced materially and in value by a new capital, even though the total sum of newly added labour is realised only in wages and surplus value, and is exhaustively expressed in the sum of these two.[36]

Fixing the subdivision into the two Departments of production and analysing all of the types of exchange and monetary mediation, Marx manages to define the fundamental point: the exchange between II c and I (v + sv). In this way, he grasps a key point not understood by the classical economists. I (v + sv) represents, in fact, the work done during a working day of the ongoing year, while II c represents the work done on a working day in the preceding year.

---

formula', according to which wages, profit, and rent would be produced by three distinct factors – labour, capital and ground – that would come to form the value of the annual social product.

35   Marx 1981a, p. 507.
36   Marx 1981b, p. 983.

Smith failed to understand exactly this key passage, which allows the work of an ongoing year to find on the market a corresponding quantity of value existing in means of consumption, and at the same time permits the necessary constant capital to be reproduced. In other words, it enables the exchange of present labour against past labour, i.e. the part of the aggregate working day of the ongoing year against a part of the working day of a previous year.[37] By grasping this temporal dimension, Marx establishes the distinction between value of the product and value-product. This distinction is obvious from the point of view of modern national accounting, but it was not understood by Smith and classical political economy, while Quesnay was able to perceive some problematics of it but not in terms of value.

The clarification of the double temporal level intrinsic to the reconstitution of aggregate social capital constitutes the presupposition of the analysis of monetary dynamics both in the exchange between the two sections – in simple and enlarged reproduction – and in the process of the reconstitution of fixed capital. These dynamics are important for understanding the problem of the endogenous disequilibrium of the capitalist economy. As we have already observed, the fulcrum of Marx's analysis of the reproduction of aggregate capital is precisely the analysis of the function of money as an essential mediating factor and at the same time as a factor of disequilibrium even in the simple, normal occurrence of the process. Behind the numerical examples it is important to observe Marx's attempt to point out the different qualitative determinations of monetary circulation in the process of reproduction. Each of these represents a different function that governs a distinct and well-determined phase of this process.

---

37   Here we can recall the differences between the perspective of single capital and that of social capital in a more analytic manner. For the single capitalist of the Department of the means of consumption (Department II), this exchange is exclusively the transformation of the part of value that represents constant capital (here always indicated as IIc) in its material elements. (This part represents for him, although existing in means of consumption, a converted form of means of production and raw materials. It can never represent a consumption fund, that is, elements in which revenue is realised). In the same way, for the single capitalist of the means of production (Department I), the exchange is simply the transformation of the part of value that corresponds to the revenue [I (v + sv)] in its material elements (for him, therefore, v + sv, although existing in the means of production, represents the converted form of the means of subsistence and is never destined for productive consumption). From the point of view of the aggregate movement, instead, IIc and I (v + sv) always and only represent, respectively, the fund of individual consumption and the fund of productive consumption. The latter can never enter into revenue and constantly remains inside of the productive process.

We take on again the exchange: 1000 I (v) + 1000 I (sv) = 2000 II (c).

The capitalists of I anticipate 1000 lst. (sterling) as wages for their workers. With this 1000 the workers buy the means of consumption from II.

With the 1000 received by the workers of I, the capitalists of II buy that part of the means of production, produced in I, that correspond to the value of labour power in I, that is, 1000 (v).

The 1000 lst. are therefore restored – through the mediation of sector II – to the capitalists of I who can newly use them for salaries, and II has substituted half of its constant circulating capital.

What remains is to exchange 1000 I (sv) against 1000 II (c):

'In actual fact,' Marx explains,

> this circulation comprises countless individual purchases and sales by individual capitalists in the two departments, and the money for this must in all circumstances originate from these capitalists, since we have already accounted for the money cast into circulation by the workers. At one time, a capitalist in category II may use the money capital that he has alongside his productive capital to purchase means of production from the capitalists of category I, while on another occasion a capitalist from category I may buy means of consumption from the capitalists of category II with the part of his money that is ear-marked for personal expenses, rather than for capital expenditure.[38]

We suppose that the circulation starts from II: the capitalists anticipate 500 lst. from their monetary fund and purchase part of the commodity production in which surplus value exists. II has therefore substituted another quarter of its constant circulating capital, and I has monetised half of its surplus value.

With this 500, I acquires the means of consumption from II. The 500 flows back in this way to II that had advanced it in circulation.

What remains is 500 I (sv) to exchange against 500 II (c). Now there are capitalists from I that advanced 500 lst. of their monetary fund and purchase means of consumption.

With this 500, the capitalists of II acquire from I the remaining part of the commodities in which the sv of I consists and in this way finish the substitution of their own constant circulating capital. The 500 lst. are in this way returned to I that had advanced them in circulation.

---

38   Marx 1981a, pp. 475–6.

In the first movement, the money represents simple wages. Already in the second movement, however, this same money, in the hands of the capitalists in II, becomes an expense of capital, a medium to substitute its own constant capital. In movements 3 and 4 the same money assumes the form of expense as capital and expense as wages depending on whether it moves from II to I or vice versa.[39]

These three determinations – the expense of income in the form of wages (workers in I), the expense of income in the form of the expense of surplus value (capitalists in I), the expense of circulating capital in the form of purchasing means of production (capitalists of II) – therefore appear, from the point of view of the movement of aggregate capital, mediated by the same money, through simple changes in function. Certainly, even on the level of the immediate process of production money is wages because it buys labour power, or is expense of capital because it buys raw material, or expense of income because it is the expense of the capitalist for his sustenance. But as money which differs at every moment, its mutation of form, its being a simple bearer of external determinations to the process of circulation cannot be grasped. It almost seems to create these determinations itself, through purely quantitative differences.

Another fundamental point that emerges from this analysis of the whole of monetary flows is that at the level of aggregate social capital, as well as the means of consumption, the purchase and sale are ultimately relations between capitalists. In fact, in the acquisition of labour power, the wages advanced from the capitalists that produce the means of production flow back, through the workers, to the capitalists that produce the means of consumption. The class relation is reproduced through the relation of exchange between commodities.[40] From this point of view, all of the categories of the market from which Marx had begun in Volume 1, in particular wages and money, lose their explicative independence.

Analogous monetary dynamics can be found in expanded reproduction and in the mechanism of the reconstitution of fixed capital. In these two processes, however, the focal point is the *non-simultaneity* inside of the cyclical process. This non-simultaneity is linked to the way in which money mediates a series of key passages of the turnover of aggregate capital and manifests itself in a series of unilateral sales and purchases *in and between* the Departments.

For example, in expanded reproduction we have a series of unilateral sales and purchases that correspond to the non-simultaneity of the times in which

39   Marx 1981a, p. 476.
40   Marx 1981a, p. 520.

the various companies of I proceed to expand production. In this sense hoarding also has a fundamental role in the field of accumulation: in fact, given certain technical conditions of production, there is a given amount of money as the necessary 'minimum' to be able to expand production. As long as this amount is not reached, the surplus value transformed into money must be hoarded. Therefore, a series of unilateral sales and purchases happens at various points of I: the companies A1...An of I sell their surplus value existing in the means of production to other companies of I (B1...Bn, which have already accumulated the sufficient monetary capital for expansion, and now subtract commodities from circulation without putting any in), and does not subtract commodities from circulation; they do not buy, but rather hoard in this way the realised money as long as the necessary sum for expansion is not reached. At this point B1...Bn could have expanded production and therefore produced additional capital-commodities, which exist in the form of the means of production.

A1...An pass now into the position of B1...Bn and buy the additional means of production, subtracting commodities from circulation without putting others in, buying and not selling, while B1...Bn, as A1...An at the beginning, now sell without buying. Furthermore, we should observe that the creation of additional money is not necessary in order to allow reproduction on an expanded scale. Now what happens is the same as what happened for the monetisation of surplus value when it was meant to be completely converted into income. A1...An or B1...Bn – given a hypothetical beginning – can originally anticipate from their reserve funds the necessary money (it can be supposed that this money was originally obtained through a sale of part of the surplus value of I existing in the means of production, directly to the gold producers who realise their surplus value in means of production and not in means of consumption) in order to expand. In the flowing of production it is reconstituted in the way we have seen, and constantly passes from A1...An to B1...Bn, accumulating in one and in the other.[41]

As in the case of simple reproduction, we can make reference to the formal model of expanded reproduction constructed by Sweezy, which disregards the numerous exhausting examples in Marx's text. We then have:

$S_{\Delta c}$ = increased consumption of capitalists
S_{av} = increase in variable capital
S_{ac} = increase in constant capital

---

41   Marx 1981a, pp. 568–77.

$$C_1 + V_1 + S_1 + S_{\Delta c1} + S_{av1} + S_{ac1} = P_1$$
$$C_2 + V_2 + S_2 + S_{\Delta c2} + S_{av2} + S_{ac2} = P_2$$

Just like in simple reproduction:
The aggregate social demand of constant capital must be equal to the product of Department I.
The aggregate demand of means of consumption must be equal to the product of Department II.

As such:

$$C_1 + S_{ac1} + C_2 + S_{ac2} = C_1 + V_1 + S_1 + S_{\Delta c1} + S_{av1} + S_{ac1}$$
$$V_1 + S_1 + S_{\Delta c1} + V_2 + S_2 + S_{\Delta c2} + S_{av2} = C_2 + V_2 + S_2 + S_{\Delta c2} + S_{av2} + Sa_{c2}$$

Eliminating from the two equations the members that appear on both sides, we achieve:

$$C_2 + S_{ac2} = V_1 + S_1 + S_{\Delta c1} + S_{av2}$$

This equation represents the general condition of reproduction on an expanded scale.[42]

It clearly results from the preceding analysis that behind these formal schemes there are, just as in simple reproduction, complex intertemporal processes. The part of surplus product that accumulates is actually produced in the ongoing year but is only realised in the following year. In general, therefore, the realisation of various components of the scale always happens in a staggered way.[43]

The analysis of reproduction on an enlarged scale, in particular in the formulation of Sweezy shown here, presents some similarities to the two sectors' models of economic growth in twentieth-century economics, and was indeed read by many interpreters as their anticipation. There are certainly points where Marx anticipates this type of problematic, highlighting various multiplicative effects, both expansive and depressive, that are linked to the modification of relationships highlighted in simple reproduction. However, this aspect is secondary in my view. As in the case of simple reproduction, beyond the numerical examples and even the general formal conditions of reproduction,

42   Sweezy 1942, pp. 162–4.
43   Reuten 1997, p. 208.

what Marx wants to show is the intrinsically monetary character of the capitalist economy and the dialectical role money always plays, determining the conditions of the normal development of equilibrium and the possibility of modification and abnormality at the same time.

The same types of monetary dynamics in enlarged reproduction are found in the mechanisms of the reconstitution of fixed capital.[44] In this case, the temporal dimension is inherent to the object itself and not to exchange. Money is hoarded, not for speculative means, but always and only in order to mediate a material process; it is therefore a hoarding, so to speak, inherent to circulation itself. A certain quantity of money must constantly exit from circulation, thereby expressing itself into a series of unilateral sales, and be accumulated over the course of time in order to reconstitute the fixed part of capital. On the other hand, if the most abstract condition of crisis is the existence itself of money – which as a medium of simple circulation (C-M-C) can break the continuity – even the process of the substitution of fixed capital contains in itself an abstract possibility of crisis. Crisis is not induced by the contingent phenomena of credit, or a real overproduction, but is linked to the particular role of money, to its particular form of circulation, which takes place through unilateral purchases and sales. In this case crisis is not due to subjective factors, to the anarchy of many individual and autonomous decisions, but to the particular form in which a material universal process is implemented on a capitalistic basis: the reproduction of the means of production.

Let us now summarise the central points of our analysis. As observed at the beginning, in Volume 2 there is still an *apparent* linear process of accumulation, but it is integrated by the cyclical processes of the reconstitution of various parts of the social product both from the point of view of value and use value. These cyclical processes define other determinations of the process of capitalist reproduction.

In the case of the reproduction of social capital, the focal point becomes the *non-simultaneity* inside the cyclical process that is linked to the way in which money mediates a series of key passages in the turnover of aggregate capital. The key point, in my view, of Marx's analysis is not the search for the conditions of equilibrium expressed by the equation I $(v + sv) =$ II (c), which represents only an accounting identity actually directed at grasping, as we have tried to show, the intertemporal dimension of reproduction. Rather, the key point is

---

44   We can only hint at this problem here. A more detailed analysis of the monetary mechanisms in the reconstitution of fixed capital can be found in the original Italian version of this paper. See Bracaletti 2013 pp. 111–14.

the essential function of money for reproduction, a function that at the same time becomes a factor of permanent disequilibrium.

On the basis of this analysis, we can even better comprehend the role of credit capital that will be analysed in Volume 3. Credit capital, as we have observed, has its origin in the necessity of the accumulation of money not for speculative ends but as an integral part of the unfolding of different phases in the productive cycle. The necessity of accumulating money for the above-mentioned needs limits the process of accumulation, because a part of re-sources must be employed in the production of gold. The credit system res-cales this necessity by reducing the effectively necessary quantity to the min-imum.[45] It therefore allows the avoidance of hoarding unproductive money and shortens the time in which the various anticipations, which mediate the exchange between Departments I and II, flow back. In addition, for the recon-stitution of fixed capital, more and more elastic financial instruments are elab-orated in order to shorten the turnover time. The complexity of these financial instruments (based on more and more structured forms, both regarding the forms of payment and of financing), their being linked to different temporal parameters, has its origin precisely in the complexity of the temporal intertwin-ing of the mechanisms of turnover, which, as I have tried to show, is itself based on continuous situations of simultaneity at a certain level and in a certain field, and on non-simultaneity in another.

Trying to manage and sort out these situations in order to reduce turnover time (whose length, as we have seen, influences the rate of profit in an inversely proportionate way), these instruments attempt to 'bypass' the necessity of real money, but by so doing they create complex mechanisms of interdependence and render the system much more vulnerable to various forms of insolvency. Ultimately credit, trying to accelerate the natural cyclical temporality of annual social capital, based on the non-simultaneity of single exchange – trying, that is, to shorten turnover time – favours the eruption and acceleration of dynamics of disequilibrium intrinsic to these processes.

From these conclusions we can therefore see that in Marx's analysis the development of the credit system is correctly posed in microfoundational terms. This is, in fact, the secondary effect of the rational behaviour of capit-alists who seek to employ the money that must be accumulated for the needs of production and circulation in a profitable manner. The fact that, ultimately, the credit system furnishes means of payment and circulation more econom-ically than actual money cannot be interpreted, as Friedman and Hicks do,

---

45   Campbell 1997, p. 146.

for example, as the result of the coordinated action of capitalists without the incentive of a private gain.[46]

To conclude, we have recalled a final point that emerges in the detail of Marx's analysis: in the cyclical dynamic of reproduction, the sale and purchase of the means of consumption are actually relations between the capitalists of Department I and II mediated by a certain quantity of money that changes its function in the course of the process. The capitalists of I anticipate a certain quantity of money in the form of wages to their workers, who acquire the means of consumption from the capitalists of II. The capitalists of II use the same money to purchase constant capital from I, in this way making the money of I flow back. Through these mechanisms, the working class is globally integrated in the productive consumption of capital and the class relationship is constantly reproduced. That is why the categories of Volume 1, in particular money and wages, lose their autonomy at an explicative level.

The Cyclical Temporality and the Concrete Mechanisms of Competition: Lean Production

We can now move from our general framework of cyclical temporality, with its various levels and determinations, to the more concrete level of competition and dynamics of the market. The series of analysis of circulation, turnover and the determinations that Marx developed to comprehend this concrete level, as well as the emphasis of the importance of reducing circulation time for the ends of valorisation, offer a coherent interpretive framework for understanding the passage from Fordism to lean production. According to Tony Smith, the latter can in fact be seen as an attempt to reduce turnover time, an objective that encountered insurmountable limits in the Fordist system of production.[47]

---

46   Campbell 1997, p. 147.

47   Smith's analysis perhaps pushes the dichotomy of Fordism and lean production to the extreme, erroneously overlapping Taylorism and Fordism which, as Krishan Kumar observes, remain two different concepts. Taylorism is applicable both for production on a large scale as well as small-scale production. Its principles can also be applied to the new forms of team work adopted by new companies we can define as post-Fordist. On the other hand, if we analyse the development of large industries in the post-World War 2 period carefully, we can observe that large-scale mass production never came to completely dominate the productive scene. Small companies and craftsmanship continued to play a substantial role. The dichotomy of mass production/lean production therefore does not correspond to the actual reality. Even the automotive industry, which is seen as

According to Smith, the form of Fordist production can be defined in terms of the following characteristics: 1) a process of labour built around the assembly line where each worker is assigned a specific task to perform in a repetitive manner; 2) a system of rigid classification of the tasks and work rules, focused on the separation between mental and manual labour; 3) a vast expansion of forms of indirect labour, such as a bureaucratic apparatus of supervisors and middle managers, quality control departments, and so forth; 4) the extensive accumulation of inventory for every phase of production so as to avoid, should any problems arise, the interruption of production and distribution; 5) the mass production of standardised commodities; 6) the separation between industries and assembly lines and their suppliers and distributors; and 7) mass consumer markets.[48]

Smith observes that this general way of organising the productive process began to show a series of limits, primarily linked to the excessive fragmentation and atomisation of labour. In order to develop new margins of growth it was therefore considered necessary to reintroduce forms of cooperation in the workplace. Even the separation between mental and manual labour had reached a limit point in the Fordist system. From various investigations, it emerged that over a long period of time, the best productivity improvements derive from small changes in the productive process. To encourage these changes, there was an attempt to stimulate the creativity of the labour force (a philosophy expressed by the Japanese term 'Kaizen', 'continuous improvement').

---

emblematic of Fordism, always used both methods (see Kumar 1995, pp. 83–4). Viewing things from a wider point of view, Kumar emphasises, the equation Fordism = rigidity of mass production is not acceptable. What came to be called the crisis of Fordism and the transition to post-Fordist forms of lean production was actually a phase of the continuous evolution and the enduring productive revolution that truly characterises Fordism. Fordism, as Gramsci had already observed, is not a new technique, but represents the systematic application of new techniques to the organisation of production in its various sectors, including relationships between management and workers. It was therefore the culmination of what Marx called the real subsumption of labour by capital. What Ford introduced was the principle of mass production. On this basis, technological innovation and the adaptability of methods of production became the basis of every entrepreneurial activity on any scale. Fordism must therefore not be seen as a static entity, but as a general project that takes the form of partial projects (see Kumar 1995 p. 84). However, despite the excessive accentuation of the 'gap' between Fordism and lean production, Smith's general framework is of great use for understanding the concrete dynamics of the reduction of turnover time.

48   Smith 1997, pp. 67–8.

The indirect costs of labour, the administration-management of one part and the maintenance of the other, were also becoming excessive in the Fordist organisation of work. These costs can be reduced if the labour of the workshop and the labour of administration-management at the intermediary level are integrated into a single entity-type of a *multi-skilled* and autonomous worker. As opposed to the fragmented worker of the Fordist system, the new multi-skilled worker also brings together the tasks of maintenance and cleaning in the productive process.

To avoid the accumulation of inventories and, therefore, in the event that these would remain unused for too long, their eventually becoming unusable and losing value, the management philosophy of lean production moves towards a new overall approach of rearranging the phases in the production process. If each of its phases and each phase of the distribution process is completed at the correct time – that is, 'just in time' – then inventories can be scheduled in moderate amounts. The final assembly is completed only when the order arrives. Commodities are produced just when they are necessary for the assembly, and suppliers deliver the parts and raw material to the plant only when required for production. Another important aspect of lean production is the different way of using fixed capital. In Fordism fixed capital was invested in single-functioning machines, that is, machines able to provide only one type of output. There was therefore the tendency to extend the productive cycle of machinery to the maximum before the standardised product became obsolete to consumer tastes, causing the consequent obsolescence of the machinery as well. This could easily bring large quantities of unsold goods along with it. In the new productive framework, multifunctional 'generalist' machine tools are introduced, that is, machines capable of adapting, through simple reprogramming, to many productive processes, without an excessive influence on unit costs.[49] These numerically controlled machine tools allow the production of small quantities of goods, both intermediate and final, which are allocated to different sectors of the market. Thanks to these tools it is possible to quickly change the product according to market opportunities and the new needs of consumers that manifest from time to time. In general, therefore, this new technology does not require new machines in order to address the changes or even the conversion and re-adaptation of old machines, a process which is usually long and costly. Everything happens through the simple modification of the computer programmes that guide production. This flexibility also allows the rapid transformation of new ideas into new products and the diver-

---

49   Smith 1997, p. 69.

sification as well as adaptation to the rapid changes in the tastes and desires of consumers. In lean production, the greatest profits are obtained by modelling commodities and services to the specific needs of particular clients according to a modality that cannot be easily reproduced by other companies. This type of productive approach does not need large facilities designed to realise economies of scale or masses of non-specialised workers such as the large Fordist factories. Instead, it requires specialisation, both in the machine and in the worker.[50]

An additional important aspect consists in the fact that, in lean production, production companies are not a totally separate reality from suppliers and distributors, as in Fordism; on the contrary, all three share technologies and personnel. This more easily allows 'fine tuning' with respect to the errors or shortages that can emerge in the course of the productive cycle. Thanks to these, closer relations among business networks, an increasing number of phases and aspects of production and distribution, can be given in outsourcing without the overall process being interrupted or affected in other ways.

Finally, in lean production, the consumer is 'integrated' into the productive process in a new way. Final consumer demand, in fact, is determined at the beginning of the 'just in time' chain of events. And because the cycles of the product shorten, lean production industries can take advantage of technologies of information in order to respond, more or less in real time, to changes in consumer demand.

If we recall the previous analysis of the general schema of the different phases of turnover, both in the production process and circulation process, lean production can be seen as an attempt to reduce the turnover time of capital in response to the crisis of Fordism. This reading allows us to appreciate Marx's insistence on this aspect even more. Indeed, the 'just in time' approach is studied in order to make every stage of the production and distribution process ready to respond to the needs of the following stage, thereby reducing the turnover time. All of the characteristics of lean production are aimed at accelerating the transformation of raw material into products, and generally at reducing the permanence of products in the sphere of production.[51] In general, the objective is to shorten product cycles and therefore also the circulation time. In vertically integrated industries, a great quantity of capital is constrained in the productive process for a long period of time before the final sale of the product. In subcontracting, on the other hand, the different stages of production and

---

50   Kumar 1995, pp. 68–9.
51   Smith 1997, pp. 70–1.

sale are assigned to different units, each of which proceeds, with regard to its own phase, at a much greater speed than that of vertically integrated industry.

Another substantial point linked to the reduction of the sum of the time of production and circulation and to the optimisation of their relationship concerns inventories. Their undesired accumulation is, as we have seen, a problem in the Fordist system. Their costs of conservation, beyond a certain limit, must be paid with quotas of surplus value. If the process of accumulation is interrupted for some reason, perishable input and output can spoil before being used or productively consumed. Furthermore, their prices can also fall significantly between the moment they are produced and the moment they are sold. From this point of view, Marx's insistence on the role of inventory and the necessity of its limitation both in the production and distribution process also comprehends different developments of contemporary capitalism, offering an overall theoretical framework for its analysis. An explicit objective of the 'just in time' system is precisely to reduce inventories at every phase in the process of production and distribution. Indeed, the quantity of raw material and intermediary parts sent by suppliers is reduced in the same way that the inventory of pieces inside the actual process of production is reduced. The relations with distributors are coordinated with the purpose of minimising the amount of unsold inventory.[52]

From a more general point of view, we can observe, among other things, that Marx grasped several concepts that would be at the basis of the modern economic analysis of the inventory cycle. In the chapter on the costs of circulation in Volume 2 of Capital,[53] he distinguishes between voluntary and involuntary inventory, and emphasises the impact of the variation of inventory on the economic cycle. In particular, Marx shows that: 1) the desired inventory is a function of the volume of probable sales; 2) the cycle of inventories is staggered with respect to the economic cycle; and 3) the breadth of the cyclical variations of inventory is greater than the general economic cycle.[54]

Taking up once more our overall schema of the different phases of circulation, we can observe that the most problematic point of the reduction of turnover time, in particular circulation time, is surely the reduction of the selling time in its most concrete dimension, that is, the purchase of commodities by the final consumer. The push towards the reduction of the cyclical time of circulation/turnover, through the adequate ideological disguise (the final

52   Smith 1997, pp. 71–3.

53   Marx 1981a, pp. 221–9.

54   Nagels 1970, pp. 201–2.

objective of the company is to better and better satisfy the needs of consumers),
is concretely manifested therefore in the attempt to integrate the consumer
into the process of production, in order to reduce the time of necessary consumption.

The first step of this process is gathering and analysing information on
consumer behaviour through various technologies which instantly monitor
purchases at the point of sale. The development of information technology
has made possible purchases via the Internet from home and the creation of
information databases on single clients. Software that enables the management and continuous updating of this data, as well as the transmission of consumer preferences directly to producers, has become available.[55] On the basis
of this work which gathers data on consumer tastes, the attempts to shorten
the time of necessary consumption follow the traditional route of advertisements that conquer greater and greater spaces in daily life (for instance, televi-
sions which transmit advertisements placed in airports, in commercial centres,
and in underground stations). This happens through ever more subtle forms
of psychic manipulation of consumers, such as the exhausting repetition of
images and musical tunes that bypass the level of conscious thought. Advert-
ising expenses in the last 15 years have increased exponentially. In the United
States, people are exposed to 3,000 advertisements per day. It was calculated
that an average 18-year-old American, when high school ends, has experienced
350 hours of public advertisements. Then, of course, there are toll-free numbers
for the questions and complaints of clients and the possibility, on the part of
the firms, to take advantage of services which sell information on consumption.
All of this aims at reaching the ideal limit of the market segment that exactly
identifies the single consumer and his or her unique and unrepeatable tastes.
All of these tendencies are further exacerbated within the overall dynamics of
lean production. The various technologies we have analysed are, from this point
of view, a great help in permitting quick adaptation of production to changes
in consumer demand. The generalist and multifunction machines we have
mentioned, CAD (computer aided design) and CAM (computer aided manufac-

---

55   An Italian example of a company that, beginning in the late 1970s, had promptly applied
      this productive philosophy was Benetton, whose facilities were supported by a very
      extensive network of small subcontractors with 30–50 employees each. Electronic cash
      registers, specifically designed for a large number of points of sale in Italy as well as abroad,
      constantly transmitted the sales data to the central office in real time. On the basis of this
      information, all subsequent decisions regarding projects and products were taken, and
      thanks to this global system, Benetton had reduced its response time to changes on the
      market to ten days. See Kumar 1995, p. 69.

ture) technologies, enable the introduction of new products without having to change the machine, but rather only the software that runs it. This means that it is no longer necessary to intensify cycles of production as much as possible in order to avoid the problems of the obsolescence of machinery. Thanks to these technologies, the design of a certain product can be more quickly transmitted from the planning-units to the computers that operate in production. In this way the time that elapses between the initial design and the concrete availability of the product is reduced. In Japan, the objective is to let out a car from the assembly line and deliver it to consumers within 72 hours from when the order was made. In general, in Japan, with the introduction of lean production, the period that elapses between the planning of a new model and its appearance on the market was 46 months as opposed to the 60 months necessary in the Fordist system in the US factories. In this way, Japanese producers could produce a smaller number of units for every model, therefore succeeding in meeting changes in the tastes of consumers more quickly.[56]

Another aspect of the reduction in necessary consumption time is the attempt to gain customer loyalty for various generations of products through support services which are always more accurate. In reality, on the one hand, just as a mythology of the consumer's centrality is created, on the other, the attempts to manipulate and control consumer preferences are always more pervasive. Moreover, the transition to lean production, behind the ideological façade of the development of worker creativity through greater conscious participation in the productive process, imposes a very high price in terms of involuntary unemployment and instability. Part-time and temporary work, forms of fixed-term contracts, are a real consequence of the way the productive process is now structured. These precarious situations, over a long period, backfire against the system because they cause a decline in demand for consumption goods by workers.[57]

The exposition of the previous paragraphs concerning lean production shows how Marxian analysis, although moving at a high level of abstraction, can be consistently connected to a more concrete dimension. Another point in this sense can be seen in the possible use of the mass of money originating from the movements and mechanisms described in the preceding pages (not only from these, of course, but also from the drainage of private savings on a small scale) through which mortgages and credit to consumers can be granted. This aspect allows us to consider in a new light the problemat-

---

56   Smith 1997, pp. 78–80.
57   Smith 1997, p. 84.

ics regarding the dynamics of the reproduction of labour power. For example, as Massimo De Angelis observes, wages are no longer enough for this reproduction. What is necessary is what Marx called fictitious capital, that is, flows of future revenues, based on forms of credit, calculated according to a given rate of current interest. On the one hand, this creates social consent and has a boosting effect on the economy, supporting precisely consumption. On the other hand, however, because the future flows of wealth and interests are often linked to highly speculative financial activities, it entails greater turbulence and instability.[58] These activities are often covered by operations of securitisation that transform an undivided credit into several securities that can find a market.[59] A widely known example is subprime mortgages, but we could also cite the operations implemented by private equity companies. These companies specialise in the financing of firms unlisted on regulated markets (for example, firms in their initial phases which are devoid of revenue, or firms with a great potential but needing liquidity in order to launch products) or in restructuring firms that have serious difficulties. Thanks to the complicity of bankers, the poor control of organs of vigilance, and the superficiality of rating agencies, private equity companies have managed to gain access to the enormous liquidity made available by aging demographics, savings in the social security system, and have used this liquidity for highly risky operations.[60] This risk is then covered and apparently neutralised through the issuing of opaque titles, in which debt, according to the modalities we have just seen, is securitised and distributed over a multitude of investors. These titles have entered bank portfolios, investment funds, and pension funds in great quantities over the past 15 years, and are continuing to create strong turbulence in the financial system today.[61]

---

58   De Angelis 2008, p. 132.

59   For example, a loan is broken into various debt securities and sold by the bank to investors who receive high interest. Ultimately, those who took on the loan mortgage become debtors to new investors and not to the bank, which therefore has lower risks in connection with the higher interest paid on these new debt securities. Simplifying to the extreme, as an additional result of this mechanism, titles are created that contain different types of promises of payment, some good and some bad. In this way, there can be securities that contain parts of low-quality loans alongside solid government bonds or shares in expanding companies. In this way the risk becomes 'democratised' but also more pervasive and subtle, and in fact uncontrollable and unpredictable, as the financial events in recent years have shown.

60   Rampini 2007.

61   A proposal made by different economists in order to partially neutralise this turbulence

Furthermore, the link between reproduction and fictitious capital sharpens the dynamics of exploitation in ways that are often subtle and indirect, such as when the worker is integrated into the dynamics of company value by encouraging productivity through premiums and incentives. De Angelis uses an example from the 1980s,[62] when, during restructuring, companies proposed to pay a part of wage increases in the form of company shares. In this way, the workers had a direct interest in improving company value and were pushed to work more. It was then the market, or better the stock market, that would define this value, and, indirectly, 'how much more' the workers had to work in order to conserve and improve it (and therefore obtain further wage increases). Another example is the part of reproduction linked, instead of wages, to pensions.[63] Even thriving pension funds are in fact increasingly linked to future interest flows. For this reason, these funds continuously shift money within financial markets in search of better investments. These funds have of course invested in developing countries, attracted by high yields guaranteed by the stiff wage control implemented in these countries, the repression of social struggles, the appropriation of common resources such as rivers (see the recent cases in China) – veritable forms of enclosure and environmental degradation. The reproduction and thriving of pension funds depends therefore on the non-reproduction and the exclusion of entire communities.

Conclusion

On the basis of the idea of cyclical temporality that underlies Volume 2, I have tried to bring out the complex intertwining of simultaneity and non-simultaneity that characterises the turnover of both individual and aggregate social capital. In the case of single capital, attention was focused on the analysis of the three cycles of productive capital, commodity capital, and money capital. Each capital fulfils all three cycles, not one after the other, but rather contemporaneously. More exactly, a fraction of every single capital is found in each of the three cycles and carries them out sequentially.

---

was in fact to create a 'bad bank' for these titles and provide a particular market for them, convincing their possessors to get ride of them instead of hiding them, due to the negative consequences for their reputation and reliability that would result if their possession were revealed.

62   De Angelis 2008, p. 133.

63   De Angelis 2008, pp. 133–4.

This dynamic is expressed in the concept of supervenience. The property of capital to be a thing in process, a value that valorises, does not completely appear in any of the cycles considered in isolation, but instead is a property that emerges from the necessary presence of a fraction of capital in all three cycles, according to the highlighted modalities of sequentiality and contemporaneity. The emerging property is the valorisation itself, which cannot be explained by any of the three forms considered separately, but manifests in the fact that capital assumes them and leaves them behind one after the other and contemporaneously. Any analysis that isolates and absolutises one of the three cycles – treating capital only as a sum of money, or only as a quantity of commodities, or only as the means of production together with labour power – results in forms of reductionism and in ideological interpretations of economic reality.

If in the case of single capital and the analysis of the three cycles, however, synchronic considerations seem to prevail (we have observed, among other things, that the simultaneity with which each capital is found in the three cycles imposes quantitative equilibria between the various fractions that can be easily disregarded), I have insisted on the fact that, in the case of the reproduction of social capital, the fundamental aspect is represented by the *non-simultaneity* inside of the cyclical process of reproduction. This non-simultaneity is intimately connected to the way in which money mediates a series of key passages of the turnover of aggregate capital. The key point for understanding these processes is the fact that the accumulation of money does not occur in a simultaneous way in all of the points of the system. This is the presupposition of the possible equilibrium. This equilibrium lies in an ideal aleatory point between an absolute non-simultaneity and an absolutely simultaneity that, if it was realised, would render the process of reproduction impossible.

Moreover, the identification of the most general condition purely at an accounting level, which allows the economic system to go through the same phases, the equation $I (v + sv) = II c$ in the exchange between the two large sections of production (means of production and means of consumption), requires, in order to make the transition from a microeconomic to a macroeconomic perspective, the comprehension of a *double temporal level*, that is, the exchange of one part of the aggregate working day of the ongoing year with the aggregate working day of the previous year. Grasping this temporal junction, Marx succeeds in defining the distinction between value of the product and value-product, which is obvious from the point of view of contemporary national accounting, but which Smith and classical political economy were unable to understand.

On the basis of these premises, Marx's analysis should not be interpreted as the identification of the conditions of equilibrium of simple and expanded reproduction, but rather as what highlights the function of money as an essential factor of mediation (and therefore the intimately monetary character of the capitalist economy) and at the same time as an intimate and inevitable factor of disequilibrium arising even in the normal flow of the process. It is therefore a theory that analyses endogenous mechanisms of the macro-circulation of money, intentionally abstracting from the credit system.

The credit system increases the disequilibrium intrinsic to these mechanisms but originates in their structural basis, because its aim is, among other things, to use the money accumulated at various points in the productive process in a profitable way rather than leaving it inactive. The credit system – whose genesis in these terms is correctly framed in microfoundational terms, as the result of the rational behaviour of possessors of money – therefore shortens the time in which various anticipations, which mediate the exchange between Departments I and II and the reconstitution process of fixed capital, flow back. This happens through increasingly elastic and complex financial instruments, which reduce the turnover time. These financial instruments are based on forms of debt that are increasingly structured and linked to temporal parameters of different natures. This aspect finds its own origin in the complexity of the temporal intertwining of the mechanisms of turnover based on continued situations of simultaneity at a certain level and in a certain field and non-simultaneity in others. Seeking to manage and compose these situations in order to shorten turnover time (whose length as we have seen influences inversely the tendency of the profit rate to fall) – searching, that is, to accelerate the natural cyclical temporality of annual social capital – these financial instruments somehow 'bypass' the necessity of real money, creating nevertheless complex mechanisms of interdependence and rendering the system much more vulnerable to various forms of insolvency and crisis.

CHAPTER 5

On Non-Contemporaneity: Marx, Bloch, Althusser*

Vittorio Morfino

Non-Contemporaneity and Untimeliness

The question of plural temporality or non-contemporaneity has emerged many times in the history of the Marxist tradition. Here I intend to focus on the question by taking as paradigmatic the different utilisations of the concept of 'non-contemporaneity' by Marx in his Introduction to the 'A Contribution to a Critique of Hegel's *Philosophy of Right*', by Bloch first in *Heritage of Our Times* and then later in 'Differentiations in the Concept of Progress', and finally by Althusser in 'The Object of *Capital*'. From the differences in these texts I will try to extract some guidelines, as well as some precautions, for the utilisation of the concept of non-contemporaneity.

Before confronting these texts, however, it is useful to draw a line of demarcation with respect to Nietzsche's concept of the 'untimely' [*unzeitgemäss*], in order to avoid some confusions and superimposed readings which are not unknown to our own time. Nietzsche's utilisation of this concept in *Untimely Meditations* and the consequent opposition of timeliness and untimeliness is pervaded by a strong dualism: what is untimely is non-contemporaneous to an inauthentic contemporaneity (the contemporaneity of 'weak spirits' or 'philistines'), and therefore in the untimely there resides a deeper, authentic contemporaneity, those 100 men of 'strong spirit' capable of acting 'counter to our time and thereby acting on our time and, let us hope, for the benefit of a time to come'.[1]

Nietzsche uses this schema, marked by a deep-seated dualism between life and science, in order to read his own time, projecting onto it his reading of the Greeks in *Birth of Tragedy*, which is dominated by the Socratic betrayal of the equilibrium between the Apollonian and Dionysian: science is separated from life and becomes the betrayal of life. In light of this, according to Nietzsche, we must therefore boldly

---

* Translated by Dave Mesing.
1 Nietzsche 1997, p. 60.

seek our models in the original ancient Greek world of greatness, natural-
ness, and humanity. *But there we also discover the reality of an essentially
unhistorical culture [wesentlich unhistorichen Bildung] and one which is
nonetheless, or rather on that account, an inexpressibly richer and more
vital culture.* Even if we Germans were in fact nothing but successors –
we could not be anything greater or prouder than successors if we had
appropriated such a culture and were the heirs and successors of that.[2]

It is in this sense that in *Untimely Meditations*, the timeliness of a Strauss ('cultural philistine') or a von Hartmann is contrasted with the untimeliness of
Schopenhauer or Wagner. In this context, it is very interesting from a theoretical point of view that in *Being and Time*, when examining the second essay,
Heidegger projects the distinction authenticity/inauthenticity onto the Nietz-
schean distinction timely/untimely:

> The possibility that historiography in general can be either an 'advant-
> age' or a 'disadvantage' 'for life' is based on the fact that life is historical
> in the roots of its being and has thus, factically existing, always already
> decided upon authentic or inauthentic historicity. Nietzsche recognised
> what is essential about 'advantage and disadvantage of historiography for
> life' in the second of his *Untimely Meditations* (1874) and stated it unequi-
> vocally and penetratingly. He distinguishes three kinds of historiography:
> the monumental, the antiquarian, and the critical, without demonstrat-
> ing the necessity of this triad and the ground of its unity. *The threefold
> character of historiography is prefigured in the historicity of Dasein.* At the
> same time historicity enables us to understand why authentic histori-
> ography must be the factical and concrete unity of these three possibilit-
> ies. Nietzsche's division is not accidental. The beginning of his *Untimely
> Meditations* makes us suspect that he understood more than he made
> known.[3]

Heidegger's reading allows us to highlight a fundamental characteristic of the
use of the distinction timely/untimely: not only is it dominated by the opposition of life and science, by will and representation – in the last instance, that
is, by a profound vitalism – but it is also dominated by a radical individualism

---

2   Nietzsche 1997, p. 103.
3   Heidegger 2010, p. 376.

(adorned here and there with a pathetic aristocraticism). Consider the follow-ing passage from Nietzsche's second essay as a *specimen*:

> To prepare the way for these creations all one has to do is to go on writ-ing history from the standpoint of the *masses* [*die Geschichte vom Stand-puntke der Massen zu schreiben*], that is to say from the laws which move the lowest mud-and-clay-strata of society. The masses seem to me to deserve notice in three respects only: first as faded copies [*verschwim-mende Copien*] of great men produced on poor paper with worn-out plates, then as a force of resistance [*Widerstand*] to great men, finally as instruments [*Werkzeuge*] in the hands of great men; for the rest, let the Devil and statistics take them![4]

The time of the masses is timely; only the great individual of strong spirit can bear the untimely. In this sense the line of demarcation with respect to Nietzsche is drawn: what we want to focus on in this chapter is precisely the non-contemporaneity of the masses.

Non-Contemporaneity in the 'Introduction to A Contribution to the Critique of Hegel's *Philosophy of Right*'

A genealogy of the concept of non-contemporaneity in the Marxist tradition cannot leave aside the use that the young Marx makes of it in one of the famous texts of the so-called 'transition to communism', the 'Introduction to A Contri-bution to the Critique of Hegel's *Philosophy of Right*', written between 1843–4 and published in the *Deutsche-Französische Jahrbücher* in 1844. Therein Marx indicates for philosophy the task of bringing the work initiated by Feuerbach through the critique of religion to completion. Once religion is shown to be a product of man, the task is to criticise the reality that has produced the reli-gious illusion. Consider this well-known Marxian passage which opens with a famous chiasm:

> It is the task of history, therefore, once the other-world of truth has vanished, to establish the truth of this world. It is above all the task of philosophy, which is in the service of history, to unmask human self-alienation in its secular forms, once its sacred form has been unmasked.

---

4 Nietzsche 1997, p. 113.

Thus, the critique of heaven is transformed into the critique of the earth, the critique of religion into the critique of law, the critique of theology into the critique of politics.[5]

Marx's introduction, however, refers to a text he wrote the year before in Kreuznach, *The Critique of Hegel's Doctrine of the State*, which does not take German reality (that is, the Prussian state) into consideration, but rather German philosophy of the state and right in their highest expression, Hegel's *Outlines of the Philosophy of Right*. It does this for the precise reason that the German reality is non-contemporaneous:

> The following exposition [Marx refers to the project of the *Critique*] – a contribution to this task – does not deal directly with the original, but with a copy, i.e. with the German *philosophy* of the state and of right, simply because it deals with Germany. If we were to begin with the German *status quo* itself, even in the only appropriate way, which is negatively, the result would still be an *anachronism* [*Anachronismus*]. For even the negation of our political present [*unsern politischen Gegenwart*] is already a dusty fact in the historical junkroom of modern nations. If I negate powdered wigs, I still have unpowdered wigs. If I negate the German conditions of 1843, I am according to French chronology barely in the year 1789, and still less at the center of the present day. Indeed, German history prides itself on a development which no other nation has previously achieved or will ever imitate in the historical firmament. We have shared in the restorations of modern nations without ever having shared in their revolutions. We have been restored, first because other nations ventured a revolution, and second because other nations endured a counter-revolution; in the first case because our leaders were afraid, and in the second case because they were not. Led by our shepherds, we have only once been in the company of liberty, and that was on the *day of its burial*.[6]

It is history itself, through its procession in modern nations, which is responsible for conducting a critique of the German reality. The German present is the past of modern nations, 'the German conditions are beneath the level of

---

5   Marx 1970, p. 132.
6   Ibid (translation modified).

history'.[7] However, a critique of the German reality is not without significance even for the other nations in in the sense that 'the German status quo is *the overt perfection of the ancien régime*, and the *ancien régime* is *the hidden defect of the modern state*'.[8]

> The struggle against the political present in Germany is the struggle against the past of the *modern* nations, who are still continually troubled by the reminiscences [*Reminiszenzen*] of this past. It is instructive for them to see the *ancien régime*, which experienced its moment of *tragedy* in their history, play its *comic* role as a German ghost. Its history was *tragic* so long as it was the privileged power in the world and freedom was a personal fancy; in short, so long as it believed, and necessarily so, in its own justification. So long as the *ancien régime*, as the existing world-order, struggled against a new world coming into existence, it was guilty of a world-historical, but not a personal, error. Its decline was, therefore, tragic. The present German regime, on the other hand – an anachronism [*ein Anachronismus*], a flagrant contradiction of universally recognised axioms, the nullity of the *ancien régime* revealed to the whole world – only imagines that it believes in itself, and demands the same imagination [*dieselbe Einbildung*] from the world.[9]

Present and reminiscence in England and France, past, anachronism, and imagination in Germany: the struggle is inscribed in this fabric of temporality.

However, there is an aspect with respect to which Germany is contemporaneous to the present: philosophy. Germans live in the present of other nations through philosophy:

> Just as ancient peoples lived their past history in their imagination, in *mythology*, so we Germans have lived our future history in thought, in *philosophy*. We are philosophical contemporaries [*Zeitgenossen*] of the present day [*Gegenwart*] without being its historical contemporaries. German philosophy is the *ideal prolongation* of German history. If, then, we criticise the *ouvres posthumes* of our ideal history, philosophy, instead of the *ouvres incomplètes* of our actual history, our criticism centers on the very questions of which the present age says: *that is the question*. What

---

7   Marx 1970, p. 133.
8   Marx 1970, p. 134.
9   Ibid (translation modified).

for advanced nations is a practical break with modern political conditions is in Germany, where these conditions themselves do not yet exist,
essentially a critical break with their philosophical reflection. *German
philosophy of right and the state* is the only German history that is *al pari*
with *official* modern times. Thus, the German nation is obliged to connect
its dream history with its present circumstances, and subject to criticism
not only these circumstances but also their abstract continuation.[10]

Marx's critique of the Hegelian philosophy of right is necessary inasmuch as,
combined with the rise of the German proletariat, it would permit Germany to
'attain a praxis *à la hauteur des principes*, that is to say, a revolution that will
raise it not only to the *official level* of modern nations, but to the *human level*
which will be the immediate future [*die nächste Zukunft*] of these nations'.[11]

The non-contemporaneity, the anachronism, of Germany with respect to
other nations, where 'other' naturally refers to France and England, combined
with the contemporaneity of German philosophy, provides the conditions for
a leap into the future of other nations:

> Just as philosophy finds its *material weapons* in the proletariat, so the pro-
> letariat finds its *spiritual weapons* in philosophy; and once the lightning
> of thought has struck deeply into this naïve soil of the people the eman-
> cipation of the Germans into men will be accomplished.[12]

We can summarise these claims with the following schema:

t1	German political present	Past of modern nations	*Ancièn régime*
t2	German philosophy of the state	Present of modern nations	Modern state
t3	Critique of the German philosophy of the state	Future of modern nations	Social revolution

In this rhetorical game of anticipations and delays, of contemporaneity and
non-contemporaneity, of reminiscences and prefigurations, of imaginations
and reality – entirely set, moreover, in old northern Europe – Marx does not,

10   Marx 1970, pp. 135–6.
11   Marx 1970, p. 137.
12   Marx 1970, p. 142.

however, renounce, as an obvious result of the schema, the idea of a fundamental time. This fundamental time gives contemporaneity and non-
contemporaneity, anticipations and delays, the predetermined phases through
which it is necessary to pass: *ancien régime*, modern state, human liberty.

Non-Contemporaneity in *Heritage of Our Times*

We now come to a second model of 'non-contemporaneity', present in Ernst
Bloch's *Heritage of Our Times*, a collection of articles written between 1924 and
1934, and published in 1935. In this text, Bloch attempts to reformulate Marx
and Engels's concept of 'survivals' in order to understand the development of
Nazism while also putting forward a political strategy in that conjuncture. The
core of the text consists, as Bloch himself declares in the preface, in the article
'Non-contemporaneity and Obligation to its Dialectic'. Here are its opening
words:

> Not all people exist in the same Now [*Nicht alles sind im selben Jetzt da*].
> They do so only externally, through the fact that they can be seen today.
> But they are thereby not yet living contemporaneously with the others
> [*Damit aber leben sie noch nicht mit den Anderen zugleich*]. They rather
> carry an earlier element with them; this interferes.[13]

This anteriority, this untimeliness, is at the centre of Bloch's analysis of German
society and Hitler's rise to power.

> The masses also streamed towards [the untimely], because at least the
> intolerable Now [*imerträgliche Jetzt*] seems different with Hitler, because
> he paints good old things for everyone. There is little more unexpected
> and nothing more dangerous than this power of being at once fiery and

---

13   Bloch 1991, p. 97 (translation modified). Laura Boella translates the opening sentence into
       Italian as follows: *L'esperienza dell'attualità non è la stessa per tutti* [The experience of
       contemporaneity is not the same for everyone], which moves non-contemporaneity from
       an objective level to the subjective or lived level. Mark Ritter's English translation and Jean
       Lacoste's French translation (*'Tous ne sont pas presents dans le même temps présent'*) both
       preserve the objective level. On this text, see Remo Bodei's *Multiversum: Tempo e storia
       in Ernst Bloch*, which offers an extremely rich historico-philosophical inventory of plural
       temporality in general. To utilise this text, however, it is necessary to draw precise lines of
       theoretical demarcation.

meager, contradictory and non-contemporaneous. The workers are no longer alone with themselves and the employers. Numerous forces, coming from the past, from a very different basis, begin to interfere.[14]

The time of the young bourgeois middle class, deprived of future bourgeois prospects,[15] the time of the peasants,[16] and the time of the impoverished middle class[17] are equally non-contemporaneous times that innervate Hitler's power: 'With the decline of Hitler the non-contemporaneous will also perhaps

---

14   Bloch 1991, p. 97 (translation modified).

15   'The keen air of youth causes left-wing fire, when it burns, to burn ever more strongly; but if there is "renewal" on the right, then the youth of bourgeois and seduced circles is all the more seducible: the blood-based, the organically young is a good soil for Nazis' (Bloch 1991, pp. 98–9).

16   According to Bloch, the peasants have a double trait of non-contemporaneity, the first linked to the private ownership of the means of production, and the second to the 'doggedness in being rooted which comes from the matter they cultivate, which directly sustains them and feeds them; they are fixed in the ancient soil and in the cycle of the seasons'. Bloch continues: 'Thus not only the agrarian crisis drives peasants to the right, where they think they are sustained by tariffs, where they are promised the precise return of the good times. Their tied existence, the relative ancient form of their conditions of production, of their customs, of their calendar life in the cycle of an unchanged nature, also contradicts urbanisation, unites with the reaction which is expert at non-contemporaneity. Even the soberness of the peasants is an anciently mistrustful, not an enlightened one, even their alert sense of ownership [...] stem from pre-capitalist times, from conditions of production which had already demanded the sharing out of land when there were as yet no individually managing bourgeois citizens' (Bloch 1991, p. 100).

17   'It is impoverished, and hence susceptible in revolutionary terms, but its work is far from the action and its memories make it completely alien to the times. The insecurity which produces merely nostalgia for what has been as a revolutionary impetus places figures in the midst of the city which have not been seen for centuries. But even here misery invents nothing or not everything, but simply blabs out, namely non-contemporaneity which long seemed latent or at most one of yesterday [*Ungleichzeitigkeit, die lange latent oder höchstens eine vom gestern schien*], but now refreshes itself beyond yesterday in an almost mysterious St Vitus's dance. Older sorts of being thus recur precisely in urban terms, an older way of thinking and older images of hate as well, like that of Jewish usury as exploitation per se. The breaking of "feudal tenancy" is believed in as if the economy were at around the year 1500, superstructures which seemed revolutionised long ago come revolving back again and come to a standstill in today's world as whole medieval townscapes. Here is the Tavern of Nordic Blood, there the castle of the Hitler-duke, there the Church of the German Reich, an earthly Church in which even city folk feel themselves to be a fruit of the German soil and worship the soil as holy, as a *Confessio* of German heroes and German history' (Bloch 1991, p. 101).

seem weaker: yet it remains as the seed and ground of the National Socialist and of every future heterogeneous surprise'.[18]

What Bloch emphasises with force in his analysis of German society is that this non-contemporaneity [*Ungleichzeitigkeit*] is not only a subjective non-contemporaneity:

> But not everything here is the little man who deceives himself [*der sich täuscht*]. Alongside the early morning arising from mustiness, depriva- tion also brings the authentic one who is to be reckoned with [*Die Not bringt neben Frühe aus Muff auch echte, mit der zu rechnen ist*]. Today there are galoshes of misery which lead just as much into past times as the galoshes of happiness in the fairytale. If misery affected only con- temporaneous [*gleichzeitige*] people, even though of a different position, origin and consciousness, it could not cause them to march in such dif- ferent directions, particularly not so far back. They could not so little 'understand' Communist language, which is in fact totally contemporan- eous [*völlig gleichzeitige*] and precisely orientated to the most advanced economy. Contemporaneous people, despite all the mid-position which keeps them economically stupid, despite all the appearance [*trotz allen Scheins*] which finds room there, could not for the most part allow them- selves to be so archaically degenerated and romanticised [*archaisch ver- wildern und romantisieren*]. Of course middle-class people also rebel dif- ferently from the proletarian against becoming a commodity because they are only indirectly involved in production. And also because the employee, at least until recently, was not yet so annulled, not yet so ali- enated in his work, not yet so unsecured in his position; moreover, unlike in the case of the proletarian, little individual possibilities of promotion existed. But even if now, after total proletarianisation and insecurity, after the decline of the higher standard of life and all prospects of a career, the masses of employees do not join the Communists or at least the Social Democrats, then there is obviously a reaction which forces the process of becoming a commodity not just in subjective-ideological terms (which was certainly solely the case with an unradicalised centre until after the war), but also in real terms, namely out of *real non-contemporaneity* [*realer Ungleichzeitigkeit*]. Impulses and reserves from pre-capitalist times and superstructures are then at work, authentic non-contempora- neities [*echte Ungleichzeitigkeiten*] therefore, which a sinking class revives

---

18   Bloch 1991, p. 103.

or causes to be revived in its consciousness. After all, not only peasants and little people, but also the higher classes have conserved their position. The road which capital cut through the 'organically' traditional land shows, as a German one at any rate, a particular large amount of byways and cracking places. [...] Germany is not only [a] big capitalist land and the caste of Junkers not only a sham.[19]

A society is therefore not a homogenous space permeated by a single time that would constitute the playing field of a simple contradiction. According to Bloch, Germany in particular is

> the classical land of non-contemporaneity [*klassiche Land der Ungleich-zeitigkeit*], i.e. of unsurmounted remnants of older economic being and consciousness. [...] The 'unequal rate of development', which Marx as-signs in the *1857 Introduction* to material production compared with the artistic kind for instance, equally existed here for long enough in material times alone and thus prevented the clearly dominating influence of cap-italist thinking and hence of contemporaneity, in the economic hierarchy of forces. With East Elbian feudalism a whole museum of German interac-tions was preserved at any rate, an anachronistic superstructure [*deutsche Wechselwirkungen und anachronistischer Überbau*] which, however eco-nomically superannuated and in need of support it may be, nevertheless prevails.[20]

Accordingly, the Marxist revolution not only finds opposition in capitalist contemporaneity, but also in the non-contemporaneity rooted in the material structure of society.

> Alongside and in much false non-contemporaneity [*viel falscher Un-gleichzeitigkeit*] there thus equally stands this certain non-contempora-neity [*diese gewisse*]: the nature, and all the more so the spectre [*Spuk*] of history comes particularly easy to the desperate peasant and bank-rupt petit bourgeois in Germany; the economic crisis which releases the spectre is taking place in a country with a particularly large amount of pre-capitalist material.[21]

---

19   Bloch 1991, pp. 105–6 (translation modified).
20   Bloch 1991, p. 106.
21   Bloch 1991, p. 107.

What Bloch calls the spectres of history, the ideologies of past epochs, recur with more ease because in Germany they are present in the material structures of those past epochs.

On the basis of this analysis, Bloch distinguishes between subjectively and objectively non-contemporaneous contradiction:

> [T]his contradictory element is *subjectively* non-contemporaneous, as an existing remnant of earlier times in the present one *objectively* non-contemporaneous. [...] The non-contemporaneous contradiction is thus the opposite of a driving, exploding one, it does not stand with the proletariat as the historically decisive class today, nor in the battlefield between the proletariat and big business as the space of today's decisions. After all, the non-contemporaneous contradiction, and its content, has released itself only in the vicinity of capitalist antagonisms and is almost an accidental, or at least warped otherness there; so that between the non-contemporaneous contradiction and capitalism there exists a hiatus, a rift which can be consoled or filled with mist.[22]

To come to grips with this conception of contradiction, Bloch develops a theory of the 'multi-layered dialectic': social development is not explainable through the famous dialectic proposed by Marx is his 1859 Preface between productive forces and relations of production, a simple dialectic which presupposes the contemporaneity of society with itself and a linear development of historical time (in the sense that the present is pregnant with the future or the future already exists within the present).[23] Rather, the explication of social development would necessarily require a dialectic which 'make[s] the turbulent Now broader':

> The subjectively non-contemporaneous contradiction is accumulated rage, the objectively non-contemporaneous one unfinished past; the subjectively contemporaneous one is the free revolutionary action of the

---

22 Bloch 1991, pp. 108–10.

23 'At a certain stage of development, the material productive forces of society come into conflict with the existing relations of production or – this merely expresses the same thing in legal terms – with the property relations within the framework of which they have operated hitherto. From forms of development of the productive forces these relations turn into their fetters. Then begins an era of social revolution. The changes in the economic foundation lead sooner or later to the transformation of the whole immense superstructure' (Marx 1977, p. 5).

proletariat, the objectively contemporaneous one the prevented future contained in the Now, the prevented technological blessing, the prevented new society with which the old one is pregnant in its forces of production.[24]

Against the model of the dialectic founded on simple contradiction, Bloch proposes a 'poly-temporal and poly-spatial dialectic', which takes into account polyrhythm and counterpoint. However, he fails to push this proposal all the way when he conceives this complexity as temporal but not structural.[25] Even in Bloch, albeit with a complication of the picture, the plurality of rhythms is only apparent, as it is in the young Marx; despite the complication, there is nevertheless a fundamental time with respect to which contemporaneity and non-contemporaneity are defined, and this fundamental time runs inexorably in the direction of communism, no matter how many surviving fragments from the past may be strewn in its path, temporarily impeding its regular course. The plurality of rhythms is a momentary condition, in expectation of the *praesens* – as Bloch says in *Eperimentum mundi* – which makes itself *praesentia*, so that it may finally say to the instant: 'stay a while, you are so beautiful!'[26]

Non-Contemporaneity and Progress

Bloch returns to the concept of 'non-contemporaneity' in a 1955 conference held at the *Akademie der Wissenschaft* of the GDR, of which he had been appointed a member. Bloch titled his presentation 'Differentiations in the Concept of Progress', and in this completely different political conjuncture, he makes use of non-contemporaneity in order to complicate the framework of an ideology of progress whose polemic objective is clearly the orthodox Marxism of the regime.

His opening move consists in emphasising the shadows inherent to any progressing, refuting the idolatry of the succession of time in itself:

---

24   Bloch 1991, p. 113.

25   See Walter Benjamin's critique, which suggests an insufficient theoretical formulation in Bloch's book, without however furnishing further tools: 'Of course, Bloch has excellent intentions and substantial insights. But he does not understand how to put them into effect. His exaggerated claims hinder him from doing so' (Benjamin 1999, p. 38). I thank Massimiliano Tomba for this reference.

26   Bloch 1975b. [Translator's note: Bloch refers to the famous line from the end of Act Five in Goethe's *Faust*: 'Verweile doch, du bist so schön!'].

[I]n this respect there is no certain chronological index of progress [*keinen sicheren Zeit-Reihen-index*], by which what happens later in history is somehow or on the whole a progressive plus compared with what has gone before. If that seems a truism, well it didn't seem so to Hegel; for the Peloponnesian War after the age of Pericles, and the Thirty Years War after the Renaissance, put serious difficulties in the way of his concept of negation – otherwise wholly in the service of progress.[27]

The second move consists in bringing the fundamental Eurocentrism of the concept of progress to light, placing Europe as the natural end of the historical process in the last instance in service of the ideology of colonial imperialism. Bloch denounces the overvaluation of the concept of the 'classic' set up by Europe. Bloch uses the Parthenon as an example of classical antiquity elevated to a normative model which ends up putting into the shadows not only other forms of extra-European art such as African sculptures, Indian temples, or Chinese pagodas, but also other forms of art which reached maturation in Europe such as the Gothic or the Baroque. Such classicism is in the service of the white man's domination.

For this reason, according to Bloch, emphasising the non-contemporaneities internal to European history helps complicate the framework in service of the white man's domination. In this regard, Bloch again evokes the passage in Marx's *1857 Introduction* in which he highlights the inequality of development between Greek art and technology in order to stress the inverse conditions present in capitalist society: namely, that there is no synchrony between progress in the structure and progress in the superstructure. Indeed, the one can be the enemy of the other:

Bach or Leibniz do not correspond in the least to the wretchedness of Germany at the time, which only, so to say, wet their feet, whereas on the other hand a fully developed state of capitalism could be damaging to the muses as well as to the masses. 'Capitalist production', Marx says with special emphasis in his *Theories of Surplus Value*, 'is inimical to certain branches of creative production such as art and poetry'. Without this insight, without this separation of an economic and State evolution from a hardly so happy development of the epic, one would have 'the fanciful imagination of the French enlightenment century which Lessing satirised so admirably'. Again this implies that politics and art were not always

---

27   Bloch 1970, p. 114.

intercommunicating channels with regard to the rising bourgeoisie. The material connection between the determinative basis and the superstructure which it determines, and which has a reciprocal effect on it, is limited; obviously progress does not occur at the same rate and at a proportionate level of achievement in the base and in the superstructure [*in gleicher Art, in gleicher Tempo und vor allem mit gleichem Rang*].[28]

However, the complication of the concept of progress not only puts the 'non-contemporaneity' of structure and superstructure into play; according to Bloch, the discontinuity among presumed states of the superstructure should also be emphasised. In this sense, new evaluations of forms long considered as the simple stages of more perfect forms can be considered as the aporias of progress. For example, the evaluation of 'Egyptian pictorial works of art [as] "crude" precursors [*steife Vorgänger*] of Greek creations' are evaluations that derive from a classic ideal of beauty that posits Greekness as a *telos*.[29] In reality, Egypt and China constitute aporias with respect to the concept of progress precisely because they resist being reduced to a pre-Greek phase in the development of humanity.

> The aporias of the concept of progress to date, the theoretical difficulties of a concept far too straight-forwardly applied [*allzu geradlinig*] to Europe, were and are a matter of the breadth of art history, and of the wholly representative and aesthetic intrinsic valuation of non-Greek [*aussergriechischer*] and above all non-European [*aussereuropäischer*] art.[30]

However, Bloch considers the colonial manipulation of progress just as reactionary as its ahistorical negation. Progress must be thought instead as a chariot with many horses. He not only replaces the notion of the Orient as prehistory with the actuality of China, India, and Africa, but also avoids thinking these cultures through the *telos* of the civilisation of man and restores to them the 'concept of the pride of people in national cultures not mediated by Europe'. In this sense Bloch argues that the Parthenon, in the measure in which it appears founded 'in ancient and pre-asiatic stylistic forms, appears in its grand true humanity, not classicist'.[31]

---

28   Bloch 1970, p. 117 (translation modified).

29   Bloch 1970, p. 118.

30   Bloch 1970, p. 120.

31   Bloch 1975a, p. 119. [Translator's note: These two passages do not appear in the English translation of the essay].

The problem is how to systematise the immense historical material. In this sense Babylon and Egypt can establish the past of Europe, but the same cannot be said of India and China. One response could be provided by the fragmentary geographism of cultural cycles, according to which Egypt, India, and China would be worlds *per se* with phases of infancy, youth, adulthood, and old age (the major reference is evidently Spengler). In this way the aporia constituted by extra-European historical material can be evaded, but the result is that history ends up being conceived as made up of islands, as a sort of 'circus'. However, Bloch adds:

> If the lack of, or disrupted, communications between nations, and above all the different stages of development, should happen to effect a sep-aration, there is no resulting disturbance to the uniform movement: a symphony (to introduce a methodically apt formal analogy) does not fea-ture a *continuo* of all voices. [...] Undoubtedly so polyphonically cohesive a picture is much more difficult in the case of universal history than in that of periodisation [*Zweifellos ist eine derart vielstimmig zusammenge-haltene Topisierung in unversalhistorischer Darstellung viel schwieriger als die Periodisierung*]; in universal historical terms, at least, it requires a *mul-tiversum* – and chronologically too.[32]

Beyond both the schema of the continuous line and the schema of epochs understood as islands (inside of which, however, the line persists under the form of phases of the life of a civilisation), history can therefore be thought through the concept of a plural temporality, represented by the metaphor of the *multiversum*, an expression Bloch takes from William James, who utilises it to think the multiplicity of spheres of experience of the psyche.

Bloch's idea is completely different from what James puts forward. The *multiversum* is not relative to experience, but rather ontological. In order to explain it, Bloch offers a reflection on time: 'Time *is* only because something happens [*Zeit is nur dadurch dass ertwass geschieht*]'.[33] Certainly, this appears clear with regard to lived time, but Bloch immediately adds that 'Mere lived time [*der bloss erlebten Zeit*] does not say anything about our problem', clearly distancing the formulation of the question of plural temporality from the terms of the philosophy of experience. On the other hand, chronological time is a

---

32   Bloch 1970, p. 123.
33   Bloch 1970, p. 124.

progression symmetrically partitioned into equal spaces and, as much as can be, traced back to numeric series regardless of their content. It is therefore a mere abstraction from the lived, and the concepts of empty or full do not suit it, because in it everything is equally full and empty:

> If it is true that the wheel of history, in the long run at least, cannot be turned back, then this wheel means the addition wholly of *tendential time* (even though it is a figure drawn from the clock wheel; and even though this retains the positive forward motion of the clock-wise clock's hand), and is therefore a very qualitative time, and not an intrinsically neutral clock-time.[34]

The mere flow of chronological time is therefore deprived of content and value. However, this does not institute a mere opposition between the time of physics and the time of history (in a Hegelian manner), because if it is true that time is uniform with respect to inanimate material (Galileo and Newton) – that is, that one of the countersigns of historical time, irreversibility, is completely lacking in the time of physics – it is also the case that new physics, characterised by relativity and quantum theory, modifies the Newtonian conception of time, understood 'as only a quantitative representation of a variable independent of events, which "of itself, and from its own nature, flows uniformly without regard to anything external," in order to permit numerically exact limit transitions'.[35]

> Einstein's critique refutes the Newtonian presupposition of a simultaneity of all – even the remotest – events [*an der Newtonschen Voraussetzung einer Gleichzeitigkeit aller noch so entfernten Ereignisse*]. As is well known, simultaneity [*Gleichseitigkeit*] exists (at least with differences so minute that they can be ignored) only for adjoining positions [...] very far distant places do not enjoy a simultaneous moment [*gleiche Augenblick*]; and not only on account of the non-measurability of this simultaneity (which in any case would be exclusively an operative-idealistic and not a factual-real confirmation). Every place, according to Einstein, has its own specific time – at least with regard to the moment.[36]

---

34   Bloch 1970, pp. 125–6.
35   Bloch 1970, p. 126.
36   Bloch 1970, p. 127 (translation modified).

In this sense Bloch believes that using Riemann's concepts of space as a parallel could help to produce 'a *non-rigid concept of* time [*unstarren Zeitbegriff*]'.[37]

> The field [...] adheres to the form [...] of changeable material events [*wechselvollen materiellen Geschehens*] [...] precisely, the space of physics can teach time something: namely, that in its historical succession, time likewise is conceivable *suo modo* as inconstant, and if not as curved, at least as 'rich in curves'. A 'multi-dimensionality' of the time-line [*eine Mehrdimensionales der Zeitlinie*], as demanded above all by the geographical richness of the historical material, is of course wholly foreign to physics itself.[38]

It is precisely the perspective of the *multiversum* and multi-dimensionality that allow Bloch to see the insufficiencies of partitioning human history into epochs such as antiquity, medieval times, and so forth. These partitions would seem to contain in their names various sets of occurrences, and yet the colouring that they give to the temporality of the epoch remains purely exterior, a mere faded tint. The time that runs through them becomes reified, persisting as an invariable substrate, despite the chronological subdivisions, 'at most something like human age is transferred to it by analogy – the Greek adolescence of the human race, and so on', while 'there is a vapid sort of pinpointing, a kind of inference of renewal in a phrase such as "the dawning of a new century" – to say nothing of mystical emphases once placed on numbers (the year 1000 and 1524)'.[39]

Instead, it is a matter of emphasising specificity.

> The 'special disciplines' of historic being and consciousness, which belong to history as a whole, have long made use of individual and *legitimate* time structures. Above all there is the very important economic concept of working time, in which the same hour is given a variant assessment according to the work performed qualitatively in it in each particular case, and is credited as a multiple. And there are also quite individual time structures in the superstructure: here one need only mention musical and verse rhythms – and in particular the structural divisions of music.

---

37   Bloch 1970, p. 128.
38   Bloch 1970, pp. 128–9 (translation modified).
39   Bloch 1970, p. 129.

There is a poised or calm time in the fugue, and a tense time in the
sonata – that is, one allowing room for tensions. There is a broad, onward
surging, exceedingly spacious time in the epic, in contrast to the drama,
which is quite materially (not artistically) compressed, or curtailed, or
skipped over, or overlapping. In the structure of the sonata as in that of
the drama, there is also an individual dominant-tonic-relationship of its
own specific time, which takes the no longer chronic but acute, because
specifically serviceable, procedural form of blow-upon-blow or stroke-
after-stroke of the approaching, then – as it were – vertically striking fall
or victory.[40]

Not only is a multiplicity given, a multi-dimensionality of times on an ontological level, but there is also a multiplicity of modes of imagining time. Bloch
underlines how not only entire civilisations exist in time, but also how these
contain, in their mythology and religion, a precise way of imagining time:

There are varied time structures [*Zeitstrukturen*] – not in the simple chro-
nology of historical succession [...] but in the above-mentioned time-
colour problem of individual historical periods, and above all, in a legitimate way, in the individual superstructures. It is these varied time structures
[...] which do not allow progress in economy, technology, and art to be
attributed simply to the same common denominator. Therefore it is also
evident that among the multifarious material which varies the form and
content of the concept of historical time and makes it accordant with
the particular material, there is ultimately to be found the still manifold
material of the goal, to which in terms of value the forward movement
of the various time series is in each case referred and directed. Precisely
these teleological relations and references, which are not yet wholly inter-
homogenous, bring about variations not only in the different types of progress – but in the time structures in which these different, so often non-
uniform types of progress (in economy, technology, art and so on) occur.
The totality of the particular social tendency – also as the total particular time-tendency – certainly overtakes the temporally layered spheres
of movement of this tendency; yet the different layer-flows (that is, the
movements of different levels) persist in the outreaching whole. And they
require most especially to be approached with considerations of time-
content that are no longer merely homogenous – they demand a kind of

---

40   Bloch 1970, pp. 129–30.

'Riemannian' time. That is: a time with a variably conceivable metrics – varying only according to the particular division, and above all according to the (still variously distant) teleological contents of the historical matter.[41]

It is in this context that Bloch considers the Leibnizian theory of time, according to which time would be, like space, an active form of forces and their movement, a mode of movement.

This is a dynamic conception of time; hence it does not see, in their consequence, the time series of human history too as unalterable and wholly similar in construction. Moreover it sees a difference between the *millions of years of pre-history* (to say nothing of the geological or cosmological milliards) and the *few millennia of cultural history* since Neolithic times. Here not only a chronometric difference but one of density in the being of time itself, above all a qualitative-structural distinction, holds sway: in short, an objective changeability in the before-and-after sequence as well. This occurs in *the overtaken unity of the developmental-historical relationship*; it is not a chronologically linear but a chronologically differentiated and federative and only thus fruitfully centered [*fruchtbar zentrierten*] relationship.[42]

Certainly against Leibniz it is possible to take a position that Bloch defines as 'formalism and categorial statics',[43] of which the perfect model would be Hartmann and his affirmation that time indifferently runs through everything: 'time is always time, and remains so whatever happens within it'.[44] In reality, there are not forms of time in itself:

There is no arguably different metrics *apart from* the social life of its 'time' – as if a time structure lived and changed as such. No more than there is a pure clock-time in history or (which comes to the same thing) time as an abstract-neutral container.[45]

---

41   Bloch 1970, pp. 130–1.
42   Bloch 1970, p. 131.
43   Bloch 1970, p. 132.
44   Ibid.
45   Bloch 1970, pp. 131–2.

Certainly, if time is only where something happens, we should ask if the rhythm of this happening influences time: for instance, does the wave crash unchangingly on the rock for hundreds of thousands of years always as enduringly and as densely as the one brief year of 1917 in Russia? It is a question that Bloch specifies in order to be understood in an objective sense and not in reference to lived time, that is, in a Bergsonian direction.

> All epochs – not only those which are humanly historical – have to be comprehended in relation to the differentiations in the density of historical and material occurrence, of its tendencies and contents. There is also an intensive and qualitative difference between *historical time itself* and natural time (particularly that in which the 'history of Nature' occurs; a time other than that characterised by the t-components of physics). It is now apparent [...] that despite its formally so very much longer durations, natural time is *less dense* than *historical-cultural time*. Though hugely inflated in comparison with the latter, natural time contains less intensive-qualitative time – just as pre-human Nature also contains less developed being. And its millions and thousands of millions of years, which are laid out in an apparently homogenous succession before the few thousand years of human history (or appear exclusively so to extend) are accordingly – to use a slightly strained though appropriate metaphor – a kind of period of inflation compared with the gold period of history and culture, an inflation-age against a gold-age.[46]

However, one should not fall into the error, in a certain sense conveyed paradigmatically by Hegel, of considering the time of nature as the past of historical time, as a sort of 'absolute preterite':

> [I]n a truly universal-historical topology of times, consideration must be given to the problem of an *individual* natural succession of time that *does not wholly pass over into the given succession of history*. The single-file succession of before-and-after is least of all tenable as a not merely finished *before* of Nature, and a not merely all-expressive *after* of cultural history. Similarly, to conceive of the immense (and tense) structure of Nature as a setting against which the corresponding drama of human history has yet to be enacted, is more appropriate than to see human-historical being and consciousness already as the opened eye of all natural being; of a nat-

---

46   Bloch 1970, pp. 133–4.

ural being which not only lies before our history (and bears it), but which for the most part continues to environ it as a history that is still hardly reconciled, in form or content, with historical time.[47]

In conclusion, according to Bloch a new Marxist anthropology is unthinkable without a new Marxist cosmology, which denies the arrow of time that runs from nature to history. It is precisely the construction of this cosmology that would also give us the instruments to negate the unilinear progress that unfolds throughout history.

The firmer the refusal of a purely Western emphasis, and of one laid solely upon development to date (to say nothing of discredited imperialism), all the stronger is the help afforded by a utopian, open and in itself still experimental orientation. Only thus can hundreds of cultures flow into the unity of the human race; a unity that only then takes shape, in non-linear historical time, and with an historical direction that is not fixed and monadic. For the very sake of the human race, Africa and Asia join in the polyphonic chorus of a polyrhythmic advance of progress towards this unity – admittedly beneath a sun which first arose, actively and in theory, in Europe, yet one which would shine upon a community that is really without slavery. In all its revolutions, the Western concept of progress has never implied a European (and of course not an Asiatic or African) vanguard, but a better Earth for all men.[48]

In *Heritage of Our Times* the explanatory model of plural temporality was utilised in order to explain the formation of Nazism in German history and society. In 'Differentiations in the Concept of Progress', the model of plural temporality is applied to *Weltgeschichte* with the precise scope of subverting the linear conception of history, typical of Hegelianism and a certain scholastic Marxism, punctuated by phases in a time temporally and geographically guided by a Eurocentric *telos*. In this text, Bloch seems to abandon the idea of a fundamental time that measures others, in favour of a temporal *multiversum* that would find a recomposition in the eschatological horizon of communism.

---

47   Bloch 1970 pp. 136–7.
48   Bloch 1970, pp. 140–1.

Althusser and Structural Non-Contemporaneity

Finally, we come to Althusser, who proposed his theory of historical time in the middle of the 1960s. In order to understand the specific Althusserian use of the concept of 'non-contemporaneity', it is crucial to return to the introduction of the concept of 'overdetermination' in *For Marx*. Althusser utilises this concept in order to draw a line of demarcation between Hegelian and Marxist contradiction: while Hegelian contradiction is the development of a simple unity in which its *telos* is inscribed *ab origine*, Marxist contradiction is always 'overdetermined' as it develops inside of a complex social whole. Drawing upon Mao's essay on contradiction,[49] Althusser affirms that in a historical process it is necessary to distinguish between the principal contradiction and secondary contradictions, as well as between the principal and secondary aspect of the contradiction, in order to grasp its unequal development. But Althusser proposes to take an additional step:

> If every contradiction is a contradiction in a complex whole structured in dominance, this complex whole cannot be envisaged without its contradictions, without their basically uneven relations. In other words, each contradiction, each essential articulation of the structure, and the gen-

---

49   Mao writes: 'But whatever happens, there is no doubt at all that at every stage in the development of a process there is only one principal contradiction which plays the leading role. Hence, if in any process there are a number of contradictions, one of them must be the principal contradiction playing the leading and decisive role, while the rest occupy a secondary and subordinate position. Therefore in studying any complex process in which there are two or more contradictions, we must devote every effort to finding its principal contradiction. Once this principal contradiction is grasped, all problems can be readily solved. [...] As we have said, we must not treat all the contradictions in a process as being equal but must distinguish between the principal and the secondary contradictions, and pay special attention to grasping the principal one. But, in any given contradiction, whether principal or secondary, should the two contradictory aspects be treated as equal? Again, no. In any contradiction the development of the contradictory aspects is uneven. Sometimes they seem to be in equilibrium, which is however only temporary and relative, while unevenness is basic. Of the two contradictory aspects, one must be principal and the other secondary. The principal aspect is the one playing the leading role in the contradiction. The nature of a thing is determined mainly by the principal aspect of a contradiction, the aspect which has gained the dominant position. But this situation is not static; the principal and the non-principal aspects of a contradiction transform themselves into each other, and the nature of things changes accordingly' (Tse-Tung 2007, pp. 88–9).

eral relation of the articulations in the structure in dominance, constitute so many conditions of the existence of the complex whole itself. This proposition is of the first importance. For it means that the structure of the whole and therefore the 'difference' of the essential contradictions and their structure in dominance, is the very existence of the whole; that the 'difference' of the contradictions (that there is a principle contradiction, etc.; and that every contradiction has a principle aspect) is identical to the conditions of the existence of the complex whole. In plain terms this position implies that the 'secondary' contradictions are not the pure phenomena of the 'principal' contradiction, that the principal is not the essence and the secondaries so many of its phenomena [...] [this] implies that the secondary contradictions are essential even to the existence of the principal contradiction, that they really constitute its condition of existence, just as the principal contradiction constitutes their condition of existence.[50]

According to Althusser, the conditions of existence spoken of in classical Marxism are not therefore the context of the contradiction's development, but the very mode in which the social whole exists, which in turn is not different from its contradictions:

If the conditions are no more than the current existence of the complex whole, they are its very contradictions, each reflecting in itself the organic relation it has with the others in the structure in dominance of the complex whole.[51]

Contradiction is therefore always, Althusser concludes, 'complexly-structurally-unevenly-determined – if you will forgive me the astonishing expression. I must admit, I preferred a shorter term: overdetermined'.[52] Such a theoretical horizon does not offer a simple contemporaneity to the game of opposites, not even in the eschatological perspective of a *praesentia* that finally resolves the complexity of temporal levels by unraveling the tangle in a full time.

The question is explicitly addressed from the perspective of a theory of temporality in one section of *Reading Capital*, the 'Outline of a Concept of Historical Time'. As in Bloch, Hegel is once again used as a 'pertinent counter-

---

50   Althusser 2005, pp. 204–5.
51   Althusser 2005, p. 207.
52   Althusser 2005, p. 209.

example'; here, it is a Hegel whose philosophy of history possesses a conception of time marked by two essential traits: 1) a homogenous continuity of time; 2) contemporaneity or the category of the historical present. These two coordinates are none other than the two coordinates of the Idea, succession and simultaneity, in its sensory form. Of the two, by far the most important according to Althusser is the second, that in which 'we find Hegel's central thought'.[53] Indeed, the category of contemporaneity precisely expresses the structure of the historical existence of the social totality:

> [T]he structure of historical existence is such that all the elements of the whole always co-exist in one and the same time, one and the same present, and are therefore contemporaneous with one another in one and the same present. This means that the structure of the historical existence of the Hegelian social totality allows what I propose to call an *'essential section'* [*coup d'essence*], i.e., an intellection operation in which a vertical break [*coupure verticale*] is made at any moment in historical time, a break in the present such that all the elements of the whole revealed by this section are in an immediate relationship with one another, a relationship that immediately expresses their internal essence.[54]

Althusser holds that it is the specific nature of this totality to allow the essential section, its spiritual nature, which makes each part a *pars totalis* in the Leibnizian sense. The continuity of time is based precisely on the continuous succession of these contemporaneous horizons, whose unity is guaranteed by the omnipervasiveness of the concept. From here, the double sense of the *moment* of the development of Hegel's Idea is as follows:

1) the moment as the moment of development that must receive a periodisation;
2) the moment as a moment of time, as the present.

This is the backdrop to Hegel's famous proposition in the *Philosophy of Right*:

> To comprehend what is, this is the task of philosophy, because what is, is reason. Whatever happens, every individual is a *child of his time*; so philosophy too is *its own time apprehended in thoughts* [*so ist auch die*

---

53   Althusser 2009, p. 94.
54   Ibid.

Philosophie, ihre Zeit in Gedanken erfasst]. It is just as absurd to fancy that a philosophy can transcend its contemporary world as it is to fancy that an individual can leap over his own age, jump over Rhodes.[55]

For Hegel, the present is the absolute horizon of all knowledge, because all knowledge is nothing but the existence, in knowledge, of the internal principle of the whole. In this horizon, a knowledge of the future is impossible and therefore so is a political science understood as 'any knowing that deals with the future effects of present phenomena'.[56] World-historical individuals do not indeed 'know' the future, but they 'divine it as a presentiment'.[57]

In this Hegelian theory of historical time that 'is borrowed from the most vulgar empiricism, the empiricism of the false obviousness of everyday life which we find in a naïve form in most of the *historians* themselves, at any rate all the historians known to Hegel himself',[58] Althusser sees the model of a conception of history in which the distinction homogeneity/contemporaneity is translated into the distinction diachronic/synchronic: 'This distinction is based on a conception of historical time as continuous and contemporaneous with itself'.[59] The synchronic is contemporaneity understood in the Hegelian sense, while the diachronic is nothing other than the becoming of this presence in the 'successive contingent presents in the time continuum'.[60] And, contrary to what one might think, this naïve representation of historical time continues to appear even in the historiography of the Annales school. Certainly, the Annales historians assert that there are different times (short, medium, and long durations) and observe their interferences as results of their encounter, but the question of the structure of the whole which causes these variations is never posed in conceptual terms. They believe that these variants can be measured by referring them to a continuous and homogenous time.[61]

According to Althusser, it is a matter of thinking through the difference with respect to Hegel of the temporality of the complex, already-given whole as it appears in Marx's thought. What is the temporality of the social whole? It is not *contemporaneity*, the Hegelian historical present, because this has

---

55   Hegel 2008, p. 15 (translation modified).

56   Althusser 2009, p. 95.

57   Ibid.

58   Althusser 2009, p. 96.

59   Ibid.

60   Ibid.

61   On the relationship between the Althusserian theory of historical time and that of the Annales school, see Schöttler 1993.

an expressive centre that irradiates uniformly outward to every point in the circumference. It is not the *synchronic*, which according to Saussure's definition occupies 'a certain span of time during which the sum of the modifications that have supervened is minimal';[62] the ontologisation of Saussurian linguistics in structuralism renders possible the tracing out in the synchronic of a sort of 'general grammar' of an epoch whose paradigm will be the Foucauldian notion of *episteme* in *The Order of Things*. It is not a *multiplicity of times* from Annales historiography, because this multiplicity maintains an essential relationship with the homogenous flow of one time that is the measure of the others. What we want to understand is which form of temporality pertains to the present moment, to the concrete situation as it presents itself to knowledge. And to do this, it is necessary to 'construct the Marxist concept of historical time on the basis of the Marxist conception of the social totality'.[63] The Marxist social totality

> is a whole whose unity, far from being the expressive or 'spiritual' unity of Leibniz's or Hegel's whole, is constituted by a certain type of *complexity*, the unity of a *structured whole* containing what can be called levels or instances which are distinct and 'relatively autonomous', and co-exist according to specific determinations, fixed in the last instance by the level or instance of the economy.[64]

Althusser brings out the Marxist conception of social totality in his comment on a passage in the *1857 Introduction* in which Marx states that 'In all forms of society there is one specific kind of production which predominates over the rest, whose relations thus assign rank and influence [*Rang und Einfluß*] to the others'.[65] The whole, for Marx, is an 'organic hierachised whole', a totality which decides precisely on the hierarchy, the grade, and the index of efficacy between the different levels of society.

What is the temporality of this hierarchised social whole? Not Hegelian contemporaneity:

> The co-existence of the different structured levels, the economic, the political, the ideological, etc., and therefore of the economic infrastructure, of the legal and political superstructure, of ideologies and theoret-

---

62   Saussure 1966, p. 101.
63   Althusser 2009, p. 97.
64   Ibid.
65   Marx 1973, p. 106.

ical formations (philosophy, sciences) can no longer be thought in the co-existence of the Hegelian *present*, of the ideological present in which temporal presence coincides with the presence of the essence with its phenomena.[66]

A continuous and homogenous time 'can no longer be regarded as the time of history'. Not only this, it is not even possible to think 'the process of the development of the different levels of the whole *in the same historical time*': each level has 'a peculiar time, relatively autonomous and hence relatively independent, even in its dependence, of the 'times' of the other levels'.[67]

Every social formation has a corresponding time and history: of the development of the forces of production, of the relations of production, of the political superstructure, of philosophy, and of artistic production. 'Each of these peculiar histories is punctuated with peculiar rhythms' and can be known only if the concept of the specificity of its temporality is defined, along with its continuous development, its revolutions, and its ruptures. Rather than independent sectors, what we have are relatively autonomous ones founded precisely on a certain type of articulation of the whole, on a certain type of dependence: 'The specificity of these times and histories is therefore *differential*, since it is based on the differential relations between the different levels within the whole'.[68] And Althusser adds:

It is not enough, therefore, to say, as modern historians do, that *there are* [*il y a*] different periodisations for different times, that each time has its own rhythms, some short, some long; we must also think these differences in rhythm and punctuation in their foundation, in the type of articulation, displacement and torsion which harmonises these different times with one another. To go even further, I should say that we cannot restrict ourselves to reflecting the existence of *visible* and measurable times in this way; we must, of absolute necessity, pose the question of the mode of existence of *invisible* times, of the invisible rhythms and punctuations concealed beneath the surface of each visible time.[69]

According to Althusser, Marx was particularly sensitive to this necessity. In *Capital* he shows that the time of economic production cannot be read in the

---

66   Althusser 2009, p. 99.
67   Ibid.
68   Althusser 2009, p. 100.
69   Althusser 2009, pp. 100–1.

continuous time of life or clocks; what we are dealing with is *a complex and non-linear time*, a time of times that must be constructed starting with the structures of production, from the various rhythms that punctuate production, distribution, and circulation. This time is essentially invisible and unreadable, opaque, a 'complex "intersection" of the different times, rhythms, turnovers, etc.',[70] a time that can be shown only by means of its concept, which much therefore be constructed, in the same way that for Freud, the time of the unconscious must be constructed in order to understand some aspects of biography. Althusser also emphasises that in the construction of this concept, the categories of *continuous and discontinuous*, 'which summarise the banal mystery of all history', are completely useless; it is a matter of constructing 'infinitely more complex categories specific to each type of history, categories in which new logics come into play'.[71]

The *present moment* is thus a differential interweaving of times. What happens if we subject this moment to an 'essential section'?

> The co-existence which can be observed in the 'essential section' does not reveal any omnipresent essence which is also the present of each of these 'levels'. The break 'valid' for a determinate level, political or economic, the break that would correspond to an 'essential section' in politics, for example, does not correspond to anything of the kind in the other levels, the economic, the ideological, the aesthetic, the philosophical or the scientific – which live in different times and know other breaks, other rhythms, and other punctuations. The present of one level is, so to speak, the absence of another, and this co-existence of a 'presence' and absences is simply the effect of the structure of the whole in its articulated decentricity.[72]

A social formation is thus *an interweaving of different times* of which it is necessary to think the displacement and torsion produced by the articulation of the different levels of the structure. What is the risk implicit in this theory of temporality? It is to think of the 'essential section' not in a linear way but in steps, thinking of the absence of one level with respect to another as forwardness or backwardness. 'If we were to accept this', Althusser writes, 'we should relapse, as even the best of our historians usually do, into the trap of

70   Althusser 2009, p. 101.
71   Althusser 2009, p. 103.
72   Althusser 2009, p. 104.

the ideology of history in which forwardness and backwardness are merely variants of the reference continuity and not the effects of the structure of the whole'.[73] To do this, we must free ourselves from the obviousness of empirical history and create the concept of history. If the different temporalities refer to the same time, we have fallen back into the ideology of a homogenous time: 'If we cannot make an "essential section" in history, it is only in the specific unity of the complex structure of the whole that we can think the concept of these so-called backwardnesses, forwardnesses, survivals and unevennesses of development which co-*exist* in the structure of the real historical present: the present of the conjuncture'.[74]

To speak using the metaphors of forwardness and backwardness, we must conceive the place and function of that different temporality in the whole, in other words, its overdetermination. A theory of the conjuncture is therefore indispensable to a theory of history. This allows us to reach two conclusions:

1) the pair diachrony/synchrony disappears;
2) history in general cannot be spoken about, only about forms of 'specific structures of historicity'.

In Althusser we therefore find the model of plural temporality used to think the specific temporality of a social formation. He categorically denies that there can be a fundamental time that measures all the others, a time that flows homogenously and linearly, concerning which the others would be earlier or later. Certainly, the structure in dominance of the social totality posits a decisive influence, in the last instance, of the time of production on the other times. However, this influence cannot be thought as the fundamental clock of being. This is the case because, on the one hand, as Althusser explicitly states, 'the lonely hour of the last instance never comes';[75] and, on the other, because the very time of production is not a simple and linear time, but a complex time, a time of times that should be built conceptually, an invisible time, not attributable to the visible time of clocks.

---

73   Althusser 2009, p. 105.
74   Althusser 2009, p. 106.
75   Althusser 2005, p. 113.

Conclusions

If we had to briefly summarise the direction of this research, which is naturally not exhaustive, but rather limited to attempting to delineate a problematic within the Marxist tradition, we could underline how we have seen the authors apply the model of plural temporality to various theoretical objects:

1) Marx uses the model of plural temporality to explain the different developments of singular nations within European history. On the one hand, Marx focuses on the non-contemporaneity of German conditions with respect to France and England. On the other hand, Marx examines the non-contemporaneity of German philosophy with respect to German society and its contemporaneity with the historical developments of France and England, and therefore its criticism with the future of these nations (which Marx identifies *tout court* with the future of humanity).

2) In the Bloch of *Heritage of Our Times*, the model of plural temporality is used to explain German history in the aftermath of World War One, and in particular the formation of Nazism. Bloch utilises non-contemporaneity on both the real and imaginary levels (or objective and subjective levels, in Bloch's traditional terminology) of determinate social classes, in order to complicate the Marxian model of the simple contradiction between capital and labour.

3) For the Bloch of 'Differentiations in the Concept of Progress', plural temporality becomes an impressive model not only for thinking a *Weltgeschichte* which refuses unilinearity and articulation into historical-geographical epochs, but also for thinking the historical *multiversum* within a cosmology marked by a time that is structurally plural.

4) Finally, Althusser utilises the model of plural temporality in 'Outline of a Concept of Historical Time' in order to think the present of each social formation. The non-contemporaneity of the constitutive elements of every social formation, while organised in a hierarchical way, do not permit a fundamental time as the measure of their flowing.

Nations, social classes, social formations, human history, and natural history must therefore be thought under the sign of non-contemporaneity. It is a non-contemporaneity thought as what Nietzsche called with contempt the 'history of the masses' and its real and imaginary productions in the light of a *multiversum*, of a concept of plural temporality that renounces every unity of transcendent and external measure, instead constructing each time the object and the complex relations of the object in its specificity. What meaning does an operation of this kind have? It means, first, renouncing a full collective subject and taking distance from the idea that, from the *Communist Manifesto* to *History and Class Consciousness*, up through Negri's latest writings, has traversed and maybe dominated the Marxist tradition, according to which the collective subject would emerge from the social structure itself, in a substance becoming subject, a becoming whose fundamental grammar was fixed by Hegel in the *Science of Logic*. It means, second, renouncing pre-established models of development, simplifications, projections of one particular reality on to another, unearthing the pitfall of a unique time, of advance and delay, of residues and survivals, giving place to a veritable archaeology; archaeology understood not in Foucault's sense (in whose sociological core there survives a sort of originary contemporaneity of the *episteme*), but in the sense in which Gramsci speaks of the person as an archaeological site. This does not mean renouncing the universality of reason, but it does mean that reason is only given inside of what the young Marx called 'the specific logic of the specific object', or which Gramsci refers to with the metaphor of 'translation', going beyond an aristocratic sentiment of 'untimeliness' with respect to our times. Disentangling the coil of times, of our times, means attempting to inherit them in Bloch's sense, while knowing that beneath them, no unbreakable time of our victory flows. It means, finally, trying to think a political strategy at the level of these complex, plural temporal interweavings.

CHAPTER 6

Fraternitas militans. Time and Politics in Ernst Bloch

Mauro Farnesi Camellone

The time of the harvest is at hand! Thus God himself has appointed me for his harvest. I have made my sickle sharp, for my thoughts are zealous for the truth and my lips, skin, hands, hair, soul, body and my life all damn the unbelievers.[1]

The political impact of Ernst Bloch's thought can be measured by highlighting the role played in his oeuvre by the production of *images*: figurations of specific historical experiences – experiences of which the unfulfilled possibilities remain latent, yet to evolve, even though they may have been *frozen* at the moment of their manifestation.[2] The Blochian image takes on the form of a historiographical construction occupying the restricted area of mediation between thought and politics. The most extensive historiographical work by Bloch is his monograph on the figure of Thomas Müntzer: the image of the German Peasants War in 1525 is seen as an appropriate *form* of political initiative applicable to the precise historical moment in which Germany found itself following the defeat of the Spartacist uprising.[3] In this work, Bloch seeks to associate the importance of the peasants' revolt in Thuringia during the sixteenth century, as an historical event, with the insurrection that took place on the streets of Berlin in 1919.

Like Furio Jesi subsequently in his *Spartakus*, Bloch seems to make the words of Carl Justi his own. Commenting on Michelangelo's monumental sculptures in San Lorenzo, he argued: 'Man lives, or ought to live, first with the dead, then with the living, and finally with himself'.[4] His *Thomas Münzer*, in effect, is an attempt to offer a communist alternative to the historicist interpretation of

---

1   Müntzer 1988, p. 46.
2   See Farnesi Camellone 2009.
3   See Bloch 1985 [1921; 1969]. As established by Boehmer 1922 and 1923, *Müntzer* is written with a *tz*, whereas Bloch always spells the name with a *z* only.
4   See Jesi 2000.

defeat, be it that of 1525, or that of 1919: it has the weight of an impassioned phenomenology of the revolt, seen as an immediate suspension of historical time, and therefore distinct from any idea of revolution that involves the formulation of a strategy, rigidly articulated in the processes of history. It is in the possibility of such a suspension that Rosa Luxemburg and Müntzer come together, and in this state of suspension that one sees the possibility of a meeting between the present and a past that is still vibrant, still unfinished; and it is precisely this that we have to explore.

But there is more. With his book on Müntzer, Bloch lays the foundations for a view of politics centred on the category of community as expectation, a category that has the power to overcome the stylemes of a clear dichotomy between revolt and revolution. Given the problem of examining both the philosophical reliability and the political import of this category, the first question to address concerns the capacity of Bloch's thought, considered in its entirety, to place the community as expectation outside the strict logic of the 'future perfect', the logic that delineates the production of power; in other words, outside the process by means of which modern order is given form.

The Future in the Past

Bloch distinguishes between a future that we see unfold with regularity and repetition, and 'the new that comes from transformation – that which has not yet appeared, while certainly having the potential to appear – or rather, that which is contained in the "now" as germinal disposition'. In the ordinary sense, the future reveals itself to us schematically, whereas the future identifiable as possibility unfolds fluidly, 'and is therefore liable to changes'. This is the future contained in 'events that are just developing, and which in terms neither of their advent nor of their content are completely conditioned or determined and therefore completely predictable'. In the future, accordingly, 'there is always the element of surprise, that is to say, in relation to the future of humankind, the element of risk or of salvation'.[5]

For Bloch, the future as a schema of repetition is 'curved' beneath the past as a mere chronological indicator of posterity. On the threshold of the future relating to uncertainty, on the other hand, there is the moment, the test, of experiment. Undoubtedly, the past can be understood as a future that has already delivered its outcome, and therefore as a future in which there is no longer any

---

5   Bloch 1985 [1975], p. 90.

tension. Even so, Bloch is interested in finding out whether in that which has been, that which seemingly could be pondered in the memory, may not also be concealed 'impulses to evolve, still inhabiting what has already evolved'. If the past is viewed only with a contemplative gaze, the risk is that of losing 'all that could have been the future in the past (*Zukunft in der Vergangenheit*)'.[6] If this type of loss occurs, the past becomes immobilised, and everything in it that has not been fully realised will be suppressed.

Bloch is in search of that past which carries 'a changeable engaging legacy'. This is not a cultural legacy having a purely ideological function, but rather, a still vibrant *in fieri*. Bloch profiles a type of historical knowledge focused on that which is recurrent in history but which, at the same time, is precursory by virtue of being a possibility, 'that which still contains in it the paradoxical condition of being, in effect, future in the past. Indeed it is precisely this utopian significativity, this seminality, this unmistakable capacity of the intentions – especially the creations – of the non-past past, to continue germinating, that constitutes the utopian surplus [...], the leaven of actuality stored in history'.[7] This type of historical knowledge is not the remembrance of a time long departed, where the dead bury their dead. On the contrary, it belongs to the threshold of the new, remaining deep in the utopian memory, which looks in all directions, *including* backwards. In short, knowledge with the faces of Janus, looking back at the unfinished business of the past, and forward to the expectancy of the future.

The utopian-concrete link proposed by Bloch is far from being the mere consequence of a succession of events that leads in purely chronological fashion to a dominant present. It is time itself, in effect, that cannot be seen as a rectilinear advance of the chronometric progression. If it is true that time exists independently of humankind, it is however not, even in its past mode, independent of the 'unconcluded', 'self-transforming' content that unfolds in humans and constitutes their concrete field.[8]

> The passage of time occurs dissimilarly on different planes that absolutely cannot be defined simply as a uniform 'before' and 'after' of a formally homogeneous sequence, which from various types of past leads to the

---

6   Bloch 1985 [1975], p. 91.

7   Bloch 1985 [1975], p. 92.

8   'The concept of chronometric time, metronomically uniform, derives from thought tied to the exchange value, which levels out all differences – even qualitative differences – in a sequence of prices characteristic only in quantitative terms' (Bloch 1985 [1975], p. 93).

future. Consequently, the different *quanta* of time are not homogeneous per se, and are also distinctly diverse qualitatively one from another, indeed so distinctly diverse that past ages of 'natural history' and 'human history', due to their radically diverse content, can definitely not be drawn on the same line.[9]

Certainly, the posthumous effects of the historical past are accompanied by ruins, wrecks and funerary remains. Even here, however, there may be elements definable as a future that could be 'reawakened' in the 'now'. Bloch turns explicitly to Walter Benjamin, exploring the idea of a singularly intensive now-time which, in the life of an individual or of a group, induces a pulsation of the past 'now' not as a memory, but as something 'vigorously re-accessed'. The explosion of the now-time produces, 'rather than the *continuum* of history, a past rich in actuality, gushing forth again, almost on the rebound'. The action of the 'now' on the ruins of the past brings with it an impact that interrupts time as a mere passage; but this means that 'both behind and before every thing that is produced' reappears the *producer*, and therefore the inconsistency of a 'contemplation interested only in its apparent disinterest'. The now-time *may* carry the impact 'of non-transcendental *praesentiae*; the plural here significant, replacing the *unum necessarium*, due to the persisting distance of that one thing missing'.[10]

In Bloch – and here one discerns a significant difference from Benjamin – the now-time as *nunc stans* is explained alone as a pre-apparition that throws its light on the darkness of the lived moment, indicating the way out from the darkness of the surplus of proximity, but never realising it in the fully practical sense.[11] The *Vor-schein* accommodates the resonance of the now-time, the now-present; in this, and only in this, Bloch sees the possibility of exploding the historical *continuum* by reactivating future-capable moments of the past. This future-related possibility of the past is the fluid and never fulfilled pre-apparition of an *ultimum*, a captured moment that in the present – without determining a necessary automatism – indicates the direction of *change*:

---

9   Bloch 1985 [1975], p. 94. See also: 'the sun of Homer enlightens us too, and can do so even without Homer, remaining literally extraterritorial relative to him, with a utopian surplus of cosmic possibility'.

10   Bloch 1985 [1975], pp. 96–7. See Benjamin 1991 [1940].

11   'The archetype of the highest good is the content of invariance of the happiest wonder; its possession, in the moment and indeed as it is this moment, *should be* that which changes into the full resolution of the fact-that' (Bloch 1985 [1959], p. 355).

This happens when the event of a former time, which is made to spring out – being not merely past, but also explosive – indicates an especially valuable asset, as if posterior time had not needed to progress that much further.[12]

Bloch therefore seeks to move beyond the perspective of a too hurried actuality, that of an inconsistent outlook on the surrounding world, the indicator of a purely contemplative attitude that remains far removed, extraneous almost, from the unfolding of the real. This is characteristic of that historical knowledge which is presumed without preconceptions, and which finds in the remote past a particular facility to sell itself as *objectivity*, as if it were 'a study of granite'.

> Ranke thought he could say, with ironic modesty, that he did not bur-
> den himself with the high office of judging the world, but wanted only
> to establish what it had been. Indeed, the aversion to judging, having
> become completely positivist (leaving aside the idealistic removal of his
> gaze from everything that for the dominators of today was already uncom-
> fortable and undesirable in the events of a former time), this aversion
> does not have the slightest interest either in preserving the memory of a
> judgement able to indicate change as something not yet liquidated, that
> is to say, something stimulated by the events of another time in their
> original locations, or in general of preserving the *memory of the future
> encapsulated in the past*. In this type of history it is mere semblances, fos-
> silized products, ideologies, that are taken without analysis for the thing
> they purport to be.[13]

It seems that Bloch's notion of the future in the past is not traceable in any way to a logic of the future perfect, that is, to a projective character of temporal-isation impressed on the productive experience of order. There is no reference in Bloch to a moment when order is founded, or any reference to the origin that is evocative of a beginning that can be referenced to produce the definit-ive order.[14] With Bloch, rather, there is the assumption, as much analytical as problematical, of the structurally impermanent nature of order, deriving from the entirely experimental and transformational character of the relationship

---

12   Bloch 1985 [1975], p. 98.

13   Bloch 1985 [1975], p. 23. For the critique of the philosophical language that subtends this
      historical science, with reference to Heidegger in particular, see Bloch 1985 [1975], pp. 33–
      8.

14   See Rametta 2006.

between man and the world, which is the way it is because both parties are always involved. Bloch's future in the past, in short, is concerned with discovering the openness of the real in the mode of temporality, considered in each and all of its ecstasies, and at the same time an assumption of risk in indicating a possible direction for change.

Eschatology and History

The notion of community is the beating heart of Bloch's *Thomas Münzer*. Around this theme, Bloch discusses the question of 'unlocking' past possibilities in their connection with the future, attempting to force the process of giving form to the politics produced by modern conceptuality. It is here that the profile of Bloch's communism takes shape. It is a communism centred on the figure of an organised subjectivity able to direct, mobilise and radicate the liberating force of an 'I' and of a 'we' in the form of a community.

In the philosophy of Ernst Bloch, the category of utopia is intended to merge eschatology, history and politics. If the principle of hope appears to be structurally intrahistorical, then hope itself, to avoid being empty passiveness, must be seen as satisfiable in potency in the eschatological goal. In Bloch's thought, there can be no separating the theme of the *novum* from the category of *ultimum*, or in effect, politics cannot be relativised through theological argument, even if important interpretations of this approach do exist.[15] The historical *novum* represents the messianic anticipation of the end time, disclosing an eternity that remains in the future, and therefore definable as 'not-yet'. This not-yet

> must not be thought of as though there already existed, say in the atom or in the subatomic 'differentials' of matter, everything that would later emerge, already present and *encapsulated* in minuscule form as inherent 'disposition'. This retrograde conception of the not-yet would suppress or fail to understand what is actually the dialectic leap of the new. Just as obvious is that in the tendency-latency of the material process, dialectical and open to the *novum*, one can find no purpose that is *preordained*, hence ready-made, in the manner of ancient theology, doubtless channelled mythologically from the top down. But to be sure, with this old theology, reminiscent also of 'Providence', the selfsame authentic theo-

---

15   See Schiller 1982.

logical problem is not discredited, as neither is the true category of the end, hence the purpose, or the sense [...]. Much less so, given that it is indeed tendency that constantly implies a reference to the end; and given that without this reference to the end, no element of progress could either be measured or be objectively and effectively present. [...] And the *truth* of theology never consists in ready-made purposes, but purposes that are formed only in the active process, always newly generated and self-enriching.[16]

Fulfilment is therefore shown always and only as expectation, since the unfulfilment of hope cannot by its very nature be accounted for dialectically: the *ultimum* can be thought of only as an interruption, as 'a total leap [...] from everything that has gone before'.[17] The utopian not-yet is thus determined by the removal of the eschatological *goal*, a deficiency that is discernible in the immanence of the historical process, and which also labels every human accomplishment as temporary. Representationally, Bloch seeks to think of 'transcending without transcendence', so that history (the not-yet) and eschatology (the *ultimum*) are held together at the highest level, with the tension of a polarity. Accordingly, Bloch does not contemplate an immanent fulfilment of immanence: the *ultimum* is the immanent limit to the very principle of hope – for the *eschaton* to be totally other is not conceivable in any place, and in any other time, other than the not-yet.[18] The *ultimum*, therefore, 'does not indicate an absolutely transcendent hereafter, but is "incarnate" in the non-yet as immanent transcendence: it manifests itself only in the form of its transcending and only in this way renders perceptible even the insufficiency and shortcoming that characterize the not-yet, despite its promise and hope of fullness'.[19] In effect, this is an attempt to think radically of a 'deviation' at the heart of the experience of the real.

We must now try to understand the significance of all this with regard to politics. Inasmuch as it is unavailable to human agency, the 'fullness of realisation' is an immanent limit to politics and therefore occupies the same place: it is the origin [*Ursprung*] of politics, in the technical and philosophical sense. For Bloch, it is about keeping faith with an *absence*, the absence of the perfection of order in human things, of its realisable fullness.[20] Only starting

---

16   Bloch 1985 [1959], p. 1626.
17   Bloch 1985 [1959], p. 233.
18   See Bloch 1985 [1959], pp. 1405–10.
19   Ganis 1996, p. 15.
20   See Bloch 1985 [1961], p. 132.

from this absence, and in the immanent operation of this absence, is it possible to think about building the *community* as a specific quality of inter-human relations.

In this passage, certainly, the myth of the foundation [*Urzustand*] has a resonance, but there is no regressive impulse at work there. In effect, this is not a case of imagining the return to an initial state, which would reduce the figure of the origin to a representation of the Edenic condition, hence to a mythology. The origin has nothing to do with a temporal provenance [*Herkunft*], with a chronological *primum* that, precisely because it has already evolved, would deny the dimension of the *novum* that utopia wishes to place at the centre of its philosophical and practical intent. If one wishes to discuss a 'naturalness of order' in Bloch, this is possible only when considering the idea as a utopian goal. That is to say, utopia remains devoid of any nostalgic trait, conscious of being unable to sit back on the preconception of a naturalness in the order of human things that has been 'known since time immemorial'. In this sense Bloch's utopia adopts the jusnaturalistic break with the ancient concept of cosmos, and radicalises it. It occupies the same plane as the modern *Zeitwende* and, precisely because of this, prevails over every position that may be externalised in relation to it and consequently incapable of overcoming it. For Bloch, it is not a question of refusing modernity, but of accomplishing it by radicalising its very premiss: the dissolving of all preconceptions, the nihilistic desertification of every root and every tradition. Thus, the *Heimat* (homeland, seen both as place of origin and as destination) cannot be sought by going back, but must be hoped for – the one inescapable supposition being its absence – having been radically removed from the equation as a condition [*Zustand*]. The *Heimat* therefore appears not as a natural state, but as part of the not-yet, never having evolved, hence as the *novum* of the utopian goal.

The strength of Bloch's approach is to occupy this same *heimatlos* ground of modernity, placing utopia at the juncture of the crisis and the break induced by it, to gain the idea of a natural order which, proceeding from a condition of absence and void of identity, does not reproduce the statal artifice of *Macht*, but a community free from the representative division in which the modern political subject is established. Bloch does not succumb to the temptation of masking the imperfection of the representative device via the pretence of an authentic substance of community. The bond *in* the community is loyalty to a fault, that is, to a universal that disallows the community to think of itself as a closed assembly or to universalise itself as a particular: on the origin side, it is open to all. That which literally disappears in this perspective is the state as 'form'. For Bloch, in effect, it is 'form' itself that is utopian, thought of perennially as in the future, never having forgotten its wellspring moment. That which Bloch subdues is the process of giving form to order by way of its representation, hence modern political theory itself, which – precisely through the concept of representation – denies the dimension of the future, embedding order in the alienating condition of an eternal present that is no longer available.[21]

The New Bond

In the first edition of *Geist der Utopie* (1918), Bloch takes Nietzsche's claim concerning the 'death of God' as a cornerstone to support the argument against what he sees as the intellectual atmosphere of his time.[22] Bloch's critique operates on an immanent plane: he does not, *contra Nihilismus*, use the 'death of God' to overturn it immediately in proposing some absolute or other, destined positively to fill the void opened up by the crisis of traditional metaphysical notions. He seems rather, Nietzsche-like, to look toward the overcoming of nihilism, in other words, toward its negation as an objectivist doctrine. The quest is that of taking on the total exploration of a world abandoned by God, consequently ridding oneself altogether of theistic *religio* – a putrescent and cumbersome corpse – and discovering space for hope in atheism.

Nietzsche's statement allows Bloch to formulate his approach to politics messianically: an approach that has its core in the utopian, atheo-religious notion of the *Heimat*, a veritable 'a-priori of all politics and culture',[23] a 'meta-religious principle of every revolution'.[24] It is in this light that the historical-philosophical position of the community is considered. The idea is therefore to reflect on the ultimate penetration of an absolute in which humanity recognises itself as an endless problem. In this way, Bloch entrusts the task of mediating between the not-yet and the *ultimum* to something which, according only to a first approximation, could be defined as 'collective subject', a recomposition of forces looking instinctively to knock down all those obstacles that stand in the way of 'becoming identical' (that is, humans by virtue of being humans), and identifiable thus with the exploited and the oppressed.

---

21   See Bernini, Farnesi Camellone and Marcucci 2010, pp. 89–120. See Tomba 2013b.

22   Nietzsche 2001, §125. See Bloch 1985 [1918], pp. 235–342, with special attention to the heading entitled 'Nietzsche, die Kirche und die Philosophie', pp. 267–70.

23   Bloch 1985 [1918], p. 341.

24   Bloch 1985 [1921; 1969], p. 210. For Bloch in later life, both the human and the natural must arrive ultimately at the unveiling of their still secret core hidden in the *Heimat*. See Bloch 1985 [1968], pp. 23–5.

With Bloch, accordingly, it is impossible to split the problem of social and economic injustice from communitarian expectation of this identity. In the historiographical exercise of 1921, Thomas Müntzer plays the key role in the necessary integrality of revolutionary action. By this stratagem, Bloch attempts to prefigure a post-metaphysical and post-statal space-time. Overcoming the 'state form' in utopia signifies unmasking the supposed substantiality of nihilism, of the void announced by the incipient violation of the modern solution to the problem of order. It is here that one has the figure of the community beyond the state, an attempt to 'cross the desert' completely, making a difference within modernity and, therefore, for the very 'salvation' of modernity. It is not against modernity, but rather, for another possible modernity. Here one sees, in all its force, the 'symbol of hope' embodied by the community, 'a bridge thrown without landing points between shadows and light, between the darkness and misery of the present time and the possibility of a new relationship with the truth'. 'An anti-tragic symbol projected toward the near-future goal of a new unity', Bloch's community is the central *category* of utopia. In the form of the not-yet, it elects to make the exodus from the modern condition of politics, from the silence of the truth, and opts for unity, seeing the possibility afforded 'in the exploration and full assumption of that nihilism from which the One must rise again, cloaked in a new myth incarnated in the meta-religious symbol of the Kingdom without God'.[25]

In the first edition of the *Geist der Utopie* it is the Christological symbol that functions as the hinge pin on which Bloch establishes the articulation between the opposing domains of life and form.[26] This articulation veers between two extremes: the negativity and immediacy of the beginning (the lived moment); and the prospect of the end, the not-yet appeared, the utopian idea. In their state of tension, these extremes live together within the Christological category, the former as 'not yet vanished darkness', the latter as a 'goal already existing', but not yet present.[27] In his bid to throw the bridge without landing points between immanence and transcendence figured by the Christological symbol,

---

25 Ganis 1996, p. 22. The relationship between the Christological figure and the notion of category is reiterated in Bloch 1985 [1975], p. 208.

26 This thought long predates the drafting of the text, and is already present in a letter of 12 July 1911 to Lukács; see Bloch 1985 [1903–75], p. 41. The theme is discussed extensively in 'Symbol: die Juden', Bloch 1985 [1918], pp. 319–32. As evident from the subsequent republication (Bloch 1964 [1923], pp. 122–47), this writing dates to the years 1912/13. For a detailed analysis of the text and the circumstances of its composition, see Bonola 2006, pp. 259–314.

27 See Bloch 1985 [1923; 1964], p. 295.

Bloch distances himself from Lukács's radicalisation of the contrast between form and life.[28] In Lukács, the concept of form has the characteristic of shaping reality, stripping it of the unknown quantity that is the possible. In form, the possible is crystallised in the sole possibility determined by the coining of form itself, that is, it becomes reality.[29] Utopia, according to Bloch, overturns this perspective entirely, discovering in form itself the abiding state of being in possibility. If for Lukács, the opacity and granularity of life may find purification in form, in Bloch, the negativity of the darkness of the lived moment does not coincide with an absolute predetermined nothingness, but with a void 'that transforms itself into a truly active background', throwing the latency of the actual subject into relief. If in the *Geist der Utopie*, any attempt at a recomposition of totality is flatly rejected, Bloch with equal firmness does not pull back from a processual restatement of immanence and transcendence, history and redemption. Bloch's project of 1918 is, in this sense, his attempt at a 'system of theoretical messianism',[30] targeting an eschatological solution for the problem of truth, 'of pure fundament, held open and yet still mysterious'.[31]

The Blochian Symbol, hinging on Christology, throws a bridge between history and redemption but, at the same time, renders the idea of conciliation utopian.[32] History and redemption, in effect, can offer neither absolute discontinuity nor dialectical *dépassement*, having the capacity, at a third and higher moment, to remove non-identity and identity. Indeed Bloch makes reference to a 'Third One, beyond the Jew and Christ',[33] and consequently to a wish for fulfilment and conciliation; this is the Messiah of a Third Testament who leads the Jew, 'an exile in the true sense, excluded from history',[34] in

---

28   See Lukács 2010. Superimposed on this contrast is the alternative between the uniqueness of sense that typifies tragedy, and the absence of sense of the *romance*, a religious drama of an age without religion. See Lukács 1971 and, more generally on these topics, Cacciari 1983.

29   See Lukács 2010 and Bloch 1985 [1923; 1964], p. 250.

30   Bloch 1985 [1918], pp. 336–8.

31   Bloch 1985 [1923; 1964], p. 135. Reaching beyond the comparison between tragedy and romance, Bloch focuses on the figure of the comic hero; see Bloch 1985 [1923; 1964], pp. 252–7. Wounded and bleeding, the comic hero contrasts with the 'complete' tragic hero, and his intangible atemporality. The incompleteness of the comic hero shines through in laughter, an omen of the positive that renders the absoluteness of tragic destiny less compact and points to a possible and different outcome, of which the comic hero is the herald. The Blochian Christ embodies this figure exactly.

32   See Krochmalnik 1993, pp. 39–58.

33   Bloch 1985 [1918], p. 329.

34   Bloch 1985 [1918], p. 327.

the exodus from the very condition of being exiled.[35] However, in accordance with Bloch's *ultimum* category, this Third One remains always and exclusively within the accomplished and simultaneously open dimension of the eschatological goal, of the not-yet.[36] In this way, Bloch absolutises neither the wound (the exile), nor the conciliation: his intention is to make the utopian not-yet a place of identification that remains open, unconcluded. Christological mediation thus presents us with a processual *Aufhebung* of the negative (a negation of negation) that is perennially about to begin. Utopia, then, does not guarantee any conciliation, but consigns it rather to the dimension of hope, thereby historicising the wound. In reality, Bloch's Christology is neither Christian, nor Jewish: the Messiah has not already come in the person of Christ, but is nonetheless proclaimed, and therefore expected, in the historical figure of Jesus.[37]

Whilst he credits Bloch with having 'denied with all his energy the political significance of theocracy',[38] Walter Benjamin nonetheless rejects the processual formulation of the relationship between history and redemption. In his *Theologisch-politisches Fragment* – from a review commenting on the first edition of *Geist der Utopie* – Benjamin highlights a *disjointed relationship* between profane time and messianic time, which denies the positive and linear articulation of history and redemption, and at the same time disallows the notion of Christological mediation between the two spheres.[39] Instead, this relationship is understood, without any element of processuality, as a sudden and unexpected upending of the two extremes one into the other. This comment by the young Benjamin is presented as an immanent critique of politics and its nihilistic essence.[40] He seeks to show the mutual affinity between nihilism and redemption since the 'messianic' is able to transcend *Gewalt* only when entirely occupying the locus.[41] The 'nullification' of state power – revolution as something other than politics signifying the seizure and retention of power – merges with the redemptive movement,[42] or rather with that other kind of

---

35   See Ganis 1996, p. 69.

36   See Bloch 1985 [1918], p. 332.

37   See Bloch 1985 [1968], pp. 70–2, 78; Bloch 1985 [1963–4; 1970], p. 185, p. 374.

38   Benjamin 1980 [1920], pp. 203–4. On theocracy and anarchy in German Judaism, essential reading is provided by Guerra 2007.

39   See Wißkirchen 1987; for a comparison between the two authors on the concept of history, see Luther 1984; Schiller 1985; Letschka 1999.

40   See Benjamin 1980 [1921].

41   See Bloch 1985 [1978], pp. 233–45.

42   See Eidam 1992.

Gewalt that invites justice, an element surplus to the form of legal order, but immanent to that order.[43] Revolution seems to interest Benjamin only for the paradoxical nature of the movement, which transcends politics, radicalising its immanence and independent direction.

Similarly, Bloch's idea of community germinates in the soil of nihilism, given its immanent subversion through the atheist symbol of meta-religion.[44] Politics and redemption cannot be reconciled by an immediate upending [*Umschlag*] of one into the other: at the centre of their relationship is the category of Christology, hence the figure of mediation.[45] From this standpoint, Bloch's Christological category contains *in nuce* the definition of politics as the 'art of the possible',[46] embracing both the subjective factor – independent subjectivity not deducible from any historical and economic determinism – and the factor of possibility that is objective – being, according to the possibility of *social matter* – hence contrary to mere subjective will. As Bloch sees it, therefore, Benjamin risks losing the sense of historical exactitude, given that by absolutising discontinuity, he separates the *Jetztzeit* from all concrete mediation.[47] To this there is the objection, no doubt effective, that 'mediation with the process and the refusal to absolutize the discontinuous, in their turn, run the risk of crushing the *Jetztzeit* between the negativity of the actual present and the negativity of the not-yet. [...] Indeed it seems that since the 1930s, there is a risk of politics being reduced simply to technicalities – the tactics of organization and propaganda – whereas the symbol of redemption, by reason of this shift, is in danger of becoming disassociated altogether from the praxis of liberation'.[48] Nonetheless, in the attempt to overcome this objection, it is possible through a synchronic consideration of Bloch's work, without wishing to conceal variations and breaks in his reflection, to discern the expansion of the function associated with the symbol of redemption in the image understood as exodus-figure – a central historical category – and with it find in the open system of experiencing the world, the appropriate *mise à jour* for the system

---

43   See Tomba 2006, pp. 205–55.

44   From this standpoint, the gap that separates the thinking of Benjamin and that of Bloch should certainly be less accentuated – a gap exacerbated by many Benjamin scholars who have often ended up producing a somewhat stereotyped version of Bloch's position.

45   See Bodei 1979, p. 78.

46   See Bloch 1985 [1970], pp. 409–29.

47   See Bloch 1985 [1935; 1962], pp. 370–1; Bloch 1985 [1975], p. 259; Bloch 1985 [1969], pp. 154–5; Bloch 1985 [1963–4; 1970], p. 322, p. 327, pp. 333–4. On Bloch as reader of Benjamin, see Farnesi Camellone 2010.

48   Ganis 1996, pp. 73–4.

of theoretical messianism. The plane on which mediation occurs is certainly shifted: the extremes between which it is placed are, in Bloch's later work, no longer history and redemption but thought and politics (history). This does not represent a betrayal of the theme of community and a reduction of politics to organisation and propaganda, but embodies the extreme bid to consider the theory-praxis relationship systematically without pushing it onto a plane of abstract and illusory necessity and closure, the very danger that the young Bloch indicated when referring to the mortiferous illusions of realised eschatologies.

In Bloch's writings during the years 1918–23, the utopian community is that in which the unitary horizon of sense exceeds every previously determined 'in-itself' and every representation of value, self-generating, rather, in the pre-conception-less decision to give history its end. The void excavated by secularisation and left open by liberal Gnosticism is one that Bloch refuses to fill in fictitiously. The theme of community, in effect, is addressed within a post-statal horizon, marked by the crisis in metaphysical notions of truth, God, and transcendence. There is no temptation to imagine an authentic substance of community, identifying it positively with people and race, blood and soil, biologistically, ethnically or culturally: a risk run throughout history, and still run today, in the perverse search for identity that immediately becomes nihilistic as it triggers the destruction of the non-identical in the name of establishing roots, a process seen as if it were a property to be protected at all costs.

In *Thomas Münzer*, Bloch distances himself decidedly from any idea of community that seeks to 'suppress the modern age rather than save it'.[49] Modernity can be saved only if the attempt to rethink politics proceeds internally of a condition characterised by the absence of a given order, so as to consume the resulting negativity processually, taking on the burden of the crisis it has produced. Focusing on the unconstructability of unity, and therefore on the inexhaustible problem of the idea of order, the symbol of community passes through the poverty of an age in which unity has always been absent and uses this deficiency as the very ground on which to base the decision, without preconceptions, in favour of sense and unity. Thus, the temporality of the symbol of community is only ever that of a living present, and of a unity that must always be newly decided, either because it exists *now*, or because it never existed before. With the words of Müntzer: '*Es ist Zeit*', Bloch removes the absoluteness of any 'bad imagination' that sees the absence and the destruction of sense as a nothing, already decided and devoid of hope – as fixation, reassuring in its

---

49   Bloch 1985 [1921; 1969], p. 165.

own way, of an irremediable loss. In the symbol of eschatological community, by contrast, one has a redeeming *destructio destructionis* that shows the nullity of the 'absence of God', so that there appears 'in the myth, the myth of this void: thus, the void will be half filled, throwing light on the next myth, that of eschatological humanity'.[50]

The space for the myth of the eschatological community opens up, accordingly, in the act of becoming distanced from all representations of good order. In short, Bloch's utopia is delineated as breaching all the rules: political form per se is seen as an unconstructable problem, like the unconstructable problem of the we (the We-Problem), as a problem of experimental experience, perennially open as far as its origin is concerned. It should be stressed that this is not a humanist vision sterilely absolutising subjectivity; on the contrary, for Bloch the symbol of community frees in man the possibility of re-establishing a collective bond with the truth and reconnecting with a praxis through which he becomes a partaker of eternity. In this, it demonstrates its extraterritoriality relative to the state, as the form of response to the historic need for a man-made order capable of controlling the religious conflict that broke the unity of Europe.[51]

This secular artifice excludes the possibility of a substantial reference to *Veritas*: since the modern State has its origins in the collapse of the *Unitas Christiana*, it must neutralise all references to theological or doctrinal substances now familiar as harbingers only of intractable conflict.[52] In the instrumentality of the modern political experience, and the '*machinique*' reduction of the political order, one measures the distance of the artifice from the substantial unity of the symbol, hence the disappearance of any relationship with eschatology.[53] Carl Schmitt is the writer who perhaps most radically has taken this loss as the genetic locus of his thought. He shows quite clearly that the detachment of the *Unitas Christiana* from the symbolic dimension represents a point of abso-

---

50   Bloch 1985 [1918], p. 341.

51   See Schmitt 2008.

52   See Koselleck 1999.

53   See Benjamin 2009, from which it emerges clearly how there is a mortiferous dimension associated coessentially with the political theology that innervates the conceptual device of the state. See Makropoulos 1989, pp. 23–59. During the Weimar years, one sees all the transitoriness of the modern response to the problem of political order, since the sovereignty of the state seems no longer to have a monopoly on the 'political', hence the reappearance of the theme of 'decision' and the absence of a presumption of sense. The artificial order instituted by the decision is always necessary, but equally, in its groundlessness, always far from the fullness of 'form'; see Schmitt 2006.

lute no return.[54] In the neutralisation and depoliticisation of the modern era, the location of the point on which order is anchored must always be shifted forward, lost and subsequently regained, but without any dialectical *dépassement*, without any reconciliation of the experience of separation and loss, the very origin of Europe as a collection of states. Schmitt rejects any prospect of refoundation and consequently denies any 'philosophy of history' inflected on the identity of modernity-decadence.[55] With Nietzsche, he is aware – as is Bloch – that the road 'leading back' cannot be taken; nonetheless, he casts a mournful gaze on the business of modernity, simply remarking with melancholy disenchantment on the fact of its being a necessary desperation.[56]

A clear distance separates Bloch's utopia from this despondent view of secularisation and its outcome. Whereas in Schmitt one has what is, effectively, almost an apologia for the *gottlos* dimension and the consequent need to think in terms of a *katechon*,[57] Bloch, conversely, attempts to draw from nihilism a notion of *unitas*, starting from the absence of the *Heimat*. In utopia, he explores the modern process of immanentisation, but overturns it, rejecting in no uncertain terms the theological schema of the fall, of which the outcome would inevitably be a justification of power. Compared to the negative apocalyptics couched in the political theology of Schmitt – intrinsically desperate and thus acting indirectly as apologist for the modern order – the politics of Bloch are characterised in reality by their essential reference to the principle of hope. The philosophical and historical significance of this principle de-absolutises the 'devoid of God' condition, pouring it into the nothingness of this same void. On this nothingness rest the foundations of the bridge thrown forward toward the *Heimat*, the homeland seen not as having been forever lost, but as being forever still to be gained.

In Bloch's notion of community, the human is emancipated from that anthropological representation, constructed by modern natural law oriented political theory, which chains him to his finitude, to his status as a being-made-for-death ... the community envisaged by Bloch elevates the human, in the full immanence of being-in-the-world, freeing the immortal in him. The relationship of the human and 'the immortal within' coincides with the substance of the communal bond that causes men to relate – in their common not-yet-being – to that which Bloch, in an essay of 1920 on the dual nature of humanity,

54   See Schmitt 2007.
55   See Schmitt 1996.
56   See Schmitt 2002.
57   See Vinx 2015.

defines as 'present and future eternity of the messianic Kingdom'.[58] This is the space of that 'new bond' [*Neue Verbindlichkeit*] that Bloch and Lukács had already discussed in 1911: a sphere of inter-human relation, originally extra-authoritarian, freed as it was from the creatural representation of man on which the artifice of power is modernly founded.

Identity, indicating the eschatological presence of the revealed face of man, is seen by Bloch as being redemptive. It is the symbol of man's participation in the immortal and not the stigma of the scission in which the subject of power is constituted in modernity, identical to itself inasmuch as it is represented by another, in the presence of which the subject appears only ever as naked mortal life. The Blochian reference here is to the symbolic and messianic core of the 'absolute natural law' of the heretical sects, which he includes in the utopian inflection of the name 'identity'. Bloch seeks in the name of identity to open the space for a new possibility – since it would seem that the monopoly of statal representation on this name might be broken – before it becomes lost to the nihilistic outcome implicit in its fascist perversion. In this, the reflection of the early Bloch is distanced completely from the reduction of the human to a passive subject, in need of an appeal to ethics and to the defence of human rights. In the Geist and Thomas Müntzer, Bloch presents the liberation of the immortal in man as a red line which, in the utopian concept of the *Selbstbegegnung* [encounter with the Self], connects the theology of revolution of the sixteenth century with our present day. In this connection, one has the exodus from creaturality and from subjection to death. The community is the space where this exodus occurs, a Christological incarnation in which man is freed from submission to the transcendence of power. Deprived of its fundament – of the representation of man as a being-made-for-death – the building of human authority is broken, leaving unencumbered space in which collectively to relaunch the bond between finite and infinite internally of an order that is, *ab origine*, extra-authoritarian.

The Dead Come Back Again

The context in which Bloch's research into the figure of Thomas Müntzer takes place goes beyond the limits of mere historical reconstruction; indeed this is a historiographical endeavour of exceptional power.[59] In effect, the task

---

58   Bloch 1985 [1969], p. 209.
59   See Taubes 2009.

undertaken is that of placing the revolutionary event of the 1525 Peasants War in contact with the revolutionary decision in the present:

We want always to be only with ourselves.

So that here too, we absolutely do not look back. But being alive ourselves, we blend with one another. And others too reappear transformed, the dead return again, their action seeks to accomplish its purpose once again with us. Münzer came to a very swift end and yet was reaching for the stars. Anyone studying him in his work sees the today and the unconditional in a more detached perspective, more complete than the too-swift lived experience, and yet equally, not attenuated. Münzer is above all history in the fecund sense, he is that which belongs to him, and all the past that merits being recorded is here to engage us, to enthuse us, to sustain always in the broadest sense that which is continually understood by us.[60]

The reading of Bloch is sustained by a 'philosophy of history' unconstrained by the illusion of a needful processuality, but which 'stirs anew that which has gone before, superseding it utopically'.[61] The present of the *Entscheidung* is the place where different but simultaneous temporalities meet; their connection is defined both as the accomplishment of that which in the past had remained unaccomplished, and as a positive legacy, to be mobilised in the present, of elements of utopian content encapsulated in this same past. Their unaccomplishedness coincides exactly with the surplus of sense contained in the not-yet that marks them out, and prompts the need to dispose ourselves as the point of conjunction between that which in history has been interrupted, and the possibility of our future. Not the past in the sense of all that has passed, therefore, but in the sense of that which, though already in the past, is 'still alive and not yet liquidated'.[62]

With this in mind, Bloch does not provide a spiritualistic vision of the theology proposed by Müntzer, which would place the sixteenth-century priest within a process connecting the heretical currents of the Reformation with neo-Protestantism and therefore with the formation of the aconfessional and secular state. Rather, he fully accentuates its intrinsically political content. In this way, he manages to show how, at the time of the Reformation, there

---

60   Bloch 1985 [1921; 1969], p. 9.
61   Bloch 1985 [1923; 1964], p. 226.
62   Bloch 1985 [1959], p. 8.

emerged different possibilities for incipient modernity, clashing bloodily one against the other. The first statement of the Müntzer heresy, in Bloch's eyes, is the stripping of all political significance from theocracy, and it is precisely this space that opens up to allow maximum politicisation of the demand for reform made by Müntzer's peasants. Conversely, Bloch sees in Lutheran theology a tendency to bring about the total neutralisation and depoliticisation of theology, opening the door to the modern secular state. Leading to this outcome is the division, in Lutheran morality, between the morals of the individual and the morals of public office, and the detachment that this creates between the world and the Christian: the introjection of the religious symbol that leads to the modern distinction between public and private.

That which in the spiritual mysticism of the Middle Ages was known as inner light, becomes in Müntzer's theology 'a consuming flame directed outwards'. As a result, the spiritualisation of the world is at one and the same time a secularisation of the spirit, and the materialisation of the spirit means the loss of this same spirit to the world. Hopes that hitherto had only been fostered internally, all of a sudden turn outward, causing historical events to unfold with particular impetus.[63] In this sense, Müntzer is seen as offering a transvaluation of the idea of Christianity, and therefore of Europe, becoming the atavistic champion of a reference to the unity of a religious symbol definable as radically *gottlos*, hence simultaneously meta-religious and meta-political, looking toward a post-statal community that is 'Lawless and Stateless'.[64]

In Bloch, the Reformation seems therefore to be marked by the complex articulation of a temporality on multiple levels. This reading disrupts every interpretation of the Reformation that tends to see the process, within a rectilinear and homogenous passage of time, as a simple progression towards modernity and the political form that identifies it, reducing it to *ex-post* justification of its historic victory. Occurring concurrently with the process that links the Reformation in its Lutheran and Calvinist guise to the birth of the modern is a different movement wherein Bloch detects the utopian traces of Müntzer's revolution theology, and his arrival at the idea of an apocalyptic community that rejects both the statal exercise of *Gewalt*, and any authoritarian dimension.

Bloch makes a veritable synchronic cut that allows him to identify the factual connection between the ambition of a minority and historically unsuccessful current of the Reformation and the community-based utopia he sought to

---

63   See Taubes 2009.
64   Bloch 1985 [1921; 1969], p. 130.

recognise as a possibility in the Germany of the Weimar Republic. In Bloch's writing we sense the resurgent agitation of the peasant war within the events of the Reformation, as the indicator of a utopian possibility for the destinies of the present. This is a utopian hermeneutic that places the non-simultaneity of sectarian emergence in the foreground of the Reformation, with respect to the modern concept of the 'political'. The surplus [*Überschuss*] of Müntzer's heresy and the possibility of inheriting his abiding presence as a utopian remnant, set against the history written by the victors, emerges with maximum impact for Bloch precisely when the process of shaping the modern liberal state appears to falter, leaving erratic masses, pockets of non-simultaneity (subordinate classes in the Germany of the early 1920s) in which awareness can be raised of a legacy encompassing the possibility of a different modernity.

The millennialist sect that gathered around the figure of Müntzer, inasmuch as it lived in expectation of that totality (the Kingdom) which is made visible in the body of the community and communitarily hoped for, is by definition universal. As a figure of the utopian not-yet, it also prefigures a form of universal order that appears, however, as a historical experience, occurring always and exclusively on the inside, in the paradoxical universal particularism by which it is characterised.[65] The sect, in its originally non-sectarian core, cannot be seen as a party politically devoid of legitimacy, in other words as a faction, along with others. But neither can it find satisfaction in being tolerated as a confession alongside other confessions, as this would signify its neutralisation in political terms. This is a group of people that cannot be viewed through the lens of modern political science, from the standpoint of statal *Gewalt* – that is, through the eyes of the victors. The Müntzer sect, in Bloch's estimation, does not see itself as a party, and accordingly, battles to establish its right to community, in short, to embody a concrete expectation of the universal. It is not a question of establishing the Kingdom by means of force, but of exercising that *Gewaltrecht des Guten* characteristic of the community wanting to become what it believes it should be. Representationally: one does not rise up against Princes because they are unfaithful, but because they prevent us from becoming that which we are.[66]

The power of Bloch's exposition rests on the placement of the otherness and surplus of Müntzer at the very heart of the nihilistic origin of the *Neuzeit*, within the same process of secularisation that was triggered by the event of the Reformation as the wellspring of the modern. The non-simultaneity of the sec-

---

65   See Bloch 1985 [1921; 1969], pp. 172–3.
66   See Bloch 1985 [1921; 1969], pp. 115–16.

tarian phenomenon is therefore synchronous with but surplus to the process of immanentisation, occupying the same time and the same place, but radically overtaking it. Only through this precise placement – not in another 'where' or in another 'when' – can the community of Müntzer, interpreted by Bloch in the light of the atheist symbol of meta-religion, represent the most profound 'otherness' in the face of the main route taken by modernity, which it seeks both to overtake and to redeem. The otherness of Müntzer stems from the fact of being in simultaneity with the emergence of the modern statal order, of which it represents, now, as then, the defeated yet still inheritable feasibility, given that it bears an imagination capable of a liberating overthrow that arises from the radicalisation of the immanentising movement of modernity. Thus, Müntzer is a figure that has the utopian pulse, beating with a different temporality beside and along the mortiferous path of non-identity and domination. The tempo of this pulse is that of communal order, in other words, the eventful temporality of the not-yet that rejects all founding rituals and any attempt to produce a definitive representation of order.

The experimental nature of the order appears as a primary characteristic of the human *multiversum*, originating in reference to a 'common' that does not occasion either the representative production of identity (the movement of identification), or a reduced visibility of the order to the reified dimension of duration. Thus, the unity of the 'common' is found entirely in the eventful temporality of the not-yet and is by definition an 'experiment'. This allows Bloch to name a 'We' that is only ever the living actuality of the connection of the many, extraneous to any idea of community-based interpersonal communication that would reduce it to a once-and-for-all foundation.

In the years 1918–23, accordingly, the political utopia envisaged by Bloch would consist in an immanent critique of modernity. Assuming the constitutivity of the crisis with/in the *Neuzeit*, even in Bloch's later writings, utopia radicalises the thrust toward emancipation contained in possibility in the modern. In the utopia of community, Bloch does not reject the modern idea of freedom in the name of organicism or paternalism, but radicalises it to the point at which, in the community, it is no longer presented as co-original with power and with objective law.[67] Freedom, therefore, is no longer that of the individual constituted by sovereignty, but that of man emancipated from the law of *subjectum*, hence from the division which, in the artifice of modern political representation, constitutes subjectivity as such. The modern neutralisation of theology in politics simultaneously produces sovereignty and the isolation

---

67   See Bloch 1985 [1959], p. 631.

of the free individual, standing before it as naked life, mortal, separated from all ties with eternity. The main purpose of Bloch's philosophy is consequently to break down the representation of man arising from an anthropology that ties the individual, without hope, to the condition of a creature, which has always been mortal because always able to be killed. From this breakage there emerges, visibly, the atheist symbol of eschatological humanity, the 'new bond' of community, which cannot but rest on the mutually experienced, common, and always new event of discovering/experimenting one's origin and destination; the 'new bond' accommodates differences and at the same time saves them, and shows itself only in the symbolic pre-apparition of a 'Tertium, beyond I and you',[68] a common not-yet that is still and always missing. It becomes a *bond* between men, thanks to which – in the form of the unconstructable problem – it is possible to name a 'we'.

Fraternitas militans

In Bloch's lengthy reflection on community, the political content of utopia is problematised and redetermined. Most of all, it is the utopian legacy of religious symbols and messianism that undergoes a profound revision,[69] though this also remains a central theme in Bloch's later work *Atheismus im Christentum*. Certainly, and especially in his writings of the Leipzig years (1949–61), there is still the problem of evaluating how the debate about real socialism may determine deep changes in Bloch's approach to politics, and how it may tend to elicit that demand for the humanisation of politics which is the driving fulcrum of *Naturrecht und menschliche Würde* (1961).[70] However, it cannot be argued that in Bloch one sees a complete functionalisation of the symbol of redemption in favour of an ethical relativisation of politics, which would accompany adherence to the minimum notion of democratic centralism.

The problem here is not that of freeing Bloch from the experience of real socialism in the Soviet bloc. Fully identifying utopia with the ethical relativisation of politics, or with the persistence of a metaphysical reserve that ought to impede the absolutisation of power, prevents the reader from seeing the real surplus of Bloch's utopia relative to any form of established order. This said, it is not possible to think of picturing a 'Western' Bloch, as proponent of a human-

---

68   Bloch 1985 [1921; 1969], p. 210.
69   See Rabinbach 1985; Mendes-Flohr 1983.
70   See Ganis 1996, pp. 106–32.

isation of the socialist experience: the natural conclusion of such a notion would be to produce an apologetical defence of moral primacy over politics, a supposed antidote to the totalitarian risk of ideologies, which in turn would be seen as ideological, being an absolutisation of the representation of the human as naked life. By declaring that it is impossible to recognise a substantial common good, ethical humanism denies man the prospect of eternity, relegating his condition to that of a creature at the mercy of death and power: it is a nihilistic humanism, drinking at the fountain of temporal inertia, of death, of nothingness.[71] A humanism of this kind is precisely what Bloch brushes aside. In effect, Bloch establishes a critical and immanent relationship with nihilism, debating its main political product: the representation of the human being as a perennially potential defenceless victim.

That said, one cannot ignore the fact that – in his book on natural law, at least – Bloch himself comes perilously close to embracing the prospect of humanism outlined above. During the Leipzig years, his political problem is to re-establish a praxis of emancipation within the framework of existing socialism, which he seems to attempt precisely by invoking moral primacy. A response dictated no doubt by the need to address the 'fact' of Stalinism, which appears, however, to be reduced to a discourse in defence of the victims of the Moscow show trials, claiming for these individuals the protection of so-called fundamental human rights – which have nothing to do with the absolute natural law of the community. A claim such as this necessarily betrays the very communism that Bloch espouses, as it rests on the premiss of the human as a passive *subjectum* at the mercy of the power of the state. That which disappears in this passage is precisely the fulcrum of the Blochian idea of community, that is, the common practice of men in the production, always open, of the truth. Thus, the recourse to human rights not only presupposes a passive humanity, but implements it, assimilating the human condition to that of mortal victim. The inconsistency in this kind of politics, which would see itself as offering resistance to power, is already there in its origin, namely that it prohibits any relation with the truth as being possible – hence imaginable or collectively practicable.

Much later, by contrast, attempting a systematic rearticulation of the theory-praxis relationship, Bloch reactivates – *contra Nihilismus* – the bond between praxis and truth.[72] If, in effect, affectedly democratic and nihilistic humanism does not reflect the last word by Bloch on politics, it is worth looking also

---

71   See Bloch 1985 [1959], pp. 1384–91.
72   Bloch 1985 [1975], pp. 239–64.

at *Naturrecht und menschliche Würde* and other contemporaneous writings for traces of a recurrent focus on the theme of community. A search of this kind could be conducted on the figure of the 'Kingdom of freedom', where the concept of *Freiheit* is connected to a form of order (more specifically, the *Reich*) placed outside the conceptual sphere of the state. The concept of *Ordnung* is readily susceptible to negative acceptations identifying it with duress, apparently signifying the exact opposite of freedom.[73] In the horizon of the state-*less* community, freedom is primarily 'freedom for' [*Freiheit-Wozu*], and refers to identity between existence and essence.[74] For Bloch, freedom in this sense is not a concept, but an *idea*,[75] an essential content of the *Reich*, in other words, a kind of order that has nothing to do with the *form* of the state.[76] The images of liberty and order that Bloch provides in his compendium of social utopias serve to indicate the possibility of an *Ordnung* that cannot be reduced to the dimension of statehood.[77]

In *Freiheit, ihre Schichtung und ihr Verhältnis zur Wahrheit* (1956), the space of the Kingdom of freedom is clearly communal, and therefore ultra-statal.[78] Here the *Gemeinde* is confirmed as being the material symbol of expectation for the *Überhaupt*, and the Christological figure occupies the threshold between what is manifested as presence and what is not yet present, as the image of inter-human relationship, extraneous to any fixity of order.[79] The political nature of this image hinges entirely on acceptance of the unconstructability of the Kingdom: it is seen as a moral relationship without the need for any external support – the moralising sphere of human rights – as it is able to contain morality in itself. Bloch's notion of community indicates a bond created by the fact of the idea – the common not-yet – becoming visible: since the idea is not deducible from the sphere of the visible, the common only ever appears, in relations between men, as an event,[80] that is, as an encounter in the innovative

---

73   See Bloch 1985 [1961], p. 258; Bloch 1985 [1959], pp. 614–21. In these writings Bloch outlines, fragmentarily, a conflictual but gradual compenetration of freedom and order, a horizon that does not coincide with the idea of community.

74   See Bloch 1985 [1969], p. 592.

75   See Bloch 1985 [1923; 1964], p. 295.

76   See Bloch 1985 [1959], p. 621. Shortly beforehand, Bloch appears to attribute the possibility of this order to the realisation of Soviet socialism; see Bloch 1985 [1959], p. 619. This seems to identify the failure of that realisation with its statalisation.

77   See the entire chapter 36 of Bloch 1985 [1959], pp. 547–729.

78   See Bloch 1985 [1969], p. 588.

79   See Bloch 1985 [1969], p. 589.

80   See Bloch 1985 [1959], p. 1492.

and future-laden dimension of repetition – the return of that which has yet to be realised.

In the book on *Naturrecht*, this prospect re-emerges together with notions of equality and fraternity. Equality in the community is not abstract equalisation imposed by a power which, in the natural law foundation of sovereignty, stems from the elimination of all articulations and differences. Rather, Bloch thinks of equality among humankind as the 'polyphony of a unison'.[81] The 'salvation' of a concrete individuality is guaranteed by the irreducible difference of the content to which the very idea of equality refers: man becoming identical to his own self. Not a static identity, a representative subtraction from the possibility of the *Begegnung*, but an *Identifizierungsprozess* that is repeated ever anew in the encounter with the other. Here one has the root of a common not-yet, the still missing *ultimum*, socially bonding but not religiously binding men to one another.[82] In the image of community,[83] identity does not occupy the place of modern sovereignty, consisting in representation as identity of the political subject, which produces the invisibility of differences – hence also that on which the dependence of man on man is based – at the price of an equal nullity in the face of *Macht*. If the modern artifice is built on the total opposition between the multiple and the single (sovereignty), unity in the community sense signifies the willingness of people to order themselves openly and *in chorus*,[84] multiversally and avoiding verticality – the self-ordering of the many where the principle of hope (identity, which is not yet, of man with himself) is seen to be operational, in the manner of immanent transcendence.[85]

The articulation of freedom and equality in an order configured as human *multiversum* in the materiality of community, is defined by Bloch as 'solidarity',[86] an expression of the multivocal interchange between the individual and the many.[87] It is the 'final rule' and, ultimately, the only rule of natural law in the 'objective radical' sense.[88] 'Fraternity', the third figure of the Republican motto, reworded by Bloch, is coextended with solidarity, based on a common situation of need or of prevarication. It passes through a determinate struggle

---

81   Bloch 1985 [1961], p. 192.

82   See Bloch 1985 [1961], p. 191.

83   See Bloch 1985 [1959], p. 235, pp. 1450–6, where this image is modelled on the archetype of the biblical *Exodus*.

84   See Bloch 1985 [1961], p. 190.

85   See Bloch 1985 [1959], p. 1516.

86   See Bloch 1985 [1959], p. 621.

87   See Bloch 1985 [1959], pp. 1137–8.

88   Bloch 1985 [1961], p. 252, p. 269.

in common in order to overcome the situation in question, and shows itself as such only on the level of concrete action, not limited to a moment of dialogue in the communicative and linguistic sense: fraternity gives an account of itself only in the concrete praxis of liberation.[89]

In Bloch's analysis of natural law, the republican images of the *citoyen* tend to conceal the sectarian and apocalyptic figure of Müntzer's *Bruder*. It is no accident that Bloch coins the expression '*citoyen des Reichs*'.[90] If liberty and equality interact in such a way as to exceed the conceptuality of the statal device, opening up the utopian-messianic horizon of the community, then fraternity evokes the image of sectarian war. Described as '*fraternitas militans*',[91] the community relationship emerges from the soil of negating everything that impedes the process whereby man identifies with himself (oppression, economics and/or politics). In this sense, fraternity also evokes a 'freedom from' [*Freiheit-wovon*] that Bloch identifies as the '*Alpha* of the revolution'.[92] However, just as in *Thomas Münzer* the revolutionary war was seen as opening space for the possibility of a community-oriented Kingdom – which therefore would have nothing to do with the purposes of seizing and keeping power – likewise in *Naturrecht und menschliche Würde*, the notion of *fraternitas militans* is subordinate to the creation of the '*fraternitas triumphans*',[93] that 'freedom to' [*Freiheit-Wozu*] that coincides with the '*Omega* of revolution':[94] the freedom of that 'new bond' embodying 'the encounter with the we'.[95]

---

89   See Cunico 1988, pp. 233–4.

90   Bloch 1985 [1959], p. 1095, p. 1413.

91   Bloch 1985 [1961], p. 193.

92   Bloch 1985 [1961], p. 188.

93   Bloch 1985 [1961], p. 193.

94   Bloch 1985 [1961], p. 189.

95   Bloch 1985 [1961], p. 192.

CHAPTER 7

Gramsci's Plural Temporalities

Peter D. Thomas

But in every age, there has been a past and a contemporaneity, and calling oneself a 'contemporary' cannot be anything but a joke. (The story is told of a little French bourgeois who put 'Contemporary' on his calling card; he had discovered that he was a 'contemporary' and bragged about it).[1]

The notion of a plurality of historical times or temporalities is now established as one of the most significant recent tendencies in the philosophy and theory of history, traversing the boundaries between otherwise conflicting paradigms of research.[2] One feature shared by most of these approaches is a commitment to the deepening of the 'spatialisation' of the notion of historical time itself. Rather than a depiction of discrete events 'punctuating' a linear temporal continuum, organised classically according to a 'before' and 'after', the pluralisation of distinct and irreducible historical times seems to configure them in more complex spatial arrangements, in either 'archaeological' or 'cartographical' models. An archaeological reconfiguration of time is thematised explicitly in the work of Koselleck, who has provided one of the most sophisticated methodological reflections on the consequences of thinking the plurality of times with his notion of 'temporal layers' [*Zeitschichten*].[3] Arguably,

---

1 Q 8, § 232, p. 1087. References to Gramsci's *Prison Notebooks* [*Quaderni del carcere*] follow the internationally established standard of notebook number (Q), number of note (§), followed by page reference to the Italian critical edition (Gramsci 1975). The English critical edition of the *Prison Notebooks*, edited by Joseph A. Buttigieg, now comprises three volumes (Gramsci 1992, 1996, 2007), containing Notebooks 1–8; notes included in those volumes can be located according to the notebook and number of note.

2 For an overview of different theories of temporal plurality or multiplicity, see Offenstadt 2011 and for a collection of recent interventions, Bevernage and Lorenz 2013. The notions of 'times' and 'temporalities' are used interchangeably throughout this text, following Althusser's usage in *Reading Capital*. Other approaches, however, have insisted upon distinguishing between them, with 'time' posited as the condition of possibility of (the experience of) 'temporality', which is then understood in a phenomenological sense. These approaches, however, are ultimately premised upon the type of philosophy of the subject that this text in part aims to place in question.

3 As Koselleck acknowledges, 'When we speak about time, we are reliant on metaphors. For

however, such a three-dimensional model is also operative in one or another form in approaches as different from each other as Bloch's study of the unevenness of German modernisation, 'classical' structuralism's distinction between synchrony and diachrony, and the Annales School's investigation of the overlayering of varying *durées*. 'Cartographical' models of plural temporality, on the other hand, seem to imply a dispersion of time in two dimensions, as different temporalities scattered across a plane, lying alongside each other in relations of indifference or antagonism.[4] Chakrabarty's distinction between 'History 1' and 'History 2', or histories 'posited by capital' and those external to or autonomous from it, but existing as 'subaltern pasts' within the 'same' time, Zerubavel's analysis of 'time maps', or Hölscher's recent proposal of the notion of 'time gardens' as a 'common ground for historical narratives, for keeping history as a universal reality together', would seem to be examples of such approaches.[5]

In all these cases, however, the spatial metaphors unify just as soon as they have divided; the pluralisation of irreducible historical times without common measure encounters, in a formulation now most often associated with Koselleck, the paradoxical notion of a 'contemporaneity of the non-contemporary' [*Gleichzeitigkeit des Ungleichzeitigen*].[6] Partially anticipated by Bloch,[7] but with deeper roots in the post-Hegelian German tradition, Koselleck's formulation aims to theorise the way in which different temporal layers emerge, or 'occur [*sich ereignen*]', 'at different times [*nicht alles zu gleicher Zeit*]', 'arising out of completely heterogeneous life contexts'.[8] Nevertheless, they all come to be 'present and effective at the same time',[9] overlaying and undermining each other, just as remnants of different historical periods can be found within the

---

time can only be made visible by means of movement in determinate units of space' (Koselleck 2000, p. 9).

4   In the former case of indifference, such a theory's primary reference would be to the autonomous duration and rhythm internal to any historical time, rather than their positioning vis-à-vis other times; it could thus be regarded as similar to Herder's suggestion (repeatedly recalled by Koselleck) that there are '*at any one time* in the universe innumerably many times', as everything has its own immanent temporal measure (cited in Koselleck 1979, p. 323). In the later case of antagonism, the intertwining of conflicting times would give rise to what Chakrabarty, following Guha, characterises as 'time-knots' of multiple times, or a notion of relative temporal autonomy. See Chakrabarty 2000, p. 112.

5   Chakrabarty 2000, p. 63, p. 112; Zerubavel 2003; Hölscher 2014, p. 591.

6   Koselleck 2000, p. 9.

7   On Koselleck's relation to Bloch, see Olsen 2012, p. 152.

8   Koselleck 2000, p. 9.

9   Ibid.

same archaeological site. 'Our own experience teaches us', Koselleck perhaps ironically remarks, 'that we still have contemporaries who live in the stone age'.[10]

The seductive formulation of the 'contemporaneity of the non-contemporaneous' thus seems to refer to two distinct registers or even conceptions of time, highlighting an ambiguity, a paradox or perhaps even a contradiction at the centre of most theories of plural historical times, both 'archaeological' and 'cartographical'. On the one hand, it posits a time of origins that phenomena carry like a birthmark, which repetition and duration may dilute or transmute, but cannot definitively efface; it is precisely this trace of the 'heterogeneous life contexts' from which they originally emerged that signals their non-contemporaneity. On the other hand, however, it also acknowledges the co-presence of such different 'times' in the 'same' time, namely, the time of the present conceived as a con-temporaneity. While non-contemporaneity derives from the continuing, substantive presence of the past in the present, contemporaneity is imposed in a purely formalist sense, as the temporal and spatial unity of whatever differences inhabit any given 'present'.

Formulated in these terms, the notion of plural temporality thus seems quickly to run the risk of relapsing into the presupposition of a type of 'History' [*Geschichte*] in the singular, within which plural histories would occur. However, rather than determination by a singular temporal line, it is instead the introduction of the notion of contemporaneity itself that here appears to subject plural historical times to a type of 'resynchronisation'. This is not simply a question of the 'work of synchronisation' of ostensibly distinct historical times affected or overdetermined by one particular time (whether the 'homogenous, linear and teleological time of progress', or the 'temporality of socially-necessary labour'),[11] or even simply a question of the construction of a form of 'achieved contemporaneity', a 'temporal order' or 'regime of historicity'.[12] Rather, it is the notion of contemporaneity itself that in this conception unites plural historical times within its single frame of reference, making possible both their non-contemporaneity (insofar as they originated at a time other than that of the present) and plurality (insofar as their plurality is determined within the unity of their con-temporaneity). The present as contemporaneity is thus conceived as a primary *Zeitschichte* or *Zeitraum* capable of encompassing and comprehending a diversity of even apparently conflict-

---

10   Koselleck 2000, p. 307.

11   Jordheim 2014, p. 502; Tomba 2013b, p. 149.

12   Osborne 2013, particularly pp. 15–36; Hartog 2003.

ing times as moments of its own coming to self-presence. It is the identity of the present with itself that here functions as a guarantee of both temporal plurality and the unity of that plurality in the notion of contemporaneity.[13] At a limit, such a notion of any given historical present as contemporaneity might even be regarded as functioning transcendentally as the condition of possibility of a theory of plural historical times; their historical pluralisation, that is, could be seen as depending on a logically prior unification in contemporaneity, as a paradigmatic form of diversity in unity.

Marxist Non-Contemporaneities

Does the Marxist tradition contain resources that might help to resolve this ambiguity, paradox or contradiction? Long considered to imply either a teleological vision of the growth of productive forces or a messianic moment of rupture with a determining temporal linearity, only relatively recently has attention turned to the much richer reflections on historical time that have accompanied the materialist conception of history since its inception. The young Marx's inheritance, mediated by Heine, of German idealism's foundational and abiding reflections on Germany's miserable non-contemporaneity, both with Europe and with itself, is only the first in a long line of Marxist reflections on the political significance of the temporal disjointedness of modern historical experience.[14] Marx's critique of political economy emphasises the centrality of differential temporal determinations in the process of capital accumulation; temporal unevenness is central to the terms in which Trotsky theorises both the reality of combined and uneven capitalist development and the possibility of permanent revolution, insights developed in related though distinct terms by the political conclusions that Lenin draws from his theory of imperialism; Lukács's historicism and Benjamin's anti-historicism alike, albeit in radically different ways, reformulated themes of temporal breaks in messianic conceptions of time; Bloch provided one of the earliest explorations of the contradictory relations between the contemporary and the non-contemporaneous, more recently extended by figures such as Daniel Bensaïd, Stavros Tombazos, Vittorio Morfino and Harry Harootunian.[15] Above all, however, it was Althusser's contri-

---

13   See in particular Derrida's critique of the 'self-presence of the present in the living present' as a 'source-point' in which 'the infinite diversity of contents is produced' (Derrida 1973, p. 9, p. 61, p. 6).

14   See Kouvelakis 2003, pp. 44–120.

15   Bensaïd 2002; Tombazos 1994; Morfino 2009; Harootunian 2015.

butions to *Reading Capital* in the early 1960s that firmly registered the theme of plural historical times as a central problem of and for the development of the materialist conception of history.

Reading Capital initially seemed to aim to distinguish Althusser's concept of historical time from other approaches then in vogue in French intellectual life, particularly the diffuse structuralism with which Althusser would come to be irrevocably associated (despite his initial and repeated protests), and the historiographical initiatives of the Annales School.[16] However, it was only in the chapter, 'Marxism is not an Historicism', that the fundamentally political motivation of Althusser's intervention became clear: namely, to provide a reformulation of a Marxist theory 'cleansed' of teleological, essentialist, and what he saw as ultimately non-revolutionary presuppositions. Rather than openly attacking the 'official' Marxist philosophy that was his true target, however, Althusser instead developed his critique in relation to a figure widely regarded in the 1960s as a viable alternative to the 'Diamat' vulgate: namely, Antonio Gramsci.

Absolute Historicism

Althusser argued that Gramsci's notion of Marxism as an absolute historicism entailed a relapse into a pre-Marxian and ultimately Hegelian conception of the present, as an essentially unified and coherent 'presence' of *Geist*, 'the ideological present in which temporal presence coincides with the presence of the essence with its phenomena'. In this perspective, the present was understood as a mere

> *'essential section'* (coupe d'essence), i.e., an intellectual operation in which a *vertical break* is made at any moment in historical time, a break in the present such that all the elements of the whole revealed by this section are in an immediate relationship with one another, a relationship that immediately expresses their internal essence.[17]

---

16   Althusser not only took his distance from structuralism in his self-critique in the late 1960s and early 1970s but, as recent research has emphasised, was openly criticising it from the early 1960s. He 'had been decrying structuralism, "idealism's last hope", as a philosophical fraud since his 1962–63 seminar on the subject' (Goshgarian 2003, p. xii).

17   Althusser and Balibar 1970, p. 94.

Althusser claimed that such an operation constituted a common element of Hegel's 'absolute knowledge' and Gramsci's 'absolute historicism'. In both, there was a particular type of 'essentialisation-spatialisation' of the present, which led to the negation of properly historical time. Ultimately, it resulted in an inability to theorise the possibility of transition or change, and the affirmation of an 'eternity' of the present in a stereotypically (and caricatured) Hegelian fashion. Althusser argued that

if Marxism is an absolute historicism, it is because it historicizes even what was peculiarly the theoretical and practical negation of history for Hegelian historicism: the end of history, the unsurpassable present of Absolute Knowledge. [...] There is no longer any privileged present in which the totality becomes visible and legible in an 'essential section', in which consciousness and science coincide. The fact that there is no Absolute Knowledge – which is what makes the historicism absolute – means that Absolute Knowledge itself is historicized. If there is no longer any privileged present, all presents are privileged to the same degree. It follows that historical time possesses in each of its presents a structure which allows each present the 'essential section' of contemporaneity. [...] Hence the project of thinking Marxism as an (absolute) historicism automatically unleashes a logically necessary chain reaction which tends to reduce and flatten out the Marxist totality into a variation of the Hegelian totality.[18]

'The present', Althusser argued, in Hegel and thus also in the 'Hegelian-Marxist' Gramsci, 'constitutes the absolute horizon of all knowing, since all knowing can never be anything but the existence in knowing of the internal principle of the whole'.[19] Althusser could therefore conclude that Gramsci's work tended to efface the decisively new conception of historical time that had emerged in the course of Marx's work, the precise delineation of which alone could guarantee the autonomy of Marxist philosophy from the incessant lures of a relapse into an 'ideological conception of historical time'.[20]

---

18   Althusser and Balibar 1970, p. 132.
19   Althusser and Balibar 1970, p. 95.
20   Althusser and Balibar 1970, p. 96.

The Impossibility of a Hegelian Politics

The opprobrium into which Althusser's work fell for a long historical period tended to work against a continuing discussion of the conceptual coherence and potential political consequences of his notion of historical time. A recent revival of interest in his later writings in particular, but also specifically in his account of plural temporalities, has reopened the debate in terms that stress Althusser's distance from the 'structuralism' to which his work was often reduced.[21] Indeed, Althusser argued that it is a unitary conception of temporal presence that presupposes an idealist conception of structure, as the express-ivist form of an essence; in its turn, this leads to an essentially aestheticised concept of history, as a succession of 'essential sections' of contemporaneity, which are always identical with each other insofar as they are manifestations of an always self-same essence. History, in the sense of causally related events, or a process of development that can be rationally explained, becomes unthink-able. Instead, each historical period would become merely a 'mobile image of eternity', in the sense ascribed to time itself in the *Timaeus*,[22] or a finite form of the infinity of the self-alienating concept, expressed in Hegel's terms. In this perspective, time is a means for the concept's re-presentation, while remaining within its own self-identical essence; as a circular process of the appearance of an essence that always returns to itself unchanged throughout the unfold-ing of its self-alienation, time is represented as merely accumulation within the concept, its mode of self-same expansion or intensification. The present would be fully identical with itself, in the sense that it would include nothing that could escape the determinations of its essence. On the basis of such an essentialisation and thus eternalisation of the present, there is no possibility of thinking change, other than in the form of the miraculous event that arrives, unexpectedly and above all inexplicably, from some beyond.[23] As *Reading Capital* declared, 'the ontological category of the present prevents any anticipation of historical time, any conscious anticipation of the future development of the concept, *any knowledge of the future*'.[24]

Furthermore, once the notion of history as development premised upon the real difference of complexity has been replaced by the indifference of 'differences' equal to each other in a 'spiritual' whole, there is little possibility of thinking transformative political practices that would usher in genuinely new

---

21   Goshgarian 2012; Chambers 2011; Morfino 2009; Hindess 2007.
22   Plat. Tim. 37d.
23   See Bensaïd 2004.
24   Althusser and Balibar 1970, p. 95.

forms of socio-political organisation. As Althusser famously remarked in *For Marx* (in 'On the Materialist Dialectic', a text that develops a 'spatial' critique of a spiritualised conception of the social formation that corresponds to the 'temporal' focus pursued in *Reading Capital*), 'It is no accident that the Hegelian theory of the social totality has never provided the basis for a *policy*, that there is not and cannot be a Hegelian politics'.[25] It would perhaps be more precise to argue that, while politics understood as a formalist repetition of existing governmental forms may indeed be possible on such a basis (as the historical record amply attests), a properly *revolutionary* or transformative politics is not, for it would seem to posit the emergence of hitherto unknown dimensions of socio-political organisation.

An essentialist theory of the social totality and its corresponding (ideological) concept of historical time could give rise, at the most, only to a politics of management, or administrative rearrangement of the status quo ('reformism'); its goal would be knowledge of the apparently diverse but essentially identical component elements of an homogenous present, in order to master them. Such an essentially 'contemplative' perspective, however, requires that the present of the social totality is represented as an 'object' [*Objekt*], in the specific sense that Marx ascribed to this concept in the first of his *Theses on Feuerbach*: the formal concept of the object of a contemplating subject.[26] Indeed, it is the implicit positing of a subject of this type that is the condition of possibility for the appearance of the world as an 'exposition' of objects for such a contemplative perspective. Conceived in these terms, politics would quickly come to function as a type of knowledge 'produced' by the subject. Formulated in Hegelian metaphors, politics would be represented as a 'self-consciousness' of the structure

---

25   Althusser 1969, p. 204.

26   Previous materialism, Marx argued, conceived of 'the object, actuality, sensuousness [der Gegenstand, die Wirklichkeit, Sinnlichkeit]' 'only in the form of the *object or of contemplation* [nur unter der Form des *Objekts oder der Anschauung*], but not as *human sensuous activity, praxis*'. Feuerbach's attempt to posit objects [*Objekte*] that are really distinct from thought-objects [*Gedankenobjekte*] is judged to fail because he does not conceive 'human activity itself [die menschliche Tätigkeit selbst] as objective activity [*gegenständliche* Tätigkeit]' (Marx and Engels 1978, p. 5). Unlike the indistinct usage of the couplet *Gegenstand/Objekt* in Kant, Marx here distinguishes between them, ascribing to the concept of *Objekt* the role of a formal comprehension of the theory-praxis nexus that he posits as designated more adequately by the active dimensions of the concept of *Gegenstand*. As João Maria de Freitas-Branco (2001) argues, Marx's subtle and often-unnoted terminological innovation plays a decisive role in the development of 'an entirely new type of materialist and dialectical gnoseology'. Regarding Kant's use of the terms, see Pradelle 2004.

of the social totality (here functioning as the equivalent of 'consciousness'), the moment that provides the social totality with knowledge of itself as unified and self-identical. As such, again following Hegel, politics would thus be the goal inscribed in the origin of the social totality, as its moment of completion or self-perfection, as fully contemporaneous with itself.

In such a perspective, the only meaningful form of political conflict would be between various claims to embody such a contemplative comprehension of the 'essential section' of the present. In other words, politics would become the clash of different particular 'subjects' claiming to have privileged knowledge of the 'object' of the present, which would be represented simultaneously as the *Kampfplatz* upon which they contend, and as the spoils of their eventual victory or defeat. Expressed in terms of a model of self-consciousness, each subject would aim to assert its claims to be recognised as the 'authentic' self-consciousness of the present, because, *qua* self-consciousness, its knowledge would ultimately be knowledge of itself, reflecting upon itself. As Althusser's expansive (and admittedly idiosyncratic) definition of 'empiricism' argues, such knowledge could be gained only by means of an 'abstraction from' or even 'extraction' of the 'essence of the object' on the part of the subject,[27] which in turn would be possible because subject and object are supposed to derive from 'an original unity undivided between subject and object', now fallen away from themselves and awaiting their unification in a redeemed, 'synchronised' present.[28] In the words of *For Marx*, at the origin of Althusser's theoretical anti-humanist offensive, 'an empiricism of the subject always corresponds to an idealism of the essence'.[29]

An Alternative Philosophical Grammar

It was this claim that constituted the most radical element of the early Althusser's theoretical anti-humanism's implications for thinking the problem of plural temporalities, which has often been forgotten in critiques of his outline of a concept of historical time that focus on the problem of transition alone.[30]

---

27   Althusser and Balibar 1970, pp. 35–6; p. 38.

28   Althusser and Balibar 1970, p. 63; see Adorno 1982.

29   Althusser 1969, p. 227.

30   For a representative example of this critique, see Osborne 1992. As Barry Hindess (2007) argues, the aim of Althusser's early project was to provide a consistently anti-essentialist theory of the social whole; critiques of its failure to account for change or transition thus arguably shoot wide of the mark, insofar as the notion of a transition (from point

Althusser's initial notion of theoretical anti-humanism was not simply a critique of the notion of the subject conceived in terms of self-consciousness, interiority, or even as a merely formal bearer of subjectivity. It was also a critique of the philosophical grammar of subject-object thought that has dominated modern Western philosophy,[31] a philosophical grammar inscribed in the very structures of what, to use the young Wittgenstein's terms, is 'sayable' and thus 'thinkable' in modern Western European languages in particular.[32] As a corollary, it was thus also a critique of any political formalism (insofar as the latter is based upon a dualism of form/content corresponding to that of subject/object). Althusser's expansion of the notion of 'empiricism' attempted to highlight a secret alliance that had united supposedly opposed materialist and idealist epistemologies; both posited knowledge as a process of the 'discovery' of an 'essence' of the object by a knowing subject, rather than as an active relationality.[33]

In *For Marx*, Althusser claimed that Marx 'drove the philosophical categories of the *subject*, of empiricism, of the *ideal essence*, etc., from all the domains in which they had been supreme ... Marx's materialism excludes the empiricism of the subject (and its inverse: the transcendental subject)'.[34] In *Reading Capital*, he argued that 'the question of the appropriation of the *real, specific* object of knowledge has to be posed: (1) in terms which exclude any recourse to the ideological solution contained in the ideological characters Subject and Object, or to the mutual mirror-recognition structure, in the closed circle of which they move'.[35] The seeming performative contradiction of this formulation was overcome with the decisive (though always unstable) transition to the concepts of articulation, torsion and relationality. *Reading Capital*'s key notion

---

A to point B) itself presupposes precisely that 'structuralist' spatialisation that Althusser's emphasis upon articulation (that is, relationality, or in the terms Althusser himself used, 'differential'; Althusser and Balibar 1970, p. 100) aimed to overcome. See also Chambers 2011. The problem of an adequate theory of the social whole, however, was for Althusser only symptomatic of the deeper problem of overcoming the deeply ingrained 'grammar' of an empiricist epistemology that marks the modern philosophical tradition.

31   Arguably, the multiple recent returns to different notions of a 'non-essentialist' subject in post-Althusserianism, from Butler to Badiou to Balibar's more critical exposition, retreat from this challenge in Athusser's work – a retreat begun by Althusser himself, after the rebuffing of his original humanist offensive in the PCF and his turn to notions of the ideological constitution of a subject-function in the late 1960s.

32   Wittgenstein 2003 [1922].

33   On Althusser's concept of empiricism, see Suchting 1997.

34   Althusser 1969, pp. 228–9.

35   Althusser and Balibar 1970, p. 55.

of the 'object of knowledge' was thereby 'demoted' to the status of a 'place-holder' indicating the relationality inscribed in knowledge itself, in what *For Marx* had characterised as a 'historico-dialectical materialism of praxis'.[36]

> The true 'subjects' (in the sense of constitutive subjects of the process) are therefore not these occupants or functionaries, are not, despite all appearances, the 'obviousness' of the 'given' of naïve anthropology, 'concrete individuals', 'real men' – but *the definition and distribution of these places and functions. The true 'subjects' are these definers and distributors: the relations of production* (and political and ideological social relations). But since these are 'relations', they cannot be thought within the category *subject.*[37]

Althusser instead proposed to explore the development of an alternative philosophical grammar, which would stress relationality over formalism, articulation over structure, displacement over localisation and torsion [*décalage*] over fixity.[38] He was aware of the immensity and perhaps even impossibility of a consistent elaboration of this project:

> It is true that much theoretical work is needed to deal with all the forms of this empiricism sublimated in the 'theory of knowledge' which dominates Western philosophy, to break with its problematic of subject (cogito) and object – *and all their variations.*[39]

The stakes, however, were high: only on the basis of resisting any reconstitution of the concept of structure, the terrain upon which 'subjects' and 'objects' could emerge, would it be possible to think the conditions for a genuinely revolutionary political engagement. The absolute historicist and absolute humanist Gramsci was the privileged object of this critique insofar as he provided the most rigorous and sophisticated formulation of such an ideological concept of historical time, its essentialist presuppositions and subjectivist consequences.

---

36   Althusser 1969, p. 229.
37   Althusser and Balibar 1970, p. 180.
38   See Althusser and Balibar 1970, p. 100; p. 104; p. 108.
39   Althusser and Balibar 1970, p. 184; my italics.

Non-Contemporaneity of the Present

Building upon recent philological work founded on Gerratana's critical edition of the *Prison Notebooks* (1975), I have argued elsewhere that the critique of *Reading Capital* ascribes positions to Gramsci that are not to be found in his texts;[40] arguably, they are not to be found in Hegel's texts either.[41] This is not to say that Althusser's reading was simply mistaken, however, in the sense of a mere misreading or epistemological failure. Rather, Althusser's interpretation has the status of one of those 'necessary failures' of any reading, a 'productive error' that has the capacity to reveal hitherto neglected elements. The great merit of Althusser's reading was precisely to have directed our attention to the themes of non-contemporaneity in Gramsci's thought; indeed, it was perhaps only the polemical force of Althusser's intervention that finally made it possible to read features of Gramsci's thought that previously had seemed illegible, beneath that level of visibility that an established interpretative tradition (the more Crocean than Gramscian historicism of the PCI) had allowed.

What emerges from this new perspective is a vision of Gramsci as a pre-eminent theorist of the non-contemporaneity of the present. Gramsci's own

---

40   See Thomas 2009, pp. 243–306. For earlier attempts to assess the cogency of Althusser's critique, see see Buci-Glucksmann 1980, Tosel 1995, pp. 5–26, Haug 2006, and Coassin-Spiegel 1997. Althusser's critique is in fact a critique of precisely those ahistorical elements of Croce's thought that Gramsci himself had subjected to a thoroughgoing refutation. For the arguably more neo-Kantian than neo-Hegelian Croce, the present is truly and necessarily identical with itself, contemporaneous in all the component parts of an omni-present *Spirito* that contains (synchronic) 'distinctions' but not (diachronic) 'real differences'; in Althusser's terms, all components within it 'always co-exist in one and the same time, one and the same present' (Althusser and Balibar 1970, p. 105). The Althusserian concept of an 'essential section' seems almost designed to capture precisely the *difference* between Croce's ostensibly 'immanentist' 'reform' of Hegelianism and Gramsci's emphasis upon the dimensions of Hegelianism ('especially ... its attempt to overcome the traditional conceptions of "idealism" and "materialism"') that could be re-proposed in a more strongly non-metaphysical and political register. See Q 4, § 11, p. 433. On Gramsci's critique of Croce, see Frosini 2003, pp. 123–7.

41   On the temporal status of Hegel's *Geist*, see Finelli 2004, pp. 102–23. Althusser not only attributed essentially Crocean positions to Gramsci; his reading of Hegel itself seems to have been fundamentally marked by positions close to those developed by Croce (see, e.g., Althusser and Balibar 1970, p. 105). As a large number of critics have pointed out, such a reductive account fails to do justice to Hegel's more complex account of historical time, in which the concept of uneven development plays a much more prominent role. For a representative example, see Hindess 2007.

proposed refoundation of Marxism involved a critique of essentialism in all its forms (in the sense of refusing not only the notion of essence, but also that of any originary or foundational moment), and a fundamental critique of 'subjectivism' (thus refusing not only a philosophy of consciousness, but also the philosophical grammar integrally related to the modern concept of the subject). Nothing could be further from the orienting perspectives of Gramsci's thought than the notions of an 'essential section', an expressivist totality, or an homogenous 'present' that could be contemporary with itself. Viewed from a certain perspective, the *Prison Notebooks* can be regarded as an immense encyclopaedia of the numerous temporal and spatial 'dislocations' that characterise the distinctive nature of modern historical experience. For Gramsci, the present is necessarily non-identical with itself, composed of numerous 'times' that do not coincide or are regulated by a common measure. Rather than being expressive of an essence equally present in all practices, the present for Gramsci is precisely an ensemble of those practices in their different temporalities, each struggling to assert their primacy in relation to the others in relational terms, and without reference to what Althusser characterised as the notion of a 'single ideological base time', against which 'backwardness' or 'forwardness' would be measured.[42] Any unity of those different times that is achieved in the notion of the present remains always provisional, and must be violently imposed against their constitutive plurality. In the terms of the late Althusser, the unification of plural times in any 'present' constitutes an achieved or 'accomplished fact'. As an historical result, such a unified configuration thus remains permanently revocable; an encounter that may or may not continue to take place.[43]

The full development of Gramsci's notion of the philosophy of praxis as 'the absolute historicism' does not reduce Marxism to a mere expression of the Hegelian matrix from which, in part, it emerged. On the contrary, with this critical appropriation of a central Crocean term, Gramsci aimed to indicate precisely the historical and theoretical distance that separated Marx's thought both from Hegel and from his latter day imitators. It was a characterisation founded upon an historical analysis of historicism as both philosophical doctrine and political current in the 'long nineteenth century'. Gramsci's argument that Marxism could be characterised as the 'absolute' form of this tradition did not imply a model of Hegelian absolute knowledge, in which Marxist theory would function as a self-consciousness of history, which, *qua* self-

---

42   Althusser and Balibar 1970, p. 105.

43   Althusser 2006, p. 169. For reflections on the notion of an 'accomplished fact' in the late Althusser, see Morfino 2009, pp. 79–99 and Morfino 2012a.

consciousness of a subject, would finally allow the object of the present to be fully contemporaneous with and transparent to itself. Rather, Gramsci deployed the adjective 'absolute' to indicate the materialist conception of history's intensification of the (German and Italian) historicist tradition's emphasis upon the historical situatedness of thought. Marxism is 'an absolute historicism', according to Gramsci, insofar as it rigorously refuses the last vestiges of an ahistorical metaphysics by historicising the realm of conceptuality itself. Rather than the consequence of an emanationist model of the social totality, Gramsci's complex identification of philosophy and history, under the aegis of politics, instead presupposes an anti-essentialist theory of translatability. In turn, this gives rise to a definition of philosophy not as the expression of an essence (the temporal and logical priority of which would guarantee the unity of the 'present's' manifold expressions, including – pre-eminently – its philosophical realisation), but as a particularly intense form of organisation – and potentially, transformation – of this constitutive heterogeneity.

La Grande Politica

Far from a negation of the possibility of revolutionary politics of the new and its replacement by modes of administration of the given, Gramsci's reflections on the non-contemporaneity of the present lead him to formulate a theory of politics as socio-political transformation aiming towards the foundation of a new 'integral civilisation'.[44] The meaning of 'politics' in the fullest sense – 'la grande politica' of struggle between major historical classes, which Gramsci distinguishes from 'la piccola politica' of intra-bourgeois intrigue – undergoes an expansion during the development of the *Prison Notebooks* research project.[45] In his historical studies and reflections on contemporary politics, Gramsci uses the term 'politics' in one of its established usages, to indicate a determinate practice (the art of 'government') occurring within a specific 'space' in the social formation (that is, within the institutions of 'political society'). In his reflections upon the nature of the modern state and its possible overcoming, however, he also increasingly uses 'politics' to signify forms of conflictual practice that are diffused throughout the 'integral state', conceived as a dialectical unity of political society and civil society.[46] These practices, *qua* practices,

---

44   Q 11, § 27, p. 1434.

45   Q 8, § 48, p. 970.

46   For one of the first attempts to think through the complexity of the vocabulary of Gramsci's state theory, see Francioni 1984.

cannot be grasped according to spatial metaphors, but need to be thought in terms of a complex overdetermined relationality of command and subordination that constitutes the integral state; it is precisely this dialectic between political and civil society as distinct modes of relationality, rather than the valorisation of one term as privileged locus of political activity, that constitutes the specificity of the Gramscian theory of hegemony.[47]

Consequently, in a critical inheritance of Hegel's state theory and of Marx's critique of it, Gramsci argues that 'political society' and 'civil society' themselves cannot simply be grasped as different 'zones' in the integral state. Rather, they need to be conceptualised as different forms of hegemonic practice, dialectically and integrally related to each other; ultimately, the relational metaphor displaces the topographical one, which nevertheless continues to be deployed in a provisional and heuristic sense.[48] Political society is comprehended as a condensation and overdetermination of the conflictuality that constitutes the quotidian weft and warp of civil society; civil society, in its turn, is thought as a mediated and ultimately subaltern form of the organising instances and political rationality elaborated most fully in the form of the relations of political society.[49] In another vocabulary, we could talk of the integral relation between organisation (from 'above') and association (from 'below'), where each instance depends upon the difference of the other in order to be itself. In the terms of a theory of plural historical times, political society and civil society represent relatively autonomous 'times' of the social formation, with differential rhythms of development and moments of efficacy.

In this perspective, the 'times' of political society and civil society necessarily do not coincide; their temporal disjunction produces their relation as always uneven and asymmetrical.[50] *La grande politica* for Gramsci becomes the struggle of the subaltern relationality of civil society to break with the impos-

---

47   For this reason, among others, *pace* Bobbio, Gramsci cannot be reduced to a proponent of civil society against that state.

48   The decisive 'transitional' note is Q 12, § 1, p. 1518.

49   In one decisive formulation, Gramsci refers to political society as the 'enwrapping' [*involucro*] of civil society; in Hegelian terms, political society as represented as the 'form' of the 'content' of civil society. See Q 8, § 130, p. 1020.

50   The early Althusser continued to think the possibility of a unifying instance of the social formation, located in the 'economic', determinant 'in the last instance'. The claim to a relational model of overdetermination was arguably thereby annulled, insofar as the economic played the role of a functional, if not essential, founding instance. Gramsci, on the other hand, by emphasising the constitutive and mutually implicated nature of civil and political society, provides a more consistently relational model.

ition by the existing political society (both as ensemble of institutions and as a relationality of 'political rationality') of an interpellating 'single ideological base time' that eternalises the existing state of affairs in an 'essential section' of relations of domination and exploitation. Such a politics 'of another type' emerges not as 'another' self-consciousness of what exists (e.g. in the form of a battle between civil society against political society), but by means of an intervention within and against the existing 'political society'. Rather than the self-consciousness of civil society (posited as the object of political society's narcissistic reflection upon its own subaltern self), political society in this perspective is instead reconfigured as a moment of organisation immanent to association, a 'time' of self-regulation internal to each of the plural times that continuously undermines their self-identity from within: a distinctive form of non-identitarian political relationality.

Given the constitutive non-contemporaneity of any social formation and of any of its constitutive elements or practices, the 'present' for Gramsci thus can only be conceived as a continual interweaving of many different 'times'. This is not simply a question of a simultaneity of diverse times, according to a model of the survival of anachronisms within what remains, 'in the last instance', a unitary and determining present, now conceived as an 'uneven' (though arguably equally 'essential') section.[51] Such a notion of the present, conceived as a structure that constitutes the shared terrain of plural times, runs the risk of surreptitiously relapsing into a notion of a fundamental contemporaneity: the present is conceived as both a *Kampfplatz* of different times, and as also constituting their common measure (*qua* structure in which their plurality is localised).[52] While elements of such a model of pro- or anachronistic time (prefigurations of the future and survivals of the past) are operative in the *Prison*

---

51   See Althusser and Balibar 1970, p. 105.

52   Althusser was well aware of this risk when he argued against relating plural temporalities to each other by means of positing the 'line of a single continuous reference time' (Althusser and Balibar 1970, p. 105). 'But this does not mean that we are dealing with an uneven section, a stepped or multiply toothed section in which the forwardness or backwardness of one time with respect to another is illustrated in temporal space in the way that the lateness or earliness of trains are illustrated in the SNCF's notice-boards by a spatial forwardness or backwardness'. As an alternative, Althusser argued that 'It is not enough, therefore, to say ... that each time has its own rhythms, some short, some long; we must also think these differences in rhythm and punctuation in their foundation, in the type of articulation, displacement and torsion which harmonises these different times with on another' (p. 100). It is an emphasis upon this notion of the primacy of articulation – and not simply a link between the theory of historical times and the theory of the social formation – that could prevent Althusser's theory from falling into a structur-

Notebooks, they are modified by Gramsci's parallel development of a theory of the 'non-presence of the present'. This perspective progressively deconstructs the notion of the present as either a point on a linear continuum, a spatial coordinate, or an archaeological layer. What is at stake in this concept is the constitutive fracturing of the 'present' itself, such that it cannot be comprehended as a 'section', whether 'essential' or 'uneven'. In other words, it cannot be comprehended with the topological metaphor of a 'structure', as a totalised hierarchy of elements whose relation is fixed prior to their relation by the totality itself. Instead, Gramsci attempts to think the 'conjunctural' dimensions of any given present (whereby conjuncture is not understood as a 'minorstructure', but as the process of active 'conjoining' of relational elements).[53] Each element in such a constellation only has meaning in terms of its dynamic relation to the others, without reference to a predetermined and predetermining structure. In Althusser's not entirely consistent terms, it is a question of the 'intertwining' and '"dislocation" (*décalage*) and torsion of the different times and temporalities produced by the different levels of the structure, the complex combination of which constitutes the peculiar time of the process's development'.[54] The present for Gramsci is ultimately to be thought not as a *Kampfplatz* of these plural times, but rather as the process of the continual interweaving and unwinding of these immanent 'relations of force' that constitute the plural temporalities of hegemony.[55]

Theoretical Anti-Humanism avant la Lettre

Gramsci develops his research on the non-contemporaneity in a series of interlocking themes throughout the *Prison Notebooks*. One of the most significant forms in which this dislocation of the present is played out occurs at the level

---

alist diachronic/synchronic distinction, and thence into the reconstitution of a notion of homogenous time. Althusser's own formulations, however, did not always draw the full implications of this insight. See Chambers 2011, p. 200 and p. 208.

53   For a survey of different meanings of the notion of 'conjuncture' in modern political and social thought that emphasise this active sense, see Koivisto and Lahtinen 2012.

54   Althusser and Balibar 1970, p. 104. The notion that such dislocation is 'produced by the different levels of the structure', rather than constituting the relations that are comprehended in formal terms by the concept of 'structure' itself, highlights the radical instability of Althusser's project in this period, as his attempt to think new problems was constrained by an older vocabulary.

55   On the concept of 'relations of force' in Gramsci, see Coutinho 2009.

of the constitution of the 'person [*la persona*]' – the Gramscian alternative to a theory of the subject, a term that is noticeable in the *Prison Notebooks* above all by its marginal usage.[56] Gramsci employs the notion of the person in terms relatively distant from its later moral dimension (from early Christian theological appropriations through to Kant) and closer to its classical theatrical sense, as a role or mask adopted in exterior relations to other roles. In terms remarkably similar to those employed by Freud's famous analogy of Rome and the Unconscious,[57] the person is not defined as a subject with a unitary and unifying essence, but as a 'living archaeological site' in which different levels of historical experience are 'at work'. Such a bizarrely composed personality contains

> Stone Age elements and principles of a more advanced science, prejudices from all past phases of history at the local level and intuitions of a future philosophy which will be that of a human race united the world over [...]. The starting-point of critical elaboration is the consciousness of what one really is, and is 'knowing thyself' as a product of the historical process to date which has deposited in you an infinity of traces, without leaving an inventory.[58]

Compiling an inventory of such an 'infinity of traces' is the starting point for elaborating a critical knowledge that forms the basis, not for mastering these contradictions in an act of self-consciousness, but rather, for the intensification of an 'element of contradiction' within the continuing 'taking hold' of the encounter that constitutes the person just as much as the history of philo-

---

56 A consolidated tradition of Gramscian commentary, with increasing frequency in recent years, has invoked Gramsci to elaborate a theory of the political subject, or a theory of political subjectivity. However, the concept of the 'subject', declined in the classical terms of introspection/self-consciousness/intentionality/authorship, appears only 15 times in over 2000 pages in the *Prison Notebooks*; in the majority of cases, Gramsci transcribes it as a part of a quotation from another writer or is stimulated to use it by the vocabulary of the writer under discussion. The mere absence of the 'word', of course, does not demonstrate the non-presence of the concept itself, traces of versions of which are arguably still operative in certain prominent passages of the *Prison Notebooks*. It does indicate, however, that Gramsci was attempting to work towards an alternative philosophical vocabulary for comprehending the conditions of political action, beyond the main currents of modern political conceptuality. On this theme, see Frosini 2010, pp. 28–9.

57 For a discussion of this elective affinity, see Urbinati 1998, p. 379.

58 Q 11, §12, p. 1376.

sophy.[59] In other words, knowledge of the lack of unity of the present is not a prelude to its unification; rather, it exacerbates its non-identity, signalling the existence of different tendencies and relations of force within each incoherent personality and posing the problem of their relative valorisation.

It may seem here that Gramsci posits a model of plural times in which archaeological diversity is underwritten by the unification implicit in the notion of the co-presence, or contemporaneity, of the person. Yet alongside such a model of the incoherent and 'bizarrely composite' person as an 'anachronism',[60] he also develops analyses of the fracturing of the person in terms of its constitutive dislocation, not simply between past, present and future, but in the present itself. Participation in numerous 'conceptions of the world' (accentuated in 'modern' societies but operative in sociality as such) occurs in the form of different practices of linguistic, social and political organisation, each with their own temporal and spatial organisation.[61] One is therefore never simply or immediately a contemporary with oneself, but is always split between the rhythms, intensities, durations and modifications of different conceptions of the world, synchronised only fleetingly and forcefully. The person is thus ultimately conceived as an unstable organisation of conflicting tendencies and times that can only be provisionally and precariously united in the contemporaneity of a consistent or 'coherent' personhood by the dominance of one temporal order: above all, that of the juridico-political practices of the state.

Gramsci thus increasingly comes to view the person as something similar to what Deleuze characterised as a 'disjunctive synthesis':[62] a relation of non-relation that does not posit difference as the condition of possibility of unity (temporal disjunction as the basis for eventual unification in the contemporaneity of the present), but as the ongoing mode of existence of the person as an organisation of conflicting tendencies.[63] As a 'conjuncture of conjunctures', the

---

59   Q 11, § 62, p. 1487.

60   Q 11, § 12, p. 1377.

61   On the distinctive notion of a 'conception of the world' in the *Prison Notebooks*, see Q 4, § 1, 419; Q 101, § 5, 1217; Q 101, § 10, 1231. On Gramsci's development of this concept in relation to the debate in Italian neo-idealism, see Liguori 2006. Nemeth 1980 explores its relation to the phenomenological tradition.

62   See Deleuze 1990.

63   Gramsci's reflections in the period leading up to a profound crisis of his health in March 1933 contain several significant notes on the constitutively conflictual formation of the person. See his letter to Tania of 6 March 1933 (Gramsci 1993) and Q 15, § 9, pp. 1762–4, where he articulates these reflections with his notion of 'molecular' composition.

'coherence' of the person is built not by effacing the different times that compose it, but by setting them to work alongside each other, interweaving their
distinctive tempos and rhythms in the form of a project.

Language as 'Metaphor'

Gramsci also finds layers or sediments of different historical experiences and
times sitting together in an uncomfortable *modus vivendi* in the formation
of languages – unsurprisingly, given Gramsci's university training in historical linguistics under Matteo Bartoli.[64] Responding to a marginal comment by
Bukharin regarding the merely 'metaphorical' use of certain terms from the
Western philosophical tradition in the work of Marx and Engels, Gramsci outlines a theory of metaphor as symptomatic of the historical nature of language,
composed of layers of inherited conventions and modes of expression interact-
ing unevenly with contemporary novelties of usage.

> Current language is metaphorical with respect to the meanings and the
> ideological content that words have had in preceding periods of civilisa-
> tion. [...] Language is transformed with the transformation of the whole of
> civilisation, through the acquisition of culture by new classes and through
> the hegemony exercised by one national language over others, etc., and
> what it does is precisely to absorb in metaphorical form the words of pre-
> vious civilisations and cultures.[65]

The notion of language as a temporal sedimentation, however, is also com-
plemented by analyses that register the internal differentiation of language in
the present, in the different linguistic communities that emerge in relation to
national languages and those languages that are retrospectively defined as their
'dialects'. Gramsci analyses dialects and national languages not in terms of hierarchical relations of degeneration or purity, but in terms of the different tempos
of historical development of regional and ultimately class formations, linked
to the conditions of political subalternity or hegemonic direction that shape
the communities of their practitioners. 'Dialects' are thus not seen as 'residues
of the past', but as actively constructed by the differential temporalities con-

---

64   On Gramsci's academic formation in historical comparative linguistics and its continuing
      influence on his prison writings, see Ives 2004; Schirru, 2011; Carlucci 2013.

65   Q 11, § 24, p. 1428.

stituting the present, 'interpellated' by the political overdetermination of the state ratification and promotion of national languages. Gramsci explores the political implications of this insight of historicist linguistics in his final notebook (Notebook 29), particularly with the elaboration of an historicist critique of normative grammar – a veritable historical materialist grammatology *avant la lettre*.[66]

The analysis of appearances of linguistic 'anachronism' as politically overdetermined relations of force leads Gramsci to move towards a model of language as the most elementary and perhaps even paradigmatic form of an organising 'conception of the world'. Above all, it prompts him to further develop his non-essentialist theory of translatability. Central here was Gramsci's continual mediation on Lenin's brief remarks on the difficulty of 'translating' the 'language' of the Russian Revolution into the languages of Western Europe.[67] Following Lenin's own metaphorical use of the notion of language in that statement, Gramsci from the outset expanded the concept of translation beyond strictly linguistic phenomena. 'Translatability' gradually comes to assume the status of a central organising perspective of Gramsci's philosophical reflections in the *Prison Notebooks*, indicating a relational and thus anti-essentialist methodology of philosophical research; in short, a dialectical method.[68] 'Translation' in this perspective is conceived as a constitutive relationality that cannot be reduced to a process of originary or retrospective unification or synchronisation. Grasped in its fullest sense, it involves the construction of lines of communication between different practices whose relations are not premised either on interiority, or an identical essence or an *Ursprache* immanently present in all, or on exteriority, in which discrete essences confront each other in subject-object relations.

---

66   Both the anarchonistic and conjunctural analysis of the times of contemporary languages are found in Gramsci's response to Croce's failure to provide an adequate definition of grammar: 'Grammar is "history" or an "historical document": it is the "photograph" of a determinate phase of a national (collective) language (which has been formed historically and is in continual development), or the fundamental features of a photograph. The practical question can be: for what end is such a photograph made? In order to write the history of an aspect of the civilisation, or in order to modify an aspect of the civilisation?' (Q 29, § 1, p. 2341).

67   See Q 11, § 46, p. 1468.

68   The theme of 'translatability' in the *Prison Notebooks* constitutes the focus of Boothman 2004. Ives 2004 examines the concept both in relation to other Marxist thinkers and significant currents in twentieth-century theories of language. Frosini also emphasises the importance of the concept of 'translatability' for the elaboration of Gramsci's philosophy of praxis (2010, pp. 31–3; pp. 167–77).

Thus, for Gramsci, the relationship between philosophy, politics and history was not to be thought in terms of a hierarchy of (either mediated and temporally distinct or immediate-expressivist) causal relations, but in terms of their dialectical interpenetration, each comprehending the others in their own particular modes. Above all, the notion of translatability is central to Gramsci's notion of the relationship of theory and practice, which he posits not as a simple *unity* of theory and practice (such a unity being premised upon their prior distinction), but as the process of their *active identification* through the intensification of relations of translation.[69] Theory and practice thus come to be immanent to each other through a process of progressive experimentation, as the practical dimensions of theory, as a form of highly mediated organisation, encounter the theoretical dimensions of emergent practices, as new forms of organisation *in nuce*.

The National and International

The non-contemporaneity of the present is starkly demonstrated in Gramsci's analysis of modern state formation and the geopolitical system. The present of individual nation states is fractured into competing times, particularly in the relations between urban centres and rural peripheries (one role of which is to provide the metropolitan present with a stereotypical image of its 'past', giving rise to and being played out in the temporal dislocations of internal migration). On an international level, the hegemonic relationships between different national formations seem to consign some social formations to the past 'times' of others, as instances of underdevelopment. Gramsci's most famous characterisation of the East in comparison to the West, which he derived from Lenin and Trotsky's reflections on the reasons for the success of the Russian Revolution and the failures of revolutions in the West, argues that

> In the East, the State was everything, civil society was primordial and gelatinous; in the West, there was a proper relationship between State and civil society, and when the State trembled a sturdy structure of civil society was at once revealed. The State was only an outer trench, behind which there was a powerful chain of fortresses and earthworks.[70]

---

69   See Q 15, § 22, p. 1780.

70   Q 7, § 16, p. 866.

This formulation has sometimes been read as presupposing a normative and progressivist notion of capitalist development, or even an 'ideal type' of the advanced modern state absent in an 'exceptional' and underdeveloped Orient. In reality, however, the distinction here between East and West, and their unification within a world system, is analytic rather than substantive; it allows us to grasp the fact that it is the tempo and efficacy of the international imperialist system that seeks to impose a unity on the disparity of different national historical experiences, as they are progressively drawn within the homogenising and synchronising dynamics of the world market. This synchronisation then serves as the basis for the subsequent production of states of 'backwardness or forwardness in time, i.e., the ideological reference time',[71] defining some social formations as of the 'East' and others as of the 'West'.[72] In this sense, Gramsci can be regarded as advancing his own theory of combined and uneven development, as a number of critics have recently begun to suggest.[73]

For Gramsci as for Trotsky and Lenin, it was thus not a question of positing the early Comintern's concrete analysis of 'East' and 'West' in the conjuncture of the early 1920s in terms of a universal model of civilisational progress, of the arguably 'orientialist' type that became prominent in oppositions that (re-)emerged later in the twentieth century, such as those between developed and underdeveloped countries, centre and periphery, North and South, and so forth. Rather, the challenge was to grasp the ways in which varying combinations of relations of force had been condensed differentially in various state formations, producing rather than being produced by an overdetermining geopolitical dynamic. Furthermore, directly referring to the terms of the early Comintern debates (that is, regarding the relative strength of state apparatuses in different countries, based on their different traditions and experiences of class struggle), Gramsci also discovers temporal disjunctions within each of his key terms. Italy is here a key instance: though seemingly of the 'West', Gramsci discovers important elements in the development of political relations in

---

71   Althusser and Balibar 1970, p. 105. On the contradictions and synchronisation of the *Weltmarkt*, see Tomba 2009.

72   Gramsci's critique of 'objectivism' also leads him to note the practical social relation embodied in such seemingly 'objective' criteria as geographical coordinates: 'I recall an affirmation of Bertrand Russell: we cannot, without the existence of man, think of the existence of Glasgow and London, but we can think of the existence of two points on the surface of the earth, one to the North and one to the South [...] But without the existence of man, what would North and South, and "point", and "surface" and "earth", mean?' (Q 4, § 41, p. 467).

73   See Morton 2010 and 2011.

Italy that seem much closer to certain 'Oriental' forms, particularly in the systematic relations of subjugation and subalternity defining the Italian South.[74] Similarly, though seemingly a stronghold of the 'West', as Gramsci's reflections on the possibility of 'Americanism' as a future civilisational model suggest, his analysis of the USA highlights key aspects that seem to place it much closer to features that a subsequent tradition of commentary has commonly associated with the 'type' of the 'East'. In particular, the apparent relative absence in the North American social formation of elaborated institutions of civil society leads Gramsci to argue that in the USA, hegemony begins directly in the factory (as opposed to the mediations of the network of 'trench systems' that characterised civil society in Europe after the French Revolution).[75] The different times of the national and international are for Gramsci thus always relative to each other, depending upon their different forms of articulation and 'intertwining' in any given conjuncture, be it always 'exceptional' national situations or geopolitical distinctions. One of the names for such 'nodal points' was, precisely, hegemony.[76]

The Philosophy of an Epoch

Althusser had feared that Gramsci's equation of philosophy and history risked reducing the former, and Marxist philosophy in particular, to the status of an 'organic ideology', the direct expression of a unified present, or merely 'its time expressed in thought', to use the often misquoted Hegelian phrase invoked by Althusser himself.[77] Yet for Gramsci, not only is philosophy not conceived as the expression of an essence of the presence, but philosophy itself is temporally split and divided; at a limit, he will come to posit a non-contemporaneity within the notion of philosophy itself. One of the central philosophical developments in the *Prison Notebooks* consists in the distinctive relationship established between philosophy and ideology. Philosophy is not defined in opposition to ideology, in a rationalist perspective. Rather, Gramsci defines both philosophy and ideology in political and historical terms, as forms of organisation of social relations, or 'conceptions of the world'. In this perspective,

---

74   Fontana 2010 explores the intertwining of the couplets of North/South and West/East,
     particularly in relation to the theme of subalternity and Gramsci's relation to more recent
     debates around the notion of Orientalism.
75   Q 1, § 61, p. 70. See Q 6, § 10, p. 692; Q 8, § 185, p. 1053.
76   See Q 14, § 68, p. 1729.
77   Althusser and Balibar 1970, p. 131.

ideology is not understood as epistemological error, but rather, in terms close to those used by the late Althusser, as a concrete form of experience – though in Gramsci's case, as an experience of the ordering of class society, rather than of the ' "world" ... experienced in its dispersion'.[78] Gramsci distinguishes philosophy from ideology only in 'quantitative', not 'qualitative', terms, with an explicitly temporal reference. He argues that 'philosophy is the conception of the world that represents the intellectual and moral life (catharsis of a determinate practical life) of an entire social group conceived in movement and thus seen not only in its current and immediate interests, but also in its future and mediated interests'. Ideology, on the other hand, Gramsci defines in this instance as 'any particular conception of groups inside the class that propose to help in the resolution of immediate and circumscribed problems'.[79]

Philosophy is not here posited as a direct expression of a unified essence of the present. On the contrary, while ideology is grasped in its contradictory (rather than organic or expressivist) relation to the present, philosophy functions to negate the present's ideological self-reference; it is constituted only insofar as it provides a conceptual comprehension of the present's internal dislocation by the historical movement between past, present and future. In another formulation, Gramsci posits an effectively nominalist definition of philosophy, as the description of an achieved ensemble of conflicting conceptions of the world, whose unity as 'philosophy' is always only retrospective, temporary and provisional. He argues that

> the philosophy of an epoch is not the philosophy of this or that philosopher, of this or that group of intellectuals, of this or that broad section of the popular masses. It is a process of combination of all these elements, which culminates in an overall trend in which the culmination becomes a norm of collective action and becomes concrete and complete (integral) 'history'. The philosophy of an historical epoch is, therefore, nothing other than the 'history' of that epoch itself, nothing other than the mass of variations that the leading group has succeeded in imposing on preceding reality. History and philosophy are in this sense indivisible. They form a 'bloc'.[80]

---

78   Althusser 2006, p. 179. While Althusser here refers to Spinoza, the terms of his discussion are very close to a phenomenological perspective of ideology as coinciding with the *Lebenswelt*.

79   Q 10I, § 10, p. 1231. The *Prison Notebooks* contain a range of 'critical', 'neutral' and 'positive' definitions of ideology. See Jan Rehmann 2008, pp. 82–101, and Liguori 2006.

80   Q 10II, § 17, p. 1255.

This is not a question of such a philosophy finally providing the adequate expression of a previously misrecognised essence, in the production of a philosophy that would be able to master its time, 'expressing' it in conceptual form and thereby completing it. The 'philosophy of an epoch' for Gramsci is not like Hegel's owl of Minerva, arriving at the close of the day in a speculative form; rather, it is an analytic description of the real existence of different philosophical practices, corresponding to different political practices, in any given conjuncture.[81] Nor is the identification of history and philosophy indicative of an expressivist relationship between the two; rather, it serves to emphasise the immanent relation to practice that sustains both philosophy and ideology, as the translation of conflicting organisational forms into 'intellectual orders'.[82]

Gramsci's decisive conceptual breakthrough consists in the redefinition of philosophy as a practice that is immanent to ideology, rather than exterior or opposed to it. Ideology is, among other things, a conception of the world; but it is confused and disorganised, lacking in the coherence that would permit it to increase the subaltern social groups' capacity to act in the face of the demobilising logic of the passive revolution.[83] The philosophy of praxis emerges as the immanent critique of ideology, re-articulating its incoherence, in the same sense that *buon senso* represents the immanent critique of the limitations of *senso comune*. Both the philosophy of praxis and *buon senso* are distinguished from their 'others' only in the sense that they represent more elaborate and critical forms of organisation. While ideology and *senso comune* fall prey to the present in a mimetic relation, philosophy and *buon senso* set to work the distinctive time of critique within and against the present, rupturing its claim to closure in self-identity and exclusion of difference.

The Plural Temporalities of Hegemony

Above all, the *Prison Notebooks* theorise the non-contemporaneity of the present in relation to the concept and practice of hegemony. As inherited by Gramsci from the debates of Russian Social Democracy and the early years of the Third International, hegemony was conceived as a form of political leadership founded upon the different historical times and temporal experiences co-present in a given national social formation. 'Advanced' social groups (the

---

81   On the notion of the conflict of different philosophical practices, see Read 2005.
82   Q 11, § 12, p. 1378.
83   Ibid.

urban industrial working classes) attempted to elaborate a political programme that would be able to gain the active support and participation of social groups still mired within 'anachronistic' social relations (particularly the rural peasantry). The non-contemporaneity of these instances – an urban 'present' seeking to guide the development of a rural 'past' – was thus understood as both index of the contradictions of 'modernisation', and as political opportunity for an ulterior development. Gramsci's reflections on the Italian 'Southern Question' in particular have seemed to many critics to explore this sense of hegemony as a 'leveraging' of temporal distinction. In this perspective, Gramsci's notion of the emergence of a 'regulated society' has been understood as a process of temporal 'synchronisation', or the affirmation of a genuine contemporaneity of a society transparent to itself, according to the terms in which some of Marx and Engels's formulations from the 1840s have often been caricatured.[84]

The *Prison Notebooks*' development of the concept of hegemony in relation to the notions of the 'integral state' and 'passive revolution', however, lead Gramsci to problematise the presupposition of such a process of modernisation: namely, the notion of a particular present of technological and sociopolitical development and organisation as a standard in comparison to which other instances represent untimely variations. In particular, Gramsci's distinction between different forms of hegemony opposes the type of historical time presupposed and enacted by the passive revolution of nineteenth-century state formation and consolidation to a type of historical time operative within what he comes to call the 'subaltern social classes' or 'groups'.[85] Passive revolution for Gramsci comes to signify a temporal regime of accumulation, repetition and hierarchical synchronisation, in which the past is 'fixed' in the present, and as inevitable future, consigning subaltern social groups to the 'margins of history'.[86] Alberto Burgio has characterised this time of state power in the *Prison Notebooks* in Benjaminian terms, as a time of 'duration', a 'development of an inert time, mere quantity adequately measured in chronological terms [...] an *empty* time'.[87] The historical time of the subaltern social groups, on the other hand, particularly as they seek forms of social and political autonomy and assert the centrality of their own histories, is represented in almost weak messianic terms. It 'implies rupturing this continuum', shattering its linearity and filling up this empty time 'with an event (an ensemble of events) which

---

84   On the notion of a (self-)regulated society in Gramsci, cf. Q 6, § 65, p. 734; Q 6, § 88, pp. 763–4; Q 7, § 33, p. 882.

85   See, in particular, Q 8, § 227, p. 1084.

86   'On the margins of history (history of subaltern social groups)' is the title of notebook 25.

87   Burgio 2002, pp. 19–20.

modifies the rhythm, the intensity, the meaning itself of historical movement, imparting to it an acceleration and determining its progress'.[88]

Hegemonic politics, born on the terrain of this clash of temporal orders, thus presupposes temporal difference between 'moments' in a hegemonic project, as both its condition of possibility, and as the 'motor' driving its development. Furthermore, each specific hegemonic project can only be grasped in terms of the particular interweaving of the differential times of the elements that constitute it; while the logic of the passive revolution of bourgeois politics aims to 'fix' those times in relations of domination, the hegemonic practice of the emergence from subalternity posits their difference as constitutive. It is this dimension that prevents the Gramscian concept of hegemony from being a leftist version of the Hobbesian covenant, or a communist reformulation of a Rousseauian General Will, both of which aim 'to synchronise' different times in a definitive political unity. Proletarian hegemony among the subaltern social groups, on the other hand, does not aim to establish or maintain a hierarchy that fixes the more 'advanced' times (those who govern) and those that are more 'backward' (the governed) in a hierarchical order.[89] Rather, Gramsci disaggregates 'leadership' from 'government'; a political practice that works towards the disappearance of the 'the necessity of the existence of [the] division' between the governors and the governed redefines leadership in relational-pedagogical terms, as the tendential emergence of practices of self-leadership. It is in this sense that the constitutively plural times and temporalities of hegemony, and the constitutive non-synchronisation of hegemony, represent a potential foundation for a distinctive mode of socio-political relationality.

The Marxist notion of class struggle is thus progressively reformulated in the *Prison Notebooks* in terms of a clash not simply between different interests, subjects or modes of production, but also between different temporal regimes. Their 'contemporaneity' is not given, but rather, only emerges temporally – and temporarily – as a function of the social and political hegemony of one social group seeking to impose its own 'present' as an insurpassable horizon for other social groups. It is precisely in its distinction from this process of synchronisation that Gramsci's conception of hegemony not as a system of power but as a strategic perspective and 'method' of political work finds its fullest meaning.

---

88   Ibid.
89   For Gramsci's reflections on this 'primordial fact' of politics, see Q 15, § 4, p. 1752.

The 'Ruse' of Structure

Gramsci should thus be regarded as a significant theorist of temporal dislocation, positing the existence of plural times and their conflictual relation as determinant of any given present. Rather than simply the contemporaneity of the non-contemporaneous, the *Prison Notebooks* attempt to think the non-contemporaneity of contemporaneity itself, of the extent to which the present is not identical with itself but is constitutively fractured between competing historical times or temporal regimes. However, has Gramsci thereby avoided the most disabling of the consequences of an expressivist and essentialist notion of the present, arriving at it, so to speak, via a long detour that turns out to have merely been another way to rejoin the main path of the modern philosophical tradition? As Althusser had noted, it is possible to produce the effects of a spiritualist conception of the social totality and its accompanying 'ideology of a homogenous-continuous/self-contemporaneous time' by other means.[90] A model of plural times, in itself, does not necessarily provide immunity against the complement of an essentialist notion of the present, or against its logical fulfilment: namely, the depiction of the social whole as an ordered field which predetermines each of its elements, (pre-)assigning them their place in the overall order. Similarly, a 'spatialisation' of multiple 'times', whether of a two-dimensional cartographical or three-dimensional archaeological model, does not on its own prevent the reconstitution of the notion of an 'essential section' of the coordinates of each particular moment of the field's historical existence; in certain 'metastructural' formulations, including Koselleck's transcendental approach, a theory of multiple times may arguably even presuppose such a theory of periodisation.[91] In this case, the plural times would be defined as 'plural' precisely due to their divergent positioning in and by the structure (of any given present, or 'period') or metastructure (of history itself), which would function as their unifying measure. In other words, these plural times would ultimately be ordered by a common measure of the 'structure' in which their plurality is localised and constituted *as* a plurality within this unity. In its turn, such a notion ultimately implies the possibility of a contemporaneity conceived as a (re-)synchronisation of the non-contemporaneous.

---

90   Althusser and Balibar 1970, p. 106.

91   For an attempt to read Koselleck's work as a theory of periodisation, see Osborne 1995, pp. 9–13. For alternative views of the import of Koselleck's metaphor, see Zammito 2004 and Jordheim 2012 and 2014.

Furthermore, as we have seen, according to Althusser's argument there is an integral link between an 'ideological conception of historical time', a spiritualist notion of the social totality, and the notion of politics as a clash between subjects, conceived as competing claims to embody the adequate self-comprehension of the present and thereby 'to complete' it. Does Gramsci avoid the depiction of politics as a struggle between subjects on the unifying terrain of the present, conceived as such a temporal structure-object? Although he rejected the explicit vocabulary of the subject, might this not simply mean that the concept of the subject constitutes the 'unthought' of his whole project? In other words, was Gramsci implicitly and perhaps unknowingly operating within the philosophical grammar of knowing and doing subjects struggling to demonstrate the authenticity of their claims of mastery of the 'object' of the social formation?

The Temporality of the Political Subject

Affirmative answers to these interrogatives yields a certain 'traditional' reading of the *Prison Notebooks*. This reading understands the politics of hegemony to involve, in the first instance, the securing of consent of a significant propor-tion of political actors in a given social formation and their unification into a 'collective political subject'; once such consent is secured, the newly con-stituted 'political subject' embarks upon a clash with another such subject formed by a similar process, each seeking to enlarge their occupation of 'territ-ory' in the social formation until they possess sufficient forces to conquer the social formation's 'centre', in the institutions of the state apparatus; in a third moment, hegemonically constructed states then engage in competition on the international terrain, in a geopolitical repetition of the originary domestic pro-cess. 'Time', conceived as singular and linear, is posited as the measure of this process, and is functional to the growth and clash of such subjects over their potential spoils.

Arguably, this reading received its most eloquent speculative formulation in what is undoubtedly one of the most influential of recent interpretations of the concept of hegemony, Ernesto Laclau and Chantel Mouffe's *Hegemony and Socialist Strategy*. Laclau and Mouffe effectively present hegemony as a pro-cess of temporal development, synchronisation and unification.[92] According to their reading, hegemony involves, first, the establishment of a 'chain of equi-

---

92   Bevernage 2016 explicitly attempts to formulate Laclau and Mouffe's theory in temporal

valence' between previously discrete social demands, each with their own histories and times; second, on this basis, their articulation and synchronisation; and third, the progressive formation of a political subject as (provisionally) achieved unity of diversity.[93] Discordant demands and their different times are thereby synchronised via hegemonic articulation in a process of implicit temporal development, leading to a moment in which a constitutively divided present becomes (even if only provisionally and contingently) present and legible to itself in the form of a clash between politically articulated subjects. Gramsci's proposals of the notion of a 'regulated society', his emphasis upon the formation of 'collective wills', and the frequent references to 'historical progress' in the *Prison Notebooks*, would all seem to provide support for such a reading. Above all, the famous figure of the 'modern Prince' as totalising principle of secularisation, appears to imply a notion of such a hegemonic political subject conceived as temporal accumulation, and as synchronisation of diverse times according to and within a common measure.[94]

> The modern Prince, as it develops, revolutionises the whole system of intellectual and moral relations, in that its development means precisely that any given act is seen as useful or harmful, as virtuous or as wicked, only in so far as it has as its point of reference the modern Prince itself, and helps to strengthen or to oppose it. In people's consciences, the Prince takes the place of the divinity or the categorical imperative, and becomes the basis for a modern laicism and for a complete laicisation of all aspects of life and of all customary relationships.[95]

For this reading, the modern Prince emerges in order violently to unify the temporal discordance of the present, mastering its contradictions and conflicts, expelling all traces of difference, finally appearing as a totalising 'subject-

---

terms, focusing in particular upon a politically constituted hegemonic coevalness, or coevalness 'effect'.

93   Laclau and Mouffe 1985. Laclau 2006 contains arguably the fullest statement of the formalist dimensions of Laclau's notion of 'the people' as political subject. Negri has argued for the continuities between Laclau and Mouffe's interpretation and that of Togliatti and the postwar PCI (Casarino and Negri 2008, pp. 162–4).

94   According to Simon Critchley, 'This act of the aggregation of the political subject is the moment of hegemony' (2007, p. 104). For a presentation of this reading that makes clear the ultimately 'Schmittian' conclusions to which it tends, see Morfino 2009, p. 99.

95   Q 13, §1, p. 1561. On the development of the figure of the modern Prince in the *Prison Notebooks*, see Frosini 2013 and Thomas 2015.

object' of history. This reading understands Gramsci to affirm not only a messianic conception of time, with the modern Prince arriving in the 'juvescence of the year', like 'Christ the tiger' in Eliot's *Gerontion*, to cure history of its ills and incompletion. It also represents the modern Prince as the mythological expression of a 'formalism of the subject'. The modern Prince, that is, is posited as the 'subject' capable of mastering the 'object' of the present, or as the 'form' that comprehends and gives expression to its 'content'. Thus, Gramsci's project in its totality is characterised as a transition from the temporal figure of the *katechon*, simultaneously promising and preventing the fulfilment of the conflicting plural temporalities, to a notion of the modern Prince as time conceived as *kairos*, the moment in which the present finally becomes fully present to itself.[96] In this case, the existence of plural temporalities is implicitly understood to be merely a ruse on the way to the reconstitution of a more fundamental and singular measure: namely, the present conceived as a structure traversed by plural times that find their telos in the conflictual formation of a subject capable of uniting them, comprehending the complexity of their articulation as a structure-object, and providing them with a consciousness of themselves.

'Prevision' as a 'Method' of Political Work

The *Prison Notebooks* undoubtedly contain formulations that are amenable to such a reading, as we have seen. However, the latter phases in particular of Gramsci's carceral research, from 1932 onwards, are characterised by an attempt to provide the outlines of an alternative conception, with the progressive development of a distinctive notion of 'prevision' [*previsione*].[97] Once

---

96 Yoshihiko Ichida has clearly delineated this problem in relation to the thinking of temporality and politics of Carl Schmitt, explicitly linking the process of subject formation to that of temporal accumulation and the emergence of a subject-object. '"Time is out of joint" precisely where the subject appears. Still, time never stops because the moment guarantees temporal flow through the very same coalescence: dividing itself into past and future, the moment is a present that alternately happens, is about to become a past, and is *always-already* past. And the subject appears finally as a knot of temporal flow, in the sense that he performs the act of the rupture and suture of time and so lives in a time he creates by himself: he is *Kairós*' (Ichida 2005).

97 On the development of the concept of prevision in the Gramsci, see Badaloni 1981. Gramsci's use of *Previsione* and the related term *prevedibilità* have most often been translated into English as 'prediction' and 'predictability' respectively. I have chosen to translate

again, Gramsci's research undergoes a development in which models of pro- and anachronistic time tend to be displaced by a model that posits constitutive non-contemporaneity as the determining dynamic of any apparently achieved present. Prevision in this latter sense is not understood as a type of prefigure- ment of the future in the graven images of the present, or a form of 'prediction' of the future predicated on the past; nor is it a response to the problem of transition, where change would be thought through relapse to a linear tem- poral model, with the sighting of the new on the far off horizon of the present, in the sense of a hermeneutical *Erwartungshorizont*; nor is it conceived in a radical modernist formulation, as the vision of that which cannot be deduced from the old. Rather, prevision is thought as 'intervention', as the modification of existing rhythms and tempos, and the 'weaving' of a new composition of the irreducible plural temporalities that denies the self-identity of the present understood as synchronisation.

The 'non-presence of the present' was a visceral theme for the imprisoned and increasingly isolated Gramsci, prompting him to reflect intensely on the tragedy of Cavalcanti in the Canto X of Dante's *Inferno*. Cavalcanti 'sees into the past and sees into the future, but does not see into the present, in a determ- inate zone of the past and of the future in which the present is located'.[98] As so often in the *Prison Notebooks*, engaging with Croce provides Gramsci with a foil for the further development of his own theory. In late 1932, objecting to Croce's depiction of Marx's theory of value as an invalid 'elliptical comparison', Gram- sci argues that the Crocean concept, applied in the field of history, would imply a dogmatic distinction between past and future and make historical develop- ment unthinkable: 'history is an implicit comparison between the past and the present [...] And why is ellipsis illegitimate when one makes a comparison with a hypothesis about the future, whereas it is legitimate when one makes a com- parison with a past fact?'[99] The Crocean concept of prevision, Gramsci argues, in fact involves an elliptical comparison that eternalises a particular concept of

---

them as 'prevision' and 'foreseeability' in order to emphasise the strongly sensual and visual dimensions of Gramsci's reflections, which go beyond the largely logical-inductive or deductive sense of prediction in English.

98   Q 4, §78, p. 517; May 1930. On the aesthetic and philosophical significance of Gramsci's 'little discovery' in Dante studies, see Rosengarten 1986. In Q 4, §85, p. 527 Gramsci recalls similar themes in his article 'Il cieco Tiresia' from 1918 discussing folklore traditions linking the gift of prevision to actual blindness. On the political significance of these studies, particularly regarding Gramsci's 'coded' communication with Togliatti, see Rossi and Vacca 2007 and Vacca 2012.

99   Q 10II, §41, p. 1310; see also Q 7, §42, p. 891.

the present, reduced to the repetition of its historical determinants: a conservative conception in which 'prevision is nothing more than a special judgement on the present'.[100]

In Bukharin, on the other hand, Gramsci detects an equally abstract conception of prevision, which is reduced to a mechanical conception of prediction. A teleological linear conception of historical time is argued to underlie Bukharin's supposed 'search of essential causes, indeed, for the "first" cause, for the "cause of causes"', sought in order 'to guarantee' predictions regarding future developments. Such an attempt 'to resolve in peremptory fashion the practical problem of the foreseeability [prevedibilità] of historical events',[101] in fact, presupposes 'criteria constructed on the model of the natural sciences',[102] which misapprehend, Gramsci later argues, the experimental nature of modern scientific practice.[103] Bukharin's invocation of Marxism as a sociology, in particular, prompts Gramsci to object, arguably in a caricatured way, that sociology is an attempt 'to derive "experimentally" the laws of evolution of human society in such a way as to "forsee" [prevedere] that the oak tree will develop out of the acorn'.[104]

Above all, it is in the critique of political economy that Gramsci finds the outlines for a notion of prevision that begins to break with a temporal linear model, even while remaining ambiguously tied to a proto-structuralist, 'synchronic' conception of the social totality. His reflections in late 1932 on the philosophical significance of Ricardo and the delineation of a non-metaphysical notion of immanence play a particularly important role in this development of 'foreseeability' as an historicist translation of the 'concept of regularity and of necessity in historical development'. In this conception, 'necessity' is understood 'in an "historical-concrete" sense', rather than 'speculative-abstract', as the presence of 'an efficient and active premise' that becomes 'operative' in a calculation of

---

100   Q 10II, § 41, p. 1311; see also Q 15, § 36, p. 1790.
101   Q 11, § 15, p. 1403.
102   Q 11, § 26, p. 1432.
103   See Q 15, § 50, p. 1811.
104   Q 11, § 26, p. 1432. The context is here important, for Gramsci's comments regard not so much any particularly tendency of modern sociology as such, but rather, his perception of the political significance of certain understandings of sociological method in the broadest sense for forms of political organisational work in the workers' movement. See Q 11, § 15, p. 1404: 'It is necessary to pose exactly the problem of the foreseeability of historical events in order to be able to criticise exhaustively the conception of mechanical causality, to deprive it of any scientific prestige and to reduce it to a pure myth that was perhaps useful in the past, in a backward period in the development of certain subaltern social groups'.

means and ends.[105] Relations of forces are posited in terms of their configuration in existing 'structures' in both productive and ideological terms. Central here is the

> Concept and fact of 'determinate market': that is, the scientific revelation that determinate decisive and permanent forces have arisen historically, the operation of which presents itself with a certain 'automatism' that allows a measure of 'foreseeability' [*prevedibilità*] and certainty for the future of individual initiatives [...]. 'Determinate market' is therefore equivalent to saying 'determinate relation of social forces in a determined structure of the productive apparatus', a relation guaranteed (that is, rendered permanent) by a determinate juridical, moral and political superstructure.[106]

The ambiguous dimensions of this formulation are soon tempered by Gramsci's forging in the same period, in his research into a praxis-oriented alternative to 'objectivist' conceptions of scientific knowledge, of a relation between prevision and political programme. The decisive moment in the development of the concept comes when it is no longer linked to temporal models of prefiguration or spatial models of localisation. Instead, Gramsci emphasises the operative dimensions of prevision as an intervention into the current articulation of plural times, as a mode of construction. He argues that

> in reality one can 'scientifically' foresee only the struggle, but not the concrete moments of the struggle, which cannot but be the results of opposing forces in continuous movement, which are never reducible to fixed quantities since within them quantity is continually becoming quality. In reality one can 'foresee' to the extent that one acts, to the extent that one applies a voluntary effort and therefore contributes concretely to creating the 'foreseen' result.[107]

---

105   Q 11, § 52, p. 1477.

106   Q 11, § 52, p. 1477; see also Q 8, § 128, p. 1018. Gramsci's use of the notion of structures (and superstructures) has earlier been modulated by his meditation of Marx's 1859 'Preface' and his 'translation' (in a directly linguistic and broader conceptual sense) of its topographical terms into the notion of forms of relationality (particularly with his decision to render the notion of superstructure as 'ideological forms'). On this dimension, see Thomas 2009, pp. 95–102.

107   Q 11, § 15, p. 1403.

Prevision is here formulated as a dimension of the notion of 'programme', as the active organisation of given relations in order to 'make victorious' a particular 'prevision'; such a practice of prevision itself may become a decisive 'element of such victory'.[108] In other words, prevision involves the construction of new relations of force that are capable of modifying the existing relations. Rather than the subsumption of the contradictions of the present in a projected unified future, the political practice of prevision instead posits the emergence of a distinctive time alongside and within the other existing plural times: the time of the intervention of an alternative. 'The time is out of joint' precisely at the moment when it is unhinged by an intervention within and against the 'accomplished' present, when alternative forms of relationality challenge the notion of a possible unifying synchronisation itself. Rather than simply negating that particular present in order to affirm another, however, the act of prevision instead actively undermines the notion of the present itself, highlighting the impossibility of its self-identity and self-presence, because always fractured by the possibility of alternative relationalities. Nicola Badaloni has aptly described this as

> a method of 'prevision' in determinate conditions, some of which are not 'given', but are constructed, or are able to be constructed, by means of the organisation, practice and formation of models of reality that are capable of disaggregating what had at first sight seemed dominated by a completely unchangeable necessity or causal order.[109]

Such a method of prevision thus does not posit the present as a *Kampfplatz* of substantively opposed but formally compatible times, nor does it envisage a moment in which the present could finally become identical with itself, with the arrival of a political subject capable of synchronising its competing times in an 'authentic' form. Rather, prevision as a method of political work presupposes the continuing existence of a plurality of times; it emerges precisely as a distinctive relation to the plurality of those times, which it aims to modify through the construction of alternative modes of their articulation. It is this method of political work, of the fracturing of the time of the present by the counter-times of alternative forms and practices of organisation, which is designated by the notion of hegemonic politics and the name of the modern Prince.

---

108   Q 15, §50, p. 1810.
109   Badaloni 1981, p. 335.

CHAPTER 8

'Space-Time' and Power in the Light of the Theory of Hegemony

Fabio Frosini

Plural Temporality and/or Contingency?

Is there a theory of plural temporality in Antonio Gramsci's *Prison Notebooks*? The answer is at first glance extremely simple: seen in the context of the notion of hegemony, every identity is the product of a political unification of hetero-genous elements. Therefore, if time is to be interpreted as the uniform rhythm of historical experience, the unity of that rhythm is the contingent outcome of a series of hegemonic practices whose sole existence is that conferred by the interweaving of these practices. Unity rises against the backdrop of plural-ity without ever cancelling it out completely. Universality is thus influenced by partiality.

This thesis, perceptively sustained by Ernesto Laclau,[1] effectively makes hegemony an equivalent of the exercise of power and a synonym of objectiv-ity. Truth, which escapes as an unavoidable deviation (according to Laclau's post-structuralist approach) from the objectivity of the meanings established by power, is pushed to the margins of full-blown hegemonic functioning. In developing a theory of the co-implication and, at the same time, mutual exclus-ivity of objectivity and truth, as well as politics and hegemony, Laclau appeals to the space/time dichotomy in which temporality is to be considered 'the exact opposite of space' and not as spatialised diachrony.[2] Therefore, if space is structure, an organisation with fixed meanings, time will necessarily be a 'dislocation of this structure'; that is, 'a maladjustment which is spatially unrep-resentable', in a word: an 'event'.[3] In this way, temporal plurality can only be located in the spatialised diachronic viewpoint in the various discourses (or stories, or 'myths') of the order,[4] while innovation, change and politics as truth in action, as alien to space, are unrepresentable and fleeting, entirely empty,

---

1   See Laclau 2000. These themes were already prefigured in Laclau and Mouffe 1985.
2   Laclau 1990, p. 41.
3   Laclau 1990, pp. 42–4.
4   See Laclau 1990, pp. 59–67.

and always identical. In a word, temporality cannot be diversified as it is indeterminable. Either it is given or it is not. There is no third way.

That the origin of this concept of temporality is to be found in the work of Bergson and Heidegger is unmistakable, as is the tension which thus arises between the contingency of hegemonic unification and the 'event' from which it always departs. If this is taken as given, the system's instability is not due to the contingency of its constitution, but to its *crisis* (unpredictable, in Bergson's terms), reactivating the contingent nature of that systematic unification is then seen as a result of this crisis. Strictly speaking, thus, in Laclau's reworking of the notion of hegemony temporality cannot be plural and vice versa, where temporal plurality exists, we are already in the field of spatiality.[5] Hegemony rests on plurality precisely because its existence depends on cancelling out every trace of the uniqueness of the event of truth.[6]

The outcome is thus that, despite the contingent feature of hegemonic unification, there is no true temporal plurality. Because of the separation between truth and objectivity, plurality is always solely that relating to the power which, however, is entirely traceable back to the same logic of 'radical alienation' in relation to the contingency of its origin. It follows that contingency is the opposite of necessity in the same way that time is the opposite of space: its absolute opposite. In this way, contingency is radicalised by Laclau to the extent of becoming an equivalent of the arbitrary nature of the 'contingent decision' whose power arises from a 'maladjustment' of the structure and which cancels itself out just by exercising this power.[7] Laclau writes that decision is 'the moment of subject before subjectivation'.[8] It is therefore not attributable to a subject, but rather it is the act of what emerges as a 'result of the collapse of objectivity' and which in this way also vanishes.[9] This does not, however, make contingency any less arbitrary in nature as it is identical with the decision.

Now – and this is my argument – what is gained and what is lost by equating the time/space couplet with that of contingency/necessity? Or in other words: what are the consequences of separating truth and objectivity? The collapse

---

5 Regarding these categories of Laclau's thought with a few oversimplifications, see Massey 1992.
6 'Power is merely the trace of contingency, the point at which objectivity reveals the radical alienation which defines it. In this sense objectivity – the essence of objects – is nothing more than a sedimented form of power, in other words, a power whose traces have been erased' (Laclau 1990, p. 60).
7 Ibid.
8 Laclau 2000, p. 79.
9 Laclau 1990, p. 61.

of the many temporalities into a single, void time reduced to simple potential freed of action is certainly the most striking. In this way, the singularity (or peculiarity) of the situation falls entirely under the category of objectivity, and it thus becomes impossible to think concretely the sphere in which political innovation erupts into the system of meanings. The fact that it may obey a certain 'logic' (the logic of equivalence versus that of difference) does not in itself imply the indiscernibility of each of its aspects in relation to any other innovation. In other words, temporal uniqueness leads to a very poor concrete analysis in which distinctions between cases and situations are reduced to the status of superficial detail and the choice of the elements that are to form part of the chains of equivalence is made arbitrarily.[10]

This, moreover, is a predictable consequence of the Bergsonian-Heideggerian notion of temporality adopted by Laclau. Seen from this perspective, contingency is bound to lose its original meaning of *contingere, cum-tangere*, that is, the non-essential unification of at least two events implying undisrupted plurality, or even an interim relationship, and therefore no longer the opposite of necessity, but a different form of it. In fact, if one wishes to use this concept in the field of historical-political analysis, it is necessary to take into account its condensation of two distinct chains of connection: on the one hand, the transience of a certain order; on the other, the arbitrary way it was established, or in other words, historicity and decision, politics and power, event and violence and so on. These two series are not identical, but rather irreducible, and contingency is the provisional and reversible way by which they can coincide. In Laclau's reworking of the logic of hegemony, historicity – to the extent that it is always 'contaminated' by internal plurality – is ejected from the political dimension and reduced to a spatialised representation of temporality. And contingency is reduced to the sole dimension of arbitrary decision. Yet, on the contrary, it is precisely the specific and ultimately unique way in which historicity and decision coincide that makes what Gramsci calls 'analysis of situations' possible.[11]

---

10   This is particularly evident in Laclau 2005.

11   Q13, § 17; pp. 1578–89. References to Gramsci's *Prison Notebooks* follow the internationally established standard of notebook number (Q), number of note (§), followed by page reference to the Italian critical edition (Gramsci 1975). Where available, a reference to an existing English translation is also provided.

Hegemony and Space

On the other hand, to insist on the opposite aspect, that of politics and historicity, by isolating two socially delimited spaces and assigning to one of them – the proletarian space – the prerogative of hegemony whilst assigning the other to the field of 'passive revolution' would not fully grasp the special features of Gramsci's approach to the issue either. Temporal plurality would no longer, in this case, be a form of radical alienation from contingency, but rather, on the contrary, precisely the way in which contingency is reaffirmed against the dominant unique and progressive temporal narrative. This interpretation, recently brilliantly proposed by Peter D. Thomas,[12] considers the reaffirmation of temporal plurality as a *strategic* matter since hegemony's place would be outside it and thus, in a sense, external to objectivity. Reaffirmation of 'temporal multiplicity', in other words, unmasks the false (ideological) a-conflictual unity of the capitalist world, but it is in its turn a step towards a true, no longer ideological, temporal synchronisation by means of the cancelling out of inequality and conflict.[13]

What this interpretation implies (and this is not a secondary issue, but rather one involving a very important aspect of Gramsci's thought and its comparison with our present) is the need – despite all the criticism of essentialism – to look for a breaking point, in other words a kind of 'pivotal' time, capable of preventing antagonism from moving the same unchanging dichotomy continually forwards or backwards without actually questioning it, as programmatically happens with Laclau. Ultimately, this is the same problem Gramsci faced with the eternity of the 'distinctions' postulated by Benedetto Croce as the transcendental motivation of the eternity of the bourgeois world.[14]

However, Gramsci does not react to this by postulating a subject capable of destroying the 'cage', or an event, however specific and occasional, which suddenly interrupts the logic by which it has been produced. On the contrary, he reacts by showing how and to what extent this cage is capable – and not only through violence – of setting up a truth, that is, a hegemony; in other words,

---

12   See Thomas 2006 and 2009.

13   See Thomas 2009, pp. 285–7.

14   It is no coincidence that Laclau as well – in reaction to Žižek's Hegelianism – retrieved the 'transcendental' aspect and defined 'radical historicism' as a 'self-contradictory enterprise' (Laclau 2000, p. 58). Ernesto De Martino's 'historicism' in his *Il mondo magico* had the same effect on Benedetto Croce. For the way in which De Martino reached Hegel despite Croce, and on Croce's reaction, see Cases 1973, pp. XVI–XXIX.

how and to what extent that cage is, in fact, an ever-changing and flexible political apparatus.[15]

This is Gramsci's starting point in his reflections on 'historicism': a preliminary refusal to distinguish in principle between objectivity and truth, that is, between power and its critique. The logic of alienation is foreign to him, and it is precisely because of this – through the development of the theory of translatability of languages – that he can conceptualise the way in which objectivity and truth – that is, decision and historicity, or better, in his own words, 'consent' and 'force' – are articulated in each moment in a specific manner with one prevailing over the other (or also with the temporary eclipse of one of the two). They are both real and always to be taken in their fullest and most authentic meaning, not as a mere appearance or a mask that conceals the truth.[16]

In the light of the translatability of languages, temporal plurality is therefore neither apparent nor strategic, but irreducible and primary. It expresses at the same time both inequality and domination, and expansive, universalistic movement – according to a prevalence which cannot be determined in advance and which cannot set in motion an end to plurality but, if anything, leads to its 'internalisation'.[17] In other words, translatability leads to the removal of domination and antagonism from plurality, and to its redefinition in solidaristic terms.[18] In a nutshell, temporal plurality is the concrete form of hegemony in all its incarnations, both bourgeois and proletarian hegemony, with the two polarities (objectivity and truth) prevailing to a different extent within it, as it is practiced in specific forms, that is, related to non-interchangeable spaces.

It is here, with this condition to which hegemony is always subject, that the spatial dimension comes into play. Contingency therefore becomes a synonym for 'differential necessity', a necessity that is historical, reversible and hypothetical, but compelling and 'equalising' all the same. A contingent bond between

---

15   This is the philosophical method of 'immanence', that is, the key to an understanding of the reformulation of Marxism as a 'philosophy of praxis'. Gramsci interprets immanence not as one of many philosophical approaches but as a political revolutionising of the status of philosophy and therefore a completely new approach to philosophy. See Frosini 2007 and 2010, pp. 112–61 (including the related bibliography).

16   For a different approach, see Tomba 2006, p. 16: 'Justice must not be understood as what needs to be progressively created, but as that whose current reality is presented as the strength of an event irreducible to the terms of law'. In Gramscian terms, it is rather a question of saying that, once expressed, the idea of justice is already a form (alternative, controversial) of law.

17   'The implementation of socialism, which is *the beginning of the end* of class struggle', is defined by Gramsci in 1922 'as an internalisation of the struggle' (Gramsci 1966, p. 446).

18   See Q19, § 5, pp. 1988–9.

historicity and decision exists *only if* a 'conjuncture' is given, that is, if there is some kind of irregularity and inequality of the surface of the social fabric.[19] A certain degree of spatiality is inextricably linked to historicity and, the other way round, there is no such thing as a 'pure' decision detached from elements of historicity. For Gramsci, the issue is not criticism of the conceptions of unitary time, but rather understanding their truth-founding capacity, that is, their political effectiveness.

An extremely important consequence follows on from what has been said thus far. Despite what is generally thought today on the basis of a successful essay by Edward Said, Gramsci was not a philosopher concerned with space – or at least no more than he was a philosopher concerned with time, or times.[20] The key to the theory of hegemony can only be grasped with an understanding of the notion of temporal plurality in different but interrelated and therefore mutually immanent (translatable) spaces, none of which is universal to the exclusion of others, but all of which are universal to the extent that they can translate all the others.

In this context the notion of space is irreplaceable. It is not only an articulation expressing order and therefore power as a system of inequalities (potentially in the form of anachronistic relations) in the reciprocal externality of its elements. Space is all of this, and at the same time the externality implicit in this encompasses the material anchor of hegemonic practices in all their both expansive and purely corporate variants. Exteriority as the dominance of a content and exteriority as the limits to this dominance are always structured into specific forms. It is precisely this that constitutes the object of the 'analysis of situations' in Gramscian terms.

In short, theorising space and politics gives us an understanding of the way in which Gramsci reworks the question of temporality in the light of the notion of hegemony by reformulating space and time as a space-time continuum.[21]

---

19   On the notion on conjuncture in Gramsci, see Portantiero 1981, pp. 177–92.

20   See Said 2001. See also Jessop 2006 and Fontana 2010.

21   By imputing to Bergson the concept of time adopted by Gramsci in his *Prison Notebooks*, Guida 2008 postulates the issue of temporal diversity in terms of general social diversity (Europe/America). However, in so doing he uses explanation precisely in lieu of what should be explained: social diversity as a relational fact (hegemonic) and not a simple juxtaposition. Guida's essay nevertheless contains observations on the time-concept and immanence-teleology relationships that merit analysis and further study (see in particular pp. 703–4).

Politics and Power

The best way to address the issue formulated above is to start from the way in which the relationship between space and politics is usually conceived of in modern philosophy, as a space-power relationship. In recent years, this issue has been the subject of some attention from scholars in the fields of history, political theory, geography, urban planning and architecture. Paul Q. Hirst's posthumous book, *Space and Power. Politics, War and Architecture*, weaves all these approaches together in an original manner and takes the form of a summary of this debate.[22] The authors that Hirst cites from a methodological point of view are the founders of the French historical geography school, Paul Vidal de la Blache and Lucien Febvre – due to the fact that they highlighted the conditioning role of space, in its specific forms, in the history of societies – and Michel Foucault's microphysics of power, because of his ability to bring out the presence of power relationships in disparate places such as prisons, churches and fortresses.[23] But while the first two are only mentioned fleetingly (suggesting that it may simply be a tribute),[24] it is actually Foucault's thought that forms the theoretical matrix inspiring Hirst's work.[25]

In actual fact, in this book the space-power relationship is considered in three different contexts: nation-states, city-states (Part I), war (Part II) and individual buildings (for example, fortifications: Part III). In all three cases, albeit in different ways, it is space whose pervasive presence determines the boundary between inside and outside. Space is therefore the set of conditions and constraints that any organism has to deal with in order to exist and survive. Space is thus the place in which power is expressed as war (which, together with borders, is, as we have seen, the subject of Part II of Hirst's book). It is the war and subjection pairing which is always the outcome of considering space and power in relation both to international space and the internal relationship between city and the territory or castle and the city. Politics, as the set of conflicts and antagonisms within a social body, is reduced following Foucault to the same categorical dichotomy of power; that is, to the internal/external dichotomy. For Foucault, power does not 'flow' from a specific sphere of social space (sovereignty), but suffuses all space homogenously. Therefore, whenever there

---

22   Hirst 2005.

23   See Hirst 2005, p. 4.

24   Hirst (2005, p. 4) cites Vidal's name incorrectly. On the latter, see Robic 2009. Regarding the relationship between Vidal and Febvre (integration of history into geography for the former, of geography into history for the latter), see Viet 1967, pp. 82–4.

25   Chapter 8 (Hirst 2005, pp. 155 ff.) is entirely dedicated to Foucault.

is a conflict within the internal space, this stems from 'resistance' encountered by power as it is exerted. However, at the precise moment that this resistance becomes organised, it is immediately transformed into power itself, that is, subordination of external to internal space.

Power is thus certainly synonymous with politics and politics with war in the sense that politics is no more than conflict aimed at setting borders, both literally as a state border, and metaphorically as an internal boundary, between the dominant classes and the dominated.

The Logic of Hegemony

But is this really so? Can it be said that every time we engage in politics power is exercised, in the sense set out here of a relationship with an external element to be defined and dominated? An answer to this question cannot be supplied if we remain within this approach. For this perspective, internal space in reality is no different from external space. On the contrary, it treats internal space as a toned down version of external space (in other, Schmittian, words: government is politics neutralised and politics shows through at the precise moment in which its essential warlike character is revealed). This approach therefore questions neither the concept of space nor that of power.

In actual fact, the reference to the category of space category has very different implications and arises in order to meet many other needs, as Vidal de la Blache and Febvre's approaches show (but Fernand Braudel should also be added). First of all, space is a category that, unlike time, encompasses a principle of multiplicity which pre-empts any attempt to lead politics back to a single, one-directional logic. Even when space is understood as static, as a territory or even as a place linked to a bloodline, it is still differentiated and concrete. Therefore, at the moment in which space is placed in relation to power, a need for concreteness arises which time as such cannot satisfy.

This requirement can be expressed as follows: power does not develop in a vacuum or in a homogenous series of equivalent places, but arises, and is organised, on the basis of specific and ultimately unique conditions. Land borders are the physical expression of this concrete organisation. It can thus be said that fixing borders is the result of a real interaction between power dynamics and space understood as the ensemble of material conditions. This is one of the needs expressed by the historical geography of Paul Vidal de la Blache and Lucien Febvre. Nevertheless, it still says nothing about the true nature of power except that it relates to an external element. This perspective sees space literally as a framework of actual places disputed by political bodies, and ultimately, by means of war.

However, if we simply transfer this spatial perspective to territorial organisms and think of politics as a form of internal war (as Foucault does), a two-fold operation is the result. First, we are taking an international projection of power as the prototype of politics (war as an expression of politics in its purest form). Second, we are tacitly switching from a literal interpretation of space to a metaphorical one and losing precisely the need for concreteness that the use of the concept of space as a variety of places expresses.

This is a very important distinction. Power relations which are internal to national space can in fact take on a geographical form – as in the case of a rich area that dominates and exploits a poor area as if it were a colony, or the relationship between wealthy neighbourhoods and ghettos – but this is not decisive. This is confirmed by the fact that internal 'boundaries' are rarely based on geographical considerations, but rather on historically established power relationships between different social groups.[26] Furthermore, such boundaries cannot be rigidly fixed given that – with some exceptions (for example, South Africa's apartheid or racial segregation in the US) – the dynamics of modern citizenship have levelled out internal national space and made it homogenous, putting its people on an equal footing in legal terms.[27]

This does not mean, however, that concrete differences with no legal foundation may not arise once again. In fact, space within national boundaries is not 'horizontal' and 'literal', but 'vertical' and 'metaphorical'. Domination is not established, as in the case of international relations, according to the availability of resources linked to specific locations, but by the ability of those dominating to build new forms of subordination within the space of homogenous citizenship continually. It is only when this difference is acknowledged that the dynamics of power within the nation-state can be specifically conceptualised. This dynamic consists in producing vertical relationships of domination/subjugation within a space (citizenship) which is in itself undifferentiated.

---

26   This can, of course, happen as in the case of the Italian 'southern question'. But this form was determined precisely by the way space was unified and hegemony constructed in Italy after 1861, that is, by a political relationship between the (northern) industrial bourgeoisie and the (southern) landowners.

27   This levelling is to some extent due to the creation of homogeneous and unified legal orders, but the organisation of a dense network of communications and transport has also played a very important role as it has 'accelerated' space by moving the link between geographical diversity and political unity onto another plane. Vidal de la Blache in particular has written about this acceleration (see Robic 2009, pp. 307–9).

For this reason, internal power does not lie in the territorial division of a space, as in the case of international relations, but in its political articulation. It is the ability of a social class to politically articulate space by building vertical relationships which enables them to establish their power and define areas of subordination. Space is not shared, but structured vertically. Places are not divided up, but one class succeeds in appropriating all the space, at the same time including other classes in it in subordinate forms. There is no legal sanction for territorial ownership, but rather political differentiation of function between the dominant/ruling class and the dominated/ruled classes. It is a sort of 'division of labour', which is not legally established, but reproduced *de facto* by effective informal selection mechanisms (belonging to family, training, opportunity for travel, connections and so forth.) and which, of course, envisages the potential for limited exceptions (molecular co-optation).

For all these reasons, finally, war is not simply extended from the external to the internal spheres, but a specific structure of power develops which we have here summarised in three elements: a) vertical articulation of space which is in itself homogenous; b) appropriation of the entire space by one class; c) non-statutory (in a formal, narrow sense), but political nature of this distribution of functions. What Gramsci calls 'hegemony' is precisely what enables differences to be engendered in a homogenous space and full possession to be taken of it without other classes being excluded from it, but rather by including them in a subordinate capacity.[28]

---

28   What has been said thus far refers to the inherent tendency of modern politics to saturate national space by moving legal segmentations outwards. A constant, formative feature of modern history has been forms of segregation and marginalisation on the margins of the bourgeois world, which Gramsci's notion of hegemony takes into account either as a prelude to a hegemonic phase or as 'national' specific forms of it. Chatterjee's (2004) attempt to redefine the concept of hegemony in the light of the limits of universalism – that is, from the perspective of the 'margins' – although it moves in the right direction, is, in my opinion, still unsatisfactory. Today the situation has changed once again: segregation and marginalisation tend today, in a new form, to generalise and impact on national space in metropolitan areas. This is due both to the new stratification caused by the illegal status of large masses of people and to the splintering of universal law into pacts or agreements with the strongest and most combative minorities. That all this happens in the presence of a new web of religion, ethnicity (culture) and politics is an extremely important fact which opens up an entire series of new research perspectives concerning the procedures and concepts involved in hegemony which, however, go beyond the approach identified here without invalidating it. For a first overview, see Balibar and Wallerstein 1991.

Marx: The Universal as 'Translation'

In his reflections on hegemony, Gramsci always works on the basis of two reference points: Hegel's *Philosophy of Right* and *The Communist Manifesto*. The
Manifesto supplies him with a theory of modernity as a history of the dissem-
ination of capitalism and the affirmation of the bourgeoisie as the new ruling
class and as a *new type* of class as well. The development of capitalism is presented as a combined structural dissolution-reconstitution of all relationships.
'The bourgeoisie', Marx writes, 'cannot exist without constantly revolutionising
the instruments of production, and thereby the relations of production, and
with them the whole relations of society'.[29] The bourgeoisie's peculiarity as
a social class derives from this. Given that in the capitalist world the state of
permanent revolution takes the place of the foundations that were previously
occupied by 'tradition',[30] the class dominating this process is defined as a class
to the extent that it changes society, not to the extent that it freezes it at any
given level. It is thus a structurally open class which continually redefines itself
on the basis of history rather than traditional ties of caste, race or religion. Its
assumption is therefore a society which is homogenous in principle, a society
into which concrete rather than abstract, material rather than formal, differences are introduced.

In short, the modern bourgeoisie encompasses a structural relationship
between social fluidity and the establishment of political difference. What is
important here is not to determine how Marx attempted, beginning with his
article on the *Judenfrage*, to establish the nexus between these two moments
of dissolutive dynamics and the re-establishment of difference. Suffice it to
say that his reading of Hegel's *Philosophy of Right*, focused as it was on the
state, and on the state as it incorporates the modern and abstract personality
of *sovereignty*, tends to reduce 'civil society' to its solely Hobbesian *facies*, and
push, as Feuerbach would, all that is 'representation' – as distinct from (and
in some sense opposed to) 'reality' – towards the category of abstraction and
impotence.[31]

Nevertheless, in the *Manifesto* and the other texts of this period (I'm thinking, first and foremost, of *Zur Kritik der Hegelschen Rechtsphilosophie. Einleitung*), there is also an attempt to understand the equivalence of theory and
practice, of speculative philosophy and politics, of an abstract state and the

---

29 *Manifesto of the Communist Party*, in Marx and Engels 1976a, p. 487.
30 See Laclau 1990, pp. 4–5, pp. 39–40.
31 See the *Addendum* to this chapter.

concreteness of the 'system of the needs' on the basis of the fact that both shape political elements from different and in contrasting angles. From the starting point of this mutual 'translation' of philosophy and politics, Germany, as the land of the abstract and speculative state, is no longer presented as a deviation from 'universal history' as embodied in the relationship between France and England, but as one potential 'national' entry route into modernity. And universality, far from being a precondition, is presented as the contingent result of the reciprocal translation of all national combinations (that is, essentially inseparable from the concrete modalities of those translations), whether these translations are centred on the language of economy, politics or philosophy.[32]

This approach sees a national language, such as German, in which the language of philosophy is dominant, as translating the modern problem of the new synthesis of non-differentiation and subordination into its own local perspective only insofar as it constructs the universal in its own way, putting itself forward as a language-archetype, source of a number of potential translations into other languages. It thereby imparts a degree of actuality to the universal by designing it in a specific 'way', but also, to some extent, increasing its rigidity and locking it into a single determination (visible especially in the 'German ideology' which is subjected to a sarcastic critique by Marx and Engels in the manuscript known by this title and in *Die heilige Familie*).

Hegel: The Dynamics of Modern Power

Gramsci's interpretation of Hegel's *Philosophy of Right* develops these ideas precisely in terms of the translatability of languages and does so primarily by changing the content of Marx's concept of 'bourgeois'/'civil' society and thereby recovering the whole inclusive power of abstraction. As Gramsci fully realises, Hegel is certainly not theorising civil society as a place of simple indifference (as Hobbes did). The 'corporations', as voluntary bodies which extended craft specialisation and articulation into the sphere of 'representation', belong to the same category as the political parties, which only established themselves later on. Corporations were therefore an early form of organisation and education which was not implemented administratively, but, so to say, 'introduced' by the ruling class into the realm of private and social life. These 'private' organisations counteracted thus the tendency to atomism inherent in

---

32   See Frosini 2009, pp. 47–62.

what Hegel calls the 'system of needs', that is, the division of labour based on the capitalist production of commodities. Gramsci writes:

> Hegel's doctrine of parties and associations as the 'private' fabric of the State. It ensued historically from the political experiences of the French Revolution and was to help give greater concreteness to constitutionalism. Government with the consent of the governed – but with organised consent, and not generic and vague as it is expressed at the moment of elections. The State has and asks for consent, but it also 'educates' this consent by means of political and trade-union associations; these, however, are private organisms, left to the private initiative of the ruling class. Hegel, in a certain sense, thus already went beyond pure constitutionalism and theorised the parliamentary State with its regime of parties. His conception of association could not help still being vague and primitive, halfway between the political and the economic, in keeping with the historical experience of the time, which was very limited and offered only one accomplished example of organisation – the 'corporative' (a politics embedded in the economy).[33]

The division of labour, and the consequent distribution of individuals into social classes,[34] cannot survive without political and pedagogical processing. Corporations operate as private mobilisation and training apparatus, as a 'veritable ideological apparatus'.[35] Corporations, these 'voluntary organizations into which persons organize themselves according to their professions, trades and interests',[36] are therefore simultaneously spheres in which state power 'rooted' in civil society is exercised and an expression of irreconcilably different and conflicting instances of civil society. They are instances both of sovereignty building and a challenge to it.

---

33   Q1, § 47, pp. 56–7 (Gramsci 1992, pp. 153–4).
34   'The infinitely varied means and their equally infinite and intertwined movements of reciprocal production and exchange *converge*, by virtue of the universality inherent in their content, and become *differentiated* into *universal masses*. In consequence, the whole complex evolves into *particular systems* of needs, with their corresponding means, varieties of work, modes of satisfaction, and theoretical and practical education – into systems to which individuals are separately assigned, i.e. into different *estates*' (Hegel 1991, § 201, p. 234).
35   Lefebvre and Macherey 1984, p. 51 (more broadly, see pp. 48–52). The reference is to §§ 253–4 of Hegel's *Philosophy of Right*.
36   Avineri 1972, p. 164. See Hegel 1991, §§ 251–5, pp. 394–5.

As they are voluntary, corporations 'produce' order and therefore a transition to the state which is far more effective than negative or paternalistic instances such the legal system and the *Polizei* can be. They produce 'satisfaction' and therefore 'consent' because they arise from the internal initiative of the social forces themselves at the very moment they take shape.[37]

The keystone of modern state power according to Gramsci lies in this mediation between plurality and order. The amphibious nature – society and state – of corporations is ultimately the dual nature of parties,[38] and more generally of all organisms 'formally' (legally) private or voluntary in which the ruling class organises and shapes, obtains and maintains consent to its hegemonic project. But in so doing, it cannot avoid pluralising that 'project', making it interact with the many demands arising from the individual and class conflicts with which society is suffused. The educational function of these organisms, on the one hand, and, on the other, the tendency of the ruling class to expand, condition one another in the sense that it is only when a class sets out to assimilate the *whole* of society (since this cannot be reduced to an inclusion/exclusion system founded on blood ties) that the question arises of educating it. It is only when it is able to educate through private organisations that this class will go beyond the corporatism consisting in identifying state and government, that is, education and constriction, and to understand the need to educate by a combination of force and consent, that is, by assuming the active collaboration of the subordinated classes (or at least, of the most socially and politically decisive subordinated classes), or, in a word, by exercising hegemony over them.

If there are no internal boundaries to bourgeois political power within the state space (in the sense that society is in principle homogenous and undifferentiated and the modern politics of citizenship, in its tendency to expand, reflects this indifference), this power will have to appeal to the totality of the 'people' precisely when it segments its unity in order to reconstitute its domination.[39]

This segmentation must however coincide with an extension of freedom and equality. It is only by presenting a universalistic perspective (in other words, by basing power on gaining consent and not on violence), that the bourgeoisie will be able to involve the other classes in its hegemonic project. The concrete form of this universal perspective is the absorption of the whole of society into

---

37 See Lefebvre and Macherey 1984, p. 49.

38 Ibid: '*not yet* in the state, they [the corporations] are no longer even part of civil society'.

39 Thus, there is a basic element of 'populism' in modern politics. Populism and the modern state are inseparable aspects of the same hegemonic dynamics, as argued by Laclau 1979 and 2005.

the bourgeoisie (as cited by Gramsci, the declaration that 'all mankind will be bourgeois'),[40] by means of an expansion of the freedom of the entire national society and an increase in its capacity for the accumulation of wealth.

Hegemony as a Theory of Modern Power

Let us go back to the three specific elements of modern power as identified above: vertical articulation of a homogenous space, appropriation of all the space by a single class, the non-statutory, but political nature of this articulation. The concept of hegemony enables us to conceptualise the link between these three aspects, because this perspective shows bourgeois power as an essentially dynamic, expansive structure legitimated by means of its own movement, which therefore constantly cancels out internal differences in the promises of shared 'progress' for all classes while at the same time reinstating class differences as the bourgeoisie is legitimated as the ruling class within this shared progressive movement.

Totalising space and its vertical articulation are one and the same thing in terms of hegemonic movement: inclusion encompasses exclusion. Winning consent, a broad base of support, is the link that organically connects these two aspects.

The metaphorical national meaning of space and its literal international connotation are also linked here. In concrete terms, hegemonic dynamics envisage an international dimension, namely, the relocation of a national state within the international framework in a manner that potentially offers development opportunities not encompassed by the previous arrangement.[41] On this level, the literal and horizontal meaning of space – as a variegated set of 'places' to be shared by states – is brought back into the equation, but in a way that shows its intrinsic connection with metaphorical and vertical connotations. In this light, in fact, international policy power is explained by the progressive-hegemonic character of politics on a national basis. In other words, war is not the foundation of power, but a derivative form of power, which can be understood only in the light of hegemonic dynamics based on the acquisition of consent. Indeed, it is because a national ruling class attempts to legitimise its internal hegemony that it undertakes a set of external actions (including war)

---

40   Q8, §179, p. 1050.

41   For an excellent reconstruction of the logic of hegemony see Balsa 2006a and 2006b. For the national/international dimension of hegemony, see Vacca 1977 and De Felice 1977.

aimed at subdividing space anew in a different way (for example, by righting an injustice perpetrated against it by the imperialism of others, as in the case of national wars of liberation).

National/International

As we have seen, the dynamics of hegemony remain incomprehensible if they are reduced to one of their two constitutive dimensions, the national and the international. If it is considered purely on a national level, its political frame-work is emphasised, that is, the fact that it succeeds in linking an extension of social rights, freedom and equality to a reaffirmation of the domination/sub-ordination relationship. But the specific and ultimately *unique* combination in which these specific hegemonic dynamics are carried out is lost: its means and resources and consequently the nature of the expansionary policy that it makes possible within the country.

Once achieved, hegemony leads to a reaffirmation of the political power of a given national bourgeoisie. But this is still not much. Not all bourgeoisies are equal. Just think of the hegemony created by the US government during the New Deal and that implemented by Italian fascism in the same period. There is an obvious analogy since in both cases a policy of active inclusion of the masses in the state through a vast campaign of public work was set in motion, which stimulated demand and social reform.[42] Nevertheless, the difference between the two regimes must be taken in account. The political weight and functions within the international division of labour of the two countries was very differ-ent. The theorists of fascism themselves, taking up a traditional vindication of Italian nationalism (but derived from Giovanni Pascoli's 'national socialism'),[43] attempted to articulate this difference by contrasting 'capital' nations to 'pro-letariat' nations.[44]

However, the contrary is also true, namely, that all the international aspects – which are ultimately 'physical' facts on which economic relations of domina-tion and difference are based – can be reduced to a sort of 'consolidation' of a number of national and international relations that ultimately belong to polit-ics. Let us consider the example of Italian fascism once again. In his *Prison*

---

42   See, for example, Schivelbusch 2005.

43   Regarding Pascoli and Corradini, see Q1, §58, pp. 68–9 and Q2, §51, pp. 205–7.

44   See the comments on the economic situation which Camillo Pellizzi and Gino Arias regularly published in the review *Gerarchia*: Pellizzi 1930 and 1931, Arias 1931a, 1931b and 1931c.

Notebooks Gramsci comments on a series of speeches given in Parliament by Foreign Minister Dino Grandi in 1932. In them, Gramsci recalls, the Minister

> posed the Italian question as a world one that had, of necessity, to be solved alongside with the others that constitute the political expression of the general post-war crisis, which in 1929 deepened to the point of near catastrophe. These questions were: the French security problem, the German equal rights problem and the problem of a new set-up for the Danube and Balkan states.[45]

Grandi stressed that, within the framework of the 'general post-war crisis', the 'local' crises are political expressions of the same 'world question', and therefore must be jointly resolved. Italy's crisis, as a nation poor in raw materials with a population which was too large to be fed, was therefore a national-local aspect of a much vaster international-global crisis.

Gramsci appreciates Grandi's ability to configure the relationship between national and international dimensions as a hegemonic political relationship:

> The way that Grandi posed the question was an able attempt to force any eventual world congress convened to resolve these problems (as well as any attempt by normal diplomatic activity) to deal with the 'Italian question' as a fundamental element of European and world reconstruction and pacification.[46]

But Gramsci also highlights an issue of political guidance of national development which illustrates fascism's serious shortcomings to the extent that it was an expression of the Italian ruling class. This was true of foreign policy:

> If it is true that general international relations, in the way that they have taken on an ever more rigid aspect since 1929, are most unfavourable to Italy (especially economic nationalism and the 'racism' that hinders the free circulation not only of goods and capital, but above all human labour), it might also be asked whether Italy's own policy has not contributed and is still not contributing to creating these new relations and making them more rigid.[47]

---

45   Q19, § 6, p. 1989 (Gramsci 1995, p. 237).
46   Q19, § 6, p. 1989 (Gramsci 1995, pp. 237–8).
47   Q19, § 6, p. 1990 (Gramsci 1995, p. 238).

There is a fundamental ambiguity between the stated policy of balance, peace and disarmament and the attempt to cast doubt on the postwar balance of power by gaining a prominent international role for Italy,[48] acting as a divisive force in the League of Nations and preparing new colonial adventures.[49] But fascism's shortcomings originated within domestic politics. In fact, Italy's 'relative poverty' was not a purely natural fact, but the result of 'socio-historical conditions that have been created and kept in being by a particular choice of political direction and that make the national economy as leaky as a sieve'.[50] The country's poverty was also (and one would say, especially) due to the inefficiency of the state's bureaucracy and the existence of a high proportion of 'parasitic', that is, non-productive, income elements. 'It may also be observed', concludes Gramsci, 'that the projection of the question onto the international field can represent a political alibi to demonstrate to the masses'.[51]

If the international dimension alone is taken into account, internal class divisions end up being brushed under the carpet together with the way in which this division was historically consolidated, so that, for example, the fascist claim to proletarian nation would have to be accepted. However, if looked at from the point of view of the concept of hegemony, the expression 'proletarian nation' means two things: a) that in the international division of labour a specific country is kept globally on the fringes and reduced to the status of a source of emigration; but also b) that a given national bourgeoisie prefers to encourage emigration (that is, the further impoverishment of its population) rather than reform the demographic structure by eliminating internal parasitism.

The link between the two aspects can in turn only be read in the light of the concept of hegemony. There were no fixed, natural constraints. The economic crisis of 1929 was actually the deepest crisis of the entire postwar period and took economic as well as a whole series of local political forms which were in turn 'worldwide' phenomena. International balance – that is, a whole series of national/international combinations – could have been rebuilt only if the Italian demand for an outlet for its emigration policy had been considered just as 'political' as, for example, French security policy. This presumes a political

---

48   The text dates back to 1934–5, but its first version, in which this judgment is already present, can be dated to June 1932. See Q9, §105, pp. 1168–9.

49   See Santarelli 1981, Vol. II, pp. 84–99.

50   Q19, §6, p. 1990 (Gramsci 1995, p. 238).

51   Ibid.

unification (of politics as an internal consent-building exercise) of all that is otherwise relegated to the sphere of 'economics', if not actually naturalised as a specific moment of the conquest of space and raw materials.

The Separation of Economics and Politics, and the International Space

The 'recombination' of a national and an international moment is, in the capitalist world, inevitably conflictual. This conflictuality stems from the fact that, within the international space, power relations – and therefore hegemony – cannot be processed in the language of politics, but are themselves forced into the language of economics as the ultimate essence of power. Geopolitics is a justification of power on the basis of economic relations and a reduction of politics to economics. Foucault's approach to space and power, as previously discussed, basically reproduces this scheme, inverting its reference values.

This reduction of politics to economics as soon as one goes beyond the national borders is not accidental. The bourgeoisie succeeds in combining the two spaces only provided that it makes them incommunicable. In fact, international projection of the internal hegemonic construction has to transform itself into a power policy changing its language in the process because internal hegemony, which power policies are designed to reinforce, also reaffirms the subdivision of space into domination and subordination relationships. The separation of economics and politics thus coincides with that of international and national space, but precisely because of the peculiar dynamics inherent in bourgeois hegemony which sets itself up in order to deny its own preconditions.

That is why the attempt – by Minister Grandi in 1932 – to introduce an explicitly political language into international space is so interesting in Gramsci's eyes. As a nation which is internationally discriminated against, Italy is forced to adopt a viewpoint 'from below' which allows it to formulate its demands in universalistic terms. The point is, however, that these premisses are then accommodated to a more modest project of national/international recombination which will keep the irrational demographic composition of the nation intact.

Gramsci cites this conflictual fate of the recombination of the two moments on the capitalist terrain, noting that there is a gulf between 'economic life' which 'has internationalism, or better still cosmopolitanism, as a necessary premiss', and the fact that 'state life has developed ever more in the direction of "nationalism" or "self-sufficiency" and so on'.[52] Economic life, as Gramsci writes elsewhere in the *Prison Notebooks*, is no stranger to politics. The 'market' is always 'determined', so much so that referring to 'the market' is equivalent to saying '"determined relation of social forces in a determined structure of the productive apparatus" that is guaranteed by a determined juridical super-structure'.[53] But while domestically the clash of social forces always acquires (or may always acquire) a political dimension – which denies the natural-ness of any 'logic' – on an international level that is infinitely more difficult.[54] The national community relies on the presupposition of its homogeneity, its indifference, namely, on the existence of a 'population' which at any time can be claimed as a benchmark to be used to measure a population which is always segmented by differences and by subordination and discriminatory structures. Internationally, this is impossible because such a community does not exist.[55]

Any attempt to regulate international space *politically* – that is, in a way that is not a simple projection of the 'nationalism' of a block of strong countries – assumes that there is a relationship of subordination to be shattered. This may occur either because of an organic crisis, such as that which occurred after 1929, in the case of war or as a reaction to the degree of organisation reached by the subordinate classes at a national level. Thinking precisely of this latter aspect, Gramsci noted the emergence, in the European postwar scenario, of a great challenge which could not be reduced to the relations to be established with the Soviet Union, but which was common to all countries struggling with the same problem and could be summarised by the expression 'trade unionism'. This should be understood not 'in its elementary sense of associationism of all social groups and for any particular purpose, but [in] its typical sense par excellence, that is, of the social elements of a new formation, which previously did not have any political authority [*non avevano "voce in capitolo"*] and which, merely by becoming united, modify the political structure of the society'.[56] 'The war itself is a manifestation of the crisis, even its first manifestation; the war

---

52   Q15, §5, p. 1756 (Gramsci 1995, p. 220).
53   Q8, §128, p. 1018 (Gramsci 2007, p. 308).
54   In the sense of Rancière 1995, pp. 36–7. A particular form of hegemony, that which Gramsci calls 'passive revolution', consists precisely in eliminating lower class demands, incorpor-ating them into a process of modernisation which is *naturalised* into an ineluctable logic, thus obtaining the result of mobilising the masses for the bourgeois project, without, however, this mobilisation *immediately* taking the shape of a political compromise.
55   See Balibar's recent claim of a post-national European populism in Balibar 2010.
56   Q15, §47, p. 1808.

was in fact the political and organisational reply of those who were responsible for the crisis'.[57]

> The war of 1914–18 represents an historical break, in the sense that a whole series of questions which piled up individually before 1914 have precisely formed a 'mound', modifying the general structure of the previous process. It is enough to think of the importance which the trade-union phenomenon has assumed, a general term in which various problems and processes of development, of differing importance and significance, are lumped together (parliamentarianism, industrial organisation, democracy, liberalism, etc.), but which objectively reflects the fact that a new social force has been constituted, and has a weight which can no longer be ignored, etc.[58]

The mere presence of this new social force, and of a state – the USSR – governed by it, makes the 'exercise of hegemony' everywhere 'permanently difficult and aleatory'.[59] The economic crisis is a signal that space in international 'economic' terms (and the dichotomy between economic and political life itself) is no longer sufficiently well-adjusted. One may talk about a new era of 'Restoration', but the analogy given by 'the attempt to give a stable legal organisation to international relations (Holy Alliance and League of Nations)' is considered by Gramsci 'the more conspicuous and superficial one',[60] because it requires in turn an explanation in the light of the 'trade union' phenomenon according to the above definition (the organisation of masses previously excluded from politics), which always comes first for him.

Bourgeois power is therefore squeezed between the growing necessity to centralise domestically, streamline and increase hegemonic strategies (this is the meaning of the passage from a war of manoeuvre to a war of position: that 'the culminating phase of the historico-political situation has begun' and that 'the siege is reciprocal, whatever the appearances', and 'the mere fact that the ruling power ha to parade all its resources reveals its estimate of the adversary'),[61] and the ineffectiveness of hegemony implemented on a national basis alone.

---

57   Q15, §5, p. 1756 (Gramsci 1995, p. 219).
58   Q15, §59, p. 1824 (Gramsci 1971, p. 106).
59   Q13, §37, p. 1638.
60   Q15, §59, p. 1824 (Gramsci 1971, p. 106).
61   Q6, §138, p. 802 (Gramsci 2007, p. 109). 'The war of position call on enormous masses of people to make huge sacrifices; that is why an unprecedented concentration of hegemony

Lenin in Italy

Italian fascism, with its demand for a balanced policy of disarmament and transition to a climate of cooperation and economic solidarity on an international level, with its vaunted adoption of a sort of hard 'productivism' on the national level and of the perspective of the 'proletariat' against the imperialist and plutocratic nations on the international level and, finally, with its 'universal' vocation,[62] represented an exceptionally important workshop for the current struggle in Gramsci's eyes, because it may have represented an expansive and 'representative' potential on a European level.[63]

However ambiguous and ultimately instrumental this claim was, fascism sought to reinstate the national-international connection by attributing a *political* nature to this link. By doing so, fascism did not frustrate the internal mobilisation of people, but rather inherently projected it outwards. The mobilised unity of the entire population and the deeply democratic aspirations of the dispossessed masses, whilst religious in origin, were condensed into the myth of the 'proletarian nation'.

In this way, fascism developed a new kind of hegemony resting on a concept of nation as the place where the aspirations of the subalterns could be fulfilled and combined non-destructively at an international level with those of other equally proletarian nations, that is, those based on production and not speculation. In this way, bourgeois politics would appropriate the visionary-religious energies and universalism of the subalterns, thus condensing into a new – populist – concept of 'nation' the need for mobilisation (acquisition of consent) on

---

is required and hence a more "interventionist" kind of government that will engage takes more openly in the offensive against the opponents and ensure, once and for all, the "impossibility" of internal disintegration by putting in place controls of all kind – political, administrative, etc., reinforcement of the hegemonic "positions" of the dominant group, etc.' (ibid.). Here Gramsci is talking about Italian Fascism.

62   Mussolini stated in 1930 that fascism 'responds to needs of a universal character' as 'it solves […] the threefold problem of relations between the state and individuals, the state and groups, groups and organised groups', and that therefore 'a fascist Europe, a Europe whose institutions are inspired by the doctrines and practice of Fascism […] i.e. which resolves, in a fascist sense, the problem of the modern state, of the twentieth century state' was imminent (Mussolini 1958, p. 283).

63   'A war of position' is currently underway, 'whose representative – both practical (for Italy) and ideological (for Europe) – is fascism' (Q10 I, § 9, p. 1229; Gramsci 1971, p. 120). There was no lack of supporters of this position at the end of the 1920s and the beginning of the following decade; see, for example, Landauer and Honegger 1928.

a domestic level and of integration and political (not merely economic, power-based) co-operation internationally.

Intervening as a leader of the Communist Party into this structure meant, for Gramsci, creating a hegemonic project starting from within Italian national life (that is, this fascist universe) capable of putting forward a more effect-ive re-combination of the national-international relationship than fascism's, whilst freeing the visionary-religious energies of the subalterns from the grip of nationalism and regressive populism. With its 'proletarian nation' demand, fascism had, as we have seen, identified the starting point of the problem, the place at which politics and religion, people and nation, national and interna-tional interweave. A completely different solution to that problem was thus required. A note by Gramsci in his ninth notebook, taken up again in his nine-teenth notebook, should probably be read in this light:

> In present-day Italy 'humanity' as an element is either 'humanity-as-capital' or 'humanity-as-labour'. Italian expansion can only be that of humanity-as-labour [...] Traditional Italian cosmopolitanism has to become a modern type of cosmopolitanism [...] The Italian people is that people which is 'nationally' more interested in a modern form of cosmo-politanism. Not only the worker but the peasant and in particular the southern peasant. To collaborate in the economic reconstruction of the world in a unitary fashion is in the tradition of Italian people and of Italian history, not in order to dominate it hegemonically and appropriate the fruits of other people's labour for itself, but in order to exist and in fact to develop as the Italian people [...] Nationalism of the French variety is an anachronistic excrescence in Italian history, typical of those who turn their heads to look back, like the damned in Dante. The 'mission' of the Italian people lies in taking up again Roman and medieval cosmo-politanism, but in its more modern and advanced form. Let it even be a proletarian nation, as Pascoli wanted: proletarian as a nation since it has constituted the reserve army for foreign capital, since it, together with the Slavonic peoples, has given the rest of the world a labour force. Exactly on this account must it take its place in the modern front of the fight to reorganise the world, including the non-Italian world, which through its labour it has contributed to create, etc.[64]

---

64   Q19, §5, pp. 1988–9 (Gramsci 1995, pp. 253–4). For a comment on this passage, see Ciliberto
        1999 and Izzo 2009, pp. 165–82.

A new type of cosmopolitanism was potentially a way of re-appropriating the whole range of issues that are tied into the myth of the 'proletarian nation' from the working class perspective. And note that this was potentially also a new form of internationalism, a response to the collapse of socialist internationalism during the Great War on which issue Comintern policy had proposed no substantial innovations.

Gramsci notes here that cosmopolitanism is the most deeply rooted feeling in a country such as Italy,[65] in which the national popular and therefore also nationalistic spirit – because of the distinguishing character of the Risorgimento and what followed it – had always remained 'an anachronistic excrescence' imported from abroad. It would not just be a case, in short, of 'overcoming' nationalism (assuming an integration of the masses on a national basis which Marx and Engels initially overlooked),[66] but of circumventing or skipping over it in exactly the same way as the Russian peasant commune could, according to Marx, avoid capitalism.[67]

Internationalism is no longer then, here, the – painfully acquired – capacity to 'go-beyond' the horizon of the nation-state by recognising the common condition of the oppressed in all nations, but a way of being *originally* a non-national specific nation, a historic achievement that had been neither chosen nor desired by the Italian people, but who could, for exactly this reason, take upon themselves a historical and political task of potentially universal significance as the only people capable, in the 'religious' clash of nationalisms, of resolving the 'proletarian nation' issue in an alternative way. This, of course, would not be a historical law, or a universally valid model, but more simply, or by contrast with infinitely greater difficulty, a possible *communist strategy* capable of creating international universality starting from Italy.

---

65 The allusion to the USSR ('the Slavonic peoples') is also evident.

66 In the *Deutsche Ideologie* (Marx and Engels 1958, p. 40) and in the *Manifesto* (Marx and Engels 1959, p. 472) proletarians were already declared as free from bourgeois prejudices such as nation, country, family, morality, religion. This is the effect of the dissolutive dynamics introduced into the world by the bourgeoisie, a dynamic force which compels everyone 'to face with sober senses [*mit nüchternen Augen*], his real conditions of life, and his relations with his kind' (*Manifesto of the Communist Party*, in Marx and Engels 1959, p. 465; Marx and Engels 1976a, p. 487). Already in the struggles of 1848–50, Marx radically revised this belief appreciating the power of ideological 'enchantments' among the masses too. But what concerns us here is the connection between this thesis and the image of civil society as the realm of generalised conflict, as seen above. See also the *Addendum* to this chapter.

67 See Marx 1987a and 1987b. Concerning these two texts, in the context of the late Marx's thought, see Sacristán Luzón 2004, pp. 333–5.

Addendum

For Marx, the two junctures of modern capitalist dynamics – the destruction and rebuilding of difference – constitute a whole as a result of the *partial* nature of the revolution carried out by the bourgeoisie. This class, he argues, proclaims universal values – *freedom, equality, fraternity* – which it immediately subordinates to *property*. Its universality is therefore false because its ability to mobilise and criticise does not go beyond the sphere of the political state, of citizenship, leaving 'civil society' in the grip of the most savage selfishness, of exploitation of man by man.[68] Rather than a legal fact, then, for Marx inequalities are *economic* and based on a pretence of contractual equality that is constantly denied in practice. Power is exerted in society through violence and since laws limit their effectiveness to the *formal aspect* of social relations alone, they merely maintain that this violence is lawful if contained within its own terms.

On this basis, a 'political' space can only be, on one hand, the pre-legal sphere of the material clash of social powers unleashed against one another and, on the other, the legal sphere of the formal equality of those same powers. In the former case, politics is resolved into economics as an accretion and organisation of private interests, whilst in the second it identifies with the idealistic public space of the modern state, which 'disregards real man or satisfies the whole of man only in imagination'.[69]

In this division of politics and its absorption into two distinct languages – economics and law-philosophy – Marx's intention is to depict the real gulf dominating the bourgeois world. But the Feuerbachian analytical framework – which Marx here follows – conditions heavily (although not completely) the result of his research. Thus, the displacement of 'consciousness' from the plane of 'the material activity and the material intercourse of men – [from] the language of real life',[70] to its 'mental production as expressed in the language of the politics, laws, morality, religion, metaphysics, etc., of a people',[71] is defined by Marx as 'sublimates' of the 'material life-process'.[72]

---

68   See *Zur Judenfrage* (1844), in Marx and Engels 1956, pp. 356–7, 365–70.

69   *Zur Kritik der Hegelschen Rechtsphilosophie* (1844), in Marx and Engels 1956, pp. 384–5 (Marx and Engels 1975a, p. 181).

70   *Die deutsche Ideologie*, in Marx and Engels 1958, p. 26 (Marx and Engels 1975d, p. 36). See also p. 30 (pp. 43–4): 'The "mind" is from the outset afflicted with the curse of being "burdened" with matter, which here makes its appearance in the form of agitated layers of air, sounds, in short, of language'.

71   Marx and Engels 1958, p. 26 (Marx and Engels 1975d, p. 36).

72   Ibid.

In direct contrast to German philosophy which descends from heaven to earth, here it is a matter of ascending from earth to heaven. That is to say, not of setting out from what men say, imagine, conceive, nor from men as narrated, thought of, imagined, conceived, in order to arrive at men in the flesh; but setting out from real, active men, and on the basis of their real life-process demonstrating the development of the ideological reflexes and echoes of this life-process. The phantoms formed in the brains of men are also, necessarily, sublimates of their material life-process, which is empirically verifiable and bound to material premises.[73]

Marx's distinction here is between what people say about themselves and what they really are, a theme to which he returns in 'The Eighteenth Brumaire of Louis Bonaparte' (1852),[74] and once again with greater force in the 'Preface' to the *Contribution to the Critique of Political Economy* (1859),[75] which separates representation and reality analytically. In 1845, Marx uses a term drawn from chemistry to describe the real status of the former: sublimation is the transformation into smoke of dry, solid matter and sublimate is the dust left over.[76] Even earlier than this, the term was drawn from alchemy: *Sublimat* is 'that which is raised, lifted and made more pure, so that it has more strength'.[77] Marx evidently tended towards the chemical sense, in which the alchemical 'lift' is reduced to a simple consequence of combustion with a corresponding loss of reality. Defining ideas as a *Sublimat* characterises the field of represent-ation as a weak copy of the original reality: a kind of reality which has *gone up in smoke*.

Thus, whilst on one hand Marx claims a real, historically effective rela-tionship between economics and politics in opposition to the philosophical idealism-legal liberalism pairing, on the other hand this claim is neutralised by his equivalence between 'abstraction' and 'alienation',[78] in such a way that thought, culture and politics are seen as antithetical to concrete reality which is in turn inescapably bound to the sphere of immediate and empirically veri-fiable practical power. The state policy sphere is therefore absorbed into the religious sphere.[79] The idea that there might be concrete power in abstrac-

---

73   Ibid.
74   See Marx and Engels 1960, p. 139.
75   See Marx and Engels 1961, p. 9.
76   See Krünitz 1773, Bd. 177, s.v., p. 653.
77   Roth 1572, s.v. (the reference is in Grimm and Grimm, 1854–1960, Band 20, s.v. *Sublimat*).
78   See *Die deutsche Ideologie*, in Marx and Engels 1958, p. 34 (Marx and Engels 1975d, p. 47).
79   See *1. Feuerbach*, in Marx and Engels 1958, p. 539 and see also *Deutsche Ideologie* (in Marx

tion, namely that the 'form' is capable of incorporating politics within it in a more effective, rather than attenuated, form, is at that moment (1844–5), for Marx, little more than a spark (we might say: an echo of the word *Sublimat* in its alchemical meaning) which is constantly frustrated and fended off by the Feuerbachian language used.[80]

The nature of the relationship between economics and politics therefore remains indeterminate. In fact, Marx oscillates (and will continue to oscillate) between a critique of political economy which shows the *political* nature, run by power relationships of scientific categories,[81] and a critique of politics and law, as limited forms and mere vehicles (in the sense of *Reflexe*, copies or indeed transcripts in another language) of economic interests.[82]

This is why Marx's notion of *bürgerliche Gesellschaft*, 'bourgeois/civil society', which he explicitly draws from Hegel,[83] is singularly impoverished when compared to the text of the *Rechtsphilosophie*. *Bürgerliche Gesellschaft* is in fact seen from the perspective of Hegel's theory of the state as a condensation of the modern state; that is, of the logic of sovereignty and therefore as atomistic disorder which the state opposes as a necessary exteriority, resulting from an overturning, from total transcendence.[84]

---

and Engels 1958, p. 31; Marx and Engels 1975d, p. 45, marginal annotation by Marx): 'First form of ideologists, *priests*'.

80   For the young Marx's attempt to develop non-Feuerbachian ideas, see Frosini 2009, pp. 47–62.

81   This emerges especially in *Misère de la philosophie* (1847) and in the *Nachwort* (1873) to the second edition of *Capital*, Vol. 1.

82   See Balibar 1991, pp. 164–5. Regarding the attempt to locate another 'place' of politics during the period of Kreuznach, see Abensour 2004.

83   See *Die deutsche Ideologie*, in Marx and Engels 1958, p. 36 (Marx and Engels 1975d, p. 50).

84   See *Kritik des Hegelschen Staatsrechts*, in Marx and Engels 1956, p. 233 (Marx and Engels 1975c, p. 31): 'Of the various elements of national life, the one most difficult to evolve was the political state, the constitution. It developed as universal reason over against the other spheres, as ulterior to them. The historical task then consisted in its [the constitution's] reassertion, but the particular spheres do not realise that their private nature coincides with the other-worldly nature of the constitution or of the political state, and that the other-worldly existence of the political state is nothing but the affirmation of their own estrangement. Up till now the political constitution has been the religious sphere, the religion of national life, the heaven of its generality over against the earthly existence of its actuality. The political sphere has been the only state sphere in the state, the only sphere in which the content as well as the form has been species-content, the truly general; but in such a way that at the same time, because this sphere has confronted the others, its content has also become formal and particular. Political life in the modern sense is the scholasticism of national life'.

In 1859 Marx uses the same wording, noting that civil society may be more precisely defined as 'the economic structure of society', formed by the 'totality' [*Gesamtheit*] of the 'relations of production'. In short, political economy anatomically breaks down 'civil society' into its essential relations, leaving out the multi-faceted surface layer of a notion that Hegel had taken over from eighteenth-century French and British writers.[85] What remains fixed, from 1844 to 1859, is the idea that civil society is limited to a 'system of needs' into which order must be introduced from the outside. Civil society includes in itself the reality (the 'material life conditions', *materielle Lebensverhältnisse*) and not the representation (the 'legal and political superstructure').[86]

Marx is not concerned with law, *Polizei* and corporations, as instances of the more or less immanent presence of the state within civil society,[87] preferring instead to emphasise conflict and its transcendent suppression. His work brings civil society back to economy, whilst the 'representative' articulations within it are simply not taken into account. This clear-cut, radical opposition between reality and representation, freed of the insight contained in the idea of the political sphere as a 'sublimation' of the economy and not a mere 'reflection', ends up ignoring the universalistic potential (and thus the *hegemonic strength*) precisely of that bourgeoisie of which Hegel is thinking in his *Grundlinien der Philosophie des Rechts*.[88]

---

85   Marx, *Zur Kritik der politischen Ökonomie*, in Marx and Engels 1961, p. 8 (Marx and Engels 1987, pp. 262–3).

86   Ibid.

87   On this subject, see Solari 1974, pp. 239–54.

88   Concerning these omissions by Marx, see Becchi 1993, p. 384, p. 390, p. 418.

CHAPTER 9

The Seeds of Ancient History: The Polemical Anachronism of Pier Paolo Pasolini

Luca Pinzolo

They who never wanted to know [...]
they shall destroy Rome
and on her ruins
they shall lay the seed
of Ancient History.[1]

In the cinematographic version of Oedipus, the protagonist is born in the 1930s and dies in Bologna at the end of the 1960s. His story, however, takes places in the past, or rather, in a sort of archaic age that cannot be precisely located either spatially or temporally.

[T]he main body of the film tells the story of Oedipus making use of an archaic setting which is at the antipodes of the neoclassic style; by means of a provocative eclecticism, elements from various cultures (African, Aztec, Japanese) are juxtaposed and interwoven in order to create a terrestrial, desertical framework rich in symbolic implications. Such a mythical story is then embedded in a modern setting, so that a fascinating back-and-forth between myth and history is created.[2]

The myth is therefore a sort of 'dream of modernity' that affects modernity itself, conferring upon it an 'oniric, sacred and hallucinatory' aura.[3]

The spectator, however, does not dream: he is awake and observes a show that unfolds in front of his eyes. He perceives a stream of images, the linearity of which is interrupted by an intertwining of heterogenous temporalities and narratological registers.[4]

---

1 'Prophecy', in Pasolini 2014, pp. 372–4.
2 Fusillo 1996, p. 36.
3 Fusillo 1996, pp. 36–7.
4 As Duflot pointed out, Pasolini's cinema is best understood as a complex of 'variations on a language'. See Pasolini 1983, p. 49.

One might refer to this simply as the nature of cinema were it not for the fact that such an experience – the actual perception of a non-contemporaneity – is exactly what contemporary humankind lives almost on a daily basis. Pasolini frequently walked through the city, passing by a *borgataro* or moving from the bourgeois neighbourhoods to the more popular ones. In doing so, he experienced the passage from the perception of a modern present to the perception of premodernity, from 'memory' to 'nostalgia'.

What is the 'pre-modern'? How are we to understand such a 'pre' and how are we to think about the possibility of grasping it within the present? The very way of formulating this question suggests that grasping the pre-modern within the modern amounts to having nostalgic perception, understood as a current perception of the past. By using such an expression, derived from Bergson,[5] my aim is to refer to the unique act that simultaneously involves perception and memory; in this case, memory is not the re-evocation of a lost past, but a specific modality of perception that is capable of grasping something in the present as if it were delayed in relation to the present itself. Pasolini refers to 'another world', whose peculiarity is to be a sort of remainder, a residue that includes within itself the world of peasants, of the lumpenprolatariat and of workers:

> up to a few years ago this was the pre-bourgeois world, the world of the
> dominated class ... the world of the peasants (to which the urban sub-
> proletarian cultures and, until a few years ago, also the working class
> minorities belonged) ... is a transnational one: it does not recognize any
> nations. It is the remainder of previous civilizations (or of an aggregation
> of previous civilizations all very similar to each other).[6]

The fundamental question is: is there something that is in relation to the present that is only the past, without being a root or origin of this present? Or, furthermore, is there anything that may be the past of no present, without being either a virtuality or a possibility, but endowed with an 'actual existence'?

This problem – the perception of the primitive within modernity – is the essential question of modernity itself, of which Pasolini is an acute observer and exegete. It is modernity that manifests itself as a disjunction of temporal

---

5 See Bergson 1975, p. 157. In this text, written in 1908 and devoted to the notion of *déjà vu*, Bergson argues that 'the formation of memory is never posterior to the formation of perception; it is contemporaneous with it'.

6 '8 Luglio 1974. *Limitatezza della storia e immensità del mondo contadino*', in Pasolini 1981, p. 62.

modes, at least if we accept the term 'modernisation' according to its immediate etymological meaning.[7] Such a disjunction, differentiating the now from
the before, eventually posits a stratified temporality.

> This is exactly what always happens in Italy, whenever one wants to dig
> further: the superficial modern layer is soon overcome, and one finds
> himself in strata of [an] inferior civilization, historically outdated.[8]

In this chapter, my aim is to flesh out this temporal complexity within the diachrony that Pasolini finds in images and in written language.[9] For Pasolini,
images and language share the fact of being writing [*la scrittura*] – understood
simply as recording and archiving, that is, transcription. Images, and particularly cinematographic images, are the written language of reality; these images
refer to reality in the way that writing refers to orality and gestures and, eventually, to an audio-visual code that in turn itself belongs to reality. Consequently,
my contribution will consist in a reading of Pasolini's writings devoted to linguistics and the semiology of cinema.

What I intend to show is that for Pasolini, writing [*la scrittura*] is the recording and the deposit of a diachrony that is amenable to a particular form of
relationship between classes, that is, one that links a proper class (endowed
with its own 'consciousness' and history) to a non-class, bereft of consciousness and history.

It is not entirely possible, of course, to deny that Pasolini resorted to religious categories for the interpretation of reality and history, combining themes
derived from Mircea Eliade with elements taken from the historicist anthropo-

---

7   See, for instance, Martinelli 2002, p. 3: 'with modernization, we mean the large-scale set of
    processes by means of which a determinate society tends to acquire the economical, political,
    social and cultural features considered central to modernity. The concept of modernization,
    then, implies the concept of modernity in the meaning that it acquired in the XVII century,
    even though its origins predate this meaning by many centuries. The late Latin word *mod-
    ernus* derives from *modo*, which means "now", "recently", and dates from the end of the V
    century A.C. It was contrasted to *antiquus*, in particular by St. Augustinus, who uses it to
    oppose the new Christian era to the old pagan times'.
8   'Prefazione' to *Le italiane si confessano*, in Pasolini 1999, p. 103, quoted in Sapelli 2005, p. 106.
9   The word 'diachrony' is used by Pasolini both to refer to the traces left in a contemporary
    image by an archaic society and in its structuralist meaning of 'revolution' and 'change'. He
    attempts to introduce diachrony in the linguistic structure, conceiving the latter 'dynamic-
    ally', as 'a structure that wants to be another structure'. See 'From the laboratory. (Notes en
    poète for a Marxist Linguistics)', in Pasolini 2005a, p. 50.

logy of Ernesto De Martino.[10] According to its own complexity, however, such
an approach is not reducible – at least not entirely – to a regressive historical
outlook centred on the idea of the 'eclipses of the sacred'. This is due to the
fact that, in its own concrete unfolding, Pasolini's approach adopts only one
aspect of 'the sacred', namely, its 'phenomenological dynamic', that is, the dis-
play of that which exceeds, which in Pasolini takes the form of the remainder
that prevents the closure of the present in an epochal totality, instead looking
for the conditions of it in the unfolding of modernity itself.

Sequence Long-Shot as 'Living Present' and Diachrony in Perception

Pasolini's notes on sequence shots in cinema can be considered as a theory
of cinema, as well as a theory of experience and of the specific temporality of
perception. Pasolini explicitly declares that 'the sequence shot is … subjective',[11]
and that, at its purest (that is, when considered only at the level of shooting
and preceding any editing), it overlaps with the entirely sensible experience.
Sensation is the capturing of the image analogous to the one performed by a
film camera. A witness of an event simply frames it and records it from the place
where they stand, that is, from a visual angle that coincides with the place in
which they are located.

> the spectator-cameramen … did not choose any visual-angles; he simply
> filmed from where he was, framing what his eyes saw – better than the
> lens.[12]

We can conceive of a plurality (even an infinite plurality) of individuals, each
one carrying a camera, each located in different points of the space, who witness and record the same event. In this case, we will have different subjective
visions, different viewpoints of the same event.[13] We can then project them in

---

10 De Martino's studies on Puglia's popular culture are mentioned in '8 Luglio 1974. Limit-
    atezza della storia e immensità del mondo contadino' and in 'Gli uomini colti e la cultura
    popolare', both in Pasolini 1981. The importance of Eliade to Pasolini is referred to in
    Pasolini 1983.
11 'Observations on the sequence shot', in Pasolini 2005a, p. 233.
12 Ibid.
13 Pasolini mentions as an example the murder of Kennedy, filmed by TV operators and
    passers-by.

succession on a screen or edit them to have a simultaneous vision in which they are all connected. In all of these cases, however, the substance remains the same. We will always have

> a series of sequence-shots which would reproduce the real things and actions of that hour, seen contemporaneously from various visual angles: seen, that is, through a series of 'subjectives'.[14]

Here, Pasolini stresses two things that need to be pointed out. First, he states that 'the subjective is therefore the realistic boundary of every audiovisual technique';[15] second, 'the reality seen and heard as it happens is always in the present'.[16]

In terms of the first statement, the expression 'realistic limit' refers both to an audio-visual technique that reproduces reality and to the 'reality' of that which (be it a person or a thing) is actually filming. In other words, the 'reality' that is at stake when an audio-visual technique is being employed is attributable both to what is filmed and to the beholder themselves, who in turn is as real as the world in which they are inserted and of which they observe a fragment from their own perspective:

> it is not conceivable to 'see and hear' reality in its development, if not from a single visual angle: and this visual angle is always that of a subject who sees and hears. This subject is a flesh and blood subject, because even if we, in a fictional film, choose an ideal point of view, and one which is therefore in a certain sense abstract and not naturalistic, it becomes realistic and, in extreme cases, naturalistic in the moment in which we place a camera and a recorder at that point of view: it will come out as something seen and heard by a subject in flesh and blood (that is, with eyes and ears).[17]

Thus, a point of view capable of overcoming the realistic limits represented by the reality of the event and by the materiality of the beholder is simply not conceivable.

---

14   'Observations on the sequence shot', in Pasolini 2005a, p. 233.
15   Ibid.
16   Ibid.
17   Ibid.

The definition of cinema according to Pasolini is well known: it represents reality through reality;[18] when it becomes a single piece of work, an *oeuvre*, it will be the 'written language' of that reality. Thus, cinema is the 'written manifestation of a natural, total language, which is the acting of reality',[19] and reality is 'cinema in nature'.[20]

If cinema is a representation of reality by means of reality itself, it follows that the image finds its origins and its content in reality itself, and not in symbolic or semiotic substitutes. To talk about 'reality as language whose words are things' amounts to saying that any and every thing is a sign of itself.[21] Thus, images are not 'signs' of things and they do not share the arbitrariness of signs; they are not substitutable in the same way that the things that they portray are, since the succession of shots follows the order of succession in which things present themselves to us,[22] and are therefore 'real' things themselves.

The expression 'by means of', as I have already suggested, not only implies that the represented coincides with the representation, but also that the place and means through which reality is turned into image is itself real; this is what Pasolini calls 'subject'.

'Subject' is therefore the limit of a subjective of reality turned into an image; such a subject is 'flesh and blood' only insofar as it is endowed with attributes that allow it to feel and observe the real (that is, an eye and an ear). If a camera-man puts a camera on a stand and leaves, this will not imply the disappearance of the subject or of the subjective character of the vision, since there will still be an eye (the lens of the camera) and an ear (the tape recorder) capable of translating a real fact into audio-visual images.

Let us consider now the second important point made by Pasolini: the space-time of vision and listening is the here-and-now, that is, the present. Every vision is a vision in the present of an event that is happening, a vision perceived by an eye that is present and located-in-the-event. Such a present eye perceives something, a gathering, so to speak, in and at the present, which is to say, now:

---

18   'Quips on the cinema', in Pasolini 2005a, p. 225.

19   'The written language of reality', in Pasolini 2005a, p. 205.

20   Pasolini 2005a, p. 198.

21   '*Res sunt nomina*', in Pasolini 2005a, p. 257.

22   'Quips on cinema', in Pasolini 2005a, p. 229 ff. See also '*Res sunt nomina*', in Pasolini 2005a, p. 259, where Pasolini argues that iconic signs are neither symbolic nor conventional. In 'The End of the Avant-garde' (in Pasolini 2005a, p. 133), he states that 'Cinema is a language ... which compels the enlargement of the concept of language. It is not a symbolic, arbitrary, and conventional system'.

the time of a sequence shot, understood as a schematic and primordial element of cinema – that is, as an infinite subjective – is therefore the present.[23]

Constitution of the subject through vision and present time is one and the same thing: subject is a 'subjective', that is, a real visual angle – in flesh and blood – on reality that translates it into an image. The time of the subject is a potentially infinite subjective, which is always in the present, a present capable of indefinite expansion; thus, the subject is the present of an inexhaustible vision:

> it is clear that reality, with all its faces, has expressed itself. It has said something to those who were present (were present as participants, because reality speaks only with itself). It has said something in his language ... All these nonsymbolic signs say that something has happened ... here and now in the present. And this present is, I repeat, the time of the various subjectives as sequence shots, shot from the various visual angles in which fate placed the witnesses.[24]

Thus far, however, we only have an event turned into a vision, a vision of a present subject, or of many subjects that occupy different spatial coordinates, but always in one present. Each vision, taken on its own, is partial and local, untrustworthy to the eye of a detective attempting to re-enact the dynamics of an event. These images are incomprehensible to a spectator watching the projection of a (or many) sequence shot(s).

The sequence shot is, therefore, 'the most naturalistic moment of the film narrative',[25] since it enables us to grasp a determined fact in its bare being-given, it is the mere manifestation of the real as a phenomenon and as such it coincides with the mechanisms of sensation and perception:

> the hypothetical pure sequence shot thus reveals, by representing it, the insignificance of life as life. But through this hypothetical pure sequence shot I also come to know ... that the fundamental proposition that something insignificant expresses 'I am', or 'there is', or simply 'to be'.[26]

---

23   'Observations on the sequence shot', in Pasolini 2005a, p. 233.
24   'Observations on the sequence shot', in Pasolini 2005a, p. 234.
25   'Is Being natural?', in Pasolini 2005a, p. 240.
26   Ibid.

The happening of an event for a subject produces an image of bare Being, a 'there is' as mere givenness bereft of any origin and goal, that is, bereft of meaning and history: it is simply a mere flux. It follows that the most neutral and accurate filming of a fact or of a real event will not be able to offer to the spectator a sense of 'reality': rather, it will produce an image of reality in its absurdity, as mere fact bereft of meaning or comprehensibility.[27]

Even if reality is 'cinema in nature' and the perception of an embodied subject is an infinite sequence shot, cinema as a 'language of reality' is at once *langue* and *parole*,[28] cinema in general, as well as 'film'. A film is realised according to a complex set of operations, from editing to the coordination of single long-shot sequences, capable of producing a discourse that is articulated and endowed with meaning. The shift from vision to an audio-visual discourse that offers itself to another present vision [*visione attuale*] is made possible by the intervention of a director, an author who has collected the traces of observations left on a film (evidence or vestiges of an experienced, hence no longer current, present) and has assembled them on the basis of a project, that is, a possible discourse. In this way, the director has worked up the evidence of the past in order to offer it as a new possible vision. In so doing, he renders the past present.[29]

> from the moment in which editing enters the picture, that is, when we pass from the cinema to a film ... it happens that the present becomes past ... a past that, for reasons immanent in the cinematographic medium, and not because of an aesthetic choice, always has the quality of the present (it is, in other words, a historical present).[30]

The cinemato-*graphic* is therefore a narrative discourse endowed with meaning, whose minimal units are nonetheless non-historical images, apparitions or, to use an expression coined by Eliade, 'ontophanies':[31] exhibitions of the phenomenal givenness of Being. With respect to history, due to reasons intrinsic to the employed technical means, it cannot but be the pre-historical: a past that can certainly be presented, but that is also to a certain extent impossible to narrate.

---

27   'Observations on the sequence shot', in Pasolini 2005a, p. 235: 'Until such living syntagmas have been placed in a relationship among themselves ... they are maimed, incomplete languages, practically incomprehensible'.

28   'Observations on the sequence shot', in Pasolini 2005a, p. 236.

29   'Observations on the sequence shot', in Pasolini 2005a, p. 235 (translation modified).

30   'Observations on the sequence shot', in Pasolini 2005a, p. 236.

31   See Eliade 1961.

We are dealing in this instance with a limit, a material residue that is contained not only in the technical tool used for the audio-visual recording, but also in the language of the script itself and even, as I will show, in language itself.

The Paradox of the Screenplay

The screenplay is first and foremost a written literary text, except for the following peculiarity: it includes 'the integrating reference to a potential cinematographic work'.[32] It therefore follows that to read a script means to read an incomplete text, a text from which something is missing, in which, however, the absence thereof is included in its very form. A screenplay therefore lacks

> an internal element of form, an element that is not there, that is a 'desire for form' ... in the details, it is only a void, a dynamic that is not made concrete; it is like a fragment of strength without destination, which is translated into a coarseness and incompleteness of form.[33]

Thus, we have a written text that, in its very form and structure, is characterised by the absence of an element that cannot be there for two reasons: because it is something that has to be 'done' and because this 'something' that has to be done is, in fact, written in another language, which the literary writing alludes to without being able to contain it. It follows therefore that

> the word of the screenplay is thus, contemporaneously, the sign of two different structures, inasmuch as the meaning that it denotes is double: and it belongs to two languages characterized by different structures.[34]

The screenplay is thus 'a diachronic structure by definition',[35] or an actual process,[36] given that it points toward a film that has yet to be made – a process without evolution. It does not move from state A to a state B and, in this

---

32   'The screenplay as a "structure that wants to be another structure"', in Pasolini 2005a, p. 188.
33   Ibid.
34   'The screenplay as a "structure that wants to be another structure"', in Pasolini 2005a, p. 193.
35   Ibid.
36   Ibid.

sense, it can be said to be a dynamism to which no destination corresponds. It is a process that does not proceed, that is, a 'tension which moves, without departing nor arriving, from a stylistic structure – that of narrative – to another stylistic structure – that of cinema – and, more deeply, from one linguistic system to another'.[37]

We thus have the paradox of a structure that coincides with a process, a structure whose structural feature is to be a process; a structure that is in itself diachronic. It is true that this paradox can be untied by the reader's capacity for imagining the passages from one state to another. In other words, the reader can define both the moment of the literary structure of the screenplay and the final moment of the cinematographic structure, and can even, eventually, internally re-enact and re-live the passages from one state to another.[38] The reader cannot avoid experimenting with the passages from the structure of written language to the linguistic structure of the images; feeling the diachronic character of the script is equivalent to experiencing it by means of the imagination. That which is given as a singular process [*processualità*] within the structure and which aims toward a specific, yet impossible goal within the 'consciousness' of the subject, in its interiority, is given as a virtually fulfilled process [*processo*]. These remarks, with all the psychological weight that they carry, are further complicated by the time in which we consider the features of the other language to which the script refers.

This is a visual language, made up of 'kinemes' or im-signs. It is these signs that constitute the minimal units of the finished film.[39] Pasolini argues that language articulates three different elements, that is, graphemes, phonemes and kinemes.[40] The latter are 'primordial images, visual monads [which are] nonexistent in reality, or virtually so. The image is born of the coordination of the kinemes'.[41]

Kinemes are 'non-existent, or almost [so]', as they are 'atoms of images', that is, virtual images forming a total image and perceptible only if coordinated

37 Ibid.

38 'The screenplay as a "structure that wants to be another structure"', in Pasolini 2005a, p. 195.

39 'The screenplay as a "structure that wants to be another structure"', in Pasolini 2005a, p. 191: 'Cinema is predicated on a "system of signs" which is different from the written-spoken one; that is, cinema is another language'.

40 'The screenplay as a "structure that wants to be another structure"', in Pasolini 2005a, p. 189.

41 'The screenplay as a "structure that wants to be another structure"', in Pasolini 2005a, p. 190.

with one another. Moreover, *qua* images, they are not 'things' but data of perception, of the imagination. Imagination is that through which a complete fusion between the code of reality and the code of audio-visual language is realised:

> an action of imagined reality and an action of imagined audio-visual language are exactly identical. To imagine a woman who looks at a plane in reality (with the lack of precision of peripheral details that always characterize our imagination) corresponds exactly to imagining said woman who looks at a 'plane' in an audio-visual representation.[42]

Here we can see that the script refers to another language in the full sense of the word, that is, to a 'primitive' language that is not translatable into the language of linguistic signs. The latter can only allude to it as something that is absent, but never translate it entirely:

> visual communication which is the basis of film language is, on the contrary, extremely crude, almost animal-like. As with gestures, and brute reality, so dramas and the processes of our memory are almost pre-human events, or, on the border of what is human. In any case, they are pregrammatical and even premorphological.[43]

Another aspect to take into account is that 'im-signs' are signs of 'impenetrable objects', which 'do not move nor do they say about themselves what they are in a particular moment'.[44] In other words, objects do not speak; however, this does not mean that they cannot be named and indeed they are; this is, however, an operation performed by us. Objects as such present themselves, but they do not name themselves and do not speak. Are we therefore to think of objects as that which resist any operation of naming? As a Real that cannot be pronounced or said and appears only through the 'holes' in language?[45] Pasolini appears to answer this question positively, at least in part. He seemingly refers to a language made out of a chain of signifiers that refer to one another and 'evoke'

---

42   'The rheme', Pasolini 2005a, p. 289. In the essay 'The "cinema of poetry"', Pasolini reiterates
      the same point: 'There is an entire world in men which expresses itself primarily through
      signifying images (shall we invent, by analogy, the term im-signs?): *this is the world of
      memory and of dreams*' (Pasolini 2005a, p. 168).

43   'The "cinema of poetry"', Pasolini 2005a, pp. 168–9.

44   'The "cinema of poetry"', Pasolini 2005a, pp. 170.

45   This is, as is well-known, the position held by the late Lacan.

(they cannot do otherwise) a primordial and pre-linguistic given, accessible to us only through the framework of imagination.[46]

However, Pasolini is also attempting to say something else: he adds that words, sentences, and so forth, are organised through grammar within a vocabulary, whereas images/signs are not. Nonetheless, when we look at an image printed on photo-paper or projected onto a screen, we already know what it is. If we see a steamship in a film, we see something that after all is part of our visual memory, that is, we see things that have 'an already lengthy and intense pregrammatical history'.[47] Two singular consequences follow: on the one hand, images are always singular and never abstract;[48] on the other, they have an oneiric physical quality.[49] In other words, they have a two-fold nature: *qua* data of imagination, they are extremely 'subjective'; *qua* images of things, they are extremely 'objective', 'to such an extent that [cinema, or the language of im-signs] reaches an unsurpassable and awkward naturalistic fate'.[50] Naturalistic fate and oneiric physical quality meet one another in the image, which is therefore not reducible either to the sole realm of dreams or to the sole realm of wakefulness. Rather, it includes both, pointing towards a dimension in which the coordinates of experience and of modern common sense have not yet taken place.[51]

The image, let us repeat, is the thing itself *qua* phenomenon offered to a beholder: it is the phenomenality of the phenomenon. In this sense, every image is objective.[52] At the same time, the image, since it originates within

---

46   Pasolini is aware that 'meaning' is itself a sign; see 'Res sunt nomina', in Pasolini 2005a, p. 258. A physical object facing an object is itself a 'living iconic sign' (ibid.); linguistic signs certainly translate the signs of non-verbal languages and the signs of reality, yet the actual place of such a translation is not in language, but in imagination (ibid.); the decoding that allows us to go backward from the linguistic sign to the referred thing is, in turn, a regressive imaginary translation of a determinate word into the image of a thing. Here we find again an apparently 'psychologistic' conception of the relationship between signs and things (signs are conventional, and the grasping of their meaning takes place in the faculty called imagination), the consequences of which for the 'language' [*lingua*] of things are crucial: reality is made up of images for which the distinction between the reality of common sense and that of dream does not hold.

47   'The "cinema of poetry"', Pasolini 2005a, p. 171.

48   'The "cinema of poetry"', Pasolini 2005a, p. 172.

49   Ibid.

50   'The "cinema of poetry"', Pasolini 2005a, p. 173.

51   The differentiation between dream and awakefulness as an acquisition of modernity is developed in De Martino 2007, particularly pp. 135–7.

52   'Quips on cinema', in Pasolini 2005a, p. 230: 'The phenomena of the world are the natural "syntagmas" of the language of reality'.

a beholder, is eminently subjective. However, Pasolini tends to emphasise the objective aspect: the beholder must not be considered a psychological subject, or as a subject capable of interpretation, but instead simply as an eye.

Yet if we rule out the idea that the capture of an image by a subject is a psychological or interpretative act, we need to think of the beholder as a place where what is produced is not an encounter, let alone a fusion of horizons (as it is the case in a translation) or a mediation of languages, but rather a difference or a bifurcation [*divaricazione*]. This is what Pasolini attempts to show when he defines the cinematographic image as free, indirect subjective [*soggettiva libera indiretta*]. It translates, in cinematographic language, the literary technique of free indirect discourse:

> it is simply the immersion of the filmmaker in the mind of his character and then the adoption on the part of the filmmaker not only of the psychology of his character but also of [their] language.[53]

In a way, this corresponds to what in literature is commonly referred to as interior monologue, except that in cinema, no interiorisation or abstraction is actually possible;[54] cinematographic images are not images contained in the mind of a subject, in the inner space of their subjectivity. They are instead images filmed by an eye, even though this eye is not entirely deprived of any features. If this is the case, is it possible to conceive of an image in which reality can show itself? Is it possible to show, through my eye, that which a peasant sees? It must be noted here that Pasolini refuses any form of sympathetic immedesimation; the borderline case of the cinematographic eye is, in fact, the total disappearance of the author into the character.[55] Pasolini also rules out any possibility of a fusion of perceptual or experiential horizons performed by language. The shift from a system of signs to another, for example, the shift from sign-reality to the film projected onto a screen, produces a semantic trans-

---

53   'The "cinema of poetry"', Pasolini 2005a, p. 175.

54   'The "cinema of poetry"', Pasolini 2005a, p. 177.

55   Ibid. On the irreducibility of the free indirect discourse to any form of human sympathy, see 'Comments on free indirect discourse', in Pasolini 2005a, pp. 88–9. To begin with, the style of an author can reveal a 'stylistic sympathy', which not only links up with the 'psychological or sociological participation to the inner world of a character', but which can also manifest an open antipathy towards him. Secondly, it must be considered that to 're-experience ... thoughts' is different from a 're-experience [of] the discourse that expresses those thoughts' (translation modified). Indirect free speech and its cinematographic equivalent are linguistic and stylistic facts, not psychological ones.

substantiation in which a 'greater inclination towards polisemy' of an already polysemic reality eventually emerges.[56]

Thus, the eye that grasps, records and reproduces reality as image is an eye that records a difference that has to do with belonging to a specific class. The differences between classes constitute the eye that films an image and offers it to us diachronously. If consciousness is there, it is a 'class consciousness' – not fusion, not immedesimation, but the recording of a bifurcation and of an internal imbalance.

> The writer has the possibility of reproducing the various languages of the different types of social conditions by reanimating them because they exist. Every linguistic reality is a totality of socially differentiated and differentiating languages, and the writer who uses 'free indirect discourse', must be aware of this above all – an awareness which in the final analysis is a form of class consciousness.[57]

The Global Eye and the Non-Contemporaneity of the Image

However, Pasolini renders his own analysis more complicated by affirming the transnational character of cinematographic language. The cinematographic look can be described in terms of class, but not in 'ethnic' terms:

> the literary language used by a writer to write a poem, a novel or an essay, is a conventional symbolic system. Moreover, any written or spoken language is defined by a set of historical, geopolitical or ... national (regional) constraints ... by contrast, cinema is a system of non-symbolic signs, of living signs, of object-signs ... cinematographic language does not express reality, then, by means of a set of linguistic symbols, but by reality itself. There is no national or regional language ... only a transnational one.[58]

The language of cinema is interclassist and international by nature. It prefigures a situation in which industrialisation and the development of the capitalist mode of production have become global, and where a general linguistic and cultural homogenisation, as well as the disappearance of national and local

---

56   'Res sunt nomina', in Pasolini 2005a, p. 258.

57   'The "cinema of poetry"', Pasolini 2005a, p. 177.

58   Pasolini 1983, p. 13.

traditions, have already taken place.[59] In sum, here we are dealing with the 'anthropological revolution' exposed by Pasolini as a form of genocide leading up to the disappearance of popular neighbourhoods, to the 'Westernisation' of the third world – what today is classified as globalisation.

The cinematographic technique anticipates globalisation, both because of its bourgeois origins and due to the exclusively technological character of its language, which is nothing else than the 'audiovisual reproduction of reality, i.e., of reality tout-court'.[60] The eye that records is merely a capturing machine and is free from ethnic and national connotations (except for the fact that it is rooted in an industrial revolution that took place in a bourgeois and capitalist world):

> a language founded on the audiovisual reproduction of reality ... cannot possess structures which are strictly homologous with those of the historically recognizable society [in which] the film is produced. The audiovisual reproduction of reality is an identical linguistic system or language in Italy, or in France, in Ghana, or in the United States.[61]

What we have then is a transnational eye bereft of national identity, capable of capturing singular data of reality loaded with chronological, ethnic and linguistic determinations. Such a look belongs to a neo-capitalist bourgeoisie that affirms itself as the sole possible perspective of visibility in the world.[62] In other words, the look of the film camera is not neutral for two reasons: first, it is material, a 'piece' of reality; secondly, it is always a particular point of view – a bourgeois class consciousness – but one that aspires to a universal status and purports to be capable of a global overview of reality. It is only possible to film differences and singularities from such a singular, yet essentially universalising consciousness.

---

59   'The end of the avant-garde', in Pasolini 2005a, p. 123.

60   'The end of the avant-garde', in Pasolini 2005a, p. 124 (translation modified).

61   Ibid.

62   This is the final result of the 'cinema of poetry' denounced by Pasolini: the cinematographic subjective perspective is a bourgeois perspective: 'in short, the bourgeoisie, also in films, identifies itself with all of humanity, in an irrational interclassism. All of these [are] part of that general attempt on the part of bourgeois culture to recover the ground lost in the battle with Marxism and its possible revolution. And it insinuates itself into that in some ways grandiose movement of what we might call the anthropological evolution of capitalism; that is, the neo-capitalism that discusses and modifies its own structures' (Pasolini 2005a, p. 185).

From the above, it follows that the character of cinematographic images with respect to the language of the audio-visual reproduction is diachronic. Such a diachronic nature refers to the pre-grammatical character of the object *qua* visual facts; to a character's spoken language, the index of their particularism, of their nation and of their ethnic group; finally, it points to the transience of the im-sign with respect to its cinematographic transcription.[63] There exists therefore a diachrony, or non-contemporaneity of the image compared to the support that films it. The filming camera, a modern tool par excellence, is capable of overcoming cultures and national limits. For this very reason, what the filming camera 'captures' is a diachronic image, an im-sign that is already old compared to the present of the look. The modern 'eye' of the filming camera can only film obsolescence, the signs of an archaic time that is but a residual production of modernity, visible in and through it only as a gap or a swerve from its temporality and its history.

Writing and Orality: The Non-Contemporaneity between Base and Superstructure

In a dense text, where Pasolini discusses the possibility of constructing a structural-Marxist linguistics,[64] he returns to the problems of the spoken language and writing, and to historical stratifications that are to be found in language itself. The declared intent is to inject some dynamism into the structuralist concept of language by inserting the diachronic dimension of becoming into the synchronic dimension of *langue*.[65]

---

63 Pasolini 2005a, p. 170: 'The filmmaker, instead of having to refine a centuries old stylistic tradition, works with one whose history is counted in decades ... His "historical addition" to the im-sign is attached to a very short-lived im-sign. Hence, perhaps, a certain sense that film is transitory proceeds from this. Its grammatical signs are the objects of a world which is chronologically exhausted each time it is depicted: the clothes of the thirties, the automobiles of the fifties'.

64 'From the laboratory. (Notes en poète for a Marxist Linguistics)', in Pasolini 2005a, p. 50.

65 'From the laboratory. (Notes en poète for a Marxist Linguistics)', in Pasolini 2005a, p. 63: 'another small and amateurish innovation ... is the diachrony (which appears in the "semantic area" of the structuralists as due to casual and inscrutable phonetic mutations) intended not as the product of an evolution of the system or of a political, and thus, schematically, linguistic revolution against the system, but as the product of an "internal revolution of the system"'.

A determinate language can only be conceived as a verbal-graphical language, that is, as a complex system where the verbal language and the written language, taken intrinsically and separate, represents only borderline cases. They are two abstractions that correspond, respectively, to the two axes of culture (writing) and nature (verbal language):

> a language in use is distinguished in this way: from the spoken-written *langue* downwards, and from the spoken-written *langue* upwards. Downwards, the purely spoken language is found, and nothing else. Upwards, the languages of culture are found, the infinite 'paroles' (that still are *never*, like spoken language, *only written and nothing other than written*: they always continue to be spoken also).[66]

At one end, we find culture, which expresses itself as writing. Such writing is to be understood as encompassing verbal and graphic language and as 'the direct and immediate product of the superstructure as [a] moment of liberation from necessity'.[67] Here, a determinate utterance is not a direct expression of natural needs, but is free and an end in itself; language is communicative insofar as it is expressive. At the other end, we find the orality, which is only 'communicative (actually on the level of biological necessity)'.[68]

Thus, the problem is now to clarify the relationship between orality and writing. Does the fact that culture is an intertwining of writing and orality turn the latter into a material structure of which the former would be the superstructure?

If this were the case, their combination would be a dialectical synthesis: culture would be the highest expression of an 'epoch', the story of the emancipation from need and the translation of such emancipation within a system of meanings. However, if this is not the case, orality would be pre-historical and only express a borderline case where language is one and the same, with a bare pre-human naturality. Whereas writing always refers to orality – if only in the sense that it attempts to subsume it and culturalise it – pure orality belongs to a pre-historical and savage world, without culture or consciousness. It is neither 'simple' nor 'complex', neither 'intelligent' nor 'non-intelligent', but a zero-degree language in which verbal expression is a natural gesture, an action like that of any other movement of the body – communication (that

---

66   'From the laboratory. (Notes en poète for a Marxist Linguistics)', in Pasolini 2005a, pp. 58–
       9.
67   'From the laboratory. (Notes en poète for a Marxist Linguistics)', in Pasolini 2005a, p. 59.
68   Ibid.

is, self-manifestation of natural being) without meaning, pure reality without concept. It is simply action.[69]

Thus, pure orality is 'included' in the concrete and verbal-graphic language only as an absence, as an index of something no longer existing and that had been marginalised by the institution of a symbolic and linguistic order: 'the "spoken" word stands there, on the two horns of the distinction, like a ghost. And in fact it is a ghost, since it is a linguistic category that is real only in the most extreme cases (primitive peoples)'.[70]

Orality cannot be the infrastructure, because it is not the base of anything; for the same reason, it cannot be the 'thesis' that finds its truth in its relationship with antithesis: it is not the foundation of anything. Because it does not have any history, because it is not history, it cannot be the origin of history in any sense; it, simply, 'is'. It follows therefore that the verbal-graphic language and the pure oral language cannot stand against each other in the form of an antithesis, nor can they be synthesised:

> such a 'langue' puts the pure 'spoken language' ... in contact with the 'spoken-written language', that is, the language of its superstructure (of its culture, be it military, agriculture, artisan, commercial, scientific, religious or literary). It does not, however, make a synthesis of them, because the two languages are not in a dialectical relation, since the first is a datum that is given and moves like a natural reality (it is in principle the relation of man to nature; it is pre-historic and unconscious – purely deterministic).[71]

We therefore need to see that written language holds in itself a sort of raw material, a purely natural facticity that cannot really be expressed, to which it is only possible to allude: a non-historical residue in the language of history, an unconscious inexpressivity that appears as a phantasm in the expressive consciousness of language. The non-historical character of this abstract dimension of pure orality is also confirmed by the fact that there is no history of orality and that there cannot be such a thing. Oral language is not subject to mutations, not even when there is a drastic revolution in language, but only to stratifications:

---

69   'The written language of reality', in Pasolini 2005a, p. 198: 'The first and foremost of the human languages can be considered to be action itself ... *Human actions in reality*, in other words, as first and foremost language of mankind. For example, the linguistic remains of prehistoric man are [a] modification of reality due to the actions of necessity'.

70   'From the laboratory. (Notes en poète for a Marxist Linguistics)', in Pasolini 2005a, p. 58.

71   'From the laboratory. (Notes en poète for a Marxist Linguistics)', in Pasolini 2005a, p. 61.

perhaps the most important characteristic of ... spoken language is that of conserving a certain metahistoric unity through the continuous stratifications and survivals of every language. No 'oral substratum' is lost: it is dissolved into the new spoken language, amalgamating itself with it, and thus representing the continuity concretely.[72]

Folk Poetry, or the Invention of the Archaic

From the very beginning of his 1955 study on Italian folk poetry,[73] Pasolini states that confronting the task of a historical reconstruction of this poetry means to confront the paradox of a literary production of an 'exquisite roughness, of a precious infantilism'.[74] Pasolini tries to avoid the idealised stereotype, romantic and Vichian in its origins, according to which the world of the people is conceived and analogous to the 'ancients' in terms of being endowed with a bright poetical fantasy and a natural simplicity foreign to the complexity of modern civilised humankind. This simplicity, which Benedetto Croce still attributes to popular modes of thinking, Pasolini argues, is a production of culture itself: only those who have a culture and a consciousness (the two things go together) can be 'simple' to the point of being naïve; where there is no consciousness or culture, there is only a complex and dramatic instinctuality:

As the naiveté ... of the popular style is in fact only the surface – simple, or simplifying due to a fusion, a fossilization – of an extremely complex and composite world, of cultural influences and stylistic stratifications, so the psychological naivety referred to by Croce, and on which he founds the only possible distinction ... between folk and high poetry, is to us only apparent. The psychological difference between bourgeois and popular is not – evidently enough – an opposition between naiveté and complexity ... it is, instead, culture, that is, consciousness, to provide men with a certain psychological naivety, not ignorance (or primitive culture): the latter leaves men, vulnerable and violent, to the obscurities of the 'complexes'.[75]

Pasolini discusses some theories on the origin of folk poetry before proposing his own. Particularly relevant among these theories is the 'monogenetic' theory

---

72   'From the laboratory. (Notes en poète for a Marxist Linguistics)', in Pasolini 2005a, pp. 61–2.
73   'La poesia popolare Italiana', in Pasolini 1994.
74   'La poesia popolare Italiana', in Pasolini 1994, p. 156.
75   'La poesia popolare Italiana', in Pasolini 1994, p. 226.

proposed in 1878 by Alessandro D'Ancona, as well as the 'bi-genetic' theory, advanced by Costantino Nigra in 1888. The former locates the origins of folk [*bassa*] poetry in Sicily, from where it would spread across the Italian peninsula during the fourteenth century to find in Tuscany its most important centre of elaboration.[76] Nigra divides folk poetry into 'two sets, lyric and epic-lyric, to which correspond[s] a geographical divide (the lyric south and the epic-lyric north)'.[77]

However, it is Croce that Pasolini addresses more attentively. Croce's studies are premised upon an anti-romantic stance that requires

a really deep review of the concept of folk poetry ... in polemics with Romantic 'mythical' understanding (of course always inspired by an anti-positivistic stance), Croce points out that such a 'myth' is premised upon an a priori attitude: folk poetry, rather than being studied historically or objectively, was forced to fit a symbolic use. The Romantics, in other words, used to turn folk poetry into the symbol of an aesthetic concept, of a political concept, or of a moral concept.[78]

Croce's perspective is that folk poetry is the expression of a mere psychological naïveté, or of a banal 'common sense'. The difference between 'high' and 'low' poetry is a matter of degrees, as is the difference between common sense and philosophical thinking.[79] From this point of view, folk poetry does not stand outside the history of literature and characterisations such as 'impersonal', 'atechnical' and 'a-historical' are by no means exclusive to it, since they can be attributed to any poetic production.

Pasolini's critique of Croce, developed through some brief and incisive remarks about various quotes, is focused exactly on these attributes. For Croce, the anonymity of folk poetry is understood only as the lack of a proper name and impersonality is considered synonymous with universality. He arguably

---

76   '*La poesia popolare Italiana*', in Pasolini 1994, p. 157.
77   '*La poesia popolare Italiana*', in Pasolini 1994, p. 159.
78   '*La poesia popolare Italiana*', in Pasolini 1994, pp. 164–5. The aesthetic concept is centred on the promotion of fantasy (closer to nature) to the detriment of intellect (product of culture); the political concept leads to the immediate identification of the people with the Nation; the moral concept is the ideal of the people as 'anti-egoistic entity – opposed to individual egoism – and almost as an incarnation of the divine' ('*La poesia popolare Italiana*', in Pasolini 1994, p. 166).
79   '*La poesia popolare Italiana*', in Pasolini 1994, p. 168.

does not understand the concept of 'anonymous',[80] and misunderstands the impersonal character of this type of literary production, equating it to the idea of 'universally human', whereas 'in the case of folk poetry, impersonal means, instead, universally pre-human'.[81] Therefore,

> the 'inventive mass' [*massa inventante*] was not to be understood as a mere quantitative association of the people gathered to make poetry, but needed to be embodied in an individual that represented the ethnic and ethical 'type', who – being undifferentiated from ... other individuals – was authorized to invent, to vary and also to scrape off, in the name of the others: he was himself 'other'.[82]

Therefore, the history of folk poetry is the history of a regress,[83] which forces the scholar to confront directly the '*miseria psicologica del popolo più basso*'.[84] While 'high' poetry is the product of a highly individualised author, capable of great originality, folk poetry is without author – it is a pre-individual, more than collective, production – characterised by the compulsive reproduction of literary stereotypes, deprived of technical freedom and incapable of stylistic innovation.[85]

Italian folk poetry did not always exist: there is no trace of it having been present during the Middle Ages. Rather, it emerged in the wake of the decadence of two great centres of power – papacy and empire – and the rise of the city-republics with their new local ruling class: a 'popular' bourgeoisie thanks to which, during the fourteenth and fifteenth centuries, folk poetry took shape. Folk poetry is therefore a product of 'the aesthetic and literary consciousness of the educated class'.[86] There is, however, a fundamental difference. The rising bourgeoisie, originally 'popular' and very close to the 'low' people, would soon distance itself from such origins and attribute to it a regressive and traditionalist character. The emergence of the bourgeoisie, bearers of an ideal of progress, will produce a set of 'remainders'; all that is left behind, or pushed to the mar-

---

80   '*La poesia popolare Italiana*', in Pasolini 1994, p. 167, nota 1.
81   '*La poesia popolare Italiana*', in Pasolini 1994, p. 167, nota 2.
82   '*La poesia popolare Italiana*', in Pasolini 1994, p. 177.
83   '*La poesia popolare Italiana*', in Pasolini 1994, p. 151.
84   '*La poesia popolare Italiana*', in Pasolini 1994, p. 154. The expression 'psychological misery', attributed by Pasolini to Ernesto de Martino, is Pierre Janet's.
85   '*La poesia popolare Italiana*', in Pasolini 1994, p. 168.
86   '*La poesia popolare Italiana*', in Pasolini 1994, p. 182.

gins of history, will be considered to be primitive by that look that instituted himself, from its inception, as archaeological.

It is as if history and the history of language unfolded along two vertical axes: one going 'upwards', leading to the formation of the consciousness, culture and the language of intellectuals, the other going 'downwards' to acquire regressive and conservative connotations in the very moment where it receives the language from 'above':

> high poetry and folk poetry essentially stem from the same kind of culture, the historical culture that belongs to [the] world in dialectical evolution, which acquires – 'descending' – regressive and primitive characters.[87]

Folk poetry, then, is born out of the relationship between the dominant and dominated class. A relationship that produces two poles and two correspondent 'psychological aptitudes': at the bottom, 'a primitive mentality' 'of archaic and primordial type, fit to produce poetry even in the most underdeveloped communities';[88] at the top, 'a mentality closer to the modern, historical life'.[89] The popular poet experiences this fracture, this non-contemporaneity; insofar as he is capable of producing verses, he participates in the high culture; as an exponent of the people, however, he cannot but attribute to himself a primitive voice and write in its name:

> a popular poet, although he occupies an ideal middle ground between the two cultures, can be at the same time a historical individual, as he belongs with the evolving culture, and [an] a-historical type, insofar as he belongs with the traditional, fixed and undifferentiating culture.[90]

Conclusion

Talking about Pasolini's 'religiousness' and his sense of the 'sacred' is beyond the scope of this chapter. Pasolini always claimed that he received a nonreligious education and that he considered himself an atheist,[91] yet at the same

---

87 'La poesia popolare Italiana', in Pasolini 1994, p. 185.
88 'La poesia popolare Italiana', in Pasolini 1994, pp. 178–9.
89 'La poesia popolare Italiana', in Pasolini 1994, p. 179.
90 Ibid.
91 Pasolini 1983, pp. 20–1.

time, he affirmed his *Weltanschauung* to be religious.[92] Alongside this feeling, however, there existed in Pasolini an 'anthropological' inclination – derived from De Martino – that allowed him to reflect on some themes strictly related to the sacred, such as the miracle, from a subjective point of view, that is, from the standpoint of their belonging to a disappearing world:

> the subjective reality of the miracle exists. It exists for the peasants of Southern Italy, as it existed for the Palestinian ones. Miracle is the innocent and naïve explanation of the real mystery that inhabits man, of the power concealed in him ... Apart from its theological feature, the revelation that takes place in the miracle belongs also to realm of magic. In any case, I purposely took a technical distance from the reality of miracles to stress that they really belong to a mentality and to a culture that are no longer entirely our own.[93]

To understand the nature of Pasolini's interest in the 'sacred' and the way in which he used it in his views of modernity, it is useful to make a detour through Mircea Eliade's studies on the history of religions, which Pasolini knew quite well.[94] Eliade, referring to the theories of Rudolf Otto, argued that the sacred is in the first place something that manifests itself in its difference from the profane:

> Man becomes aware of the sacred because it shows itself, as something wholly different from the profane. To designate the act of manifestation of the sacred, we have proposed the term hierophany. It is a fitting term, because ... it expresses no more than is implicit in its etymological content, i.e., that something sacred shows itself to us ... [the] manifestation of something of a wholly different order, a reality that does not belong to our world.[95]

---

92   Pasolini 1983, p. 22.

93   Pasolini 1983, p. 23.

94   Pasolini mentions among his resources Eliade's treatises on religions, where he found his own idea of the non-natural character of nature for the primitives: 'the characteristic of agricultural civilizations, i.e., of sacred civilizations, is to consider nature as something non-natural. I think that, on this point, I have but rediscovered what was already known' (Pasolini 1983, p. 78).

95   Eliade 1961, p. 11.

The sacred is thus conceived phenomenologically as a modality of the manifestation: the sacred is the 'manifestation of the sacred' – hierophany – where
Being manifests itself as power and fullness – ontophany:

> for primitives as for the man of all premodern societies, the sacred is
> equivalent to a power, and, in the last analysis, to reality. The sacred is
> saturated with being. Sacred power means reality and at the same time
> enduringness and efficacity.[96]

Such a manifestation entails the production of a heterogenous and discontinuous space, a space that is traversed by hierarchical tensions and by vectors that
orient the profane space upward, displacing and relativising it with respect to a
fixed point serving as centre.[97] Such heterogeneity is not only spatial, but also
temporal: sacred time suddenly appears as 'a primordial mythical time made
present'.[98]

> It is a mythical time, that is, a primordial time, not to be found in the
> historical past, an original time, in the sense that it came into existence
> all at once, that it was not preceded by another time, because no time
> could exist before the appearance of the reality narrated in the myth.[99]

We can now reassess Pasolini's theoretical gesture: he recuperates, so to speak,
the phenomenological dimension of the sacred, depriving it of all connotations in terms of values (still present in Eliade's idea of a hierarchical organisation of the space around a centre, which entails its division between high
and low, a centre and a periphery) and turns it into a hermeneutic of modernity. All hierarchies are embedded in a narrative in which there is an origin and an end, a telos: they are part of history and of historiography, to
which is nonetheless opposed a pure nonsensical, ahistorical and non-natural
Being. Hence, Eliade's order of terms – hierophany, ontophany – needs to be
overturned: only an authentic ontophany appears to a laical man as hierophany.

The problem for Pasolini was to consider the insertion of the heterogenous
into the homogenous, starting from class struggles understood as the con-

---

96   Eliade 1961, p. 12.
97   Eliade 1961, p. 15.
98   Eliade 1961, p. 68.
99   Eliade 1961, p. 72.

tinuous displacing and bifurcating of temporalities, subjects and places. The development of capitalism, with the ensuing need for enlarging the army of the labour force and of consumers, led to the urbanisation of rural populations and to the creation of a sub-proletariat.[100]

The occupation of spaces brings about a plurality of tempos and leads to a paradoxical phenomenology of class struggle, which finds itself confronted by an absolute conflict where no recognition between the conflicting parties is possible and where there is no common stake. It is the conflict between those who fight and those who are always already excluded from the fight, on the margins of it. What is a fight between those who live in a temporality oriented towards the goal of progress and development, and consequently look and fight for *something*, and those who do not fight because they live in a temporality from which the idea of becoming is absent? In fact, it can only be a frozen conflict where the fighting attitude of one part meets only the preliminary surrender of the other.[101] What Pasolini wrote about the people of Naples is revealing:

> Neapolitans are today a big tribe that instead of living in the savannah like the Touareg or the Beja, live in the womb of big city on the sea. This tribe decided – as such, without taking responsibility for its forced mutations – to fade away, refusing the new power, that is, what we normally call history or modernity.[102]

Let us turn now to the hermeneutics of modernity, which finds its expression in Pasolini's use of myth. The myth is a product of modernity – the ancients did not live in a 'mythical' or 'natural' world – and is, so to speak, a void of and in the modern historiographical discourse. This void is produced by this discourse, it is the result of its attempt to utter the pre-modern, to express its living on as a 'not-yet'.

Myth allows us to see the modern and pre-modern, the now and the not-yet/no-longer together, but not in a (impossible) totality. The process of modernisation unfolds precisely as a progressive demarcation from the ancient. In

---

100   See Sapelli 2005, pp. 1–2: 'the poet grasps the culture of the *lumpenproletariat* as continuous and secular, and locates its distinctiveness in the moving from the countryside to the city. Such a movement, which led to a ruralization of the city, also led to an anthropological rupture'.

101   See Pasolini 1961, p. 37: 'Their mercy is in their being merciless, /their strength in their levity, / their hope in their being hopeless'.

102   'La napoletanità', in Pasolini 1999, p. 230.

this sense, as Roberto Esposito argues, myth fulfils a double function: metahistorical and infrahistorical, insofar as it accounts for the specificity of its own events and exposes the unavoidable dispersion of the remainders of progress.[103]

In other words, the primitive is not the origin of the modern, nor is it that which comes before; rather, it is what the modern had to differentiate itself from and reject within the past. In the face of the modern, it is the outcast more than the enemy. The following is an excerpt from a poem collected in *The Religion of My Age*:

> they came out of their mothers' womb
> to find themselves on footpaths and pre-historical
> meadows, and written in a civil registry
> that wants them ignored by any history[104]

This is why Pasolini's *Oedipus* can be born and die in the nineteenth century, but live within a primitive world: his story unfolds in times and places that are not modern. Oedipus enters the modern world only to be born and die – the primitive, evoked by the modern, makes its appearance only to disappear.[105] It is against this backdrop that Pasolini's remarks on the variability peculiar to the contemporary age must be read. The contemporary age was for Pasolini a continual transition in which the ancient appears only insofar as it is going to disappear and where the validity of values is affirmed only through a process of uninterrupted de-valorisation. 'Today we are plunged in a (transitional) world in which old values hold their validity while they crumble in front of us'.[106] Modernisation is nothing but the very movement of demarcation from the past, which is made visible in its chronological and axiological difference: modern temporality is therefore in itself non-contemporaneous.

---

103   Esposito 2010, p. 200. 'Pasolini does not use the myth in [an] anti-historical way, but rather in a metahistorical or in an infrahistorical way, in the sense that it is embedded in history as an archaic fragment'.

104   Pasolini 1961, p. 46.

105   Esposito's interesting remarks on the 'unconscious impulse towards sacrifice that pervades nearly all of Pasolini's characters ... it is not that single life that is violent, but life in itself, once left to itself and subtracted from the course of history, like the one of the "ragazzi di vita" [literally boys of life, hustlers], all devoted to death, understood as the force that leads life at one and the same time towards its animal regression and to its sacral excess' (Esposito 2010, p. 196).

106   Pasolini 1983, p. 45.

What happens, however, when the idea of progress is reduced to mere economic and pragmatic development,[107] the consequence of which is the blockage of the historical process and the exhaustion of any utopian project?[108] The end of history entails an increasing homogenisation that nonetheless leaves out some wastes [*scarti*]: the difference reappears and is repeated in new forms, for example, in the difference between development and underdevelopment.[109]

In the motionless background of triumphant modernity, the non-contemporaneous keeps revealing itself, even if only as a 'false note':

> between body and history, there is this
> musicality out of tune,
> wonderful, in which are the same
> what ends and what begins – and such
> remains over the centuries: the given of existence.[110]

---

107   'Sviluppo e progresso', in Pasolini 1981, p. 216.

108   'Neo-capitalism seems to follow the path that coincides with aspirations of the masses. So disappears the last hope of a renewal of values through a communist revolution' (Pasolini 1983, p. 46).

109   But we may list other couples, such as 'possession/poverty', 'happiness/struggle', which seem to point towards the more radical opposition 'nature/consciousness' or 'unconsciousness/thought'. See for instance the famous lines of *Gramsci's Ashes* (Pasolini 2014, p. 177): 'drawn to a proletarian life/ from before your time, I take for religion/ its joyousness, not its millenial/ struggle: its nature, not its/consciousness'. See also *Riches* (Pasolini 2014, p. 235): 'Yet in this this world/which has nothing/not even the awareness of poverty,/ I, cheerful, hard, and lacking all faith,/ was rich. I had something!'; and p. 237: 'Oh, to withdraw into oneself and think!/ To say to oneself: there, now I'm thinking [...]/ I can think! [...]/ gusts of gold/ on bridle paths over which horses with beautiful/ brown cruppers run, mounted by boys/ who look younger still, and know not/ what light is in the world around them'.

110   'Il glicine', in Pasolini 1961, p. 166.

CHAPTER 10

Modern Times: Sociological Temporality between Multiple Modernities and Postcolonial Critique

Nicola Marcucci

Over the last decades, sociological theory, as well as political philosophy, has attempted to rethink a linear and mono-directional conception of temporality by advocating instead a plural conception. For sociological theory, the concept of modernity is essential and strategic because it represents both an interpretative canon (implicitly referring to a political philosophy able to distinguish 'normatively between what is modern and what is not), and the condition of its own experience'.[1] Thus rethinking the notion of temporality from a sociological point of view means discussing the very notion of modernity.

The benefit of looking at the conception of plural temporalities from and for a sociological perspective is twofold: first, because sociological epistemology has been grounded on the relationship between the experience of moderns and the political expectations of modernity, sociology is able to take into consideration aspects of reality that political philosophy has often considered to be pure ideological manifestation; second, because the pluralisation of temporality involves a deep revision of the notion of modernity, provoking in this way a revision of the constitutive relation between sociology and political philosophy.

I propose in this chapter a reflection on plural temporalities focused on the attempt to pluralise the concept of modernity presented in the sociological theory of multiple modernities and the critique of this concept supported by postcolonial theory.

---

1 'The relation between modernity and the social sciences is marked by an inherent tension. On the one hand, "modernity" is the condition that allows the social sciences, as the reflexive knowledge of the human social world, to emerge and exist. On the other hand, it is the objective and task of the social sciences to conceptualise and analyse "modernity" as an historical social formation. In the first meaning, "modernity" refers to a philosophical and, in particular, an epistemological condition. In the second meaning, it refers to an historical, empirical instance' (Wagner 2001, p. 3). See also Wagner 2008.

After Postmodernism: Modernity

The debate on multiple modernities can be considered as a response to the simplifications with which postmodernism intended to replace the very concept of modernity itself or – taking for granted the previous distinction between the experiences of the moderns and the political expectations of modernity – to emphasise the de facto pluralism of modern experiences by cancelling out universalism and emancipation from the modern political agenda.

Postmodernism – notably opposed to the unitary and progressive conceptions of history from nineteenth and twentieth centuries – foregrounds a plural and topological conception of time made of infinite series of local temporalities. These include, notably, the unique temporality of modernity versus the plural temporalities of postmodernity; the reification of a fictional occidental temporality established by a totalitarian metanarrative versus the postmodern consciousness of the plural linguistic character of identities; and the progressive and divisible time of 'Fordism' versus the compressed and flexible time of late capitalism.

Postmodernism can be considered as a denunciation (and radicalisation) of the nominalist nature of modernity. If modernity needs inescapably to conceive its own temporality through the acknowledgment of paradigmatic events, postmodernism dissolves the materiality of history via the free narrative choices of subjects and melts the acknowledgment of events and concrete subjects into a blurred plurality.

It is well known that postmodern perspectives were significant for a season in many disciplines. The social sciences are no exception. Nonetheless in the case of sociology, the reflection on the concept of modernity played a very specific role. Although classical sociology discourses have been grounded in highly differentiated cultural and institutional conditions, all these different conditions were involved in the late nineteenth century crisis of liberalism and in sociology's renewal of two of the main assumptions of modernity:

1. The legitimation of a new temporality as a break with the theological conception of temporality.[2]
2. The acceleration of historical time by the invention of the idea of progress.[3]

---

2   Blumenberg 1983.
3   Sociology grounds its temporality on an aspect considered by Koselleck to be foundational to the modern notion of history. This can be understood both as *Geschichte*, meaning the series

The break with theological temporality and the acceleration of historical time have been considered by sociology as the conditions of possibility of its own scientific project. Sociology transformed the modern political break with theological temporality into a theory of rationalisation and the acceleration of historical time into a conception of social change that obliterated its extreme possibility – revolution.[4] Unlike the early modern universalistic natural law rationality that proclaimed the end of theological time with the voluntarily institution of the commonwealth, sociological reason understands modernity as historically embedded in religious institutions.

Modern auto-determination by will is not exclusively provoked by modern rationality but is sociologically understood as a belief. This aspect does not undermine either the modern aim of autonomy or the rationality of modern will, but it does radically transform the relation between autonomy and the will.[5] Will is not opposed to traditional forms of authority, but is understood as a specific form of authority, which makes modern institutions comparable – because based themselves on beliefs – and the absoluteness of modern rationality self-reflexive. The self-reflexiveness of sociological reason transforms our relation to modernity, and highlights the political contents of the social sciences. Consequently, looking at classical sociology as a specific kind of political self-consciousness, I consider the philosophical denunciation of the positivist (objectifying) nature of classical sociology to be a partial and misleading vision of its epistemological aim.

I do not follow these interpretations regarding the birth of sociology as merely the outcome of conservative post-revolutionary thought.[6] Instead, I understand the birth of European sociology as a chapter of modern enlightenment thought that aimed to overcome modern abstract universalism by means of a critique of liberal conceptions of formal freedom.[7] Certainly, sociology's reflection on authority started at the beginning of the nineteenth century via the rise of conservative thought in the aftermath of the French Revolution.[8]

---

of events and objects of understanding; and as *Histoire*, meaning the form of understanding of this object itself. This double connotation of history has to be considered a prerequisite for understanding the ambivalent notion of modernity as both experience and sociological interpretation. For this characterisation of the notion of history, see Koselleck 1975.

4　For an interesting account of the relation between revolution, temporality and French conservative thought, see Brahami 2011.

5　On this aspect in relation to Durkheimian sociology, see Callegaro 2015.

6　Nisbet 1966.

7　On this perspective, see Seidman 1983, pp. 21–73.

8　For a strong argument reconstructing the relation between conservative thought and classical sociology, see Spaemann 1959.

Nevertheless, sociology opposed the conservative nature of this reflection and interpreted its role as the reopening of the modern project started by natural law theories.[9] In this sense, sociology represents an intellectual deepening and a political radicalisation of the modern quest for autonomy.

Although Marxism had earlier advocated this criticism of formal freedom, it seems to me that the essential distinction of sociological theory (and for this reason, the canonical association of Marx with key founders of sociology such as Durkheim, Tönnies, Simmel and Weber in the history of social theory is problematic) consists in the fact that it does not contemplate a revolutionary subversion of temporality. Instead, it advocates what I would call an epistemological renewal of the covenant, that is, a critique of contractual theory and the overcoming of the notion of natural law by means of the invention of a *sui generis* kind of reality immanent to both morality and law, namely, *society*. The sociology tradition also aimed, by way of its own epistemology, to overcome normative philosophy and political economy and in this way to reinvent the very grounds of modern obligation.

The entire project of classical sociology has been confronted with this reinvention of modern obligation. What Giddens calls the reflexive character of sociology is founded on the requirement that modern time is both an intellectual condition and an empirical object of sociology. For this reason, sociological reflexivity can be opposed to political performativity. That which we can call the political philosophy of classical sociology is grounded in this surrender to the political time of modernity – what Bruno Karsenti has defined as 'a political surrender to politics' – transforming modern temporality, grounded in break and acceleration, in its object and condition.[10]

Beyond the political justification of modern times, sociology defined its field by a theory of modernisation that defined modernity historically and then 'hypostatised' its assumption, thus transforming modern temporality itself in terms of its horizon of expectation.[11] All classical sociologies – Tönnies, Simmel, Durkheim, Weber – are historical sociologies because they assume certain narrations of modernity that identify specific events-processes as their standpoints. It is exactly this narrative that has become the target of postmodern critique.

Nevertheless, given the double definition of modernity as a condition and as an object of sociology, postmodern critique that denies the very reality of

---

9   On the relation between modern natural law and social theory, see Chernilo 2013.

10   See Karsenti 2006. On the political relevance of the modern invention of the social in
      French intellectual history, see Terrier 2011.

11   This expression is notably the one invented by Koselleck (1985, pp. 255–75).

these modern events-processes implicitly leads to the obliteration of sociology itself.[12] This last aspect has provoked a debate in which multiple modernity theories and postcolonial thought, even as they criticise the notion of temporality specific to classical sociology, propose to recover the concept of modernity itself.

Axial Age and Multiple Modernities

The expression 'multiple modernities' was invented by the Israeli sociologist Shmuel Noah Eisenstadt and began spreading rapidly in sociological debates in the middle of the 1980s.[13] This theory was born in the research programme in 'comparative cultural studies' headed by Eisenstadt at the Hebrew University of Jerusalem.[14] It is founded on a critical recovery of the notion of an 'axial age', first used by Karl Jaspers in *Vom Ursprung und Ziel der Geschichte*, published in 1953.[15] Jaspers's goal in this text was to investigate what he called the 'structure of universal history'.

Jaspers's research must be considered first as a critique of the nineteenth-century conception of *Weltgeschichte*.

> Thus in the nineteenth century world history was regarded as that which, after its preliminary stages in Egypt and Mesopotamia, really began in Greece and Palestine and led up to ourselves. Everything else came under the heading of ethnology and lay outside the province of history proper. World history was the history of the west proper (Ranke).[16]

Despite these criticisms of nineteenth-century world history, Jaspers does not give up as an 'article of faith' the idea that the global history of 'mankind has one single origin and one goal',[17] which is unknown to humanity.

---

12   For this reason, Wittrock 2000 distinguishes, using the distinction of Yack, between temporal and substantive conceptions of modernity. On the postmodern vanishing of sociology, see Brym 1990, pp. 329–33.

13   Eisenstadt 2002. On Eisenstadt, see Turner and Sussen 2011.

14   Preyer 2007.

15   Even if Jaspers characterises with precision the existence of the axial age, the use of this concept is common to many authors such as Mumford, Voegelin and more recently Gauchet. For a useful survey of the uses of axial age, see Szakolczai 2003, pp. 80–6.

16   Jaspers 2011 [1953], p. XIV.

17   Jaspers 2011 [1953], p. XV.

The objects of historical study are, according to Jaspers, human civilisations. Nevertheless, rather than pointing to a process in which those theories of history substantialise civilisations and transform them into 'cultural totalities' (as, for example, in Spengler's *Decline of the West*), Jaspers argues instead that 'only ideas of a relative spiritual whole and schemata of such ideas in ideal-typical constructions' exist.[18]

How, then, are civilisations born? How could their histories be synchronically understood without overlooking their diachronic development? The axial age consists of a section of global history between 800 and 200 BC, a period when events of extraordinary importance for world spiritual life occurred: Confucius and Lao-tse in China, Buddha in India, Zarathustra in Iran, Jewish prophets in Palestine and the generations between Homer and Plato in Greece. These figures contributed to the formation of some of the major global civilisations – different paths and different civilisations developing synchronically. According to Jaspers, in this period the 'spiritualisation of collective life' began. He argues:

> These paths are widely divergent in their conviction and dogma but common to all of them is man's reaching out beyond him self by growing aware of himself within the whole of Being and the fact that he can tread them only as an individual of his own.[19]

According to Jaspers, the axial age furnishes a cognitive pattern that makes it possible to conceive of history globally. The theoretical utility of an axial age of humanity would then consist in:

1. Furnishing a universal history common to all humankind, beyond relative beliefs.
2. Identifying a framework for global communication of civilisations and establishing a ground for intercultural dialogue.

This cognitive pattern has been the object of deep criticisms and revisions, and even when it has been adopted it has been used only as a putative paradigm.[20] Recently, underlining the heuristic utility of this concept, Björn Wittrock has

---

18   Jaspers 2011 [1953], p. 277, note 3.
19   Jaspers 2011 [1953], p. 4.
20   'To sum up, the chronological demarcation of the Axial Age is bound to be fluid and contested, even more so in some cases than others, and more work on its prehistory is likely to raise new questions about its claims to exceptional significance' (Arnason 2005, p. 59).

referred to the axial age as an 'epoch in global history that involved profound shifts in at least three fundamental and inescapable dimensions of human existence, namely *reflexivity, historicity* and *agentiality*'.[21]

I will now focus on the use that theorists of multiple modernities have made of this version of history. In order to define the genesis and the sense of the concept of multiple modernities, it is necessary to situate this concept in some of the open questions that have characterised the social sciences debate since the second half of the 1980s. As previously noted, during this period sociological theories of modernisation were subjected to direct attacks by postmodern theorists.

Nevertheless, these are not the only kinds of criticism targeting the very notion of modernity. The increasing success of intellectual history and history of human sciences operating with Foucauldian and Koselleckian frameworks – that is, historical approaches stressing the autonomy of 'discourses' for the definition of modern practices – challenges sociological approaches that typically take 'discourses' as ideological representations of social and institutional macro-transformations.[22] The plural character of modern 'discourses', the fragmented and anti-teleological time of modernity, does not seem to fit with the empty and homogenous time of modernisation.[23] As Wittrock puts it,

> For Koselleck, contrary to Parsons and a number of earlier scholars, the French revolution per se is a symptom rather than a cause of the arrival of new expectations and new imaginations of temporality, of the sense of contemporaneity of the non-co-temporal, 'die Gleichzeitigkeit des Ungleichzeitigen'.[24]

Another factor that certainly influenced the emergence of the paradigm of multiple modernities is the reflection on globalisation that shaped the debate in the 1990s. In the political context post-1989, theorists quickly agreed on the necessity of establishing a non-Eurocentric conception of modern temporality that had both true global ambition and the ability to pluralise local experiences. In these years, global history and the critiques of 'methodological nationalism' arose in debates, and new concepts such as 'glocal', which aimed to re-

---

21 Wittrock 2005, p. 107.

22 'Begriffgeschichte and Social History', in Koselleck 2004, pp. 75–92.

23 On historical sociology's need to rethink the theory of modernity and the history of concepts, see Wagner 2008.

24 Wagner 2008, p. 84.

embed locality in globalism, started to emerge in the literature.[25] Nevertheless, a consistent part of the theory of globalisation actually has a crucial feature in common with classic issues of modernisation theories. To put it bluntly, if the invention of society could be read (as in Durkheim, for example) as a new kind of universalism, one that is able to overcome the philosophy of history embedded in Kantian cosmopolitism, the emergence of a global standpoint reinforced this classical sociological ambition and tried to overcome the supposed paradoxes of sociological and state Eurocentrism of classical sociological theories.[26]

This double movement – the pluralisation of modern temporality and the unification of the social in a global pattern – determines the conditions and the problematic dimension according to which theorists of multiple modernities try to develop their own position.

The notion of axial civilisation was introduced in this context in order to furnish an historical frame of the *longue durée*. The theory of the axial age, founded on the hypothesis of a differentiated access of each civilisation to its own historical consciousness – Jaspers spoke of a differentiation in the passage from myth to logos – suggests the existence of a long lasting period of pre-modern 'cultural crystallisation' that contributed to the de facto pluralisation of the modern 'project'. We are then confronted with a culturalisation of the idea of modernity by the development of heterogenous civilisational projects:

> While the common starting point was once the cultural program of modernity as it developed in the West, more recent developments have seen a multiplicity of cultural and social formations going very far beyond the homogenising aspects of the original version.[27]

It is not difficult to understand the polemical target of this theory that in many aspects can be called neo-Weberian.[28] On the one hand, it is a critique

---

25 Beck 2005.

26 One of the interpreters who insisted most on this transformation of the concept of modernity in literature and the contemporary sociological imaginary is certainly Delanty. See Delanty 1999; 2011. On the invention of a new sociological cosmopolitism, alternative to the Kantian one, see Delanty 2009.

27 Eisenstadt 2000, p. 24.

28 Boatcă and Costa 2010. On the centrality of Max Weber's sociology of religion, see Preyer 2007, pp. 11–12.

of a false unity imposed by globalisation, that is, the very idea that globalisation would correspond to the 'end of history',[29] and thus to the uncontested
domination of liberal modernity. Contrary to these theories, it defends the
idea according to which a pluralisation of modern temporalities would be
supported by an original multiplicity of cultural projects. On the other hand,
it is a critique of a false conception of a plurality of civilisations, according
to which the global post-ideological era would ensure a re-culturalisation of
politics and an unavoidable clash of civilisations.[30] Contrary to this prophecy,
the concept of an axial age and its use in the theory of multiple modernities
both emphasise the elements of co-determination of the concept of civilisation.

Furthermore, the possibility of topologically decomposing modern temporality is not the only possibility suggested by those theories. According to Eisenstadt, European temporality itself is made of different stratified modernities.
We could, for example, distinguish between a liberal modernity and a totalitarian modernity, which would render collectives 'entities ontologically distinct'
but nonetheless, as shown by Arendt and Bauman, still understandable as modern political societies.[31]

Postcolonial Temporalities and the Critique of Multiple Modernities

Despite the attempt to pluralise the concept of modernity according to the
theory of multiple modernities, European modernity conserves an effective
primacy. In fact, the qualification of European modernity given by Eisenstadt
sounds canonical: the rise of nation-state; industrialisation; market; representative institutionalisation of politics. According to this picture, despite the
apparent refusal of the implicit evolutionism of theories of social change, the
main aspects characterising modernity originate *in* Europe and have been historically justified *by* Europe.

Along the lines of these reflections, in the same years of the development
of theories of multiple modernities, another kind of critical theory – that of
postcolonial studies – has targeted modern conceptions of temporality and
thus the sociological conceptions of it.

---

29   Fukuyama 1992.
30   Huntington 1996.
31   Arendt 1958; Bauman 2001.

Like the theorists of multiple modernities, postcolonial readers offer a critique of the notion of temporality implicit in a large part of modern historicism. There are many differences between these two reflections on the concept of modernity, but the most relevant is the specific (political) relevance that postcolonial theorists attribute to modern temporalities.

As in the case of Foucauldian modern disciplinarian power, postcolonial interpreters face the question of how the subalterns can speak, performing the same institutions that have produced and still reproduce their silence and exclusion.[32] The telling of the history of subjectivation seems paradoxically to annihilate the autonomy of subjects themselves, whether those of modern psychiatry or the workers of colonial India.[33] This issue shapes the entire postcolonial conception of subjectivity and temporality:[34] the main problem is how to think critique without introducing metanarratives that would reduce the plurality of modern temporalities to the unique time of European modernity.

In contrast to sociological theories of multiple modernities, postcolonial theorists avoid the possibility of decomposing analytically modern time by pluralising modern spaces and cultures. According to some versions of postcolonial theory, modernity as object and subject of enunciation is necessarily made of the connection between cultural singularity and the universality of political claims.

Even if postcolonial perspectives substantially differentiate themselves from multiple modernities, they share an essential aspect that we can call the 'cultural qualification of temporality'. The difference, however, is that the culturalisation of modern temporality supported by multiple modernities legitimated by the de-culturalisation of European modernity inevitably produces a depoliticising of different modern temporalities. In contrast, one of the most significant ambitions of postcolonial theory consists precisely in politicising cultural diversity – understood to be an internal and conflictive differentiation of the uniqueness of modern time.

The refusal of an empty and homogenous conception of modern time determines the valorisation of the cultural dimension in the definition of modernity. According to theories of multiple modernities, this happens through the acknowledgment of a plurality of civilisations composing modernity, while postcolonial thinkers offer a definition of heterogenous postcolonial temporality, understood as opposed to the empty time of capital. As Chakrabarty puts

---

32   Spivak 1988.
33   Trouillot 1995.
34   On the relation between temporality and postcolonial subjectivity, see Mezzadra 2008, pp. 56–72.

it, modern time 'acts as a bottomless sack' into which it is possible to put an infinite series of events, and it is homogenous 'because it is not affected by any particular events'.[35]

In *The Politics of the Governed*, Chatterjee tries to describe 'popular politics in most of the world' without the use of any kind of 'particular institutional form or process of politics'.[36] The question posed is then: can the governed speak? In this sense the *pars destruens* of Chatterjee's argument questions whether classical concepts of social theory are able to express contemporary political subjectivities.[37] Chatterjee, taking seriously Anderson's analysis of the invention of the imaginary community of nation,[38] shows how one of the main assumptions for the production of a national community is the construction of the simultaneity of political time reproduced by the media. According to Chatterjee, the strategy deployed by capital to maintain a disqualification of plural temporalities corresponds to a kind of 'ethnicisation of differentiated time':

When it encounters an impediment, it thinks it has encountered another time – something out of pre-capital, something that belongs to the pre-modern. Such resistances to capital (or to modernity) are therefore understood as coming out of humanity's past, something people should have left behind but somehow haven't. But by imagining capital (or modernity) as an attribute of time itself, this view succeeds not only in branding the resistances to it as archaic and backward, but also in securing for capital and modernity their ultimate triumph, regardless of what some people may believe or hope, because after all, time does not stand still.[39]

The main effect of this ethnicisation of differentiated temporalities is that it makes real the fiction of the homogenous and empty time of modernity, neutralising the plural political temporalities by which it is in reality composed. The aim of postcolonial history becomes then one of reconstructing and defending the 'heterogeneous time of modernity' and the possibility of this operation is

---

35 Chakrabarty 2000, p. 85. More generally on the postcolonial critique of the historicist conception of modernity, see pp. 47–113. The expression 'empty and homogenous time' is taken from Benjamin's *Theses on the Philosophy of History*.

36 Chatterjee 2004, p. 3.

37 In this respect, see again Spivak 1988.

38 Anderson 1991. On the relation between nationalism, temporality and modern history in a postcolonial perspective, see Bhabha 1990, pp. 291–322.

39 Chatterjee 2004, p. 5.

proved by the fact that these temporalities are not only removed from modernity, as the unique time of capitalism claims, but are co-extensive with this time, bearing the possibility of political conflict. This nomination of the plural temporality of subalterns represents the emancipatory potential embedded in postcolonial critique: namely, the political requalification of culturalised temporalities. This exercise in requalification has an ambivalent and critical relation to the concept of modernity. On the one hand, it expresses a resistance to the annihilating power of modern time; on the other, it represents an appropriation of modernity by histories and practices able both to embody the modern quest for emancipation and to criticise the abstractions of modern universalism.

This perspective makes visible a variety of examples: the events excluded by the spontaneous colonial ontology of modern history such as the Haitian revolution, forgotten because of its diachronic relation to European progressive temporality and its critique of the racial borders of the Enlightenment ideal of emancipation;[40] the modern subjection of the Atlantic slave trade;[41] or forms of micro-resistance such as the appropriation of colonial sporting practices like cricket or other cultural practices. In all these cases, the plurality of modern temporalities is not simply reified beyond the uniqueness of modern time, as in postmodern theories, nor differentiated within the paradigmatic temporality of European modernity, as in theories of multiple modernities; rather, it is performed by the diachronic singularisation of modern emancipation.[42]

The question is: what kind of consequences can this type of critique of sociological theory produce?

As observed, classical sociology is constituted by the break of the theological conception of temporality and the acceleration of historical time. If we take the revision of the notion of modernity produced by theories of multiple modernities and postcolonialism seriously, the questions that arise are: do sociological conceptions of modernity really correspond to the homogenisation and emptying of the modern temporalities, or do they instead represent an attempt to pluralise them? How can a sociological perspective promote an effective pluralisation of modern temporality without renouncing the consideration of modernity as a tool to think, promote and defend political emancipation?

As suggested by the postcolonial theorist Gurminder Bhambra in her *Rethinking Modernity: Postcolonialism and the Sociological Imagination*, the social

40   James 2006.
41   Gilroy 1993.
42   In this perspective, postcolonial historiography can be considered, according to Gilroy himself, an 'anti-anti-essentialism'.

sciences have historically distinguished the concept of modernity according to two different aspects: historical break and difference.[43] According to the first, dealing with time, modernity distinguishes what is traditional and what is not. According to the second, dealing with space, the distinction operates between European modernity and its beyond. This distinction deeply influenced both colonisers and colonised forms of knowledge. According to Bhambra, the imaginary of social sciences is entirely entangled in this political knowledge of colonialism. An obvious example of this specific epistemological politics is Edward Said's conception of orientalism.[44]

One of the main problems of postcolonial theory is the fact that the historical distinction of modernity and the anthropological difference of moderns is possible only analytically – not historically. To define modern temporality means to establish a distinction between moderns and non-moderns. This represents the limit of a European universalism that has denied its own aspirations by *ethnicising* the temporalities of others.

The mutual implication of a temporal and spatial conception of modernity becomes particularly explicit, according to Bhambra, in the theory of modernity that originated in the Scottish and French Enlightenments,[45] although there are different attitudes and condemnation of slavery and colonialism, from the less explicit (Locke) to the more vigorous (Montesquieu).[46]

Nevertheless, this implicit genealogy – from Enlightenment philosophy of history to classical sociology's conceptions of historicity – is problematic. Deriving the sociological conception of temporality from progressive and stadial conceptions of history developed throughout the eighteenth and nineteenth centuries can reproduce a teleological conception of sociological epistemology. I am convinced that what I have called an epistemological doubling of the pact produced by classical sociology must be considered not as the simple reproduction of the main assumptions of political modernity, but as an attempt to elaborate a situated conception of universalism.[47]

---

43   Bahmbra 2007.

44   Said 1978.

45   On this topic in the Scottish Enlightenment, see Sebastiani 2008.

46   Landucci 1972.

47   This aspect is briefly annotated by the author herself when she says: 'As Helbron suggests, "the idea that human beings can be understood from the social arrangements they form" means that modern societies are not "the same sort of units as states". However, the extent to which this is the case in practice is open to question, as most social theorists continued to delineate their conceptions of society in terms of national boundaries' (Bahmbra 2007, pp. 48–9). It must be said that the author accepts some problematic assumptions of

Bhambra's criticisms target the fact that the standpoint of this situated conception of universalism is in itself mystified. In this sense, all sociological reflexivity is viciously conditioned by the fact that it is not able to understand its
own (colonial) conditions of possibility. For this reason, sociological epistemologies are inescapably Eurocentric. Classical sociology defines its own concept
of temporality-defining events – processes of European history able to define
the semantics of modern time – and these events are inevitably embedded in
the dominant temporality of modern capitalist Europe.

According to Bhambra, theories of multiple modernities fail in their attempt
to pluralise modern temporality. The heart of Bhambra's criticism focuses on
sociological uses of the notion of the ideal-type and on sociological comparativism. In this perspective, Eisenstadt and other defenders of multiple modernities cannot afford to think of global modernity without a misleading use of
the notion of modernisation:

> Understanding modernity in this way allows scholars to situate European
> modernity – seen in terms of a primary combination of the institutional
> and the cultural forms – as the originary modernity and, at the same time,
> allows for different cultural encodings that result in *multiple* modernities.
> The idea of multiple modernities, then, is consistent with the idea of a
> common framework of modern institutions – for example, the market
> economy, the modern nation-state, and bureaucratic rationality – which
> originated in Europe and was subsequently exported to the rest of the
> world.[48]

Sociological comparativism implicitly emphasises Eurocentrism in the very
notion of modernisation. By distinguishing between the unique (European)
structure of modernity and the plurality of its (cultural) *discourses*, sociology
reifies the structure of European modernity and denies its colonial assumptions. According to the theory of multiple modernities, the use of ideal-types
instead of the notion of evolution enables us not to think of 'other' modernities as a deviation from an original model. However, according to Bhambra,
this conception is not capable of understanding the real process of pluralisa-

---

Nisbet's history of sociology: 'This is because sociology was conceived to understand
"modern" society in the context of perceiving it also to be the displacement of a "lost"
community – thus, in its very conceptualisation, sociology set up understanding modern
society not on its own terms, but as the loss of something other, something authentic'
(p. 53).

48   Bahmbra 2007, p. 69.

tion of temporalities across modernity determined by the interconnection of modern times – an interconnection that can only be understood by politically qualifying the practices of heterogenous time.

The ideal-type of European modernity thus maintains a priority over other modernities. The multiple modernities paradigm is anti-teleological, but de facto Eurocentric when its Eurocentrism is carried into its methodology through the failure to recognise connected histories. In order to rescue a plural notion of temporality that escapes this Eurocentric conclusion of sociological theories of modernity, Bhambra defends the necessity of thinking modern orders in terms of the connections of different histories.[49] This re-connection operates via a deconstruction of the foundational paradigms (those events-process quoted above) of European modernity – which Bhambra calls 'myths of European cultural integrity'. It provincialises the political knowledge of colonialism and positively practises a different historiography grounded on connection of histories and orders instead of on the modelisation of the order and temporality of modern Europe.

The connected postcolonial history aims to re-politicise our relation to history, unambiguously producing a refusal of modern sociology. Nevertheless, as stated at the beginning of this chapter, sociology itself consists of a political appropriation of modernity, beyond the absoluteness of its rational auto-determination. Certainly, classical sociology passed through a 'naturalisation' of modernity as a break and as progress, but its politics consisted exactly in making these transformations (undoubtedly based on violence and expropriation, that is to say, on colonialism) understandable and comparable from another standpoint. This standpoint consists exactly in refusing a conception of progress based on linear conceptions of temporality.

Condemning this very kind of reflexivity because it is implicitly embedded in modern philosophies of history would be the same as refusing connected history because it is inevitably embedded in imperial history. Meanwhile, the argument of postcolonial conceptions of history runs the other way around: according to them, it is only by taking seriously power relations and colonial domination developed throughout global history that we could allow what is political and unseen in the interconnection of modern temporalities to re-emerge. Why, then, instead of renouncing this specific standpoint of modern sociology, do we not try to present its political content, partially unseen and certainly changed in contemporary global world, more explicitly? If that is pos-

---

49   Among the works focusing on the critique of multiple modernities in a postcolonial perspective, see Boatcă, Costa and Guitiérrez Rodriguez 2010; Boatcă and Spohn 2010.

sible, and I am firmly convinced that it is, postcolonial theory could understand sociology as an ally rather than an enemy in transforming political standpoints on modernity.

References

Abensour, Miguel 2004, *La Démocratie contre l'État. Marx et le moment machiavelien*, Paris: Èditions du Félin.

Adorno, Theodor 1982, 'Subject and Object', in *The Essential Frankfurt School Reader*, edited by Andrew Arato and Eike Gebhardt, New York: Continuum.

Althusser, Louis 1969, *For Marx*, London: Verso.

Althusser, Louis 1996, 'Le "Piccolo", Bertolazzi et Brecht (Notes sur un théâtre matérialiste)', in *Pour Marx*, Paris: La Découverte.

Althusser, Louis 1999 [1995], *Machiavelli and Us*, edited by F. Matheron, London: Verso.

Althusser, Louis 2005 [1965], *For Marx*, translated by Ben Brewster, London: Verso.

Althusser, Louis 2006, *Philosophy of the Encounter: Later Writings 1978–1987*, edited by François Matheron, translated and introduced by G.M. Goshgarian, London: Verso.

Althusser, Louis 2009 [1968], 'The Object of *Capital*', in Louis Althusser and Étienne Balibar, *Reading Capital*, translated by Ben Brewster, London: Verso.

Althusser, Louis and Étienne Balibar 1970, *Reading Capital*, London: NLB.

Anderson, Benedict 1991, *Imagined Communities: Reflections on the Origin and Spread of Nationalism*, London: Verso.

Anderson, Kevin 2002, 'Marx's Late Writings on Non-Western and Precapitalist Societies and Gender', *Rethinking Marx*, 14(4).

Anderson, Kevin 2010, *Marx at the Margins: On Nationalism, Ethnicity, and Non-Western Societies*, Chicago: University of Chicago Press.

Arendt, Hannah 1958, *The Origins of Totalitarianism*, New York: Meridian Books.

Arias, Gino 1931a, 'Il significato storico della crisi economica', *Gerarchia*, 11: 482–7.

Arias, Gino 1931b, 'Problemi economici mondiali', *Gerarchia*, 11: 643–50.

Arias, Gino 1931c, 'Cronache economico-finanziarie. La sterlina e la crisi inglese', *Gerarchia*, 11: 780–5.

Arnason, Johann P. 2005, 'The Axial Conundrum: between Historical Sociology and the Philosophy of History', in *Comparing Modernities: Pluralism vs. Homogeneity. Essays in Hommage to Shmuel N. Eisenstadt*, edited by E. Ben-Rafael and Y. Sternberg, Leiden: Brill.

Arnold, N. Scott 1990, *Marx's Radical Critique of Capitalist Society*, London: Oxford University Press.

Arthur, Christopher J. 1997, 'The Fluidity of Capital and the Logic of the Concept', in *The Circulation of Capital: Essays on Volume Two of Marx's* Capital, edited by Christopher J. Arthur and Geert Reuten, London: Palgrave Macmillan.

Assoun, Paul-Laurent 1978, *Marx et la répétition historique*, Paris: PUF.

Augustine 1993, *Confessions*, Indianapolis, IN: Hackett.

Avineri, Shlomo 1972, *Hegel's Theory of the Modern State*, Cambridge: Cambridge University Press.

Baczko, Bronislaw 1997, *Job, mon ami. Promesses de bonheur et fatalité du mal*, Paris: Gallimard.

Badaloni, Nicola 1981, 'Antonio Gramsci. La filosofia della prassi come previsione', in *Storia del marxismo Vol. III – Il marxismo nell'eta' della terza internazionale*, edited by Eric J. Hobsbawm et al., Turin: Einaudi.

Bagu, Sergio 1949, *Economia del la societad colonial*, Buenos Aires: Ateneo.

Balibar, Etienne 1991, 'From Class Struggle to Classless Struggle?', in Etienne Balibar and Immanuel Wallerstein, *Race, Nation, Class. Ambiguous Identities*, London and New York: Verso.

Balibar, Etienne 1992, *Les frontières de la démocratie*, Paris: La Découverte.

Balibar, Etienne 1993, *La philosophie de* Marx, Paris: La Découverte.

Balibar, Etienne 2010, 'Europe: Final Crisis? Some Theses', *Theory & Event*, 13 (http://z3950.muse.jhu.edu/journals/theory_and_event/v013/13.2.balibar.html).

Balibar, Etienne and Immanuel Wallerstein 1991, *Race Nation Class: Ambiguous Identities*, London: Verso.

Balsa, Javier 2006a, 'Las tres lógicas de la construcción de la hegemonía', *Revista THEO-MAI/THEOMAI Journal*, 14: 16–36.

Balsa, Javier 2006b, 'Notas para una definición de la hegemonía', *El Nuevo Topo. Revista de historia y pensamiento crítico*, 3: 145–66.

Basso, Luca 2008–9, 'Marx: quale libertà?', *Quaderni materialisti*, 7/8: 69–87.

Basso, Luca 2012 [2008], *Marx and Singularity. From the Early Writings to the 'Grundrisse'*, Leiden-Boston: Brill.

Basso, Luca 2015 [2012], *Marx and the Common. From 'Capital' to the Late Writings*, Leiden-Boston: Brill.

Bastid, Paul 1970, *Sieyès et sa pensée*, Paris: Hachette.

Bauman, Zygmunt 2001, *Modernity and the Holocaust*, Ithaca: Cornell University Press.

Becchi, Paolo 1993, 'Distinciones acerca del concepto hegeliano de sociedad civil', *Doxa. Cuadernos de Filosofía del Derecho*, 14: 1993: 379–419.

Beck, Ulrich 2005, *Cosmopolitan Vision*, London: Polity, 2005.

Bellofiore, Riccardo 2009, 'A Ghost Turning into a Vampire: The Concept of Capital and Living Labour', in *Re-reading Marx. New Perspectives after the Critical Edition*, edited by Riccardo Bellofiore and Roberto Fineschi, New York: Palgrave.

Bellofiore, Riccardo and Massimiliano Tomba 2013, 'The "Fragment on Machines" and "The Grundrisse": The Workerist Reading in Question', in *Beyond Marx: Confronting Labour-History and the Concept of Labour with the Global Labour-Relations in the Twenty-First Century*, edited by Marcel van der Linden and Karl Heinz Roth, Leiden and Boston: Brill.

Bellofiore, Riccardo and Roberto Fineschi (eds) 2009, *Re-reading Marx. New Perspectives after the Critical Edition*, New York: Palgrave.

Benjamin, Walter 1980 [1920], *Theologisch-politisches Fragment*, in *Gesammelte Schriften*, II, 1, edited by R. Tiedeman and H. Schweppenhäuser, Frankfurt a.M.: Suhrkamp.

Benjamin, Walter 1980 [1921], *Zur Kritik der Gewalt*, in *Gesammelte Schriften*, II, 1, edited by R. Tiedeman and H. Schweppenhäuser, Frankfurt a.M.: Suhrkamp.

Benjamin, Walter 1991 [1940], *Über den Begriff der Geschichte* (1940), in *Gesammelte Schriften*, I, 3, edited by R. Tiedeman and H. Schweppenhäuser, Frankfurt a.M.: Suhrkamp.

Benjamin, Walter 1999, 'W. Benjamin a A. Cohn, 6 Feb 1935', in *Gesammelte Briefe*, Band 5, Frankfurt: Suhrkamp.

Benjamin, Walter 2009, *The Origin of German Drama*, translated by John Osborne, London: Verso.

Bensaïd, Daniel 1995a, *La discordance des temps. Essai sur les crises, les classes, l'histoire*, Paris: Les Éditions de la Passion.

Bensaïd, Daniel 1995b, *Marx l'intempestif. Grandeurs et misères d'une aventure critique (XIXe–XXe siècles)*, Paris: Fayard.

Bensaïd, Daniel 2002, *A Marx for Our Times. Adventures and Misadventures of a Critique*, London: Verso.

Bensaïd, Daniel 2004, 'Alain Badiou and the Miracle of the Event', in *Think Again: Alain Badiou and the Future of Philosophy*, edited by Peter Hallward, New York: Continuum.

Bergson, Henri 1975, 'Memory of the present and false recognition', in *Mind-Energy. Lectures and Essays*, Westport-London: Greenwood Press.

Bernini, Lorenzo, Mauro Farnesi Camellone and Nicola Marcucci 2010, *La sovranità scomposta. Sull'attualità del 'Leviatano'*, Milano: Mimesis.

Bevernage, Berber 2016, 'Against Coevalness: A Belated Critique of Johannes Fabian's Project of Radical Contemporaneity and a Plea for a New Politics of Time', *Anthropological Theory* (forthcoming).

Bevernage, Berber and Chris Lorenz (eds.) 2013, *Breaking Up Time: Negotiating the Borders between Present, Past and Future*, Göttingen: Vandenhoeck & Ruprecht.

Bhabha, Homi K. 1990, 'DessemiNation: Time, Narrative and the Margins of Modern Nation', in *Nation and Narration*, London: Routledge.

Bhambra, Gurminder K. 2007, *Rethinking Modernity: Postcolonialism and the Sociological Imagination*, New York: Palgrave.

Bloch, Ernst 1964 [1923], *Durch die Wüste. Kritische Essays*, Frankfurt a. M.: Suhrkamp.

Bloch, Ernst 1970 [1955], 'Differentiations in the Concept of Progress', in *A Philosophy for the Future*, translated by John Cumming, New York: Herder and Herder.

Bloch, Ernst 1975a, *Differenzierungen im Begriff Fortschritt*, in *Werkausgabe* Band 13, Frankfurt: Suhrkamp.

Bloch, Ernst 1975b, *Experimentum mundi*, in *Werkausgabe* Band 15, Frankfurt: Suhrkamp.

Bloch, Ernst 1985 [1903–75], *Briefe 1903–1975*, Volume I, edited by U. Opolka, Frankfurt a. M.: Suhrkamp.

Bloch, Ernst 1985 [1918], *Geist der Utopie. Erste Fassung*, in *Werkausgabe* Band 16, Frankfurt a. M.: Suhrkamp.

Bloch, Ernst 1985 [1921; 1969], *Thomas Münzer als Theologe der Revolution*, in *Werkausgabe* Band 2, Frankfurt a. M.: Suhrkamp.

Bloch, Ernst 1985 [1923; 1964], *Geist der Utopie. Zweite Fassung*, in *Werkausgabe* Band 3, Frankfurt a. M.: Suhrkamp.

Bloch, Ernst 1985 [1935; 1962], *Erbschaft dieser Zeit. Erweiterte Ausgabe*, in *Werkausgabe* Band 4, Frankfurt a. M., Suhrkamp.

Bloch, Ernst 1985 [1959], *Das Prinzip Hoffnung*, in *Werkausgabe* Band 5, Frankfurt a. M.: Suhrkamp.

Bloch, Ernst 1985 [1961], *Naturrecht und menschliche Würde*, in *Werkausgabe* Band 6, Frankfurt a. M.: Suhrkamp.

Bloch, Ernst 1985 [1963–4; 1970], *Tübinger Einleitung in die Philosophie*, in *Werkausgabe* Band 13, Frankfurt a. M.: Suhrkamp.

Bloch, Ernst 1985 [1968] *Atheismus im Christentum. Zur Religion des Exodus und des Reichs*, in *Werkausgabe* Band 14, Frankfurt a. M.: Suhrkamp.

Bloch, Ernst 1985 [1969], *Philosophische Aufsätze zur objektiven Phantasie*, in *Werkausgabe* Band 10, Frankfurt a. M.: Suhrkamp.

Bloch, Ernst 1985 [1970], *Politische Messungen, Pestzeit, Vormärz*, in *Werkausgabe* Band 11, Frankfurt a. M.: Suhrkamp.

Bloch, Ernst 1985 [1975], *Experimentum Mundi. Frage, Kategorien des Herausbringens, Praxis*, in *Werkausgabe* Band 15, Frankfurt a. M: Suhrkamp.

Bloch, Ernst 1985 [1978], *Tendenz-Latenz-Utopie*, in *Werkausgabe Ergänzungsband*, Frankfurt a. M.: Suhrkamp.

Bloch, Ernst 1991 [1932], 'Non-contemporaneity and Obligation to its Dialectic', in *Heritage of Our Times*, translated by Neville and Stephen Plaice, Cambridge: Polity Press.

Blumenberg, Hans 1983, *The Legitimacy of the Modern Age*, Cambridge, MA: MIT Press.

Boatcă Manuela and Willfried Spohn 2010, *Globale, multiple und postkoloniale Modernen*, Munich: Hampp.

Boatcă Manuela, Sérgio Costa and Encarnación Gutiérrez Rodríguez 2010, *Decolonizing European Sociology: Transdisciplinary Approaches*, London: Ashgate.

Boatcă, Manuela and Sérgio Costa 2010, 'Postcolonial Sociology: A Research Agenda', in Manuela Boatcă, Sérgio Costa and Encarnación Gutiérrez Rodríguez, *Decolonizing European Sociology: Transdisciplinary Approaches*, London: Ashgate.

Bodei, Remo 1979, *Multiversum: Tempo e storia in Ernst Bloch*, Naples: Bibliopolis.

Boehmer, Heinrich 1922, *Studien zu Thomas Müntzer*, Leipzig: Koehler & Amelang.

Boehmer, Heinrich 1923, 'Thomas Müntzer und das jüngste Deutschland', *Allgemeine Evangelisch-Luterische Kirchenzeitung*, 56: 187–222.

Bonefeld, Werner 2014, *Critical Theory and the Critique of Political Economy*, New York and London: Bloomsbury.

Bongiovanni, Bruno 1989, *Le repliche della storia. Karl Marx tra la Rivoluzione francese e la critica della politica*, Torino: Bollati Boringhieri.

Bonola, Gianfranco 2006, 'L'impulso dello spirito ebraico all'utopia. Ernst Bloch letto da Walter Benjamin e Gershom Scholem (1919/1920)', in *Teologia e politica. Walter Benjamin e un paradigma del moderno*, edited by M. Ponzi and B. Witte, Torino: Aragno.

Boothman, Derek 2004, *Traducibilità e processi traduttivi. Un caso: A. Gramsci linguista*, Perugia: Guerra.

Boutang, Yann Moulier 1998, *De l'esclavage au salariat. Economie historique du salariat bridé*, Paris: PUF.

Bracaletti, Stefano 1990, *L'analisi del capitale complessivo sociale in Marx*, unpublished dissertation, Università degli studi di Milano.

Bracaletti, Stefano 2013, 'Per un'analisi della temporalità nel *Capitale*' in *Tempora Multa. Il governo del tempo*, edited by Vittorio Morfino et al., Milano: Mimesis.

Brahami, Frédéric 2011, 'Déchirure et production politique du temps. Science et volonté autour de la révolution française', *Incidence*, 7: 249–90.

Bredin, Jean-Denis 1988, *Sieyès. La clé de la Révolution française*, Paris: Editions de Fallois.

Brym, Robert J. 1990, 'The End of Sociology? A Note on Postmodernism', *The Canadian Journal of Sociology/Cahiers Canadies de Sociologie*, 15(3): 329–33.

Buci-Glucksmann, Christine 1980 [1975], *Gramsci and the State*, London: Lawrence and Wishart.

Burgio, Alberto 2002, *Gramsci storico. Una lettura dei 'Quaderni del carcere'*, Rome-Bari: Laterza.

Cacciari, Massimo 1983 'Metafisica della gioventù', in Georg Lukács, *Diario (1910–1911)*, Italian translation by G. Caramore, Milano: Adelphi.

Callegaro, Francesco 2015, *La science politique des modernes: Durkheim, la sociologie et le projet d'autonomie*, Paris: Economica.

Campbell, Martha 1997, 'Money in the Circulation of Capital', in *The Circulation of Capital: Essays on Volume Two of Marx's* Capital, edited by Christopher J. Arthur and Geert Reuten, London: Palgrave Macmillan.

Carlucci, Alessandro 2013, *Gramsci and Languages: Unification, Diversity, Hegemony*, Leiden: Brill.

Casarino, Cesare and Antonio Negri 2008, *In Praise of the Common: A Conversation on Philosophy and Politics*, Minneapolis, MN: University of Minnesota Press.

Cases, Cesare 1973, 'Introduzione', in Ernesto De Martino, *Il mondo magico. Prolegomeni a una storia del magismo* (1948), Turin: Boringhieri.

Certeau, Michel de 1994, *La prise de parole et autres écrits politiques*, Paris: Seuil.

Chakrabarty, Dipesh 2000, *Provincializing Europe: Postcolonial Thought and Historical Difference*, Princeton, NJ: Princeton University Press.

Chambers, Samuel A. 2011, 'Untimely Politics *avant la lettre*: The Temporality of Social Formations', *Time and Society*, 20(2): 197–223.

Chatterjee, Partha 2004, *The Politics of the Governed: Reflections on Popular Politics in Most of the World*, New York: Columbia University Press.

Chernilo, Daniel 2013, *The Natural Law Foundations of Modern Social Theory: A Quest for Universalism*, Cambridge: Cambridge University Press.

Chignola, Sandro 2004, *Fragile cristallo. Per la storia del concetto di società*, Napoli: Editoriale Scientifica Italiana.

Ciliberto, Michele, 'Cosmopolitismo e Stato nazionale nei "Quaderni del carcere"', in *Gramsci e il Novecento*, Volume I, edited by Giuseppe Vacca in collaboration with Marina Litri, Rome: Carocci.

Coassin-Spiegel, Hermes 1997 [1983], *Gramsci und Althusser. Eine Kritik der Althusserschen Rezeption von Gramscis Philosophie*, Hamburg-Berlin: Argument.

Cobban, Alfred 1964, *The Social Interpretation of the French Revolution*, Cambridge: Cambridge University Press.

Coutinho, Carlos Nelson 2009, 'Rapporti di forza', *Dizionario gramsciano 1926–1937*, edited by Guido Liguori and Pasquale Voza, Rome: Carocci.

Critchley, Simon 2007, *Infinitely Demanding: Ethics of Commitment, Politics of Resistance*, London: Verso.

Cunico, Gerardo 1988, *Critica e ragione utopica. A confronto con Habermas e Bloch*, Genova: Marietti.

Darwin, Charles 1988, *The Origin of Species by Means of Natural Selection*, in *The Works of Charles Darwin*, Volume 16, London: William Pickering.

De Angelis, Massimo 2001, 'Marx and Primitive Accumulation: The Continuous Character of Capital's Enclosures', *The Commoner*, 2, available at: http://www.commoner.org.uk/02deangelis.pdf

De Angelis, Massimo 2008, 'Crisi dei sub-prime impasse neoliberale e commons', in *La lunga accumulazione originaria. Politica e lavoro nel mercato mondiale*, edited by Devi Sacchetto and Massimiliano Tomba, Verona: Ombrecorte.

De Felice, Franco 1977, 'Rivoluzione passiva, fascismo, americanismo in Gramsci', in *Politica e storia in Gramsci*, edited by Franco Ferri, Volume 1, Rome: Editori Riuniti.

De Martino, Ernesto 2007, *Il mondo magico*, Torino: Bollati Boringhieri.

Delanty, Gerard 1999, *Social Theory in a Changing World: Conceptions of Modernity*, Cambridge: Polity Press.

Delanty, Gerard 2009, *The Cosmopolitan Imagination: The Renewal of Critical Social Theory*, Cambridge: Cambridge University Press.

Delanty, Gerard 2011, 'Modernity and the Escape from Eurocentrism', in *Handbook of Contemporary Social Theory*, edited by Gerard Delanty and Bryan Turner, London: Routledge.

Deleuze, Gilles 1990 [1969], *The Logic of Sense*, New York: Columbia University Press.

Del Lucchese, Filippo 2004, *Tumulti e indignatio. Conflitto, diritto e moltitudine in Machiavelli e Spinoza*, Milano: Ghibli.

Derrida, Jacques 1972, *Positions*, Paris: Les Editions de Minuit.

Derrida, Jacques 1973, *Speech and Phenomena and Other Essays on Husserl's Theory of Signs*, Chicago: Northwestern University Press.

Derrida, Jacques 2002, *Positions*, London: Continuum.

Diderot, Denis 1916 [1746], 'Philosophical Thoughts', in *Diderot's Early Philosophical Works*, edited by Margaret Jourdain, Chicago: Open Court Publishing Company.

Dussel Enrique and Augustin Yanez 1990, 'Marx's Economic Manuscript of 1861–63 and the "Concept" of Dependency', in *Latin American Perspectives*, 17: 62–101.

Eidam, Heinz 1992, *Strumpf und Handschuh. Der Begriff der nichtexistenten und die Gestalt der unkonstruierbaren Frage. Walter Benjamin Verhältnis zum Geist der Utopie Ernst Blochs*, Würzburg: Königshausen & Neumann.

Eisenstadt, Shmuel N. 2000, 'Multiple Modernities', *Daedalus*, 129.

Eisenstadt, Shmuel N. 2002, *Multiple Modernities*, Piscataway: Transaction Publishers.

Eliade, Mircea 1961, *The Sacred and the Profane*, New York: Harper and Row.

Engels Friedrich 1975 [1845], *The Festival of Nations in London, To Celebrate the Establishment of the French Republic*, in *Marx and Engels Collected Works*, Volume 6, Moscow: Progress Publishers.

Esposito, Roberto 2010, *Pensiero vivente. Origine e attualità della filosofia italiana*, Torino: Einaudi.

Farnesi Camellone, Mauro 2009, *La politica e l'immagine. Saggio su Ernst Bloch*, Macerata: Quodlibet.

Farnesi Camellone, Mauro 2010, 'Categories as Images: Bloch and the Hand of Benjamin', in *Le vie della distruzione. A partire da Il carattere distruttivo di Walter Benjamin*, edited by Seminario di studi benjaminiani, Macerata: Quodlibet.

Feher, Ferenc 1990, 'Marx et les Révolutions françaises permanents', *Actuel Marx*, 9: 45–66.

Finelli, Roberto 2004, *Un parricido mancato*, Turin: Bollati Boringhieri.

Fineschi, Roberto 2009, '"Capital in General" and "Competition" in the Making of Capital: The German Debate', *Science & Society*, 73(1): 54–76.

Fontana, Benedetto 2010, 'Political Space and Hegemonic Power in Gramsci', *Journal of Power*, 3(3): 341–63.

Francioni, Gianni 1984, *L'officina gramsciana. Ipotesi sulla struttura dei 'Quaderni del carcere'*, Naples: Bibliopolis.

Freitas-Branco, João Maria de 2001, 'Gegenstand', in *Das historisch-kritische Wörter-*

buch des Marxismus, Band 5, edited by Wolfgang Fritz Haug, Hamburg-Berlin: Argument.

Frosini, Fabio 2003, *Gramsci e la filosofia. Saggio sui 'Quaderni del carcere'*, Roma: Carocci.

Frosini, Fabio 2007, 'Dialettica e immanenza da Labriola a Gramsci', in *Dialettica. Tradizioni, problemi, sviluppi*, edited by Alberto Burgio, Macerata: Quodlibet.

Frosini, Fabio 2009, *Da Gramsci a Marx. Ideologia, verità e politica*, Rome: Derive-Approdi.

Frosini, Fabio 2010, *La religione dell'uomo moderno. Politica e verità nei 'Quaderni del carcere' di Antonio Gramsci*, Rome: Carocci.

Frosini, Fabio 2013, 'Luigi Russo e Georges Sorel: sulla genesi del "moderno Principe" nei *Quaderni del carcere* di Antonio Gramsci', *Studi storici*, 54: 545–89.

Fukuyama, Francis 1992, *The End of History and the Last Man*, New York: Free Press.

Furet, François 1986, *Marx et la Révolution française*, Paris: Flammarion.

Furet, François and Denis Richet 1970 [1965], *The French Revolution*, New York: Macmillan.

Fusillo, Massimo 1996, *La Grecia secondo Pasolini. Mito e cinema*, Scandicci: La Nuova Italia.

Gambino, Ferruccio and Devi Sacchetto 2013, 'The Shifting Maelstrom: From Plantations to Assembly-Lines', in *Beyond Marx: Theorising the Global Labour Relations of the Twenty-First Century*, edited by Marcel van der Linden and Karl Heinz Roth, Leiden: Brill.

Ganis, Stefano 1996, *Utopia e Stato. Teologia e politica nel pensiero di Ernst Bloch*, Padova: Unipress.

Gauchet, Marcel 1989, *La Révolution des droits de l'homme*, Paris: Gallimard.

Gilbert, Alan 1981, *Marx's Politics: Communists and Citizens*, New Brunswick, NJ: Rutgers University Press.

Gilroy, Paul 1993, *The Black Atlantic: Modernity and Double Consciousness*, London: Verso.

Glassman, Jim 2006, 'Primitive Accumulation, Accumulation by Dispossession, Accumulation by "Extra-Economic" Means', *Progress in Human Geography*, 30.

Goshgarian, G.M. 2003, 'Introduction', in Louis Althusser, *The Humanist Controversy and Other Writings 1966–67*, London: Verso.

Goshgarian, G.M. 2012, 'The Very Essence of the Object, the Soul of Marxism, and Other Singular Things: Spinoza in Althusser 1959–67', in *Encountering Althusser. Politics and Materialism in Contemporary Radical Thought*, edited by Katja Diefenbach, Gal Kirn, Sara R. Farris and Peter D. Thomas, New York: Bloomsbury.

Gramsci, Antonio 1966, *Socialismo e fascismo. L'Ordine Nuovo 1921–1922*, Turin: Einaudi.

Gramsci, Antonio 1971, *Selections from the Prison Notebooks*, edited and translated by Quentin Hoare and Geoffrey Nowell Smith, New York: International Publishers.

Gramsci, Antonio 1975, *Quaderni del carcere*, edited by Valentino Gerratana, Turin: Einaudi.

Gramsci, Antonio 1992, *Prison Notebooks*, Volume 1, edited by Joseph A. Buttigieg, translated by Joseph A. Buttigieg and Antonio Callari, New York: Columbia University Press.

Gramsci, Antonio 1993, *Letters from Prison*, 2 Volumes, edited by Frank Rosengarten, translated by Raymond Rosenthal, New York: Columbia University Press.

Gramsci, Antonio 1995, *Further Selections from the Prison Notebooks*, edited and translated by Derek Boothman, Minneapolis, MN: University of Minnesota Press.

Gramsci, Antonio 1996, *Prison Notebooks*, Volume 2, translated and edited by Joseph A. Buttigieg, New York: Columbia University Press.

Gramsci, Antonio 2007, *Prison Notebooks*, Volume 3, translated and edited by Joseph A. Buttigieg, New York: Columbia University Press.

Grimm, Jacob and Wilhelm Grimm 1854–1960, *Deutsches Wörterbuch*, 16 Bände in 32 Teilbänden, Leipzig: S. Hirzel.

Groethuysen, Bernard 1956, *Philosophie de la révolution française*, Paris: Gallimard.

Guerra, Gabriele 2007, *Judentum zwischen Anarchie und Theokratie. Eine religionspoltische Diskussion am Beispiel der Begegnung zwischen Walter Benjamin und Gershom Scholem*, Bielefeld: Aisthesis Verlag.

Guida, Giuseppe 2008, 'La "religione della storia". Aspetti della presenza di Bergson nel pensiero di Gramsci', in *Gramsci nel suo tempo*, edited by Francesco Giasi, Rome: Carocci.

Häberle, Peter 1987, 'Die verfassungsgebende Gewalt des Volkes im Verfassungsstaat', *Archiv für öffentliche Recht*, 112: 54–92.

Hall, Derek 2012, 'Rethinking Primitive Accumulation', *Antipode*, 44(4): 1188–208.

Harootunian, Harry 2015, *Marx after Marx: History and Time in the Expansion of Capitalism*, New York: Columbia University Press.

Hartog, François 2003, *Regimes d'historicité: Présentisme et experiences du temps*, Paris: Seuil.

Haug, Wolfgang Fritz 2006 [1996], *Philosophieren mit Brecht und Gramsci*, Hamburg-Berlin: Argument.

Hecker, Rolf 1987, 'Zur Entwicklung der Werttheorie von der 1. zur 3. Auflage des ersten Bandes des "Kapitals" von Karl Marx (1867–1883)', *Marx-Engels-Jahrbuch*, 10: 147–96.

Hegel, Georg Wilhelm Friedrich 1991, *Elements of the Philosophy of Right*, edited by Allen W. Wood, translated by Hugh Barr Nisbet, Cambridge: Cambridge University Press.

Hegel, Georg Wilhelm Friedrich 2010 [1820], *Outlines of the Philosophy of Right*, translated by T.M. Knox, revised by Stephen Houlgate, Oxford: Oxford University Press.

Heidegger, Martin 2010 [1927], *Being and Time*, translated by Joan Stambaugh, revised by Dennis J. Schmidt, Albany, NY: State University of New York Press.

Heinrich, Michael 2009, 'Reconstruction or Deconstruction? Methodological Controversies about Value and Capital, and New Insights from the Critical Edition', in *Re-reading Marx: New Perspectives after the Critical Edition*, edited by Riccardo Bellofiore and Roberto Fineschi, New York: Palgrave.

Heinrich, Michael 2013, 'The "Fragment on Machines": A Marxian Misconception in the *Grundrisse* and its Overcoming in *Capital*', in *In Marx's Laboratory: Crtitical Interpretations of the Grundrisse*, edited by Ricardo Bellofiore, Guido Starosta and Peter D. Thomas, Leiden: Brill.

Hincker, François 1990, 'Droidloms, Droits de l'homme et du citoyen', *Actuel Marx*, 8: 159–73.

Hindess, Barry 2007, 'The Althusserian Moment and the Concept of Historical Time', *Economy and Society*, 36(1): 1–18.

Hirst, Paul Q. 2005, *Space and Power: Politics, War and Architecture*, Cambridge: Polity Press.

Hobsbawm, Eric J. 1990, *Echoes of the Marseillaise: Two Centuries Look Back on the French Revolution*, London: Verso.

Hölscher, Lucian 2014, 'Time Gardens: Historical Concepts in Modern Historiography', *History and Theory*, 53.

Howitt, William 2010 [1838], *Colonization and Christianity: A Popular History of the Treatment of the Natives by the Europeans in all their Colonies*, London: Nabu Press.

Hunt, Richard N. 1975, *The Political Ideas of Marx and Engels*, London: Macmillan.

Huntington, Samuel P. 1996, *The Clash of Civilizations and the Remaking of World Order*, New York: Simon & Schuster.

Ichida, Yoshihiko 2005, 'Subject to Subject: Are we all Schmittians in Politics?', *borderlands*, 4(2).

Ives, Peter 2004, *Gramsci's Politics of Language: Engaging the Bakhtin Circle and the Frankfurt School*, Toronto: University of Toronto Press.

Izzo, Francesca 2009, *Democrazia e cosmopolitismo in Antonio Gramsci*, Rome: Carocci.

James, C.L.R. 2006, *I giacobini neri*, Roma: DeriveApprodi.

Jaspers, Karl 2011 [1953], *The Origin and Goal of History*, London: Routledge.

Jaurès, Jean 1968 [1922–4], *Histoire socialiste de la Révolution française*, Paris: Éditions Sociales.

Jesi, Furio 2000, *Spartakus. Simbologia della rivolta*, edited by A. Cavalletti, Torino: Bollati Boringhieri.

Jessop, Bob 2006, 'Gramsci as a Spatial Theorist', in *Images of Gramsci: Connections and Contentions in Political Theory and International Relations*, edited by Andreas Bieler and Adam D. Morton, London and New York: Routledge.

Jordheim, Helge 2012, 'Against Periodization: Koselleck's Theory of Multiple Temporalities', *History and Theory*, 51: 151–71.

Jordheim, Helge 2014, 'Introduction: Multiple Times and the Work of Synchronization', *History and Theory*, 53: 498–518.

Karsenti, Bruno 2006, *Politique de l'esprit. Auguste Comte et la naissance de la science sociale*, Paris: Hermann.

Koivisto, Juha and Mikko Lahtinen 2012, 'Conjuncture', *Historical Materialism*, 20(1): 267–77.

Koselleck, Reinhardt 1975, 'Geschichte, Histoire', in *Geschichtilche Grundbegriffe. Historisches Lexikon zur politisch-sozialen Sprache in Deutschland*, edited by in O. Brunner, W. Conze, R. Koselleck, Stuttgart: Ernst-Klett.

Koselleck, Reinhardt 1979, *Vergangene Zukunft. Zur Semantik geschichtlicher Zeiten*, Frankfurt am Main: Suhrkamp.

Koselleck, Reinhardt 1999, *Critique and Crisis: Enlightenment and the Pathogenesis of Modern Society*, edited by Victor Gourevitch, Cambridge, MA: MIT Press.

Koselleck, Reinhardt 2000, *Zeitschichten*, Frankfurt/M: Suhrkamp.

Koselleck, Reinhardt 2004 [1979], *Futures Past: On the Semantics of Historical Time*, New York: Columbia University Press.

Kouvelakis, Stathis 2003, *Philosophy and Revolution: From Kant to Marx*, London: Verso.

Krochmalnik, Daniel 1993, 'Ernst Bloch Exkurs über die Juden', *Bloch Almanach*, 13: 39–58.

Krünitz, Johann Georg 1773, *Oekonomisch-technologische Encyklopädie, oder Allgemeines System der Staats-, Stadt-, Haus- und Landwirthschaft, und der Kunstgeschichte*, Berlin: Pauli (Hildesheim & New York: Olms, 1970–).

Kumar, Krishnan 1995, *From Post-industrial to Post Modern Society: New Theories of the Contemporary World*, Oxford: Blackwell.

Laclau, Ernesto 1979, *Politics and Ideology in Marxist Theory: Capitalism, Fascism, Populism*, London: Verso.

Laclau, Ernesto 1990, *New Reflections on the Revolution of Our Time*, London: Verso.

Laclau, Ernesto 2000, 'Identity and Hegemony: The Role of Universality in the Constitution of Political Logics', in Judith Butler, Ernesto Laclau and Slavoj Žižek, *Contingency, Hegemony, Universality: Contemporary Dialogues on the Left*, London: Verso.

Laclau, Ernesto 2005, *On Populist Reason*, London: Verso.

Laclau, Ernesto 2006, 'Why Constructing a People is the Main Task of Radical Politics', *Critical Inquiry*, 32(4): 646–80.

Laclau, Ernesto and Chantal Mouffe 1985, *Hegemony and Socialist Strategy: Towards a Radical Democratic Politics*, London: Verso.

Landauer, Carl and Hans Honegger (eds.), *Internationaler Faschismus. Beiträge über Wesen und Stand der faschistischen Bewegung und über den Ursprung ihrer leitenden Ideen und Triebkräfte*, Karlsruhe: G. Braun.

Landucci, Sergio 1972, *I filosofi e i selvaggi 1580–1780*, Bari: Laterza.

Lefebvre, Georges 1962 [1951], *The French Revolution*, New York: Columbia University Press.

Lefebvre, Jean-Pierre and Pierre Macherey 1984, *Hegel et la société*, Paris: PUF.

Letschka, Werner 1999, 'Geburt der Utopie aus dem Geist der Destruktion. Anmerkungen zu allegorische Strukturen in der Geschichtsphilosophie Blochs und Benjamin', *Bloch Almanach*, 18: 43–69.

Liguori, Guido 2006, *Sentieri gramsciani*, Rome: Carocci.

Löwy, Michael 1989, 'The Poetry of the Past: Marx and the French Revolution', *New Left Review*, 177: 111–24.

Lucretius 1924, *De Rerum Natura*, translated by W.H.D. Rouse, London: William Heinemann/G.P. Putnam's Sons (Loeb Classical Library).

Lukács, Georg 1971, *The Theory of the Novel*, translated by Anna Bostock, Cambridge, MA: MIT Press.

Lukács, Georg 2010, *Soul and Form*, translated by John T. Sanders, New York: Columbia University Press.

Luther, Andreas 1984, 'Variationen über die Endzeit. Bloch contra Benjamin', *Bloch Almanach*, 4: 57–73.

Maguire, John M. 1978, *Marx's Theory of Politics*, Cambridge: Cambridge University Press.

Maihofer, Andrea 1992, *Das Recht bei Marx. Zur dialektischen Struktur von Gerechtigkeit, Menschenrecht und Recht*, Baden-Baden: Nomos-Verlag.

Makropoulos, Michael 1989, *Modernität als ontologischer Ausnahmenzustand? Walter Benjamins Theorie der Moderne*, München: Fink.

Mao Tse-Tung 2007, *On Practice and Contradiction*, London: Verso.

Marini, Ruy Mauro 1991, *Dialéctica de la dependencia*, México: Ediciones Era.

Martinelli, Alberto 2002, *La modernizzazione*, Roma-Bari: Laterza.

Marx, Karl 1970 [1843], 'A Contribution to the Critique of Hegel's Philosophy of Right. Introduction', in *Critique of Hegel's 'Philosophy of Right'*, translated by Annette Jolin and Joseph O'Malley, Cambridge: Cambridge University Press.

Marx, Karl 1972 [1941], *Ethnological Notebooks of Karl Marx*, edited by L. Krader, Assen: Van Gorcum.

Marx, Karl 1973, *Grundrisse*, translated by Martin Nicolaus, London; Penguin.

Marx, Karl 1975a [1843], *Critique of Hegel's Philosophy of Right*, in *Marx and Engels Collected Works*, Volume 3, Moscow: Progress Publishers.

Marx, Karl 1975b [1844], *On the Jewish Question*, in *Marx and Engels Collected Works*, Volume 3, Moscow: Progress Publishers.

Marx, Karl 1975c [1844], *Contribution to the Critique of Hegel's Philosophy of Law, Introduction*, in *Marx and Engels Collected Works*, Volume 3, Moscow: Progress Publishers.

Marx, Karl 1975d [1844], *The King of Prussia and Social Reform*, in *Marx and Engels Collected Works*, Volume 3, Moscow: Progress Publishers.

Marx, Karl 1976 [1847], *Moralising Criticism and Critical Morality*, in *Marx and Engels Collected Works*, Volume 6, Moscow: Progress Publishers.

Marx, Karl 1977 [1859], *A Contribution to the Critique of Political Economy*, Moscow: Progress Publishers.

Marx, Karl 1977a [1848], *The Bill Proposing the Abolition of Feudal Obligations*, in *Marx and Engels Collected Works*, Volume 7, Moscow: Progress Publishers.

Marx, Karl 1977b [1848], *The Bourgeoisie and the Counter-Revolution*, in *Marx and Engels Collected Works*, Volume 8, Moscow: Progress Publishers.

Marx, Karl 1979 [1852], *The Eighteenth Brumaire of Louis Napoleon*, in *Marx and Engels Collected Works*, Volume 11, Moscow: Progress Publishers.

Marx, Karl 1981a, *Capital*, Volume 2, translated by David Fernbach, New York: Penguin Books.

Marx, Karl 1981b, *Capital*, Volume 3, translated by David Fernbach, New York: Penguin Books.

Marx, Karl 1986 [1871], *Address of the General Council of the International Working Men's Association on the Civil War in France*, in *Marx and Engels Collected Works*, Volume 22, Moscow: Progress Publishers.

Marx, Karl 1987, *Outlines of the Critique of Political Economy* [1857–8], in *Marx and Engels Collected Works*, Volume 29, London: Lawrence & Wishart.

Marx, Karl 1987a, Letter to the Editor of the *Otecestvennye Zapiski*, November 1877, in Karl Marx and Friedrich Engels, *Werke*, Volume 19, Berlin, Dietz.

Marx, Karl 1987b, Letter to Vera Zasulich, 8th March 1881, in Karl Marx and Friedrich Engels, *Werke*, Volume 19, Berlin, Dietz.

Marx, Karl 1989, 'Letter from Marx to Editor of the Otechestvennye Zapiski' [1877], in *Marx and Engels Collected Works*, Volume 24, London: Lawrence & Wishart.

Marx, Karl 1989a, 'First Draft of Letter to Vera Zasulich', in *Marx and Engels Collected Works*, Volume 24, London: Lawrence & Wishart.

Marx, Karl 1996 [1867], *Capital*, Volume I, in *Marx and Engels Collected Works*, Volume 35, London: Lawrence & Wishart.

Marx, Karl 1996 [1867], *Capital, Volume I*, in *Marx and Engels Collected Works*, Volume 35, Moscow: Progress Publishers.

Marx, Karl and Friedrich Engels 1956, *Werke* (*MEW*), Volume 1, Berlin: Dietz.

Marx, Karl and Friedrich Engels 1958, *Werke* (*MEW*), Volume 3, Berlin: Dietz.

Marx, Karl and Friedrich Engels 1959, *Werke* (*MEW*), Volume 4, Berlin: Dietz.

Marx, Karl and Friedrich Engels 1960, *Werke* (*MEW*), Volume 8, Berlin: Dietz.

Marx, Karl and Friedrich Engels 1961, *Werke* (*MEW*), Volume 13, Berlin: Dietz.

Marx, Karl and Friedrich Engels 1975–, *Gesamtausgabe* (= MEGA^2), edited by Institut für Marxismus-Leninismus, Berlin: Dietz Verlag [now Akademie Verlag].

Marx, Karl and Friedrich Engels 1975a [1845], *The Holy Family*, in *Marx and Engels Collected Works*, Volume 4, Moscow: Progress Publishers.

Marx, Karl and Friedrich Engels 1975b [1845], *The German Ideology*, in *Marx and Engels Collected Works*, Volume 5, Moscow: Progress Publishers.

Marx, Karl and Friedrich Engels 1975c, *Collected Works*, Volume 3, London: Lawrence and Wishart.

Marx, Karl and Friedrich Engels 1975d, *Collected Works*, Volume 5, London: Lawrence and Wishart.

Marx, Karl and Friedrich Engels 1976 [1848], *On the Polish Question*, in *Marx and Engels Collected Works*, Volume 6, Moscow: Progress Publishers.

Marx, Karl and Friedrich Engels 1976a, *Collected Works*, Volume 6, London: Lawrence and Wishart.

Marx, Karl and Friedrich Engels 1978, *Werke*, Band 3, Berlin: Dietz.

Marx, Karl and Friedrich Engels 1987, *Collected Works*, Volume 29, London: Lawrence and Wishart.

Marx, Karl and Friedrich Engels 1983, *Werke* (*MEW*), Volume 42, Berlin: Dietz.

Marx, Karl and Friedrich Engels 1989 [1879], *Circular Letter to August Bebel, Wilhelm Liebknecht, Wilhelm Bracke und Others*, in *Marx and Engels Collected Works*, Volume 24, Moscow: Progress Publishers.

Massey, Doreen 1992, 'Politics and Space/Time', *New Left Review*, I/196: 65–84.

McLellan, David 1970, *Marx Before Marxism*, London: Macmillan.

Mendes-Flohr, Paul R. 1983, '"To Brush History against the Grain": The Eschatology of the Frankfurt School and Ernst Bloch', *Journal of the American Academy of Religion*, 51: 631–50.

Mezzadra, Sandra 2008, 'Tempo storico e semantica politica nella critica post-coloniale', in *La condizione postcoloniale. Storia e politica nel presente globale*, Verona: Ombre corte.

Miaille, Michel 2001, 'Sur la citoyenneté: en relisant la question juïve', in *Le droit dans la mondialisation. Une perspective critique*, 'Actuel Marx' Confrontation, Actes du Congrès Marx International II, edited by Monique Chemiller-Gendreau-Yann Moulier-Boutang (eds.), Paris: PUF, pp. 39–54.

Michel, Jacques 1983, *Marx et la société juridique*, Paris: Publisud.

Mohri, Kenzo 1979, 'Marx and "Underdevelopment"', *Monthly Review*, 30(11): 32–42.

Momigliano, Amaldo 1966, 'Time in Ancient Historiography', *History and Theory*, 6: 1–23.

Morfino, Vittorio 2004–5, 'La sintassi della violenza tra Hegel e Marx', *Quaderni materialisti*, 3–4: 285–302.

Morfino, Vittorio 2005, *Il tempo della moltitudine*, Roma: manifestolibri.

Morfino, Vittorio 2007, 'La "filosofia" di Darwin', *Quaderni materialisti*, 6: 205–18.

Morfino, Vittorio 2009, *Spinoza e il non contemporaneo*, Verona: Ombrecorte.

Morfino, Vittorio 2012a, 'History as "permanent revocation of the accomplished fact": Machiavelli in the last Althusser', in *Encountering Althusser: Politics and Materialism in Contemporary Radical Thought*, edited by Katja Diefenbach, Gal Kirn, Sara R. Farris and Peter D. Thomas, New York: Bloomsbury.

Morfino, Vittorio 2012b, 'Le cinque tesi della "filosofia" di Machiavelli', in *Machiavelli: tempo e conflitto*, edited by R. Caporali, V. Morfino, S. Visentin, Milano: Mimesis.

Morton, Adam 2010, 'The Continuum of Passive Revolution', *Capital & Class*, 34(3).

Morton, Adam 2011, *Revolution and State in Modern Mexico: The Political Economy of Uneven Development*, Lanham, MD: Rowman & Littlefield.

Moseley, Fred 1997, 'Marx's Reproduction Schemes and Smith's Dogma', in *The Circulation of Capital: Essays on Volume Two of Marx's 'Capital'*, edited by Christopher J. Arthur and Geert Reuten, London: Palgrave Macmillan.

Müntzer, Thomas 1988, *The Collected Works of Thomas Müntzer*, edited by P. Matheson, Edinburgh: T&T Clark.

Murray, Patrick 1997, 'Beyond the "Commerce and Industry" Picture of Capital', in *The Circulation of Capital: Essays on Volume Two of Marx's 'Capital'*, edited by Christopher J. Arthur and Geert Reuten, London: Palgrave Macmillan.

Mussolini, Benito 1958, 'Messaggio per l'anno IX del 27 ottobre 1930', in *Opera Omnia*, edited by Edoardo and Duilio Susmel, Volume 24, Florence: La Fenice.

Nagels, Jacques, *Reproduction du capital selon Karl Marx*, Bruxelles: Université libre de Bruxelles.

Negri, Antonio 1999 [1992], *Insurgencies: Constituent Power and the Modern State*, Minneapolis, MN: University of Minnesota Press.

Nemeth, Thomas 1980, *Gramsci's Philosophy: A Critical Study*, Brighton: Harvester.

Ngai, Pun 2005, *Made In China: Women Factory Workers in a Global Workplace*, Durham, NC: Duke University Press.

Nietzsche, Friedrich 1997 [1873–6], *Untimely Meditations*, translated by R.J. Hollingdale, Cambridge: Cambridge University Press.

Nietzsche, Friedrich 2001, *The Gay Science*, edited by Bernard Williams, Cambridge: Cambridge University Press.

Nisbet, Robert 1966, *The Sociological Tradition*, New York: Basic Books.

Offenstadt, Nicolas 2011, *L'Historiographie*, Paris: Presses Universitaires de France.

Olsen, Niklas 2012, *History in the Plural: An Introduction to the Work of Reinhart Koselleck*, New York: Berghahn.

Osborne, Peter 1992, 'Modernity is a Qualitative, not Chronological, Category', *New Left Review*, I/192.

Osborne, Peter 1995, *The Politics of Time: Modernity and Avant-Garde*, London: Verso.

Osborne, Peter 2013, *Anywhere or Not at All: Philosophy of Contemporary Art*, London: Verso.

Pasolini, Pier Paolo 1957, *Le ceneri di Gramsci*, Turin: Einaudi.

Pasolini, Pier Paolo 1961, *La religione del mio tempo*, Garzanti: Milano.

Pasolini, Pier Paolo 1981, *Scritti Corsari*, Milano: Garzanti.

Pasolini, Pier Paolo 1983, *Il sogno del centauro*, Roma: Editori Riuniti.

Pasolini, Pier Paolo 1994, *Passione e ideologia*, Milano: Garzanti.

Pasolini, Pier Paolo 1999, *Saggi sulla politica e la società*, Milano: Mondadori.

Pasolini, Pier Paolo 2005a, *Heretical Empiricism*, Washington: New Academia Publishing.

Pasolini, Pier Paolo 2005b, *Gramsci's Ashes*, translated by Michelle Cliff, PN Review, 31(3).

Pasolini, Pier Paolo 2014, The *Selected Poetry of Pier Paolo Pasolini*, Chicago: University of Chicago Press.

Pasquino, Pasquale 1998, *Sieyès et l'invention de la constitution en France*, Paris: Odile Jacob.

Pellizzi, Camillo 1930, 'La "grande proletaria" e la crisi mondiale', *Gerarchia*, 10: 724–7.

Pellizzi, Camillo 1931, 'Considerazioni sulla crisi britannica', *Gerarchia*, 11: 813–17.

Picavet, Emmanuel 1996, 'Sur la justification des droits de l'homme', *Archives de philosophie*, 2: 249–71.

Portantiero, Juan Carlos 1981, *Los usos de Gramsci*, Mexico City: Folios Ediciones.

Pradelle, Dominique 2004, 'Gegenstand/Objekt', in *Vocabulaire Européen des Philosophies: Dictionnaire des Intraduisibles*, edited by Barbara Casin, Paris: Editions du Seuil.

Preyer, Gerhard 2007, 'The Paradigm of Multiple Modernities', *ProtoSociology. An International Journal of Interdisciplinary Research*, 24: 5–18.

Rabinbach, Anson 1985, 'Between Enlightenment and Apocalypse: Benjamin, Bloch and the Modern Jewish Messianism', *New German Critique*, 34: 78–124.

Rametta, Gaetano 2006, 'Le difficoltà del potere costituente', *Filosofia Politica*, 20(3): 391–402.

Rampini, Federico, 2007 'La bolla dei titoli spazzatura così può colpire i risparmiatori', *Corriere della Sera*, 5 August.

Rancière, Jacques 1995, *La Mésentente. Politique et philosophie*, Paris: Galilée.

Read, Jason 2005, 'The Althusser Effect: Philosophy, History, and Temporality', *borderlands*, 4(2).

Rehmann, Jan 2008, *Einführung in die Ideologietheorie*, Hamburg-Berlin: Argument.

Reuten, Geert 1997, 'The Status of Marx's Reproduction Schemes: Conventional or Dialectical Logic?', in *The Circulation of Capital: Essays on Volume Two of Marx's 'Capital'*, edited by Christopher J. Arthur and Geert Reuten, London: Palgrave Macmillan.

Robic, Marie-Claire 2009, 'De la relativité ... Elisée Reclus, Paul Vidal de la Blache et l'espace-temps', in *Elisée Reclus – Paul Vidal de la Blache. Le Géographe, la Cité et le Monde hier et aujourd'hui. Autour de 1905*, ouvrage collectif édité par Jean-Paul Bord, Raffaele Cattedra, Ronald Creagh, Jean-Marie Miossec, Georges Roques, Paris: L'Harmattan.

Rosengarten, Frank 1986, 'Gramsci's "Little Discovery": Gramsci's Interpretation of Canto X of Dante's Inferno', *boundary 2*, 14(3): 71–90.

Rossi, Angelo and Giuseppe Vacca 2007, *Gramsci tra Mussolini e Stalin*, Rome: Fazi editore.

Roth, Regina 2009, 'Karl Marx's Original Manuscripts in the Marx-Engels-*Gesamtausgabe* (MEGA): Another View on Capital,' in *Re-reading Marx: New Perspectives after the Critical Edition*, edited by Riccardo Bellofiore and Roberto Fineschi, New York: Palgrave.

Roth, Simon 1572², *Ein Teutscher Dictionarius*, Augsburg: Michael Manger.

Rousseau, Jean-Jacques 1964, *Œuvres complètes*, edited by Bernard Gagnebin and Marcel Raymond, Paris: Pléiade-Gallimard.

Rousseau, Jean-Jacques 1997 [1761], *Julie, Or the New Heloise*, in *The Collected Writings of Rousseau*, Volume 6, edited by Philip Stewart and Jean Vaché, Hanover: University Press of New England.

Rousseau, Jean-Jacques 2000 [1782], *The Reveries of the Solitary Walker, Botanical Writings, and Letter to Franquières*, in *The Collected Writings of Rousseau*, Volume 8, edited by C. Kelly, translated by Charles E. Butterworth, Alexandra Cook and Terence E. Marshall, Hanover: University Press of New England.

Rousseau, Jean-Jacques 2003 [1762], *The Social Contract or Principles of Political Right*, translated by G.D.H. Cole, Mineola, NY: Courier Dover Publications.

Sacristán Luzón, Manuel 2004, *Escritos sobre El Capital (y textos afines)*, introduced and edited by S. López Arnal, Barcelona: El Viejo Topo.

Said, Edward 1978, *Orientalism*, New York: Pantheon.

Said, Edward 2001, 'History, Literature and Geography', in *Reflections on Exile and Other Literary and Cultural Essays*, London: Granta.

Santarelli, Enzo 1981, *Storia del fascismo*, Rome: Editori Riuniti.

Sapelli, Giulio 2005, *Modernizzazione senza sviluppo. Il capitalismo secondo Pasolini*, Milano: Bruno Mondadori.

Saussure, Ferdinand de 1966 [1916], *Course in General Linguistics*, translated by Wade Baskin, New York: McGraw-Hill Book Company.

Schiller, Hans-Ernst 1982, *Metaphysik und Gesellschaftskritik. Zur Konkretisierung der Utopie im Werk Ernst Blochs*, Königstein/Ts: Athenaeum-Hain-Scriptor-Hanstein.

Schiller, Hans-Ernst 1985, 'Jetzeit und Entwicklung. Geschichte bei Ernst Bloch und Walter Benjamin', in *Ernst Bloch Text+Kritik*, edited by H.L. Arnold, München: Text+Kritik.

Schirru, Giancarlo 2011, 'Antonio Gramsci studente di linguistica', *Studi storici*, LII, 925–73.

Schivelbusch, Wolfgang 2005, *Entfernte Verwandtschaft. Faschismus, Nationalsozialismus, New Deal. 1933–1939*, München: Hanser.

Schmitt, Carl 1996, *Roman Catholicism and Political Form*, translated by G.L. Ulmen, Westport: Greenwood Press.

Schmitt, Carl 2002, *Ex Captivitate Salus. Erfahrungen der Zeit 1945/47*, Berlin: Duncker & Humblot.

Schmitt, Carl 2006, *Political Theology: Four Chapters on the Concept of Sovereignty*, translated by George Schwab, Chicago: University of Chicago Press.

Schmitt, Carl 2007, *The Concept of Political*, expanded edition, translated by George Schwab, Chicago: University of Chicago Press.

Schmitt, Carl 2008, *The Leviathan in the State Theory of Thomas Hobbes: Meaning and Failure of a Political Symbol*, translated by George Schwab, Chicago: University of Chicago Press.

Schöttler, Peter 1993, 'Althusser and Annales Historiography. An Impossible Dialogue?', in *The Althusserian Legacy*, edited by E. Ann Kaplan and Michael Sprinker, London: Verso.

Scuccimarra, Luca 2002, *La sciabola di Sieyès. Le giornate di brumaio e la genesi del regime bonapartista*, Bologna: il Mulino.

Sebastiani, Silvia 2008, *I limiti del progresso. Razza e genere nell'illuminismo scozzese*, Bologna: il Mulino.

Seidman, Steven 1983, *Liberalism and the Origins of European Social Theory*, Berkeley, CA: University of California Press.

Shanin, Teodor 1983, *Late Marx and the Russian Road: Marx and 'the Peripheries of Capitalism'*, New York: Monthly Review Press.

Shaw, William H. 1984, 'Marx and Morgan', *History and Theory*, 23(2): 215–28.

Sieyès, Emmanuel 1970 [1789], *Qu'est-ce que le Tiers Etat?*, edited by R. Zapperi, Geneva: Droz.

Smith, Tony 1997, 'The Capital/Consumer Relation in Lean Production: The Continued Relevance of Volume Two of *Capital*', in *The Circulation of Capital: Essays on Volume Two of Marx's Capital*, edited by Christopher J. Arthur and Geert Reuten, London: Palgrave Macmillan.

Soboul, Albert 1975 [1948], *The French Revolution, 1787–1799*, New York: Random House.

Solari, Gioele 1974 [1931], 'Il concetto di società civile in Hegel', in *La filosofia politica, Volume II: Da Kant a Comte* edited by Luigi Firpo, Rome-Bari: Laterza.

Spaemann, Robert 1959, *Der Ursprung der Soziologie aus dem Geist der Restauration*, München: Kösel-Verlag.

Spivak, Gayatri Chakravorty 1988, 'Can the subaltern speak?', in *Marxism and the Interpretation of Culture*, edited by C. Nelson and L. Grossberg, Urbana, IL: University of Illinois Press.

Stamford Raffles, Thomas 1817, *History of Java and its Dependencies*, London.

Starobinski, Jean 1971, *J.-J. Rousseau, La transparence et l'obstacle*, Paris: Gallimard.

Starobinski, Jean 1988, *Jean-Jacques Rousseau: Transparency and Obstruction*, Chicago: University of Chicago Press.

Steiner, Udo 1966, *Verfassunggebung und verfassunggebende Gewalt des Volkes*, Berlin: Duncker & Humblot.

Suchting, Wal 1997, 'Empirismus', *Das historisch-kritische Wörterbuch des Marxismus* Band 3, edited by Wolfgang Fritz Haug, Hamburg-Berlin: Argument.

Sweezy, Paul M. 1942, *The Theory of Capitalistic Development*, London: Dennis Dobson Limited.

Szakolczai, Árpád 2003, *The Genesis of Modernity*, London: Routledge.

Taubes, Jacob 2009, *Occidental Eschatology*, translated by David Ratmoko, Stanford, CA: Stanford University Press.

Terrier, Jean 2011, *Visions of the Social: Society as a Political Project in France 1750–1950*, Leiden: Brill.

Thomas, Peter D. 2006, 'Althusser, Gramsci e la non contemporaneità del presente', *Critica marxista*, 44: 71–9.

Thomas, Peter D. 2009, *The Gramscian Moment: Philosophy, Hegemony and Marxism*, Leiden: Brill.

Thomas, Peter D. 2015, 'Gramsci's Machiavellian Metaphor: Restaging *The Prince*', in *The Radical Machiavelli: Politics, Philosophy and Language*, edited by Fabio Frosini, Filippo Del Lucchese and Vittorio Morfino, Leiden: Brill.

Tomba, Massimiliano 2006, *La 'vera politica'. Kant e Benjamin: la possibilità della giustizia*, Macerata: Quodlibet.

Tomba, Massimiliano 2009, 'Historical Temporalities of Capital: An Anti-Historicist Perspective', *Historical Materialism*, 17(4): 44–65.

Tomba, Massimiliano 2011, *Strati di tempo. Karl Marx materialista storico*, Milan: Jaca Books.

Tomba, Massimiliano 2013a, 'I tempi storici della lunga accumulazione capitalistica', in *Tempora Multa. Il governo del tempo*, edited by Vittorio Morfino et al., Milano: Mimesis.

Tomba, Massimiliano 2013b, *Marx's Temporalities*, Leiden: Brill.

Tombazos, Stavros 1994, *Le temps dans l'analyse économique: les catégories du temps dans le Capital*, Paris: Société des saisons.

Tombazos, Stavros 2014, *Time in Marx: The Categories of Time in Marx's 'Capital'*, Leiden: Brill.

Tomich, Dale W. 2003, *Through the Prism of Slavery: Labor, Capital, and World Economy*, Lanham, MD: Rowman & Littlefield.

Tosel, André 1995, 'In Francia', in *Gramsci in Europa e in America*, edited by Eric J. Hobsbawm, Rome-Bari: Laterza.

Trouillot, Michel-Rolph 1995, *Silencing the Past: Power and the Production of History*, Boston: Beacon Press.

Turner, Bryan S. and Simon Susen (eds.) 2011, 'Special Issue: Shmuel Noah Eisenstadt', *Journal of Classical Sociology*, 11(3).

Urbinati, Nadia 1998, 'From the Periphery of Modernity: Antonio Gramsci's Theory of Subordination and Hegemony', *Political Theory*, 26(3).

Vacca, Giuseppe 1977, 'La "quistione politica degli intellettuali" e la teoria marxista dello Stato nel pensiero di Gramsci', in *Politica e storia in Gramsci*, Volume I, edited by Franco Ferri, Rome: Editori Riuniti.

Vacca, Giuseppe 2012, *Vita e pensieri di Antonio Gramsci (1926–1937)*, Turin: Einadui.

Vegetti, Mario 2000, 'Tempo e storia nell'esperienza greca', in *Memoria e scrittura della filosofia*, edited by S. Borutti, Milano: Mimesis.

Viet, Jean 1967, *Le scienze dell'uomo. Indagine francese per l'Unesco sulle tendenze e l'organizzazione della ricerca*, translated by Paola Cusumano, Milan: Jaca Book.

Vinx, Lars 2015, *The Guardian of the Constitution: Hans Kelsen and Carl Schmitt on the Limits of Constitutional Law*, Cambridge: Cambridge University Press.

Vovelle, Michel 1984 [1972], *The Fall of the French Monarchy, 1787–1792*, Cambridge: Cambridge University Press.

Wada, Haruki 1983, 'Marx and Revolutionary Russia', in *Late Marx and the Russian Road: Marx and 'the Peripheries of Capitalism'*, edited by Teodor Shanin, New York: Monthly Review Press.

Wagner, Peter 2001, *Theorising Modernity*, London: Sage.

Wagner, Peter 2008, *Modernity as Experience and Interpretation: A New Sociology of Modernity*, Cambridge: Polity Press.

Wainwright, Joel 2008, 'Uneven Developments: From *Grundrisse* to *Capital*', *Antipode*, 40(5): 879–97.

Wainwright, Joel 2010, 'On Gramsci's "conceptions of the world"', *Transactions of the Institute of British Geographers*, 35: 507–21.

Wallace, David Foster 1996, *Infinite Jest*, New York: Little, Brown and Company.

Wißkirchen, Hubert 1987, 'Die humane Kraft des Denkens. Die frühen Philosophie Blochs und Benjamins', *Bloch Almanach*, 7: 53–79.

Wittgenstein, Ludwig 2003 [1922], *Tractatus Logico-Philosophicus*, New York: Barnes and Noble.

Wittrock, Bjorn 2000, 'Modernity: One, None or Many? European Origins and Modernity as a Global Condition', *Daedalus*, 129(1): 31–60.

Wittrock, Bjorn 2005, 'Cultural Crystallization and Civilization Change: Axiality and Modernity', in *Comparing Modernities: Pluralism vs. Homogeneity. Essays in Homage to Shmuel N. Eisenstadt*, edited by E. Ben-Rafael and Y. Sternberg, Leiden: Brill.

Wright, Steve 2002, *Storming Heaven: Class Composition and Struggle in Italian Autonomist Marxism*, London: Pluto Press.

Zammito, John 2004, 'Koselleck's Philosophy of Historical Time(s) and the Practice of History', *History and Theory*, 43: 124–35.

Zerubavel, Eviatar 2003, *Time Maps: Collective Memory and the Social Shape of the Past*, Chicago: University of Chicago Press.

Zweig, Egon 1909, *Die Lehre vom 'pouvoir constituant'. Ein Beitrag zum Staatsrecht der Französischen Revolution*, Tübingen: Mohr.

Index